Advanced Maya®
Texturing and
Lighting

Third Edition

Advanced Maya®
Texturing and Lighting

Third Edition

Lee Lanier

SYBEX®
A Wiley Brand

Acquisitions Editor: MARIANN BARSOLO
Development Editor: JIM COMPTON
Technical Editor: STANLEY "GREY" HASH
Production Editor: CHRISTINE O'CONNOR
Copy Editor: ELIZABETH WELCH
Editorial Manager: MARY BETH WAKEFIELD
Production Manager: KATHLEEN WISOR
Associate Publisher: JIM MINATEL
Compositor: MAUREEN FORYS, HAPPENSTANCE TYPE-O-RAMA
Proofreader: JOSH CHASE, WORD ONE NEW YORK
Indexer: NANCY GUENTHER
Project Coordinator, Cover: BRENT SAVAGE
Cover Designer: WILEY
Cover Image: LEE LANIER

Copyright © 2015 by John Wiley & Sons, Inc., Indianapolis, Indiana

Published simultaneously in Canada

ISBN: 978-1-118-98352-2

ISBN: 978-1-118-98353-9 (ebk.)

ISBN: 978-1-118-98354-6 (ebk.)

For general information on our other products and services or to obtain technical support, please contact our Customer Care Department within the U.S. at (877) 762-2974, outside the U.S. at (317) 572-3993 or fax (317) 572-4002.

Wiley publishes in a variety of print and electronic formats and by print-on-demand. Some material included with standard print versions of this book may not be included in e-books or in print-on-demand. If this book refers to media such as a CD or DVD that is not included in the version you purchased, you may download this material at http://booksupport.wiley.com. For more information about Wiley products, visit www.wiley.com.

Library of Congress Control Number: 2015933608

10 9 8 7 6 5 4 3 2 1

Art is always worth the effort.

 ## Acknowledgments

Many thanks to all those who've bought previous editions of this book. What can I say? You rock. Thanks to the fine Sybex staff and freelancers, including Mariann Barsolo, Christine O'Connor, Jim Compton, Liz Welch, Josh Chase at Word One, Maureen Forys at Happenstance Type-O-Rama, as well as my technical editor Grey Hash.

About the Author

Lee Lanier has worked as a professional computer animator and visual effects artist since 1994. While at Buena Vista Visual Effects at Walt Disney Studios, he created VFX for numerous feature films. While at PDI/DreamWorks, he served as a senior animator on *Antz* and *Shrek*. Along the way, he directed a series of independent, animated short films that went on to play 200+ film festivals, museums, and art galleries worldwide. His work has been featured at such venues as Sundance, Slamdance, SXSW, the Ottawa International Animation Festival, Boston Museum of Fine Arts, and the Smithsonian Institution. As a world-renowned expert in the VFX field, Lee has written high-end software books that have sold 30,000 copies, has authored VFX training videos for lynda.com, has taught VFX compositing at the Gnomon School of Visual Effects in Hollywood, is a member of VES (Visual Effects Society), is the executive director of the Dam Short Film Festival, and co-manages the Boulder City branch of Dr. Sketchy's Anti-Art School. He has worked on over 70 features, shorts, music videos, trailers, and commercials.

Contents

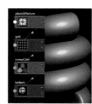
CONTENTS ∎

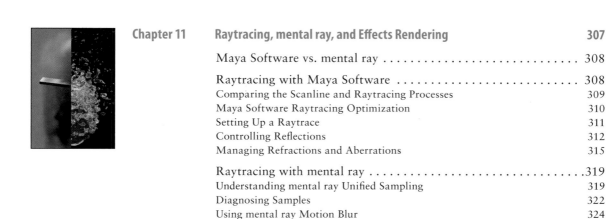

CONTENTS ■

Introduction

There's nothing quite like turning a gray-shaded model into something that looks real—or that could be real.

When I wrote the first edition of *Advanced Maya Texturing and Lighting* in 2006, it was to shed more light on the powerful lighting and texturing systems found in the Autodesk® Maya® program. I'm very flattered to meet people to this day who drag around old dog-eared copies of that book. Yet the success of this book is not so much a compliment to my writing skills as it is a nod to the amazing possibilities within the reach of any animator willing to put in hard work and long hours. After all, there's almost nothing you *can't* create with a good 3D package like Maya.

I should stress that I am self-taught. In 1994, I sat down at a spare seat of Alias PowerAnimator 5.1 and started hacking away. After several years and various trials by fire, 3D became a livelihood, a love, and an obsession. Along the way, I was fortunate enough to work with many talented artists at Buena Vista Visual Effects at Walt Disney Studios and Pacific Data Images (which became PDI/DreamWorks). In 2000, I switched from PowerAnimator to Maya and have since logged tens of thousands of hours with the subject of this book.

Because of my unusual combination of an informal and professional background, I do not profess to know everything there is to know about Maya. However, I've made a point to cover the most critical aspects of texturing, lighting, and rendering, at least from my personal and professional perspective.

Third Edition

The first edition of *Advanced Maya Texturing and Lighting* was written with Maya 7.0 and published in 2006. The second edition was written with Maya 2008 and published in 2008. This edition represents a major revision and is written with Maya 2014 and Maya 2015. Although the core functions of Maya have remained the same since 2006, you'll find many significant updates that are worth learning. These include new Maya utility nodes, upgraded mental ray® shaders, nDynamics simulation tools, the new Node Editor window, the Bifröst fluid simulation system, advanced indirect illumination components like importons and irradiance particles, more robust viewport rendering options, and expanded render pass support.

Who Should Read This Book

Advanced Maya Texturing and Lighting, Third Edition, is designed for anyone with a working knowledge of Maya. Specifically, this book was written with the following people in mind:

- Students who are reaching the upper levels of their 3D curriculum

- Hobbyists or amateurs who are self-starters and would like to rapidly refine their Maya skills
- Professionals working in other areas of Maya, such as animation or rigging, who would like to expand their knowledge of texturing and lighting

Although most of the information in this book is Maya-specific, you can apply the texturing and lighting theories and approaches to other 3D programs. This book also refers to digital image manipulation software such as Adobe Photoshop and compositing software such as Adobe After Effects. Basic knowledge of such programs is useful but not mandatory when using this book.

How to Use This Book

Advanced Maya Texturing and Lighting, Third Edition, is divided into 13 chapters.

Chapter 1 discusses lighting history, technique, and application, as well as basic color theory. Naturalistic, stylistic, 1-point, 2-point, and 3-point lighting are covered in detail. If you are new to lighting, this is the best place to start.

Chapters 2 and 3 detail Maya lights and shadows and how to apply them properly. Specialized effects, such as Environment Fog, Light Fog, Paint Effects, Maya Fur, and Maya nHair, are also covered.

Chapters 4 through 8 delve deeply into Maya materials and utilities. Most Maya books barely scratch the surface in this area. If you've ever wondered what each Maya node actually *does*, check out these chapters. Custom networks are also discussed at length. Numerous examples are provided with clearly labeled illustrations, and you'll find that the examples are easy to follow (as much as such a complex subject allows). I've also included detailed information on the Node Editor.

Chapter 9 takes a detour and reviews UV texture space issues. It also covers bump, normal, and displacement mapping.

Chapter 10 concentrates on scene optimization and batch rendering preparation.

Chapters 11 and 12 delve deeply into raytracing, mental ray shaders, Global Illumination, and Final Gathering. Here you'll find many of the important new Maya 2015 features.

Chapter 13 looks at color management within Maya, as well as HDR workflow and mental ray render pass management.

If you're fairly new to Maya or 3D in general, I suggest starting with Chapter 1 and then work your way through the book. If you're experienced with Maya, I recommend hitting the chapters that contain information that's poorly documented by other sources. In this case, Chapters 6, 7, and 8 should prove the most interesting.

Eleven chapters of *Advanced Maya Texturing and Lighting, Third Edition,* contain tutorials. These tutorials allow you to practice advanced techniques that are employed regularly in the visual effects and animation industries. Each tutorial is accompanied by ample illustrations and completed Maya scene files. In addition, short step-by-step guides are included for specific tasks in every chapter.

Tutorial Files

Several gigabytes of Maya scene files, texture bitmaps, and QuickTime movies accompany this book. Many of the book's figures include the original Maya scene file, which is listed with the figure captions. (Note that some of these files contain simplified geometry.) The tutorial files are hosted on the official Sybex *Advanced Maya Texturing and Lighting, Third Edition* website, which is:

www.sybex.com/go/advancedmaya

The tutorial files are organized in the following manner:

Directory	Contents
Project_Files\Chapter_*n*\scenes\	Maya 2014 and Maya 2015 scene files saved in the MA format
Project_Files\Chapter_*n*\images\	Reference and high-dynamic range bitmaps saved as TIFF and HDR files
Project_Files\Chapter_*n*\textures\	Texture bitmaps saved as TIFF, PSD, and JPEG files
Project_Files\Chapter_*n*\movies\	Sample QuickTime MOV movies

No chapter has all of these folders, but most have at least two of them.

To avoid lost or missing texture bitmaps, I recommend copying the files for a given chapter to your desktop and setting the Maya project to the appropriate chapter directory. For example, if you are reading Chapter 2, choose File > Set Project in Maya and select the /Project_Files/Chapter_2/ directory before opening any Chapter 2 files. You can find more information on bitmap use in Chapter 4.

Maya Versions

The scene files included with the tutorial files are saved in the Maya 2014 or Maya 2015 MA text format. (MA stands for Maya ASCII.) The files have been tested with versions 2014 and 2015. Any significant differences between the two versions are noted in the text.

You can open newer versions of Maya scene files with an older version of the software. To do so, choose Window > Settings/Preferences > Preferences, click on the File/Projects section, and select the Ignore Version check box.

Abbreviations

Since Maya requires a three-button mouse for proper operation, the abbreviations LMB, MMB, and RMB are used and stand for Left-Mouse-Button, Middle-Mouse-Button, and Right-Mouse-Button, respectively.

Contact the Author

Feel free to contact me at www.BeezleBugBit.com. You can also find me on popular social networks. For any updates that may accompany the book, go to the book's website at www.sybex.com/go/advancedmaya.

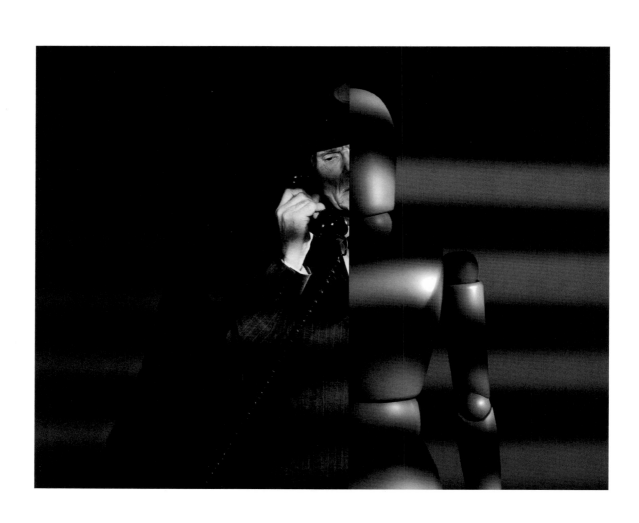

Understanding Lighting and Color

1

Lighting is a cornerstone of any 3D project. Although you can easily create and position lights within a scene, an understanding of lighting theory will help you make aesthetically solid choices. The history of art and cinema is full of inspiring examples to choose from. Although 3-point lighting is a mainstay of 3D, 1-point, 2-point, and naturalistic lighting provide alternative lighting methods that better match the real world and the art traditions of the past. On the other hand, stylistic lighting can free an artist from traditional bounds and thereby place no limits on expression.

Chapter Contents
Common lighting terms
An overview of 1-, 2-, and 3-point lighting
An exploration of naturalistic and stylistic lighting
A quick review of color theory and monitor calibration
Exploring the art of lighting

Like every aspect of 3D, lighting must be created from scratch. Unfortunately, the techniques for emulating the real world are not always obvious or intuitive. Luckily, a wealth of lighting theory exists in the form of historical artwork, photography, and motion pictures.

For the sake of clarity, I've broken the discussion of lighting theory into the following categories: 1-point, 2-point, 3-point, naturalistic, and stylistic. The first three categories refer to the number of lights employed. The last two refer to a particular style. Before delving into 1-point lighting, however, I'll define a few common lighting terms:

Key The most intense light in a scene. The key light's source is generally identifiable (the sun, a lamp, and so on). The key light usually produces the strongest shadow in the scene.

Fill A secondary light that is less intense than the key. This light "fills" in the dark areas of a subject and the shadows produced by the key. Fill lights often represent light from a key that has bounced off a surface, such as a wall.

Rim An intense light source placed behind a subject that strikes the subject along the edge. Rim lights are often employed as hair lights. When a rim light strikes the side of a subject, it's also referred to as a kicker. Note that you can refer to any light arriving from behind the subject as a backlight.

Using 1-Point Lighting

The 1-point lighting scheme is dramatic, sometimes stark, and often foreboding. The lighting involves a single, easily identifiable key light source, with no significant supplemental sources. You can find 1-point lighting in the following situations:

- A man lights a cigarette in an otherwise dark alley.
- A woman drives a car down a dark country road, lit only by the car's instrument panel.
- Sunbeams burst through the window of an otherwise unlit interior.
- A theater audience is illuminated by the light of the movie screen (see Figure 1.1).

The motion picture genre that most closely emulates 1-point lighting is film noir. Film noir is a style historically associated with crime dramas of the 1940s and '50s. The style is typified by black-and-white film stock, sparsely lit characters, and deep black shadows. Aesthetically, the lighting stemmed from stories with cynical, paranoid, or nihilistic outlooks. Technically, the stark lighting was the result of placing only a few lights on the set, in some cases because of budgetary restrictions. Although multiple lights were generally needed for any given shot for proper exposure, the result often *appears* as if a single light source exists. For example, in Figure 1.2 a key light strikes a man from screen right, thereby creating a dark shadow on the wall; however, the horizontal streaks of light from a set of Venetian blinds originates from a weaker fill light.

Figure 1.1 A woman is lit by a movie screen in a 1-point lighting setup.

Figure 1.2 Stark lighting in a film noir–style photo

Classic film noir films include *The Maltese Falcon* (1941), *Double Indemnity* (1944), and *Touch of Evil* (1958). More recent examples include *Blade Runner* (1982) and *Sin City* (2005). The lighting style employed by film noir is often referred to as low-key lighting, where there is a strong key light and little, if any, fill.

Film noir is closely related to German expressionism, which was an art movement popular in Germany from 1905 to 1925. German expressionism was dominated by the dark, sinister aspects of the human psyche. The movement is known for its bold, simplified woodcuts and its atmospheric horror cinema (for example, *The Cabinet of Dr. Caligari*, 1919).

The roots of expressionism can be traced to the chiaroscuro painting style of the 15th and 16th centuries in Italy and Flanders. Chiaroscuro is defined by a bold contrast between lights and darks (the word is Italian for light-dark). This is often characterized by figures in bright pools of light jutting through dark spaces. Chiaroscuro reached its pinnacle with the baroque art movement (17th and 18th centuries in Europe) and is exemplified by master painters Caravaggio (1573–1610) and Rembrandt (1606–1669).

When painters push for stronger contrast, unlit areas of the scene are rarely painted with pure black. In Figure 1.3, an unidentified key light arrives from above and to the left. No other source of light is apparent. Yet, a background wall is dimly visible thanks to a faint fill. In addition, the right sides of the character faces are seen in the shadows. Hence, such paintings bridge the gap between 1- and 2-point lighting.

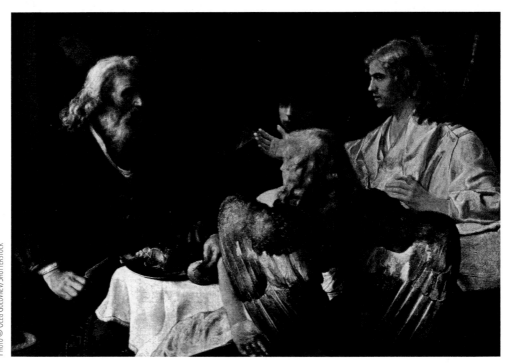

Figure 1.3 Rembrandt, *Abraham and the Three Angels*, ca. 1630–1640, oil on canvas. State Hermitage Museum, Saint Petersburg.

In comparison, true 1-point lighting is sometimes found in portraiture. For example, in Figure 1.4 there is a single light source to the left and in front of the couple. A secondary light source is not identifiable. The painter Anthony Van Dyck (1599–1641) was an influential baroque portraitist.

Figure 1.4 Van Dyck, *Princess Mary Stuart and Prince William of Orange*, 1641, oil on canvas. Rijksmuseum, Amsterdam.

You'll see 1-point lighting in contemporary photography and videography. In particular, this technique is used in work created for the fashion industry, commercial advertising, and music videos. A strong, diffuse key light, sometimes in the form of a "soft box" light diffuser or a large ring of fluorescent lights, is placed around, beside, or above the camera. This setup creates evenly lit faces with little sense of additional lighting (see Figure 1.5).

Figure 1.5 A fashion photograph displays 1-point lighting.

It's easy to set up 1-point lighting in 3D. The most difficult aspect of the scheme is the creation of aesthetic patterns of light and dark. For example, Figure 1.6 shows the film noir–style photo from Figure 1.2 re-created in Autodesk® Maya®. A series of trial-and-error renders were necessary to position a spot light in a satisfactory manner. The horizontal shadows are created by shadowing primitive geometry in the foreground (out of the camera's view). The intensity of the key should be high enough to illuminate the parts not in shadow but not so high as to "blow out" or overexpose some areas.

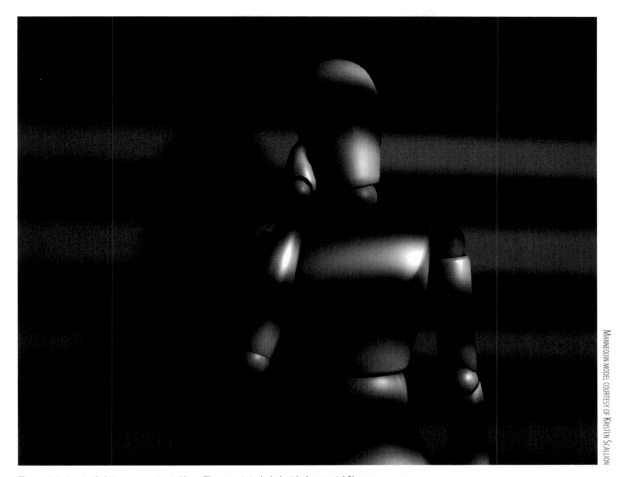

MANNEQUIN MODEL COURTESY OF KRISTEN SCALLION

Figure 1.6 1-point lighting re-creation in Maya. The scene is included with the tutorial files as 1_point.ma.

Using 2-Point Lighting

The 2-point lighting scheme matches many of the lighting scenarios we encounter in our everyday lives. The scheme often involves a strong key and an extremely diffuse fill. The following are examples of 2-point lighting:

- Sunlight streams through a window. The light bounce from the interior walls serves as a fill.

- Office workers sit in a windowless room lit with overhead fluorescent lights. The light bounce from the walls, desks, and floor serves as a fill.
- A cat walks down a sidewalk on a sunny day. The light bounces off the concrete, providing fill to the bottom of his neck and belly (see Figure 1.7).

Figure 1.7 A cat receives sunlight from above and as a bounced fill from the sidewalk. The lighting is a 2-point setup.

You'll often see 2-point lighting in painted portraits. For example, in Figure 1.8 a man is lit by a strong key light arriving from the left. A second light source delivers fill from the right; thus, no part of the person or his outfit is left unlit. This painting was created by Frans Hals (1582–1666), a baroque painter whose loose, powerful brushstrokes inspired the impressionism movement. This style of lighting is called broad lighting, whereby the side of the head facing the viewer receives the key. The opposite style of lighting is called short lighting, whereby the side of the head facing away from the viewer receives the key.

Figure 1.8 Left: Hals, *Portrait of a Member of the Haarlem Civic Guard*, ca. 1636/1638, oil on canvas. National Gallery of Art, Washington, DC.; Right: 2-point lighting re-creation in Maya. The scene is included with the Chapter 1 tutorial files as 2_point.ma.

The intensity of the key light as compared to the fill (key-to-fill ratio) should vary with the subject and location. The optimum intensity of any light used in a scene depends on its position and the qualities of the materials involved. Nevertheless, as a rough rule of thumb for an initial lighting pass, you can set the intensity of a fill light to at least half that of the key. For the 3D reproduction illustrated in Figure 1.8, a directional light serves as the key. The directional light's Intensity value is set to 1.75. An ambient light, which serves as the fill, is placed screen right with its Intensity value set to 0.2 (see Figure 1.9).

The 2-point lighting scheme is not limited to portraits. Many outdoor scenes exhibit two distinct sources of light. For example, in Figure 1.10 a watercolor scene portrays a strong key light in the form of the sun arriving from the left. An even fill along the front of the building represents the bounced sunlight, which serves as the second light source.

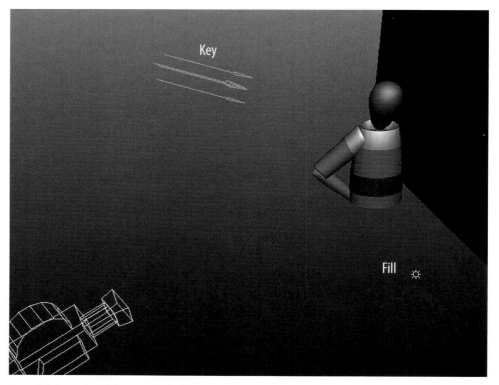

Figure 1.9 Two-point lighting set up for the Hals painting re-creation

Figure 1.10 A painting of the outdoors shows 2-point lighting.

Using 3-Point Lighting

Perhaps the most commonly discussed and applied lighting technique is 3-point lighting. Descriptions can be found in numerous 3D, film, and video instructional materials. Although 3-point lighting is a reliable way to light many scenes, it has inherent drawbacks.

In the standard 3-point lighting scheme, a strong key is placed to one side of a subject (approximately 15 to 45 degrees off the camera axis). A fill light is placed on the opposite side and is at least half the intensity of the key (see Figure 1.11). A rim light is placed behind the subject so that it grazes the subject's edge.

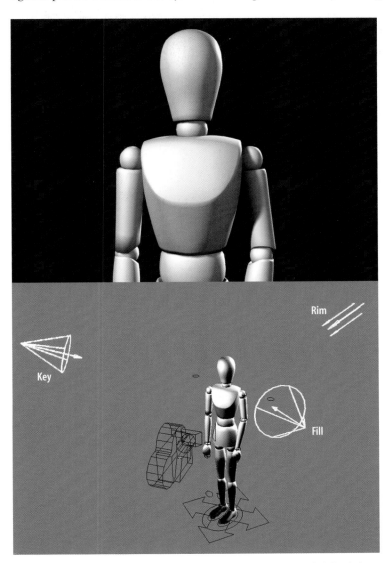

Figure 1.11 Standard 3-point lighting applied to a mannequin. This scene is included with the Chapter 1 tutorial files as 3_point_man.ma.

The 3-point lighting scheme is popular in the realm of 3D because it lends depth to a potentially flat subject. For example, in Figure 1.12 a sphere is given additional roundness with three lights. A spot light, which serves as the key, is placed screen left (that is, at the left side of the frame). An ambient light, which serves as a fill, is placed screen right. A directional light, which functions as a rim light, is placed behind the sphere. The balance between the key and fill creates a slightly dark "core" down the center of sphere. The bright edge created by the rim helps separate the sphere from the dark background.

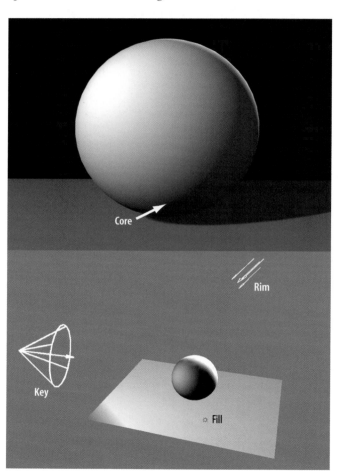

Figure 1.12 Standard 3-point lighting applied to a primitive sphere. This scene is included with the Chapter 1 tutorial files as `3_point_sphere.ma`.

Three-point lighting was developed in the "Golden Age of Hollywood," which refers to the period between the advent of "talkies" and the years immediately following World War 2. Studio cinematographers developed the technique as an efficient way to light scenes when time was somewhat limited and production schedules had to be met. When lighting actors, cinematographers often sought out the "Rembrandt patch," which is a triangular patch of light on the cheek opposite the light source (see Figure 1.13). The patch was named after the painter, who often featured such a pattern in his portraits.

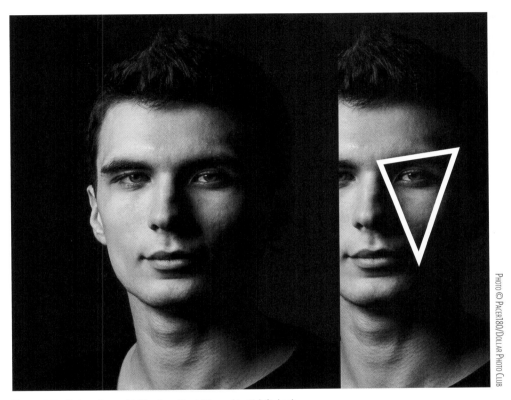

Figure 1.13 Modern photo with "Rembrandt patch" on subject's left cheek

Rim lights, in particular, were developed to separate the actor from a dark or cluttered background. Rim lights (and other fundamental aspects of lighting design) can trace their roots to early theatrical stage lighting. Early examples of their use in motion pictures include, but are not limited to, *Old and New* (1929), directed by Sergei Eisenstein, and the 1920s comedies of Charles Chaplin (*A Woman of Paris*, *The Gold Rush*, and so on). Eventually, rim lights were used to impart a fantastic glow to the hair of heroines such as Ingrid Bergman in *Casablanca* (1942), Rita Hayworth in *Gilda* (1946), and Grace Kelly in *Rear Window* (1954). The use of rim lights does not necessitate the use of a definitive fill light. Glamour lighting, a name loosely given to the lighting style of publicity photography of American motion picture studios from the 1920s to the 1940s, often used only a key and a rim (see Figure 1.14).

Figure 1.14 A variation of glamour lighting using a key light (high and to the right) and a kicker (a rim light hitting the left side of the model's face)

Proper 3-point lighting is fairly difficult to find in the world of painting. Clearly defined rims are not generally painted in. In many cases, a portion of a subject that is dark is allowed to blend into a dark background (refer back to Figure 1.3). In other situations, the chosen background is bright enough to delineate the outline of the subject (see Figure 1.4).

On the other hand, rim lighting can often be found in nature. For example, in Figure 1.15 clouds cover the sun and pick up bright rims. The plane gains a similarly bright edge. A girl's hair is lit from the sun that sets behind her. These natural occurrences, however, do not fit the standard 3-point lighting system. None of the subjects are affected by more than two distinct sources of light—the key light and the fill light. (Note that professional photographers sometimes add to the fill light by using a reflector; even so, 2-point lighting is often maintained, as is the example of the girl in Figure 1.15.)

Figure 1.15 Naturally occurring examples of rim lighting

Many contemporary cinematographers and videographers consider 3-point lighting either antiquated or unsatisfactory for many lighting situations. The necessity of specific positions for key, fill, and rim lights guarantees that 3-point lighting does not match many real-world situations. The alternative to 3-point lighting is thus naturalistic lighting.

Using Naturalistic Lighting

Naturalistic lighting is an adaptable scheme that matches the natural lighting scenario of the subject location. Any light that is visible is logically driven by a recognizable source. Naturalistic lighting is sometimes called "transparent" in that no artificial lighting methods can be detected. Another way to define naturalistic lighting is to list what it *lacks*:

- Unmotivated shadows
- Impossibly distinct rim light
- Perfectly placed lights that never permit a character to fall into shadow or be unglamorously lit

The field of motion pictures has numerous examples of non-naturalistic lighting. Many films feature stylized or exaggerated lighting. This is particularly evident with musicals, which are fantastic by their very nature. Such films as *The Band Wagon* (1953) and *Silk Stockings* (1957) employ high-key lighting, in which the fill light is intense and there is a low key-to-fill ratio. The characters in these films are therefore evenly lit and carry a minimum number of deep, dark shadows. High-key lighting is also evident in many television sitcoms, in which it is necessary to keep a character well lit at all positions on the set. Similar lighting is employed for advertising and catalog art (see Figure 1.16).

Figure 1.16 High-key lighting demonstrated by ad photography

In other situations, non-naturalistic lighting is a result of technical limitations or time and budget restrictions. A common problem with older motion pictures is the unintended creation of unmotivated, multiple shadows. For example, light representing the sun casts multiple shadows of a character on the ground. More commonly, a lamp casts multiple, distinct shadows of its own fixture (see Figure 1.17). This is caused by a need to illuminate a set with multiple lights to attain correct exposure even though the desired light source—in terms of the story—is singular.

Figure 1.17 A lamp unrealistically casts three sharp shadows of itself (as seen in a frame blowup from a 1950s motion picture).

In contrast, naturalistic lighting is often found in post-1950s historical dramas, particularly those set in times before the advent of the lightbulb. Prime examples include *Barry Lyndon* (1975), directed by Stanley Kubrick (1928–1999), and *1492*

(1992), directed by Ridley Scott (1937–). In these works, lighting is motivated by combinations of sunlight, moonlight, candlelight, and firelight. Keys, fills, and their resulting shadows are often extremely soft. The naturalistic lighting approach is not limited to historical drama, however. Kubrick also employed naturalistic lighting in such films as *A Clockwork Orange* (1971) and *The Shining* (1980).

In the world of art, naturalistic lighting can be found in any of the painting genres that placed a premium on accurate lighting. For example, Jan van Eyck (1385–1440) was an early adopter of physically accurate painting. In Figure 1.18, the light from several windows bounces through a room, creating soft shadows along the way. Van Eyck helped to establish the style of the Early Renaissance, which placed an importance on the study of the natural world. Note that the subtleties in lighting are easily seen even when the painting is reproduced in black and white.

Figure 1.18 Van Eyck, *The Arnolfini Portrait*, 1434, tempura on wood. National Gallery, London.

In addition to chiaroscuro works, the baroque movement produced many naturalistic paintings. The movement placed an emphasis on emotionally and physically accurate portrayals of subjects. Two Dutch painters, Jan Vermeer (1632–1675) and Pieter de Hooch (1629–1684), were particularly successful at rendering soft, naturally lit interiors and exteriors.

Realism, as an art movement, appeared in the mid-19th century and placed a premium on an accurately portrayed world with no hint of idealism or romanticism. Realist artists include George Caleb Bingham (1811–1879) and Jules Breton (1827–1906), both of whom are noted for their accurately rendered outdoor scenes. Impressionism, centered in France in the 1860s and considered a branch of realism, sought to faithfully portray light and color as perceived by the human eye.

Naturalistic lighting, by its very nature, does not dictate a fixed number of lights or specific light locations or intensities. However, you can use the following guidelines to assist you during setup:

- Determine what the strongest light is and where it should be coming from. Is the light source visible within the frame or is it arriving from offscreen? Set one or more key lights in appropriate locations. Match the type of light to the type of source. (See Chapter 2, "Applying the Correct Maya Light Type," for more information on Maya light types.) Render tests to determine the appropriate intensities of the key or keys before adding fill lights.

- Determine what secondary light sources are needed. Are these sources physical (that is, a lamp, a candle, and so on), or are they actually the bounced light of the strongest light source? Set fill lights in the appropriate locations. If you are copying an existing location, replicate the key-to-fill ratio. If the scene you are creating does not exist in the real world, apply a key-to-fill ratio that is similar to an equivalent location in the real world.

- When applying shadows, replicate the type of shadow that is naturally produced by a specific light source. For example, midday sunlight creates hard-edged parallel shadows (see Figure 1.19). An artificial source close to the subject, such as a lightbulb, produces a shadow that widens and softens over distance. (See Chapter 3, "Creating High-Quality Shadows," for information on shadow creation in Maya.)

- Color is equally important when reproducing a particular location. Different light sources create different wavelengths of light, which in turn produce specific hues that are perceived by the human eye or recorded on a medium such as film or video. (See Chapter 2 for information concerning Maya light color. For information on color temperature, see "A Note on Color Temperature" at the end of this chapter.)

Figure 1.19 Left: The sun creates parallel shadows of stone columns; Right: An artificial light source creates a shadow that widens and softens over distance.

Using Stylized Lighting

Stylized lighting pays no heed to the real world but fabricates fantastic sources of light or simply ignores the lighting information altogether.

The oldest form of stylized lighting can be called 0-point lighting. In this case, lighting plays no part in the artistic representation. You can see this in prehistoric art, as well as in the art of ancient or primitive cultures (see Figure 1.20). To this day, 0-point lighting survives as cartoons and comic strips where no shading is added.

Figure 1.20 Petroglyphs, hieroglyphics, and some comic art carry no lighting information.

Stylized lighting is well suited for 3D animation, since the medium places no limitation on the type of lighting employed. For 3D examples of this style, see the section "Step-by-Step: 3D Lighting Examples" at the end of this chapter.

Understanding Color

Successful lighting does not depend on appropriate light placement alone. One crucial component is color. Color theory is an enormous topic, and it is beyond the scope of this book to cover more than the basics. However, a discussion of the RYB and RGB color models, color wheels, color space, color temperature, and light color is worth a look.

Color Theory Overview

In the traditional color theory model, red, yellow, and blue are considered primary colors. As such, they follow these rules:

- No combination of any two primary colors can produce a third primary color.
- Combinations of all three primaries can produce a wider range of colors than any other combination of colors.

You can form secondary colors by mixing together primary colors, which produces orange, green, and violet (purple). You can form tertiary colors by mixing primary colors and secondary colors; the resulting colors are generally given hyphenated names, such as blue-green. The primary, secondary, and tertiary colors are often represented by a 12-step color wheel (see Figure 1.21).

The red-yellow-blue (RYB) color theory model evolved in the 18th century and was based on color materialism, which assumes that primary colors are based on specific, indivisible material pigments found in minerals or other natural substances. The popularization of specific RYB colors was aided by printmakers such as Jakob Christoffel Le Blon (1667–1741), who developed the color separation printing process. The color wheel itself was invented by Sir Isaac Newton (1642–1727) in 1704, although his variation contained seven hues visible when white light was split by a prism.

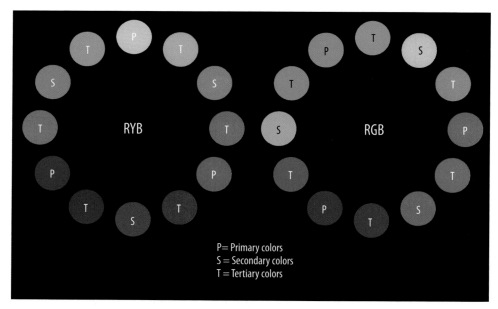

Figure 1.21 Left: Red-yellow-blue (RYB) color wheel re-created in Maya. The scene is included with the Chapter 1 tutorial files as RYB_wheel.ma; Right: Red-green-blue (RGB) color wheel re-created in Maya. The scene is included with the Chapter 1 tutorial files as RGB_wheel.ma.

The development of computer graphics, however, has added a new set of primary colors: red, green, and blue, or RGB. This produces its own unique color wheel (see Figure 1.21). Through an additive process, computer monitors mix red, green, and blue light to produce additional colors. Added in equal proportions, RGB primaries produce white. In contrast, the RYB color theory model is subtractive in that the absence of red, yellow, and blue produces white (assuming that the blank paper or canvas is white). In this case, if colored paint or ink pigments are present, they absorb certain wavelengths of light, thus preventing those wavelengths from being reflected back at the viewer. When combined in equal proportions, the RYB primaries produce black (having absorbed *all* visible wavelengths of light). Modern printing techniques follow the subtractive model by using cyan, magenta, and yellow primary inks, with the addition of black ink (CMYK, where K is black). Cyan, magenta, and yellow happen to be secondary colors on the RGB color wheel. The Color Chooser window in Maya represents the RGB color wheel as a circular shape, with red in the 3 o'clock position. (For more information on the Color Chooser, see Chapter 6, "Creating Custom Connections and Applying Color Utilities."

Despite the disparity between color theory models, methods of using a RYB color wheel are equally applicable to RGB color wheels. As such, the goal of color selection is color harmony, which is the pleasing selection and arrangement of colors within a piece of art. The most common methods of choosing harmonic colors produce the following color combinations with the RGB color wheel:

Complementary Colors   A pair of colors at opposite ends of the color wheel. For example, in Figure 1.22, the blue-cyan body and red-orange head of a bizarre character compose a complementary color set.

Figure 1.22 A blue-cyan body and a red-orange head form complementary colors. This still is taken from the short film *7 Deadly Sins for the 21st Century.*

Split Complement   One color plus the two colors that flank that color's complementary color (for example, green, blue-violet, and red-violet).

Analogous Colors   Colors that are side-by-side. For example, in Figure 1.23 the leaf color varies from red-orange to yellow-orange. In RGB, red-orange is a mixture of primary red and tertiary orange; yellow-orange is the mixture of secondary yellow and tertiary orange. If compared to the RYB color wheel, the colors correspond to secondary orange and tertiary yellow-orange, which are also analogous.

PHOTO © KIRILART / DOLLAR PHOTO CLUB

Figure 1.23   The colors of the leaves on the ground in a painting form analogous colors, both in RGB and RYB.

Diad   Two colors that have a single color position between them (for example, secondary violet and primary red on the RGB color wheel).

Triad   Three colors that are equally spaced on the wheel.

N o t e :   A common mistake made by many 2D and 3D animators is the overuse of pure primary and secondary colors in their designs. Colors located between the secondary and tertiary elements will provide a more diverse palette. For instance, instead of choosing 1, 0, 1 in Maya RGB color space, try selecting 0.5, 0.4, 0.8 for a more muted variation of violet.

Checking Color Calibration

Maya operates in RGB color space. Color space represents all the colors that a device can produce. The color space available to various output devices varies greatly. For example, the color space that a television can display is significantly different from the color space available to a computer monitor or a printer.

Never assume that a computer monitor is displaying your renders correctly. If you are creating an animation for video, it's best to check the resulting edit on a professional broadcast monitor. If you are creating a render for print, bring the render into Adobe Photoshop or a similar program, convert the RGB color space to CMYK color space, and choose the correct color profile. If you are creating the animation for motion picture film, calibrate your monitor based on the suggestions of the service or personnel transferring the frames. In many cases, a lookup table (LUT) is developed to properly map the gamma of the computer monitors used by animators. Portable calibration hardware, and matching software, is also used to check the calibration result. (The color displayed by a monitor "drifts" over time.) Although monitor calibration equipment may be impractical for an independent animator, calibration shortcuts can be taken.

A quick-and-dirty method of checking the color calibration of a monitor involves the use of a chip chart. For example, in Figure 1.24 a chart runs from black to white in 11 distinct steps and in a continuous gradient. When displayed on a monitor, a portion of the chart may appear "crushed." (Certain steps may no longer be visible, and the gradient may no longer be smooth.) If this is the case with your monitor, you might unintentionally base a scene's lighting on an inaccurate view of the scene's actual color space. The end result might be an animation that appears too dark and muddy on video or too bright and washed out on film. Adjusting the brightness, contrast, gamma, and color temperature of the monitor can alleviate this problem. Although you can usually adjust the brightness and contrast through a monitor's external control panel, the gamma and color temperature are usually controlled through a piece of calibration software (for example, the Windows 8 operating system provides color management software tools). For more information on gamma, see Chapter 6.

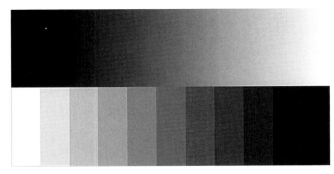

Figure 1.24 A calibration chip chart. This file is included with the Chapter 1 tutorial files as `chip_chart.tif`.

A Note on Color Temperature

Color temperature is based on the wavelength of light emitted by a material when it is heated. Technically speaking, if a light source is said to be 5500 Kelvin (K), it emits the same wavelength of light, and the same color of light, as a black body radiator heated to 5500 K. A black body radiator is a theoretical material that absorbs 100 percent of the radiation that strikes it when the body is at absolute zero (−273 C°). Although there are no true black bodies in the real world, graphite and various metals come close. In the original experiments by William Kelvin (1824–1907), a block of heated carbon was used. The Kelvin, on the other hand, is a measurement of temperature that adds 273 to the temperature read in Celsius. The Kelvin measurement only refers to the thermal temperature of the theoretical black body radiator and is not the actual temperature of a light source. In other words, a fluorescent lightbulb does not have to reach a real-world 4000 K to produce the same color of light as the black body radiator at 4000 K; instead, the color of the bulb is roughly correlated to the color of the heated black body.

When a material is heated to a temperature above 700 K, it emits visible light. At temperatures close to 700 K, the light wavelength is long and the perceived light is red. At temperatures above 6000 K, the wavelength becomes shorter and the perceived color shifts to blue. The chart in Figure 1.25 indicates the color temperature of various light sources and their perceived colors. The colors represented are only a rough approximation. In addition, the color temperatures listed for each light source are an average; depending on the circumstance or the method of manufacture, color temperatures can easily vary by hundreds of Kelvin. Light-emitting diode (LED) lightbulbs are also rated for specific temperatures. For example, a "warm" LED bulb may be 3000 K whereas a "cool white" LED may be 4100 K to 5000 K. Some LED lamps offer the ability to shift between color temperatures.

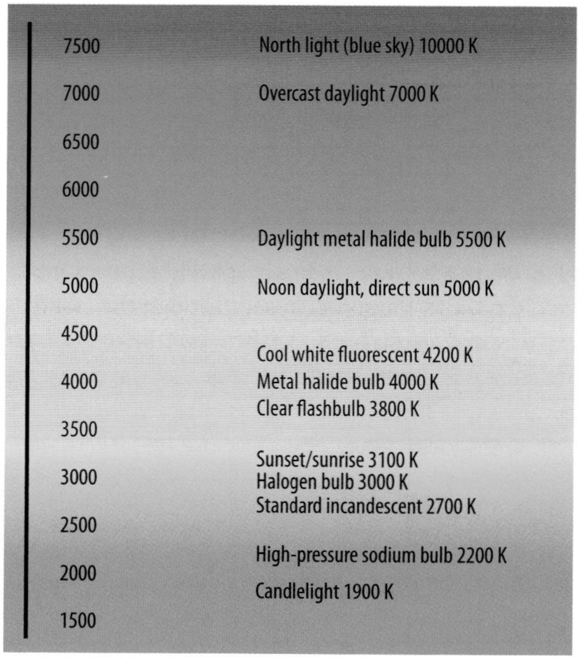

7500	North light (blue sky) 10000 K
7000	Overcast daylight 7000 K
6500	
6000	
5500	Daylight metal halide bulb 5500 K
5000	Noon daylight, direct sun 5000 K
4500	Cool white fluorescent 4200 K
4000	Metal halide bulb 4000 K Clear flashbulb 3800 K
3500	
3000	Sunset/sunrise 3100 K Halogen bulb 3000 K Standard incandescent 2700 K
2500	
2000	High-pressure sodium bulb 2200 K Candlelight 1900 K
1500	

Figure 1.25 Color temperatures of common light sources. This image is included with the Chapter 1 tutorial files as color_chart.tif.

Setting a White Point (White Balance)

When you work with monitor calibration, color temperature is used to set the white point of the hardware. (Setting the white point is also commonly referred to as *setting the white balance*.) A white point is a coordinate in color space that defines what is "white." If a monitor is given a white point with a high Kelvin value, the display has a blue cast. If a monitor is given a white point with a low Kelvin value, the display has a yellow cast. The flexibility of the white point is necessary to match potential output formats. For example, graphic artists might set their monitors to 5500 K to better match the appearance of physical paper or canvas in a common work environment. For 3D animation intended for video, 6500 K generally works, because 6500 K is a common setting for SDTV and HDTV television sets. Many HDTV sets, both consumer and broadcast, offer the option to switch to 5400 K to better match motion picture film or 9300 K for cooler colors.

When lighting in Maya, you do not need to know the Kelvin temperature of a light source. What is important, however, is that the color of the light logically fits the type of source. For example, daytime sunlight varies from white to blue. Firelight varies from red to orange. Older incandescent lightbulbs are yellowish. If a light color is out of place, a scene may appear incorrect to the viewer. Obviously, if you are matching 3D to a live-action plate, colors should be replicated regardless of what they might be. However, if the 3D is only meant to *look* real, colors—as they're perceived by the human eye—should be matched.

For more information on color manipulation, see Chapter 6. For information on color bit depth, see Chapter 10, "Prepping for Successful Renders."

Step-by-Step: 3D Lighting Examples

In this section, I'll discuss the lighting approach of various independent animations I've worked on. The lighting ranges from naturalistic to stylized.

Millennium Bug featured a series of otherworldly characters inserted into photographs of San Francisco. Simple naturalistic lighting was employed to match the cloudy, overcast weather conditions of the photos. As the film was presented in black and white, light color was not important. However, attention was given to the relative intensities of the lights to re-create the light levels at the actual locations. In one shot (see Figure 1.26), a 3D head was added to a preexisting crane. A single spotlight, positioned high and to the right, served as a key and emulated the sun diffused through the clouds. A very low intensity fill light was placed low and to the left to emulate the net fill arriving from the ground. The shadow of the head on the building was added in the composite. Film grain and an artificial camera move were also added in postproduction.

Mirror employed an extreme example of chiaroscuro lighting. Many shots possessed only a single key with a limited cone size and no fill. With this project, lighting decisions were purely aesthetic and stylistic and were not intended to match any specific location. That said, the goal was to make the lighting somber and foreboding, much like film noir movies. In Figure 1.27, a woman is lit with a single spotlight from screen left. The shadow directly behind the woman was fabricated in the composite and is hence less dense than other shadows in the shot.

Figure 1.26 *Millennium Bug*

Figure 1.27 *Mirror*. A QuickTime movie excerpt is included on the CD as `mirror.mov`.

In *Day Off the Dead*, a combination of naturalistic and 2-point lighting was used. For exteriors, one to four lights were placed to emulate a bright, sunlit day (see the top of Figure 1.28). For the interiors, rarely more than two lights were used; in each case, there was always a strong key. Much as in *Mirror*, the goal was to create a somewhat stylistic and somber look that fit the deathly topic. Many of the shadows were created during the composite, which allowed the shadow shapes to go off in unrealistic and inappropriate directions (see the bottom of Figure 1.28). Depth of field was added for many shots in postproduction.

Figure 1.28 *Day Off the Dead*. A QuickTime movie excerpt is included in the Chapter 1 tutorial files as `dotd.mov`.

Weapons of Mass Destruction employed high-key lighting with supersaturated colors. The film was constructed as a series of short vignettes, many of which served as bizarre commercials from the future. In one shot (see Figure 1.29), a worm was lit with a strong key from the front. The ambience and incandescence of the character's material prevented the need for any additional lights. The background, which started as a 3D piece, was eventually converted to a digital matte painting.

Figure 1.29 *Weapons of Mass Destruction.* A QuickTime movie excerpt is included in the Chapter 1 tutorial files as womd.mov.

Little Dead Girl made use of stylistic lighting. In many cases, the light hitting the characters had little to do with the environment. In the two shots featured in Figure 1.30, the Little Dead Girl, the Lab Frog, and the Eyeball Child were each given their own sets of key lights, fill lights, and rim lights. The goal of the lighting was simply to model the characters in an interesting fashion. The colors employed by many of the lights were tied to specific story locations or times of day (for example, blue rims for moonlight). In other instances, colors were selected that formed complementary or analogous sets with other lights or with the modeled and textured background. In the end, the animation took on the feel of stop-motion cinematography.

Figure 1.30 *Little Dead Girl*

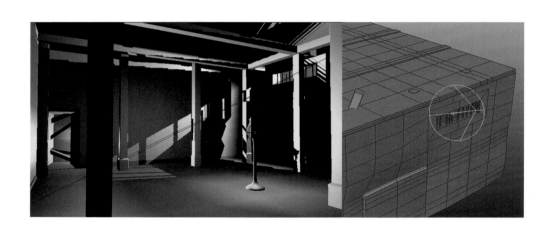

Applying the Correct Maya Light Type

2

Autodesk® Maya® offers six types of lights that emulate a wide range of real-world lighting situations. Familiarity with the way light interacts with various environments will benefit your 3D lighting. Light Fog and Light Glow effects are also available through Maya lights, giving you even more flexibility when re-creating specific lighting situations. The Relationship Editor can link lights to objects, allowing you to create multiple lighting setups in a single scene.

Chapter Contents
Qualities of each of the six Maya light types
Real-world equivalents for each light type
Linking and unlinking lights
Creating Light Fog and Light Glow
A review of Environment Fog and Volume Fog

Reviewing Maya Light Types

The six Maya light types have unique sets of qualities and are thus appropriate for different situations. Although spot and ambient lights receive the most use, directional, point, area, and volume lights are equally valuable. Despite their differences, the six types share many common attributes, which are discussed in the next section.

If no lights are present in a scene, Maya creates a default lighting scheme. Once a light is created, the default lighting scheme is overridden. You can turn off the default scheme at any time by deselecting the Enable Default Light attribute in the Render Options section of the Common tab in the Render Settings window.

When you choose Shading > Smooth Shade All from a viewport menu, Maya ignores any lights you may have added to the scene and continues to use the default lighting. To see the added lights working in the viewport, choose Lighting > Use All Lights from the viewport menu.

N o t e : Any given viewport has three different interactive render modes. By default, Maya 2014 viewports are set to Default Quality Rendering, which is the fastest but least accurate hardware rendering method. You can switch to High Quality Rendering through the viewport Renderer menu. High Quality Rendering creates surface shading with greater accuracy. Viewpoint 2.0, also available through the Rendering menu, offers the best optimization for complex scenes and is able to display bump and normal maps. Viewport 2.0 also supports motion blur and anti-aliasing if those attributes are selected through the Hardware Renderer 2.0 Settings window (choose Renderer >Viewport 2.0 > ❏) .

With Maya 2015, Viewport 2.0 is the default setting. Default Quality Rendering is renamed Legacy Default Viewport and High Quality Rendering is renamed Legacy High Quality Viewport. None of the render modes will incorporate cast shadows unless you select Lighting > Shadows through the viewport menu.

Investigating Common Light Attributes

This section describes common attributes shared by all Maya lights. These are found in the Light Attributes section of the lights' Attribute Editor tabs (see Figure 2.6 later in this chapter).

Color   Sets the color of the light. If you map a texture to this attribute, the result is similar to a slide projector and the texture appears on the surfaces that the light strikes.

You can emulate the shadow of an object that does not exist by mapping a black-and-white texture to the Color attribute. For example, in Figure 2.1 a bitmap featuring black leaves on a white background is mapped to a spot light, which creates a simulated, treelike shadow. In this case, the Color Gain attribute of the File texture that carries the bitmap is tinted blue to replicate moonlight. (When mapping the Color attribute of a point or ambient light, the texture becomes distorted because both lights are omnidirectional. Area lights also produce a distorted image due to their design.)

Figure 2.1 The shadow of a tree is created by mapping the Color of a spot light. The scene and image are included with the Chapter 2 tutorial files as `spot_leaves.ma` and `leaves.tif`.

If the Color attribute is not mapped, you can animate the color value changing over time by setting several keys. To set a key, move the timeline to a desired frame, RMB-click over the Color attribute name in the Attribute Editor tab, and choose Set Key from the menu. To edit the resulting red, green, and blue animation curves, select the light and open the Graph Editor (choose Window > Animation Editors > Graph Editor).

Intensity Controls the brightness of the light. You can apply a texture to this attribute to vary the intensity across the throw of the light. The texture serves as a multiplier. If Intensity is set to 2 and the texture is 50 percent gray, the intensity of the light will only be 1.0 when it strikes a surface.

Illuminates By Default Serves as an on/off switch for the light.

Emit Diffuse and Emit Specular Determine whether the light will affect the diffuse and specular calculations of a material during a render. You can deselect each attribute independently. If only Emit Specular is selected, the specular highlights render by themselves; however, the alpha channel will include the entire surface. Controlling the render of diffuse and specular components may be useful for setting up render passes, which are discussed in Chapter 12, "Working with mental ray Shaders, Global Illumination, and Final Gathering."

Activating Light Manipulators

Maya lights offer manipulator handles to make the positioning of the light icons easier. You can activate a manipulator by selecting the light and choosing Display > Rendering > Camera/Light Manipulator > *manipulator name*. (To hide the manipulator, choose it again it from the menu.) The following manipulator handles are available for all six lights:

Cycling Index Displays an upside-down Q-shaped icon that, when clicked, cycles through all the other available manipulators (see Figure 2.2). This is perhaps the most efficient way to use the light manipulators.

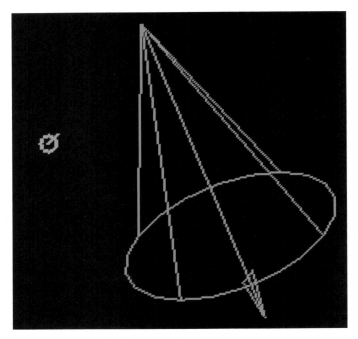

Figure 2.2 A spot light's Cycling Index manipulator

Center Of Interest   Displays a Center Of Interest manipulator and an Eye Point manipulator (see Figure 2.3). When the Center Of Interest is translated, the light rotates automatically to follow. You can also translate the Eye Point manipulator and thus move the body of the light.

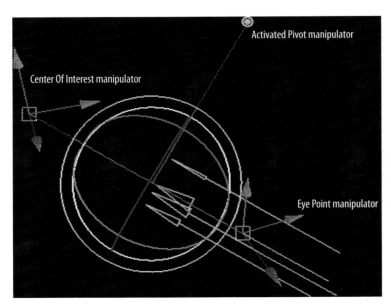

Figure 2.3   A directional light's Center Of Interest and Pivot manipulators. The Pivot manipulator handle is activated so that the Rotate tool operates around the new pivot point.

Pivot Displays a handle that sets the light's pivot point. You can drag the handle's small circle across the light's Center Of Interest line, which is automatically displayed with the Pivot manipulator (see Figure 2.3). You can set the pivot in front of or behind the light. To rotate the light with the new pivot point, click the small circle so that its center becomes solid yellow and choose the Rotate tool. To return the rotation to the light's origin, click the small circle a second time. If the Pivot manipulator is hidden while it is active (that is, solid yellow at the center), the Rotate tool will continue to operate around the new pivot point.

Working with Light Decay

By default, the light of ambient, directional, point, and spot lights never decays. That is, its intensity appears the same whether an object struck by the light is one world unit from the light or a million world units from the light. However, with point and spot lights you can force the light to lose intensity by changing the Decay Rate attribute to Linear, Quadratic, or Cubic. The Decay Rate options are ordered from the mildest to the harshest (see Figure 2.4). With Quadratic, the intensity decreases proportionally with the square of the distance (Intensity = $1/\text{distance}^2$), which matches light within the Earth's atmosphere. When using any decay, you will need to raise the Intensity value of the light. For example, in Figure 2.4 each light is given an Intensity value of 150. Even so, the light with the Cubic Decay Rate manages to illuminate no more than 12 world units from its origin.

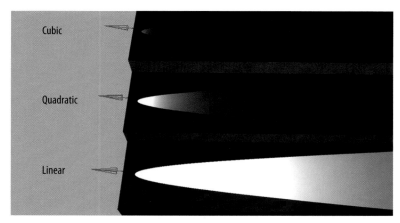

Figure 2.4 Linear, Quadratic, and Cubic decay rates for a spot light. This scene is included with the Chapter 2 tutorial files as `spot_decay.ma`.

Note: Area lights naturally decay over distance. Nevertheless, area lights carry a Decay Rate attribute to speed the decay process. In contrast, directional and ambient lights have no natural decay. However, you can create decay through a custom shading network. See Chapter 7, "Automating a Scene with Sampler Nodes," for an example using the Light Info utility. Volume lights, on the other hand, are constrained by their sphere, box, cylinder, or cone light shape.

Using Spot Lights

Maya spot lights are named after the spotlights used on stage and in motion pictures. As opposed to their real-world counterparts, however, the light rays from a Maya spot light are born at an infinitely small point in space. The light rays quickly diverge and follow the shape of the spot light cone. Although the cone has a finite length, the light rays continue on indefinitely.

Note: The scale of a light icon does not affect the light quality of a spot, directional, ambient, or point light. However, the scale of an area or volume light icon does affect their light quality. Light icon rotation affects a spot, directional, and area light, but does not affect a point or ambient light. Each light is discussed in more detail in this chapter.

Spot lights are ideal for emulating light that possesses one or more of the following traits:

- Naturally divergent rays
- Close proximity to the subject
- Identifiable transition between 0 and 100 percent intensity

Hence, flashlights, car headlights, recessed lighting, lamps with shades, overhead lighting that "pools," and sunlight diffusely bounced through a window are all good candidates for spot lights (see Figure 2.5).

Figure 2.5 Real-world lighting situations that match the qualities of Maya spot lights

In addition to standard attributes, Maya spot lights carry Cone Angle, Penumbra Angle, and Dropoff attributes (Figure 2.6).

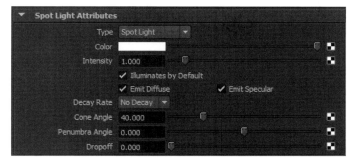

Figure 2.6   The Light Attributes section of a spot light's Attribute Editor tab

Cone Angle sets the diameter of the spot light throw. The Penumbra Angle represents the transition from full light intensity to no light intensity. The larger the Penumbra Angle value, the softer the edge of the spot light. If the Penumbra Angle value is smaller than the Cone Angle value, Cone Angle establishes the outermost limit of the spot light's illumination (see Figure 2.7). If the Penumbra Angle value is larger than the Cone Angle value, Penumbra Angle establishes the outermost limit of the spot light's illumination. The Dropoff attribute also affects the softness of the spot light edge. However, Dropoff only determines the rate at which the light Intensity degrades from the light center to the Cone Angle edge. If Dropoff is set to 1.0, there is no degradation.

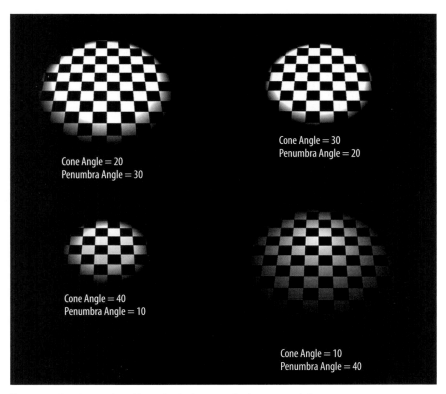

Figure 2.7   Four Cone Angle and Penumbra Angle settings for the same spot light

Spot lights are unable to emulate daytime sunlight accurately, since the spot light rays can never be parallel. Additionally, if the Cone Angle of a spot light is set to a large value, such as 120, the resulting shadows are distorted. (For more information on shadows, see Chapter 3, "Creating High-Quality Shadows.")

Employing Spot Light Manipulators

In addition to standard light manipulators, Maya spot lights include Cone Angle, Penumbra, Look Through Barn Doors, and Decay Regions manipulators. You can activate one of these manipulators by selecting the light and choosing Display > Rendering > Camera/Light Manipulator > *manipulator name*. The manipulators are described here:

Cone Angle Creates a circular handle at the edge of the light cone that allows you to interactively increase or decrease the Cone Angle attribute. If you click-drag the small cyan cube, the cone size will change.

Penumbra Creates a circular handle at the center of the light cone that allows you to interactively increase or decrease the Penumbra Angle attribute.

Look Through Barn Doors Toggles on virtual barn doors for the spot light. In the real world, barn doors are rectangular metal flaps that control the light throw of a spotlight. In Maya, barn doors allow a normally circular light to be square. To see the Look Through Barn Doors manipulator, you must select the Barn Doors attribute in the Light Effects section of the spot light's Attribute Editor tab, choose Panels > Look Through Selected through a viewport menu, and choose Display > Rendering > Camera/Light Manipulator > Look Through Barn Doors.

The barn doors are represented by two horizontal and two vertical cyan lines. If you reduce the values of the Left Barn Door, Right Barn Door, Top Barn Door, or Bottom Barn Door attributes in the Light Effects section, the barn door lines move closer to the center of the light. The smaller the remaining "hole," the smaller the rectangular light shape when the light strikes a surface. If a barn door line extends past the circular edge of the light, the circular edge serves as the cutoff point for that section of the light (see Figure 2.8). You can interactively click and drag the barn door lines in the viewport when Panels > Look Through Selected is activated for the light.

Decay Regions Displays circular handles that represent decay regions. You can force the light to possess specific decay regions by selecting the Use Decay Regions attribute in the Decay Regions section of the spot light's Attribute Editor tab. Three regions, labeled 1, 2, and 3, are provided. Each region has a Start Distance and an End Distance attribute. Both attributes represent a specified number of world units from the light's origin. The section between the Start Distance and End Distance represents the area where the light is active. The gaps between these sections represent the areas that receive no light. Hence, you can force the light to "skip" across surfaces (see Figure 2.9). You do not have to use all three regions. If the End Distance and Start Distance values of two neighboring regions are identical, the decay between the regions is nonexistent. You can LMB-drag the Decay Regions manipulator circles to interactively resize the regions. The Use Decay Regions and Decay Rate attributes are compatible. However, shadows are unaffected by the use of the Use Decay Regions attribute.

Figure 2.8 Top: Look Through Barn Doors manipulators for two spot lights; Bottom: The corresponding light shapes made by the spot lights.

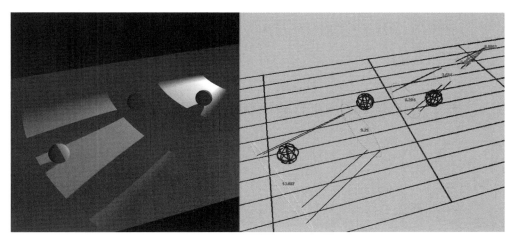

Figure 2.9 Light "skips" across a plane when the Use Decay Regions attribute for a spot light is selected.

Controlling Spot Light Decay and Color with Curves

For a more subtle decay with Maya spot lights, you can create custom curves with the Intensity attribute. To do so, click the Intensity Curve Create button in the Light Effects section of the light's Attribute Editor tab. A curve node is automatically created (see Figure 2.10). By default, the curve is given an excessive number of keyframes. Nevertheless, you can delete or add keys as necessary in the Graph Editor (choose Window > Animation Editors > Graph Editor). The Intensity of the light is represented by the down-to-up Y direction of the graph. The distance the light travels in world units from its origin is represented by the left-to-right X direction of the graph. The distance is determined with the aid of a Light Info utility. (For more information, see Chapter 7.) By default, the curve starts at 1.0 and ends at 100 in the X direction, but you can scale the curve or move keyframes if necessary.

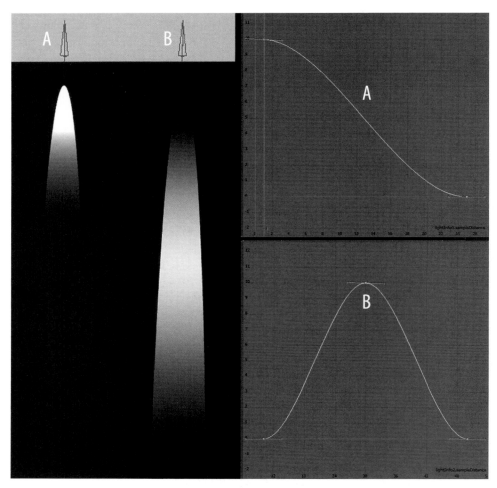

Figure 2.10 Two spot lights are given custom Intensity curves. This scene is included with the Chapter 2 tutorial files as `spot_curves.ma`.

You can create similar curves for the light's Color. To do so, click the Color Curves Create button in the Light Effects section of the light's Attribute Editor tab. In this situation, separate curve nodes are created for the Red, Green, and Blue channels. Once again, the default curves will have an excessive number of keyframes; these can also be edited in the Graph Editor.

Using Directional Lights

Directional lights provide light direction without light position. That is, they are infinite and constant in one direction. The position and the scale of the directional light icon do not affect the light's intensity. Thus, the primary control for a directional light is its rotation.

Directional lights are ideal for emulating light that possesses one or more of the following traits:

- Naturally parallel rays
- A source that is a great distance from the subject
- No identifiable edge or falloff

Hence, direct sunlight and moonlight are the best candidates for directional lights (see Figure 2.11).

Figure 2.11 Real-world lighting situations that match the qualities of Maya directional lights

Directional lights are ideal for set pieces that are large in world space. In the same situation, a spot light would have to be placed extremely far from the subject or have its Cone Angle increased to a very large value, which in turn would cause the light's shadows to become even less parallel (see Chapter 3 for a comparison of shadows).

Using Ambient Lights

Ambient lights create a diffuse light emanating in all directions. Ambient lights do not contribute to specular or bump map calculations. If a scene is lit solely with ambient lights and a material has a bump map, the bump map will not be visible.

Ambient lights are ideal for emulating light that possesses one or more of the following traits:

- Extremely diffuse or random rays
- Little, if any, variation in intensity
- Visible in areas that are shadowed by other lights

Hence, ambient lights are well suited for fill light. In particular, light that bounces off walls and light that bounces off the ground are appropriate for ambient lights (see Figure 2.12). As discussed in Chapter 1, "Understanding Lighting and Color," fill lights are often the least intense light in a scene.

Figure 2.12 Real-world lighting situations that match the qualities of Maya ambient lights. Details visible in the cast shadows of the key light (the sun) indicate the presence of fill light (reflected sunlight).

By default, ambient lights are not truly omnidirectional. The Ambient Shade attribute, found in the Ambient Light Attributes section of the Attribute Editor tab, controls the balance between omnidirectional and directional light rays for the light.

The default Ambient Shade value of 0.45 mixes omnidirectional and directional rays (see Figure 2.13). If Ambient Shade is 0, the light is read with equal intensity at all points in the scene. This creates a flat, "toon" style of render which may be appropriate for special render passes (discussed in Chapter 12). If Ambient Shade is 1.0, the light emanates from the current position of the light icon; in this situation, the light is identical to a point light. If Ambient Shade is 0, it does not matter where the light icon is placed. In general, a default Ambient Shade value is suitable for most renders.

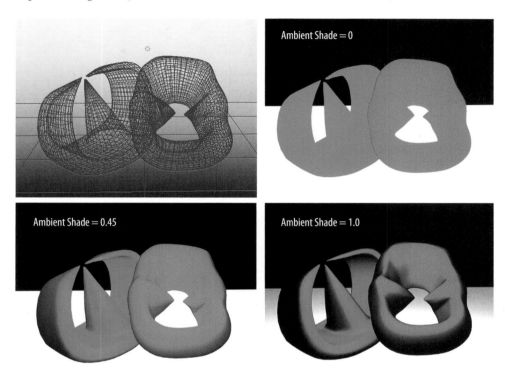

Figure 2.13 Various Ambient Shade values for an ambient light. This scene in included with the Chapter 2 tutorial files as `ambient_shade.ma`.

Using Point Lights

Point lights represent a light source at a fixed position. Light emanates in all directions from the light icon. The light is generated from an infinitely small point at the center of the icon.

Point lights are ideal for emulating light that possesses one or both of the following traits:

- Omnidirectional
- Physically represented by a spherical shape

Hence, incandescent lightbulbs are the perfect candidate for point lights. Point lights can also emulate LEDs and compact fluorescent lighting (see Figure 2.14).

Figure 2.14 Real-world lighting situations that match the qualities of Maya point lights

Using Area Lights

Area lights are physically based lights that emanate from a confined, flat area. Area lights can be scaled in two directions (X and Y). Area lights have a center pointer that indicates the direction in which the light is flowing.

Area lights are ideal for emulating light that possesses one or more of the following traits:

- Emanates from a flat or narrow source
- Bounces off or transmits through a large, flat surface
- Possesses decay that is affected by distance and angle

Hence, area lights match light filtering through a window or bouncing off a large wall. Area lights can also re-create fluorescent lighting fixtures, strips of neon light, backlit signs, and large, dense banks of incandescent bulbs (see Figure 2.15).

Area lights do not produce parallel light rays. Instead, area lights create a series of rays that emanate from the light icon at sampled positions along the height and width. In essence, area lights function as an array of stacked point lights (see Figure 2.16).

The intensity of an area light is affected by its Intensity attribute *and* its relative angle and size. That is, if the angle between the surface normal and the light direction vector of a single ray is large, the light intensity contribution of the ray is low. If the angle between the surface normal and the light direction vector of a single ray is small, the light intensity contribution of that ray is high. Since area lights produce a series of rays that are sampled across the height and width of the light icon, a unique light direction vector exists for each ray of the series. In addition, the net amount of light an area light contributes to a scene is dependent on its light icon size.

Figure 2.15 Real-world lighting situations that match the qualities of Maya area lights

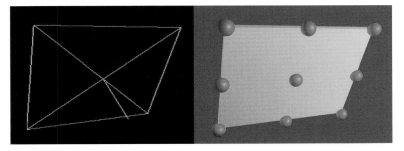

Figure 2.16 Left: Area light icon; Right: A simplified representation of an area light array. Red spheres represent sampled positions that generate light rays.

Because the light rays of an area light diverge from their origins, the edge of the area light's throw is soft. The degree of softness depends on the distance between the light and the surface. For example, the higher the light is raised above a surface, the more diffuse the edge (the divergent rays have the opportunity to overlap to a greater degree). Although area lights are either square or rectangular, the edge is always rounded at the corners. For a perfectly square pattern, you can use a spot light with barn doors.

Area lights, by their nature, decay automatically. Nevertheless, a Decay Rate attribute is provided to accelerate the decay process.

Using Volume Lights

Volume lights possess a shape icon that dictates the extent of their light throw (how far light radiates omnidirectionally). You can scale and translate the shape icon to achieve different light falloffs. By default, the light's Light Shape attribute is set to Sphere. You can switch the attribute to Box, Cylinder, or Cone. You can find the Light Shape attribute in the Volume Light Attributes section of the light's Attribute Editor tab.

By default, a volume light shoots light rays from the center of its shape icon in an outward direction; in this way, the volume light is similar to a point light. However, the light will never escape from or exceed the boundary of the shape icon. You can force the light rays to shoot inward from the boundary of the shape by changing the Volume Light Dir attribute to Inward. On the other hand, if Volume Light Dir is set to Down Axis, the light rays will be generated in parallel and will all follow the light shape's down axis. By default, the down axis points toward negative Y. The axis is indicated by the shape icon's green arrow when Down Axis is chosen (see Figure 2.17). You can rotate the shape icon if need be.

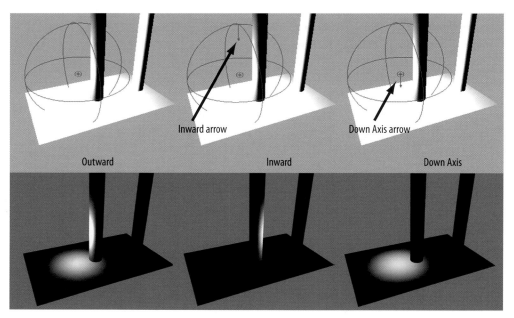

Figure 2.17 Volume light with Volume Light Dir set to Outward, Inward, and Down Axis. The light intersects a plane and one of two cylinders. This scene is included with the Chapter 2 tutorial files as `volume_axis.ma`.

Note: If a volume light's illumination fails to appear in a Maya Software render, temporarily deactivate the Mayatomr.mll plug-in (choose Windows > Settings/Preferences > Plug-In Manager).

By default, the volume shape is closed. However, if Light Shape is set to Sphere, Cylinder, or Cone, you can reduce the Arc attribute and thus use only a section of the light. For example, if Light Shape is set to Sphere, Volume Light Dir is set to Outward, and Arc is set to 90, a pie-shaped wedge of light is created on an intersecting plane.

You can add additional ambient light to the volume shape by checking the Emit Ambient attribute in the Color Range section. In this situation, ambient light is added to all points within the volume shape.

The quality of the light produced by a volume light is controlled by two ramp graphs: Penumbra and Color Range. The Penumbra ramp, which is available to Cylinder and Cone shapes, controls the light falloff. The left side of the ramp represents the intensity of the light at the volume shape's outer edge. The right side of the ramp represents the intensity of the light at the shape's center. You can insert additional handles into the Penumbra ramp by clicking the ramp field. If a handle is pulled down to 0, the light will have zero intensity at that point. Additionally, you can widen the end of the Cone shape by raising the value of the Cone End Radius attribute. In its default state, the Cone shape's down axis extends from the point of the cone.

The Color Range ramp controls the color of the light. As with the Penumbra ramp, the left side corresponds to the volume shape's outer edge. You can insert additional handles into the Color Range ramp by clicking the ramp field. The color of each handle is set by the Selected Color swatch. If a handle is set to black, it effectively reduces the light's intensity to zero at that point. For example, in Figure 2.18 the Light Shape of a volume light is set to Box, Volume Light Dir is set to Outward, and Emit Ambient is checked. Three additional color handles are inserted into the Color Range ramp. The result is a stylized light emanating from the center of the cube.

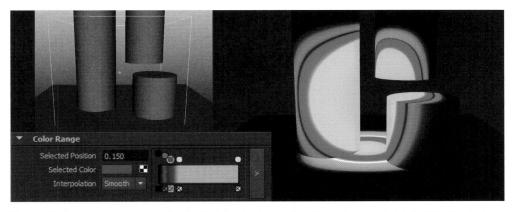

Figure 2.18 A custom Color Range ramp tints the light of a cube shaped volume light. This scene is included with the Chapter 2 tutorial files as `volume_color.ma`.

The main advantage of a volume light is the ease with which the light falloff can be adjusted through the shape icon and the Color Range and Penumbra ramps. Thanks to the flexibility of the light's attributes, a volume light can function in a similar manner to an ambient, a point, or a directional light within a contained (volumetric) space.

Linking and Unlinking Lights

In Maya, there are several ways to link and unlink lights and geometry. By default, a light is linked to all geometry within a scene when it is created. If a light is unlinked from a geometry node (that is, unlinked from a surface), it no longer illuminates that surface. The option is useful for lighting complex scenes where a light may be adversely affecting some surfaces while lighting others properly. In addition, it allows different elements within a scene to have the dedicated set of lights. For example, one character may be given one set of lights with specific settings, whereas a second character is given a separate set of lights with a completely different settings.

The quickest way to unlink a light from a surface is to select the light and surface, switch to the Rendering menu set, and choose Lighting/Shading > Break Light Links. Unlinking affects the Render View and any batch renders but is not reflected in the viewport views unless you activate Smooth Shade All, Use All Lights, and Legacy High Quality Viewport or Viewport 2.0 through the viewport menus (for more information, see the "Reviewing Maya Light Types" section earlier in this chapter). To relink the light and surface, choose Lighting/Shading > Make Light Links.

If Break Light Links fails to work, or if you are linking and unlinking multiple lights and surfaces, it is more efficient to use the Relationship Editor. For example, to unlink a light from multiple surfaces, follow these steps:

1. Select a light. Choose Window > Relationship Editors > Light Linking > Light-Centric. The Relationship Editor window opens (see Figure 2.19 later in this section).

2. The left column of the window lists all the lights in the scene. The right column lists all the geometry nodes, shading group nodes, and assigned materials in the scene. To see only the light you selected, choose List > Manual Load from the left-column menu. This option loads into the column only the lights that are currently selected. The Manual Load option is also available in the right-column List menu.

3. Click the light name in the left column. A blue bar highlights it. At the same time, each surface, shading group node, and assigned material in the right column receives a blue bar, indicating that the light is linked to those items. To break a link, click a name in the right column, which removes the blue bar. You can restore a link by re-clicking a name in the right column. If a long list exists in the right column, you do not have to click each name individually. Instead, click the topmost name and drag the mouse downward; all the names under the mouse arrow are automatically highlighted or unhighlighted.

You can also choose Window > Relationship Editors > Light Linking > Object-Centric, which opens the Relationship Editor with the geometry on the left and the lights on the right. When you do so, you can break the links by clicking the light names. You can switch from Light-Centric to Object-Centric at any time by choosing the option from the window's upper-left drop-down menu.

Note that you do not have to unlink shading group nodes or materials—only the geometry node names. If you do click a highlighted shading group name, all the surfaces assigned to the shading group are unlinked (in fact, the assigned geometry node names are automatically unhighlighted). If you click a geometry node name, only it is unlinked; the other surfaces assigned to the shading group are unaffected.

To simplify the view within the columns of the Relationship Editor window, choose Show > Objects > *object type* from the column menu. If an object type has a check mark beside it, the object type is displayed in the column.

As a working example, in Figure 2.19 two heads and two point lights are placed in the scene. The left light is green and is linked only to the left head. The right light is red and is linked only to the right head. Light linking allows two models to have independent lighting even when they share close proximity. This is often useful when making fine adjustments to models that carry different materials and textures or carry stylistic differences.

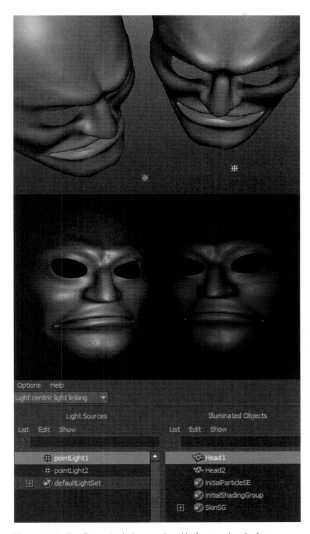

Figure 2.19 Top: Two point lights are placed before two heads; Center: Thanks to light linking, the left green light illuminates only the left head whereas the red right light illuminates only the right head; Bottom: The Light-Centric view in the Relationship Editor showing how pointLight1 is linked to Head1 and no other node. This scene is included with the Chapter 2 tutorial files as `light_linking.ma`.

In addition, it's possible to link and unlink shadows from surfaces. For more information, see Chapter 3.

Generating Fogs and Glows

Maya spot lights, point lights, and volume lights support Light Fog and Light Glow. In addition, Maya area lights support Light Glow. Light Fog creates a virtual fog in a specific volume. Light Glow creates a postprocess light effect (postprocess effects are added at the end of complete renders). In contrast, volume primitives create Volume Fog within specialized containers. In addition, the Maya Software renderer provides the Environment Fog option, which creates fog throughout an entire scene.

Creating Light Fog

To create Light Fog, click the Light Fog checkered attribute button in the Light Effects section of the light's Attribute Editor tab. A Light Fog material, named lightFog, is automatically created and is accessible in the Materials tab of the Hypershade window. The lightFog material node is connected to a new light fog shading group node but has no visible connection to the light itself.

If the light is a spot light, a cone-shaped fog icon instantly extends itself from the original light cone. The new cone, drawn in blue in the viewport views, represents the area in which the fog appears (see Figure 2.20). Scaling the entire spot light increases or decreases the fog area. The fog will not extend past the end of the fog icon but abruptly ends. A utility node named coneShape generates the fog icon.

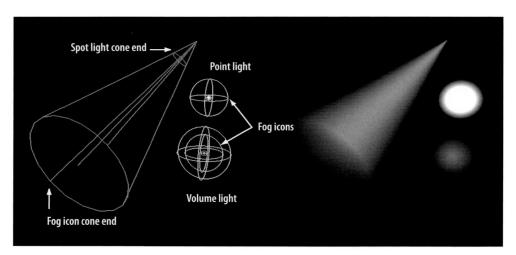

Figure 2.20 Fog icons and default fog renders for a spot light, point light, and volume light. This scene is included with the Chapter 2 tutorial files as `light_fog.ma`.

If the light is a point light or a volume light, a sphere-shaped fog icon is added. Initially, the fog icon for a volume light is the same size as the volume light itself, but the fog icon is scalable. (It's a separate utility node parented to the light shape node.) However, if the fog icon for a volume light is scaled larger than the volume light, the fog is no longer illuminated and is no longer visible in the alpha channel. You can also scale the fog icon of a point light, in which case the size of the icon is not restricted.

Adjusting the Light Fog Material

The Light Fog material carries the following attributes in the Light Fog Attributes and Matte Opacity sections of the Attribute Editor tab:

Color This attribute is multiplied by the light's Color attribute to determine the color of the fog. For example, if the Light Fog material Color is set to yellow and the light's Color attribute is set to cyan, the fog will appear green and the illuminated objects will be struck by cyan light. If the light's Color attribute is left as white, the fog will pick up the color of the Light Fog material Color.

Density   This attribute sets the density of the fog. The higher the value, the more opaque the fog. The density is consistent throughout the entire fog volume. You can set the Density value higher than 1.0.

Color Based Transparency   If selected, this attribute bases the fog's transparency on its color. Bright areas of the fog are the most opaque and dark areas are the most transparent. If deselected, the fog becomes 100 percent opaque within the alpha channel and the colors of the surfaces trapped within the fog are ignored.

Fast Drop Off   When selected, this attribute causes the occlusion of objects within the fog to vary with their distance from the camera (see Figure 2.21). This closely copies the physical nature of real fog. If deselected, the amount of occlusion is consistent and the object's distance from the camera is ignored. If selected, the Density attribute is ignored.

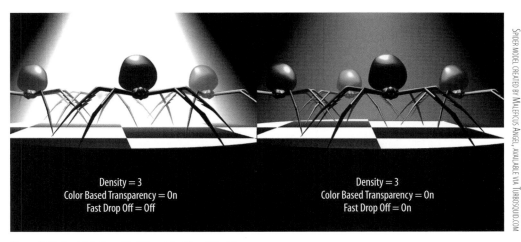

Figure 2.21   Spot light fog with different Fast Drop Off settings

Matte Opacity Mode   This attribute determines how the fog will render in the alpha channel. (*Matte*, *mask*, and *alpha* are interchangeable words when discussing 3D rendering.)

Opacity Gain, which is the default option, renders alpha based on the fog transparency. Opacity Gain is appropriate for most renders. Pixel values used for the Opacity Gain calculation are multiplied by the Matte Opacity attribute.

The second option, Solid Matte, ignores transparency information and bases the alpha solely on the Matte Opacity value. If Matte Opacity is set to 1.0, the fog will be 100 percent opaque in the alpha channel.

The third option, Black Hole, works like Solid Matte, but in reverse. By default, the fog is rendered as 100 percent transparent in the alpha, "punching" a hole into all objects that intersect its throw.

Additional Light Fog Attributes

In addition to the options available through the Light Fog material, spot lights possess Fog Spread and Fog Intensity attributes in their Light Effects section. Fog Spread controls the width of the fog within the fog icon; low values cause the fog to form at the icon's center, away from the icon edges. Fog Intensity controls the fog's brightness; higher values cause the fog to become more opaque. The Fog Intensity attribute is provided for point lights and volume lights. In place of Fog Spread, point lights have Fog Radius. Fog Radius interactively scales the fog icon of the point light. In addition, point lights have the Fog Type attribute. When Fog Type is switched from Normal to Linear or Exponential, there are minor variations in the fog quality at the edge of the fog icon.

When a texture is mapped to the Color of a light with Light Fog, the color of the texture is streaked through the fog, making the effect similar to a movie projector in a smoky room (see Figure 2.22).

Figure 2.22 Light Fog with a bitmap mapped to the Color attribute of a spot light. This scene and image are included with the Chapter 2 tutorial files as `fog_bit-map.ma` and `countdown.tif`.

By default, Light Fog ignores all surfaces in a scene and passes through objects. However, if shadows are turned on for the light, the fog stops appropriately. For details on rendering fog with shadows, see Chapter 3.

Note: The brightness of Light Fog is ultimately dependent on the light's Intensity value. If the light's Intensity is set to 0 or is reduced to 0 through a mapped Color or Intensity bitmap, the fog ceases to exist.

An Introduction to Environment Fog

Environment Fog produces a fog effect similar to Light Fog. Environment Fog, however, occurs at all points within the camera view between a camera's near and far clipping planes. You can create Environment Fog by clicking the Environment Fog attribute button in the Render Options section of the Maya Software tab in the Render Settings window.

Environment Fog consists of four nodes: envFogLight, environmentFog, environmentFogShape, and envFogMaterial. The envFogLight node is an ambient light placed to illuminate the fog. The environmentFogShape node is a render utility that connects the fog to a shading group node; in the viewport, it is represented by a disc that surrounds the ambient light. The environmentFog node carries the fog's transform information. (For more information on nodes, see Chapter 6, "Creating Custom Connections and Applying Color Utilities.") The envFogMaterial node controls the look of the fog and includes the following sections and attributes:

Simple Fog   This section represents the default Environment Fog type. Simple Fog has a limited number of attributes and is efficient to render. Color sets the fog color. Color Based Transparency works the same way as the Light Fog attribute. Saturation Distance determines the distance from the camera at which the fog becomes 100 percent opaque. The Use Layer attribute, when selected, acts as a multiplier for the fog's density. If a 3D texture is mapped to the Layer attribute, the fog density varies throughout its mass (see Figure 2.23). (For more information on 3D textures, see Chapter 5, "Applying 3D Textures and Projections.")

Figure 2.23 Simple Fog with Color set to green, Saturation Distance set to 1.0, Use Height selected, Min Height set to 0, Max Height set to 1.0, Blend Range set to 0.5, and a Cloud texture mapped to the Layer attribute. This scene is included with the Chapter 2 tutorial files as `ground_fog.ma`.

The Use Height attribute, when selected, limits the fog to a certain height off the ground (the XZ plane). Min Height and Max Height determine the fog's range in Y. Blend Range determines the speed with which the fog transitions at the borders of Min Height and Max Height. A value of 1.0 causes the fog to end abruptly. Lower values create a more gradual transition between fog and no fog.

Physical Fog Toggles off and on physically based Environment Fog. If Physical Fog is selected, Simple Fog attributes cannot be accessed. Physical Fog has seven Fog Type fogs. Uniform Fog creates fog with density equal in all directions. Atmospheric, Sky, Water, Water/Fog, Water/Atmos, and Water/Sky fogs are designed to emulate real-world situations (see Figure 2.24). The attributes for these fogs are listed in the Air, Water, and Sun sections. These attributes control color, opacity, density, and light scatter, as well as the color, intensity, and position of an artificial sun.

Figure 2.24 Left: Physical Fog with Water/Atmos Fog Type. Camera is below the virtual water level. Right: Same fog, but with the camera placed just above virtual water level. This scene is included with the Chapter 2 tutorial files as `physical_fog.ma`.

Note: You can apply Environment Fog as a postprocess by selecting the Apply Fog In Post attribute in the Render Options section of the Maya Software tab in the Render Settings window. In this section, you also have the option to increase the softness of the fog by increasing the Post Fog Blur attribute. When selecting Apply Fog In Post, you may need to increase the Saturation Distance value, because the fog will become extra dense through the postprocess composite.

An Introduction to Volume Fog

Maya provides volume primitives for the express purpose of containing Volume Fog within specific shapes. You can create a volume primitive by choosing Create > Volume Primitives > *shape*. The resulting primitive, whether it is a sphere, cube, or cone, is automatically assigned to a Volume Fog material that is named after the shape (for example, cubeFog). The Volume Fog material carries standard material and fog attributes such as Color, Transparency, Incandescence, and Density. In addition, the material provides a Color Ramp graph. If the Color Ramp Input attribute is set to Ignore, the color of the fog is taken from the Color attribute. However, if Color Ramp Input is set to Transparency, Concentric, or Y Gradient, the color of the fog is taken from the ramp (see Figure 2.25). The left side of the ramp represents the color of the fog at its center (Concentric) or bottom (Y Gradient). If Color Ramp Input is set to Transparency, the most transparent areas of the fog receive colors from the left side of the ramp and the more opaque regions of the fog receive colors from the right side of the ramp. The Transparency attribute affects this calculation.

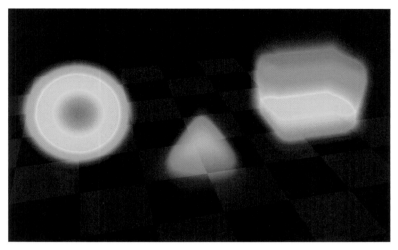

Figure 2.25 Left to Right: Sphere volume with Concentric fog, Cone volume with Transparency fog, and Cube volume with Y Gradient fog. This scene is included with the Chapter 2 tutorial files as `volume_fog.ma`.

Creating Light Glow

Light Glow is a postprocess that creates various lighting effects. To create a Light Glow, click the checkered Map button beside the Light Glow attribute in the Light Effects section of a spot, point, volume, or area light's Attribute Editor tab. An Optical FX utility is connected automatically to the light. The controls for Light Glow are broken into five sections in the Optical FX utility's Attribute Editor tab: Optical FX, Glow, Halo, Lens Flare, and Noise.

The Optical FX Attributes section controls the global qualities of the Optical FX utility (see Figure 2.26). By default, the node creates a four-pointed star with a glow at the center of the light. Star Points sets the number of "arms" visible on the star. You can remove the star point effect by setting Star Points to 0. Rotation controls the orientation of the star points. The glow is controlled by the Glow Type attribute. In addition, you can add a halo glow with the Halo Type attribute.

Figure 2.26 The Optical FX Attributes section of the optical FX utility's Attribute Editor tab

You can choose one of six Glow Type glows: None, Linear, Exponential, Ball, Lens Flare, and Rim Halo. You can also choose one of six Halo Type halos: None, Linear, Exponential, Ball, Lens Flare, and Rim Halo. The halos roughly correspond to the glows with the same name. The halos, however, are more diffuse and extend farther from the light's center. The exceptions to this are the Lens Flare and Rim Halo options, which do not render in multiple colors. Halo Type does not have to match Glow Type (see Figure 2.27). If Glow Type is set to None, Halo Type will not produce star points.

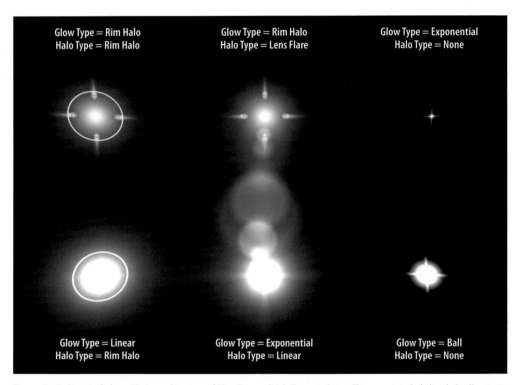

Figure 2.27 Six point lights with six combinations of Glow Type and Halo Type attributes. This scene is included with the Chapter 2 tutorial files as `glow_halo.ma`.

Glow and halo effects have their own sections in the Optical FX utility's Attribute Editor tab. The attributes in these sections are fairly self-explanatory and determine the intensity, spread (diameter), internal noise, and additional star arms of the glow and halo. The color of the glow or halo is derived from the multiplication of the light Color value and the Glow Color and Halo Color attributes of the Optical FX utility.

By default, the Optical FX glow includes star points (the outward extending arms). To alter the number of star points, adjust the Star Points value in the Optical FX Attributes section. To adjust the intensity of the points (which impact the intensity of the spherical glow), adjust the Glow Star Level in the Glow Attributes section. The various glow noise attributes affect the quality of the star points.

You can create a lens flare with the Optical FX utility by selecting the Lens Flare attribute in the Optical FX Attributes section. The quality of the flare is controlled by the attributes in the Lens Flare Attributes section. Once again, the attributes are fairly self-explanatory and determine the flare's color, intensity, spread, and included components.

There are several Optical FX utility attributes that add noise to the glow effect. To take advantage of this noise, follow these steps:

1. Raise the value of Glow Noise, in the Glow Attributes section, above 0.

2. Adjust the value of the Noise Threshold attribute, in the Noise section, to fine-tune the strength of the noise.

3. Adjust Noise Uscale and Noise Vscale, in the Noise section, to adjust the size of the noise. The higher the values, the smaller the noise "grains." To offset the noise pattern left, right, down, or up, adjust Noise Uoffset and Noise Voffset.

When the Optical FX utility is created for a point or volume light, a sphere-Shape render utility node is also placed in the scene. This node connects the opticalFX node to a shading group node and is necessary for the glow or halo to render. A spot light receives a directedDiscShape node. Although you can scale these specialized utility nodes, the scale does not affect the size of the glow or halo (adjust the Glow Spread or Halo Spread attributes instead). That said, the glow and halo of a spot light are not visible unless the spot light is pointing toward the camera. Note that it may be useful to render an Optical FX as a separate render pass. The glow- or flare-like nature of the FX makes them ideal for placing them on top of a scene through compositing. Render passes are discussed in Chapter 12.

Chapter Tutorial: Lighting an Interior

In this tutorial, you will light the interior of a room, mixing moon light and incandescent light (see Figure 2.28). You will use spot lights and point lights. In addition, you will apply Light Fog and Light Glow effects.

Figure 2.28 The lit room

1. In Maya, choose File > Set Project. In the Set Project window, browse for the Project_2 directory, select the directory name, and click the Set button. This ensures that the texture bitmaps will be correctly located. Open `room.ma` from the Chapter 2 scenes folder. Spend a few minutes familiarizing yourself with the model's various parts. All the surfaces have been assigned to Blinn materials with bitmap textures. There are two cameras: persp and WorkingCamera. Use persp for rendering. Use WorkingCamera to move around the scene.

2. Create a point light via the Create > Lights menu. Name the light **BackHallLight**. Move BackHallLight into the back hallway on the screen-left side of the model (roughly –9, 3.75, –29 in X, Y, Z). Through the light's Attribute Editor tab, set the Color to orange-yellow and Intensity to 1.5. Render a test frame through the Render View (choose Window > Rendering Editors > Render View). Note that the render is set to Maya Software with high-quality settings. (Render settings are discussed in more detail in Chapter 10, "Prepping for Successful Renders.") The light from the point light reaches into the main room. To prevent this, activate shadows. Scroll down to the Shadows section of the Attribute Editor tab. In the Depth Map Shadows Attributes subsection, select Use Depth Map Shadows. Set Resolution to 1024 and Filter Size to 24. A large Filter Size softens the shadow edge. (Shadow settings are further explored in Chapter 3.) Render a test frame. The light illuminates the back hallway but no other part of the model.

3. Create a second point light and name it **RedLight**. Move RedLight behind the foreground pillar on the left (roughly –11, 6.5, 1.75 in X, Y, Z). Set the light's Color to red. Render a test frame. The red light reaches the far corners of the room with full strength. Change the Decay Rate attribute, below Color, to Linear. Increase the Intensity to 3. Despite the higher Intensity, the light is only dimly seen along the back wall. The red light adds an interesting accent to the foreground. Select the light's Use Depth Map Shadows attribute. Leave the Resolution set to 512 and change the Filter Size to 24. This prevents the red light from unrealistically appearing on the wall behind the pillars.

4. Create a third point light and name it **LightBulb**. Move LightBulb so it sits directly above the LightStand geometry (roughly 2.4, 5.7, –2.4 in X, Y, Z). The top of Figure 2.29 shows the point light positions. Change the light Color to pale yellow, the Intensity to 4.5, and the Decay Rate menu to Linear. Select Use Depth Map Shadows, and set Resolution to 1024 and Filter Size to 24. Render a test frame. Although the light illuminates the room in a believable fashion, the light itself is not visible. To remedy this, click the checkered Map button beside Light Glow in the Light Effects section. An Optical FX node is created. You can find this listed as opticalFX1 in the Lights tab of the Hypershade window. In the opticalFX1 Attribute Editor tab, change the Glow Type menu to Ball. In the Glow Attributes section, set the Glow Color to pale yellow. Set Glow Intensity to 10. Set Glow Spread to 0.35 (values below 1.0 erode the rendered glow). In a viewport, interactively select the LightBulb light icon. Note that the opticalFX1

node adds a spherical handle around the light. Interactively scale the light until the spherical icon intersects the LightStand slightly. Render a test frame. The opticalFX1 glow is added as a postprocess, appearing at the end of the render. The Ball glow creates the illusion that there is an illuminated bulb or bulb housing in the scene. The bottom of Figure 2.29 shows a render at this point.

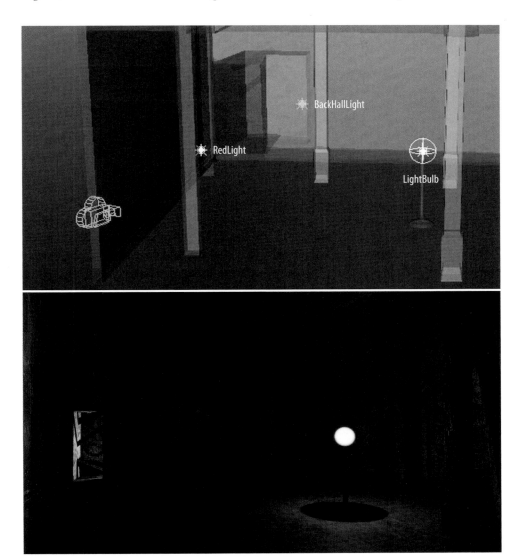

Figure 2.29 Top: Point light positions; Bottom: Resulting render

5. Create a spot light and name it **MoonLight**. Scale the spot light so that it is easy to work with. Set the light Color to pale purple, the intensity to 3.0, and the Cone Angle to 60. Select Use Depth Map Shadows, and set Resolution to 1024 and Filter Size to 24. Position MoonLight outside of the narrow window along the right side of the model. Rotate the light so it strikes the back wall through

the window. To make the adjustment easier, go to the persp viewport menu and choose Lighting > Use All Lights and Lighting > Shadows. A simplified version of the shadowed light appears on the geometry (see the left of Figure 2.30). Note that this is only visible while Viewport 2.0 is used. Optionally, you can select MoonLight, go to a different viewport, and choose Panels > Look Through Selected through that viewport's menu. You can then use the standard Alt/Opt+mouse buttons to move the light as you look through it. (To return to the previous viewport view, choose Panels > Perspective > *camera name*.) In the finished example scene file, the light is placed at approximately 24, 18.8, –5.7 with a rotation of –27, 63, 4.4 (see the right of Figure 2.30). Feel free to experiment with different positions and rotations, and then render a test frame.

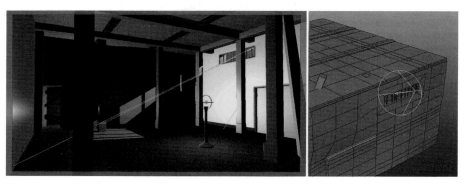

Figure 2.30 Left: The persp viewport with Use All Lights and Shadows selected; Right: The positioned MoonLight spot light

6. At present, the MoonLight light enters through the window to strike the back wall. However, the light itself is not visible in the air. You can emulate a light beam by activating Light Fog. Light Fog re-creates participating media, whereby small particulates in the air, such as water vapor, dust, or smoke, reflect light. In the Light Effects section of MoonLight's Attribute Editor tab, click the checkered Map button beside Light Fog. A lightFog1 material is created and appears in the Materials tab of the Hypershade window. In addition, the light's icon receives an extended, blue cone indicating where the fog will form. Interactively scale the light icon so that the fog cone extends past the floor of the model. Open the lightFog1 material in the Attribute Editor. Change the Color to dark blue-purple. Increase Density to 2.0. Render a test frame. A bluish fog appears as a narrow beam between the window and the wall (see Figure 2.31). Note that the depth map shadows of Moonlight restrict the fog to the window area.

Figure 2.31 Light Fog creates a light beam between the window and wall.

7. The lighting is complete! The render should look similar to Figures 2.28 and 2.31. If you get stuck, take a look at a finished version of this scene, which is saved as room_finished.ma in the Chapter 2 scenes folder.

Creating High-Quality Shadows

3

Shadows are an inescapable part of the physical world. Unless an animation is intended for a stylized look, high-quality shadows are a necessity for a professional rendering. Depth map and raytrace shadows can be fine-tuned to match many lighting scenarios. In addition, you can shadow advanced effects in Autodesk® Maya®, including Light Fog, Fur, Paint Effects, nHair, and nCloth. To make the shadow-rendering process more efficient, you can link shadows.

Chapter Contents
Depth map methodology
Fine-tuning and troubleshooting depth maps
Adjusting raytrace shadows
Linking and unlinking shadows
Applying shadows to Light Fog
Creating shadows with Paint Effects
Creating shadows with Maya Fur and nHair System

Rendering Depth Maps

Depth maps are easy to apply and efficient to render. Unfortunately, their default quality is generally poor. You can improve the quality by adjusting various attributes and applying specific lighting strategies.

Understanding Depth Maps

When the Use Depth Map Shadows attribute is selected for a spot, directional, point, area, or volume light, Maya creates a temporary depth map (see Figure 3.1).

Figure 3.1 The Depth Map Shadow Attributes section of a spot light's Attribute Editor tab

The depth map represents the distance between surfaces in the scene and the shadow-casting light from the light's point-of-view. This information is stored as a monochromatic Z-depth buffer (see Figure 3.2). Objects far from the light receive dark pixels, and objects closer to the light receive light pixels.

Figure 3.2 A depth map

When a surface point is rendered, its distance to the shadowing light is compared to the distance encoded in the corresponding depth map pixel. If the distance is greater than that encoded in the depth map pixel, it's assumed that another surface occludes the surface point's view of the light and the surface point is therefore shadowed. For example, in Figure 3.2 a distant building is partially occluded by a pair of gas pumps. The gas pumps are assigned brighter pixels because they are fairly close to the light. The part of the building that's not occluded has fairly dark pixels. Since the distance value of the dark pixels is equal to the actual distance that the surface points are from the light, no shadows occur in that area (with the exception of self-shadowing, which is discussed later in this section).

Reusing and Overwriting Depth Maps

By default, depth maps are temporarily written to disk during a render but are not saved. You can force Maya to save the depth map as a Maya IFF bitmap by switching the Disk Based Dmaps attribute (found at the bottom of the Depth Map Shadow Attributes section) from Off to one of the two following options:

Reuse Existing Dmap(s)   With this option, the depth map is written to the project folder with a name established by the Shadow Map File Name field (see Figure 3.3). You can automatically add suffixes to the map name by selecting the Add Scene Name and Add Light Name attributes. Each subsequent time the scene is rendered, the written depth map is retrieved. This option is appropriate if the light position does not change between renders. You can change light attributes, such as Intensity, and material attributes (with the exception of displacement maps) between renders with no penalty. In addition, cameras can be repositioned.

Figure 3.3   The Disk Based Dmaps section of a spot light's Attribute Editor tab

Overwrite Existing Dmap(s)   With this option, a new depth map is written with each render. If an old map exists with the same name, it is overwritten. The new map name is set by the Shadow Map File Name attribute.

If you batch-render an animation, the Disk Based Dmaps attribute will reuse or re-render the depth map for the first frame and apply it to all the frames. This is appropriate if objects are static (however, you can animate the camera). If objects are in motion, and their motion does not change between batch renders, select the Add Frame Ext attribute. Add Frame Ext adds a frame number to the depth map filename. The first time the animation is rendered, a depth map is rendered for each frame. For each subsequent render, the series of depth maps is either reused—Reuse Existing Dmap(s)—or re-rendered—Overwrite Existing Dmap(s).

By default, Maya writes out at least two IFF files per depth map. The following naming convention is used:

ShadowMapFileName_lightName_sceneName.SM.iff*frameNumber*

ShadowMapFileName_lightName_sceneName.MIDMAP.SM.iff*frameNumber*

When a depth map is calculated, Maya shoots a shadow ray from the light view plane through each pixel of the depth map. The first surface point that the ray encounters is recorded in the SM map. The MIDMAP.SM map is created by the Use Mid Dist attribute.

Note: If the Disk Based Dmaps menu is set to Reuse Existing Dmap(s), you can use the Use Macro field (below Add Frame Ext). This field allows you to list a script that Maya will apply to the stored depth maps each time they are called for a render. For example, you can list a Perl or Python script that alters or postprocesses the depth maps. For demonstration scripts, see the "Shadow Attributes" page of the Maya Help files.

Note: The depth map scene name suffix used by the batch render process differs from the scene name suffix used by the Render View window. The batch render uses the temporary scene filename, such as test__1740, whereas the Render View uses the letters. Maya writes temporary scene files to disk with every batch render, even when no depth map shadows are present. This difference in suffix names may potentially confuse the Reuse Existing Dmap(s) and Overwrite Existing Dmap(s) options.

Adjusting Use Mid Dist and Bias

By default, Use Mid Dist is selected for each light type that supports depth map shadows. This attribute significantly reduces self-shadowing artifacts, which often appear as bands across flat surfaces or a degradation of the shadow as it wraps around a curved surface (see Figure 3.4).

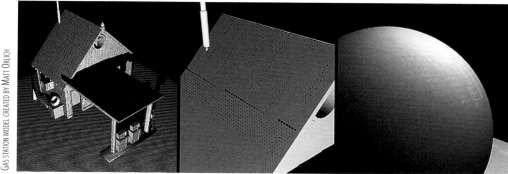

Figure 3.4 Extreme to subtle depth map artifacts

The artifacts are generally the result of one of two factors:

- Surface points are misinterpreted as existing "below" or "behind" adjacent surface points. This can occur when surface points are sampled within the boundary of a depth map pixel and are discovered to be farther from the light than the distance value encoded in that pixel (see Figure 3.5). Since the distance value stored in a depth map pixel is based on a single sample—one taken at the point at which the shadow ray intersects the surface—this problem occurs frequently.

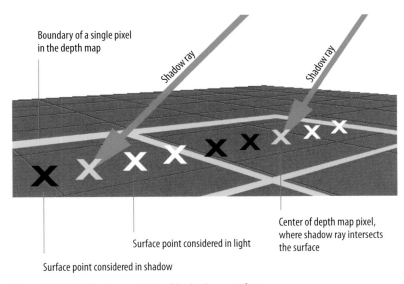

Figure 3.5 A simplified representation of the depth map artifacts

- The pixels of a depth map, which may cover relatively large surface areas, are unable to accurately sample areas of high curvature. In such a case, surface points are incorrectly considered "behind" or "below" adjacent surface points.

In either of these situations, the artifacts are not visible in the depth map bitmap itself. The artifacts occur only during the render of the final image. You can increase the depth map Resolution value as a solution. Unfortunately, doing so reduces the size of the artifacts but will not necessarily eradicate them. In addition, an increased Resolution increases render times. The Use Mid Dist attribute, on the other hand, artificially pushes the surface points closer to the light by determining the average distance from the light to the surface point and the distance from the light to the second surface encountered (see Figure 3.6). The second surface encounters are recorded in the MIDMAP.SM depth map.

If a second surface is not encountered, the light's far clipping plane value is used. The only surfaces considered by the depth map process are those whose Cast Shadows attribute is selected (which is the default state of a surface). Again, the basic depth map algorithm works in the following manner:

- If the distance between a surface point and the light is *less* than or *equal* to the distance encoded in the depth map pixel that contains the surface point within its boundary, the surface point is in light.

- If the distance between a surface point and the light is *greater* than the distance encoded in the depth map pixel that contains the surface point within its boundary, the surface point is shadowed.

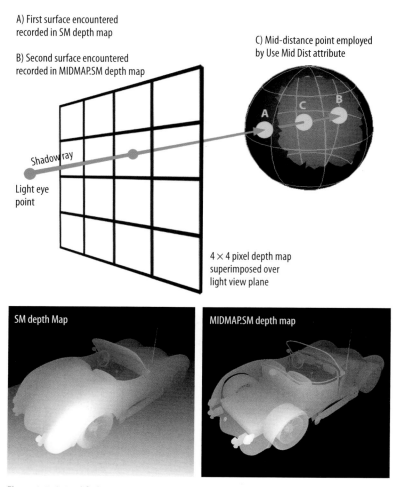

Figure 3.6 A simplified representation of the Use Mid Dist process

In this situation, Use Mid Dist forces the depth map to encode distances that are greater than the actual distance to the first surface encountered. Hence, surface points sampled during the render have a greater likelihood of possessing a smaller distance value when compared to the distance encoded in the corresponding depth map pixel.

Although Use Mid Dist is responsible for a significant improvement in the quality of a render, it cannot eliminate 100 percent of the artifacts. The Bias attribute, which operates on similar principles, is designed to work in conjunction with Use Mid Dist.

Bias holds true to its name and "biases" the surface point position. Whereas Use Mid Dist forces the depth map to take its distance value from an averaged distance between the first encountered surface and the second, Bias simply offsets the actual surface point value, thus virtually transforming it closer to the light.

Trial-and-error is often the best solution when choosing a Bias value. When changing the value, incrementally step from 0.001 to 1.0. For example, in Figure 3.7 depth map artifacts appear along the edge of a convoluted surface. Although a 0.25 Bias value reduces the problem, a value of 0.5 removes the artifacts completely. Higher values erode the self-shadowing on the surface.

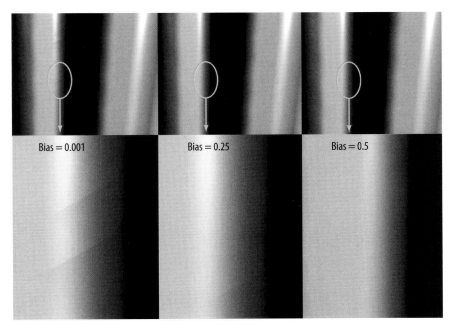

Figure 3.7 Depth map artifacts are eliminated by adjusting the Bias attribute. This scene is included with the Chapter 3 tutorial files as `bias_values.ma`.

With most scenarios, selecting Use Mid Dist and leaving Bias set to its default value is satisfactory. However, if you find it necessary to change the Bias value, proceed with caution. A Bias value that removes an artifact at one point on a surface can introduce an artifact at another point. For example, an incorrect Bias value will often "disconnect" a surface from a ground or floor. In Figure 3.8, a thin NURBS leg loses its connection with a plane.

Figure 3.8 Three Bias values affect the connection of a depth map shadow to a NURBS leg. This scene is included with the Chapter 3 tutorial files as `bias_leg.ma`.

Creating Multiple Depth Maps

If necessary, you can generate more than two depth maps per spot light or point light. If a scene is large in world space or necessitates a large Resolution size, you can deselect the Use Only Single Dmap attribute. When this attribute is deselected, six additional attributes become available with the following naming convention: Use *Axis*+/– Map (see Figure 3.9).

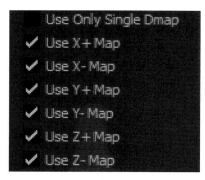

Figure 3.9 The Use Only Single Dmap section of a shadow-casting spot light's Attribute Editor tab

If any individual axis attribute is selected, a depth map is rendered from the point of view of the light in one axis direction. For example, Use X+ Map writes a depth map aligned to the positive X axis. If Use Mid Dist is selected and Disk Based Dmaps is not set to Off, two depth maps are written out to the disk with the following names:

```
ShadowMapFileName_lightName_sceneName.XP.iffframeNumber
ShadowMapFileName_lightName_sceneName.MIDMAP.XP.iffframeNumber
```

P stands for positive axis direction. *P* is replaced by *N* if the axis direction is negative. The ability to choose direction is particularly useful for a spot light that must cover a large model. For example, in Figure 3.10 a spot light with a 120-degree Cone Angle value is placed close to the model of a building. Use X+ Map, Use X– Map, and Use Z– Map are selected. The resulting render creates two depth maps—one standard and one for Use Mid Dist—in each axis direction. If Use Only Single Dmap had been selected, the left and right sides of the model would have been excluded from the depth map. If the spot light were moved farther from the model to avoid this problem, a significantly higher Resolution value would be required to maintain the map's detail.

By default, point lights create six standard depth maps and six corresponding depth maps for Use Mid Dist. These maps surround the point light in a virtual cube. You can turn off particular directions to save render time. For example, if no critical geometry exists below the point light, you can deselect Use Y– Map. If a particular direction is completely empty, the corresponding depth map is ignored automatically.

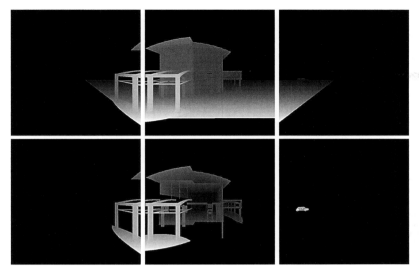

Figure 3.10 Six depth maps are generated for one spot light.

You can view a depth map IFF file by choosing File > View Image and browsing for the filename. The FCheck window opens. Press the Z key while the mouse arrow is over the window or click the Z Buffer button. Since the depth information is stored in the Z channel of the IFF file, the depth map cannot be seen in Photoshop or other standard digital-imaging program. However, if you choose File > Save Image in FCheck while the depth map is visible, you can export the monochromatic image to any of the image formats supported by Maya. In this case, the information is written as RGB. Unfortunately, the converted file cannot be read by a Maya renderer because a depth map with an IFF extension and a Z channel is expected during the shadow-casting process.

Refining Depth Maps

Maya depth maps possess other attributes that are critical to the quality of their render. These include Resolution, Filter Size, Shadow Color, and Use Auto Focus. These attributes are located in the Depth Map Shadow Attributes section of the light's Attribute Editor tab. In addition, a specialized mental ray depth map and area light offers an alternative approach to creating shadows.

Setting the Resolution, Filter Size, and Shadow Color

Resolution sets the pixel size of the depth map. Filter Size controls the amount of edge blur applied to the shadow. As a general rule of thumb, you can follow this guideline:

- A crisp edge requires high Resolution and low Filter Size.
- A soft edge requires low Resolution and high Filter Size.

Aside from softening the shadow's edge, the Filter Size attribute is designed to disguise depth map limitations. Since depth maps are restricted by a fixed number of pixels, the pixels are often visible in the render. For example, in Figure 3.11 three different Filter Size values are applied to a depth map with its Resolution set to the default value of 512.

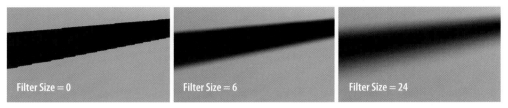

Filter Size = 0   Filter Size = 6   Filter Size = 24

Figure 3.11 A depth map with a 512 Resolution and three different Filter Size values

The blur created by Filter Size is applied to the shadow map equally at all edge points. Hence, it cannot replicate a diffuse shadow that changes edge quality over distance. You can overcome this limitation, however, by using a mental ray® area light. This light is demonstrated in the "Converting to mental ray Area Lights" section later in this chapter.

Shadow Color tints the color of the shadow, thus emulating bounced light. Choosing a lighter color also creates a shadow that is less intense and gives the appearance that a greater amount of fill light is present. (In general, the default Shadow Color is suitable for most scenes.)

Setting a Spot Light's Focus

The Use Auto Focus attribute automatically fits objects in the light's view to the resolution of the depth map. That is, if the objects are surrounded by empty space, the light view is "zoomed" in to maximize the number of pixels dedicated to the objects. Use Auto Focus is available on spot, directional, and point lights. Area and volume lights do not possess the attribute.

Note: If the cone of a spot light cuts objects out of the spot light's view, the Use Auto Focus attribute will not widen the view for the depth map. To avoid this problem, you will have to increase the light's Cone Angle, move the light backward, or manually set the light's Focus attribute.

In some situations, a scene will benefit if Use Auto Focus is deselected and the light's Focus value is set manually. For example, if a depth map shadow is not critical for objects on the fringe of a scene, you can choose a Focus value that allows the light to concentrate on the scene's most important elements.

To choose an appropriate Focus value for a spot light in any given scene, take the following steps:

1. Select the spot light and open its Attribute Editor tab. Deselect Use Auto Focus. The Focus attribute becomes available.

2. With the light selected, choose Display > Rendering > Camera/Light Manipulator > Cone Angle. In a viewport, choose Panels > Look Through Selected. The view through the light appears.

3. LMB-drag the Cone Angle manipulator until the cone circle surrounds the objects in the scene that require a depth map shadow. Do not allow the cone circle to "split" a shadow-casting object in half; the resulting shadow will come to an abrupt stop in the render. Note the Cone Angle value and enter the number in the Focus attribute field. Move the manipulator back to its original position so that the original Cone Angle value is once again achieved.

4. Switch Disk Based Dmaps to Reuse Existing Dmap(s), enter a name into the Shadow Map File Name field, and render a test frame. Double-check the resulting depth map with FCheck. In the viewport used to look through the light, choose an orthographic camera through the Panels menu; this removes the temporary camera attached to the light by the Look Through Selected command.

Setting a Directional and Point Light Focus

Although directional lights possess the Focus attribute, choosing an appropriate value requires a different strategy. By default, directional lights possess direction but have no true position; despite the location of the light icon, they are considered to be an infinite distance from the subject. Hence, a directional light automatically includes all the objects in a scene for a depth map shadow. As a result, two new attributes become available when Use Auto Focus is deselected: Width Focus and Use Light Position. Use the following steps to set these attributes:

1. Select the directional light and open its Attribute Editor tab. Deselect Use Auto Focus and select Use Light Position.

2. Through a viewport, choose Panels > Look Through Selected. The view through the light appears. With Alt/Opt+RMB, dolly the light in or out so that the shadow-casting objects fill the view.

3. Using the viewport menu, choose View > Camera Attribute Editor. In the camera's Attribute Editor tab, scroll down to the Orthographic Views section. Select Orthographic (if it is not already selected). Note the value in the Orthographic Width field. The Orthographic Width attribute represents the width of the visible scene as measured from the left side to the right side of the current view. Enter the value into the Width Focus field, in the directional light's Depth Map Shadow Attributes section.

4. Switch the Disk Based Dmaps menu to Reuse Existing Dmap(s), enter a name in the Shadow Map File Name field, and render a test frame. Double-check the resulting depth map with FCheck. If the foreground appears clipped, the light icon is below, intersecting, or otherwise too close to the clipped surface. Simply dolly the light back in the viewport view and render another test. If shadow-casting objects are cut off at the left or right side of the depth map, gradually increase the Width Focus value and render additional tests.

You can use the same four steps to determine the Focus value of a point light. However, the Orthographic Width value, when used for the point light's Focus value, does not produce the expected result. You can work out a rough formula that relates the world width across the shadow-casting objects and the distance the light is from those objects. However, the math becomes fairly convoluted. For example, if the light distance is 10 units and the object width is 10 units, a Focus value of approximately 50 works. Yet if the light distance is 5 units and the width remains 10 units, a Focus value 75 produces similar results. Hence, trial-and-error is generally necessary to determine the appropriate Focus value for a point light.

Switching to mental ray Shadow Maps

The mental ray renderer supports standard Maya depth maps. In addition, mental ray can produce its own shadow map variation. To render the mental ray light variations, switch the Render Using attribute, in the Render Settings window, to mental ray.

When selected, the Use mental ray Shadow Map Overrides attribute overrides the standard Maya depth map shadow. (You can find the attribute in the mental ray > Shadows subsection of a spot, directional, area, or point light's Attribute Editor tab.) The Shadow Map Format attribute, found directly above Use mental ray Shadow Map Overrides, controls the type of mental ray shadow map. The Regular Shadow Map option produces mental ray depth maps, which are more advanced than the Maya equivalent, thanks to additional attributes. The Detail Shadow Map option supports object transparency and is discussed in Chapter 11, "Raytracing, mental ray, and Effects Rendering." If you click the Take Settings From Maya button (directly below Use mental ray Shadow Map Overrides), the applicable values from the Depth Map Shadow Attributes section are transferred to the mental ray Shadow Map Overrides subsection (see Figure 3.12).

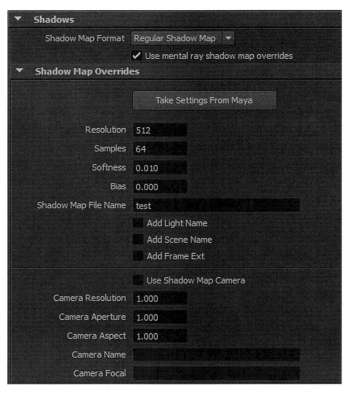

Figure 3.12 The Shadows and Shadow Map Overrides subsections of a light's Attribute Editor tab

The following attributes control the look of the resulting mental ray shadow:

Resolution   Sets the pixel size of the depth map.

Samples   Sets the number of subpixel samples taken per pixel. Low values create grainy results.

Softness   Controls the spread of the light. Values above 0 create a softer, more diffuse shadow edge. Higher values necessitate higher Samples values to create acceptable results (see Figure 3.13). High values tend to smear the shadow at surface corners.

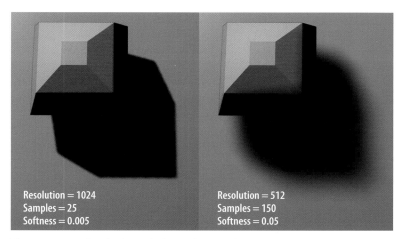

Resolution = 1024
Samples = 25
Softness = 0.005

Resolution = 512
Samples = 150
Softness = 0.05

Figure 3.13   mental ray depth map shadows with two attribute settings

Bias   Functions in the same manner as the default Maya depth map Bias attribute by offsetting surface points to avoid self-shadowing artifacts. This attribute, if above 0, overrides the Shadow Map Bias attribute (Render Settings window > Options tab > mental ray Overrides section > Shadow Map subsection). Maya documentation recommends a Bias value that is less than the world distance between the light and the shadowed object. (Additional shadow attributes, including those found in the mental ray tab of the Render Settings window, are discussed in detail in Chapter 11.)

Shadow Map File Name   When a name is entered into this field, mental ray shadow maps are written to disk in the \renderData\mentalray\shadowMap\ folder within the project directory. The maps are overwritten with each new render. The depth map files are written in a native mental ray format and cannot be viewed with FCheck. Point lights automatically produce six depth map files, while other lights produce one each.

Note: If you are rendering mental ray shadow maps with a directional light, you have the option to render the depth map with a shadow map camera. A shadow map camera provides an "auto focus" functionality by allowing you to choose a camera focal length, aperture size, and independent map resolution. You can activate the camera by selecting the Use Shadow Map Camera attribute found in the Shadow Map Overrides subsection. For more information on the shadow map camera settings, see the "mental ray Attributes For Lights" section of the Maya Help Files.

Converting to mental Ray Area Lights

You can convert a spot light into a mental ray area light by selecting the Area Light attribute (found in the mental ray > Area Light subsection of a spot light's Attribute Editor tab). You can convert a standard Maya area light into a mental ray area light by selecting Use Light Shape (found in the same subsection). Although area light icons remain unaffected, spot lights are given an additional area light shape (see Figure 3.14). You must use the mental ray renderer to take advantage of these light variations. Although mental ray can render standard Maya area lights, this option gives you the ability to use mental ray's more advanced lighting and shadowing capabilities. For more specific information on area lights and their general uses, see Chapter 2, "Applying the Correct Maya Light Type."

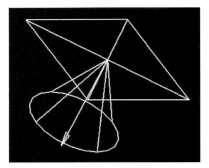

Figure 3.14 When the Area Light attribute is selected, a mental ray light is grafted onto the spot light icon.

The mental ray area light, when used in conjunction with raytrace shadows, acts as a light spread, creating a diffuse, soft-edged shadow. This is advantageous when using raytrace shadows with default quality settings, which normally produce hard-edged shadows. Although you can soften a raytrace shadow by adjusting the Light Radius and Shadow Rays attributes, the Area Light offers alternative controls that can potentially render with greater efficiency (see Figure 3.15). (For more information on raytrace shadow settings, see the "Raytracing Shadows" section later in this chapter.)

You can adjust the resulting shadow with the following attributes:

Type   Determines the shape of the area light. Options include Rectangle, Disc, Sphere, Cylinder, and Custom (listed as User with prior versions). If Type is set to Cylinder, the area light sends shadow rays above, below, and behind the parent light. If Type is set to Sphere, the area light sends shadow rays in all directions. The Custom option allows you to apply a custom mental ray light shader to the area light.

High Samples   Sets the number of shadow rays emitted from the area light, as measured in the X and Y directions of the light's icon. Default values leave the shadow very grainy. High values create an excellent result but slow the render.

Figure 3.15 Left: Raytrace shadow with a mental ray area light activated for a spot light; Right: Default raytrace shadow with same spot light. This scene is included with the Chapter 3 tutorial files as `area_spot.ma`.

High Sample Limit Represents the maximum number of times a shadow ray is permitted to reflect or refract before it must employ the Low Samples attribute. By switching to Low Samples, fewer shadow light rays are involved when calculating reflections and refractions.

Low Samples The number of shadow rays employed when the High Sample Limit is reached.

Visible If the parent light is a Maya area light, the Visible attribute determines whether the mental ray area light icon is visible in the render. If Visible is selected, Shape Intensity becomes available and controls the strength of the visibility. If Shape Intensity is set above 0, the icon renders as a solid white rectangle but does not affect the light striking surfaces in the scene. Maya documentation recommends using the mental ray area light in conjunction with the Maya area light because it requires lower sampling levels to produce higher-quality shadows. Note that the light is only visible in the render if the camera faces its front side (the side with the directional pointer).

> **N o t e :** The mental ray renderer provides a set of physically-based light shaders that are designed to work with advanced rendering systems, such as Global Illumination. These are discussed in Chapter 12.

Addressing Light Gap Errors

Light gaps, which look like thin, bright lines, often appear along the intersection of two surfaces. For example, in Figure 3.16 two primitive planes sit at a right angle and intersect slightly. A spot light, placed behind the surfaces, casts a default depth map shadow. A light gap appears along the intersection seam. Such gaps are due to a mismatch of the depth map to the render of the geometry. Depth maps do not receive anti-aliasing, which leads to stair-stepping. (See Chapter 10, "Prepping for Successful Renders," for information on render quality issues.) In this situation, the depth map will not accurately line up with the anti-aliased render, and the bright surface appears in the resulting "gap." The light's Filter Size attribute, which blurs the shadow edge, widens the gap if raised above 0.

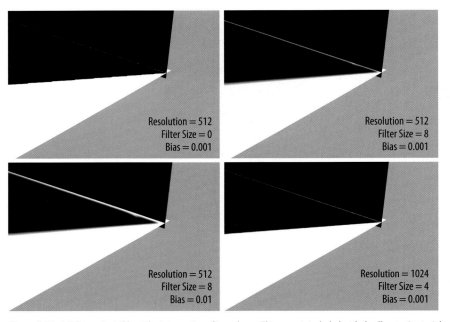

Figure 3.16 A light gap is visible at the intersection of two planes. This scene is included with the Chapter 3 tutorial files as `light_gap.ma`.

In this situation, higher Bias values make the error worse. You can increase the light's Resolution value, which will reduce the strength of the light gap. However, the increased Resolution will not make the error disappear completely (see Figure 3.16). Switching to raytrace shadows will solve the problem but requires a more time-intensive render. Another solution involves the following steps:

1. Open the shadow-casting light's Attribute Editor tab. In the Depth Map Shadow Attributes section, set the shadow attributes to create a satisfactory shadow.

2. Switch Disk Based Dmaps to Reuse Existing Dmap(s). Enter a name in the Shadow Map File Name field. Render a test frame. The render will write the depth maps to the project folder.

3. Select the vertical surface in a workspace view. Translate the surface away from the light. In the example illustrated in Figure 3.16, the plane needs to be translated only 0.2 units in the Z direction. When the plane is moved away from the light, the gap is covered by the geometry and is no longer visible in the render. The depth map is not updated since the Reuse Existing Dmaps(s) option retrieves the map after it has been written out the first time.

Comparing Shadows

Each light in Maya imparts distinctive qualities to the shadow it casts. Familiarity with the quirks and strengths of each light will help you make the proper decisions when lighting a scene. As a side-by-side comparison, each light type has been placed in an identical location on a test set (see Figure 3.17). A row of vertical cylinders illustrates the omnidirectional or multidirectional qualities of many of the lights.

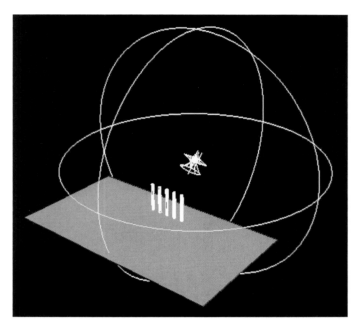

Figure 3.17 The light test set

All the lights, except for the ambient, cast depth map shadows with a Resolution set to 2048 and a Filter Size set to 2 (see Figure 3.18). The ambient light, which cannot cast depth map shadows, casts raytrace shadows with the default setting. The area light casts both depth map and raytrace shadows since it possesses a unique, physical-based lighting method. The spot light is rendered with two cone sizes. All the lights, except for the volume, are left at their default scale. The volume light is scaled to surround the test set. The lights are turned on, one at a time, with the Illuminates By Default check box.

When the shadows of each light are compared, many qualities are identical; a few, however, stand out. In particular, the short shadows of the directional display the parallel quality of the light type. Even though the directional has the same Intensity value as all the other lights, it imparts the most illumination to the surface. In terms of realism, the area light with raytrace shadows is by far the best. Even though the raytrace attributes are left at their default settings, the area shadows become more diffuse with distance, mimicking light properties in the real world. In comparison, the area light with a depth map shadow creates a look similar to the volume light. Both the area and the volume have the most aggressive light decay.

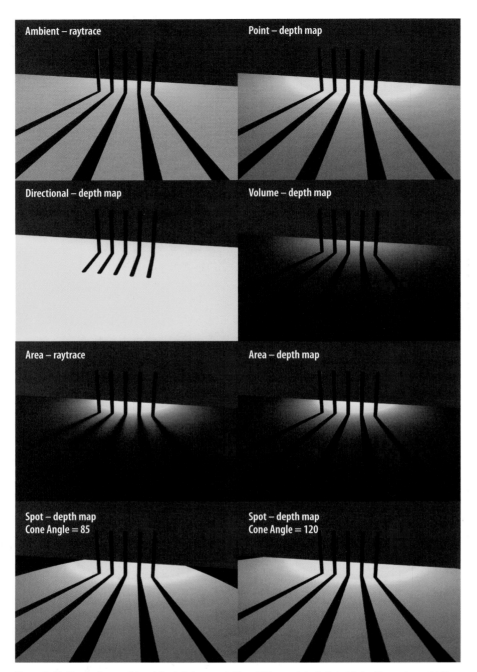

Figure 3.18 The shadow qualities of the six light types in Maya. This scene is included with the Chapter 3 tutorial files as light_set.ma.

With the exception of the directional light, the lights produce almost identical shadow patterns. If you were to move any nondirectional light farther from the cylinders, its shadows would become more parallel and less spread out. The spot light shows slight variations in the pattern when its Cone Angle is increased from 85 to 120. The directional and ambient lights provide the most even lighting, with the intensity of the surface changing little over its length and width; the other lights create hot spots near the cylinders.

For specific examples of what types of lights are appropriate for various locations and scenes, see Chapter 2.

Raytracing Shadows

Raytraced shadows are more physically accurate than depth map shadows but are generally more processor-intensive. Raytraced shadows represent the one type of shadow that is available to all light types, including ambient. For a raytraced shadow to be calculated, the Raytracing attribute must be selected in the Maya Software tab of the Render Settings window. In contrast, the mental ray renderer raytraces by default. (For information on the raytracing process, see Chapter 11.) To activate raytraced shadows, select the light's Use Ray Trace Shadows attribute (found in the Shadows > Raytrace Shadow Attributes subsection, as seen in Figure 3.19).

Figure 3.19 The Raytrace Shadow Attribute subsection of a directional light's Attribute Editor tab

In addition, each light carries a set of raytrace shadow attributes.

Shadow Radius/Light Radius/Light Angle These attributes control the softness of the shadow edge by virtually scaling the width of the light (see Figure 3.20). Large light sources, such as a theater marquee or a window with sheer curtains, produce naturally diffuse, soft-edged shadows. Shadow Radius is provided for ambient lights. Light Radius is provided for spot, point, and volume lights. Light Angle is provided for directional lights. With each of these attributes, the larger the value, the softer the resulting shadow. Shadow Radius and Light Radius have a range from 0 to 1.0. Light Angle has a range from 0 to 360. Area lights do not possess any of these attributes—the softness of their shadows is determined by the position and rotation of the light icon.

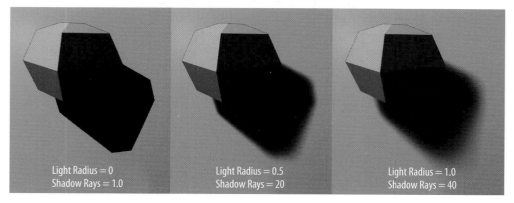

Figure 3.20 A raytrace shadow created by a spot light with three different Light Radius and Shadow Rays attribute values. Note that the softness of the shadow edge increases with distance from the shadow-casting object.

Shadow Rays   Sets the number of rays employed to calculate the shadow edge. The higher the value, the more refined the result.

Ray Depth Limit   Sets the number of times a camera eye ray can reflect and/or refract and still cause objects to cast raytrace shadows within the reflections or refractions. That is, higher values allow raytrace shadows to appear within a greater number of recursive reflections and refractions. If Ray Depth Limit is set to 1.0, no shadows appear within reflections or refractions.

You can find additional depth map and raytrace shadow attributes in the mental ray tabs of the Render Settings window. These are discussed in detail in Chapter 11.

Linking and Unlinking Shadows

With Maya, you can make or break shadow links between lights and surfaces. If a shadow link is broken, the surface no longer casts a shadow for that light. For complex scenes, the ability to pick and choose which surfaces cast shadows can save render time and improve render quality.

By default, all surfaces cast shadows for shadow-producing lights that strike them. To break a shadow link for a surface while using the Maya Software or mental ray renderer, follow these steps:

1. If you are using Maya Software, open the Render Settings window, switch to the Maya Software tab, and expand the Render Options section. Change Shadow Linking to Shadows Obey Shadow Linking.

2. If you are using mental ray, open the Render Settings window, switch to the Quality tab, and expand the Shadows section. Switch Shadow Linking to On.

3. Select the light and the surface whose shadow link you want to break. Switch to the Rendering menu set, and choose Lighting/Shading > Break Shadow Links. The surface will no longer cast a shadow for the selected light. To restore the shadow, select the surface and light and choose Lighting/Shading > Make Shadow Links.

Breaking a shadow link does not prevent a surface from receiving a shadow from another object. If Shadow Linking is set to Shadows Obey Light Linking (Maya Software) or Obeys Light Linking (mental ray), the surface will *not* cast a shadow *only* if it is unlinked from the light in the Relationship Editor or through the Break Light Links tool (see Chapter 2). Note that a viewport's Lighting > Use All Lights and Lighting > Shadows options may ignore broken shadow links unless you choose Renderer > Viewport 2.0.

 Note: To prevent a surface from casting a shadow for any and all lights, regardless of shadow linking, deselect Casts Shadows in the Render Stats section of the surface's Attribute Editor tab. To prevent a surface from receiving shadows from all other surfaces, deselect Receive Shadows.

Creating Effects Shadows

The Light Fog, Paint Effects, Fur, and nHair systems create an amazing range of render effects. Although it is beyond the scope of this book to go into great detail for these effects, shadow creation for each is covered. Simple Paint Effects, Fur, and nHair tutorials are included so that prior knowledge is not a prerequisite. (Light Fog is introduced in Chapter 2.)

Note: The nCloth system in Maya deforms polygon geometry as if it was fabric. Because nCloth geometry remains polygonal, it automatically casts depth map and raytrace shadows. (Nevertheless, you'll see those elements demonstrated as part of the tutorial at the end of this chapter.) The Toon system, on the other hand, renders geometry as if it's a 2D cartoon with nonshaded colors. You can create shadows with the Toon system if the surfaces are assigned to the Shaded Brightness Two Tone or Shaded Brightness Three Tone shaders (these are found in the Toon > Assign Fill Shader menu). Particle and nParticle rendering is demonstrated in Chapter 7, "Automating a Scene with Sampler Nodes." Rendering Fluid Effects and Bifröst liquids are discussed in Chapter 11.

Shadowing with Light Fog

You can render Light Fog with the Maya Software or mental ray renderers. However, to produce cast shadows within the body of the fog, you must use depth map shadows with Maya Software. (The mental ray renderer offers alternative methods of rendering fog, which are discussed in Chapter 12, "Working with mental ray Shaders, Global Illumination, and Final Gathering.")

Two additional fog attributes, Fog Shadow Intensity and Fog Shadow Samples, are included in the Depth Map Shadow Attributes section of spot, point, and volume lights. Fog Shadow Intensity dictates the darkness of shadows appearing in the body of the fog (see Figure 3.21).

Figure 3.21 Light Fog shadow with three different Fog Shadow Intensity settings. This scene is included with the Chapter 3 tutorial files as `fog_shadow.ma`.

The higher the Fog Shadow Intensity value, the less fog remains in the shadowed area. A value of 10 generally removes all the fog in the shadowed area and leaves a clean alpha channel (assuming there are no objects behind the fog).

Fog Shadow Samples, on the other hand, reduces potential fog graininess by applying additional sampling. Although there is no built-in maximum for the attribute, the default value of 20 is generally sufficient for a smooth render.

Shadowing with Paint Effects

Paint Effects is a powerful tool that allows you to interactively paint specialized strokes that create complex geometry as a postprocess. Numerous Paint Effects brushes are included with Maya and are grouped in such categories as grasses, trees, fire, and fibers.

An Introduction to Paint Effects

To create a simple Paint Effects scene, you can follow these basic steps:

1. Create a primitive, such as a sphere. Select the primitive, switch to the Rendering menu set, and choose Paint Effects > Make Paintable.

2. Choose Paint Effects > Get Brush. The Visor window opens. Select a brush folder, such as *trees*. Select a brush style by clicking a Paint Effects icon. Close the Visor.

3. LMB-drag the mouse arrow over the primitive. The Paint Effects stroke is laid over the surface. Each viewport shows a simplified version of the Paint Effects tube or sprite growth. To see the final quality, render with Maya Software in the Render View window. (Note that Viewport 2.0 only shows the Paint Effects stroke as you draw it.)

A Paint Effects stroke is a specialized set of nodes. The *stroke* shape and transform nodes generate the geometry visible in the viewports. A hidden *curve* node controls the shape of the stroke path. The brush node, which carries all the brush attributes, is connected to the stroke shape node. You can view the brush node in the Hypergraph: Connections or Node Editor windows; in addition, the brush node appears beside the stroke shape node in the Attribute Editor. The brush node is named after the brush type (for example, *rope1*). If a Paint Effects brush is applied to a surface through Make Paintable, the stroke geometry automatically deforms and moves with the surface. You can apply Paint Effects brushes to any surface that has a valid UV layout.

The majority of Paint Effects brushes grow special tube geometry as part of the postprocess. This is most noticeable with brushes that create plant life. A long list of attributes controls the tube growth; these can be found in the Tubes section of the brush node's Attribute Editor tab. Tubes can generate higher-quality shadows. A few additional brushes create simple non-tube geometry (for example, those in the *cityMesh* folder). These are also capable of creating accurate shadows. In contrast, a few Paint Effects brushes create sprites (for example, the *hands* brush). With these brushes, a bitmap is applied to a flattened tube with alpha information. No matter what direction the camera points, the sprite bitmap always faces the camera. Although sprites can cast shadows, the shadows take on the shape of the flattened tubes.

Note: Although mental ray is unable to render Paint Effects in their native state, you can convert Paint Effects strokes into renderable polygons. To do so, select the stroke and choose Modify > Convert Paint Effects To Polygons. The Convert Paint Effects To Polygons Options window includes attributes for controlling the number of polygons produced (a high polygon count may be necessary to accurately reproduce the Paint Effects tubes). In addition to creating a polygon node for each Paint Effects component (such a branches, leaves, and so on), the Convert tool creates a material network that emulates internal Paint Effects shading and texturing. You are free to adjust the resulting materials or assign new ones.

Note: Paint Effects brushes can be adapted or written from scratch. Each Paint Effects brush exists as a MEL text file in the *brushes* folder of the Maya program directory.

Creating 2D and 3D Paint Effects Shadows

Paint Effects strokes cannot cast raytraced shadows (unless the Paint Effects are converted to polygons). However, two attributes are provided to create depth map and fake shadows. They can be found in the Shadow Effects section of the brush node's Attribute Editor tab (see Figure 3.22).

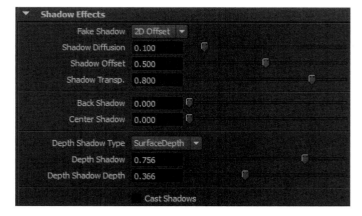

Figure 3.22   The Shadow Effects section of a Paint Effects brush node's Attribute Editor tab

Cast Shadows   If selected, the Paint Effects stroke is included in the depth map calculation. If the depth map's Resolution is sufficiently large, the result is accurate (see Figure 3.23).

Figure 3.23 Left: A Paint Effects plant casts depth map shadows through the Cast Shadows attribute; Right: Same stroke with a 3D Cast shadow. This scene is included with the Chapter 3 tutorial files as `Paint_Effects.ma`.

Fake Shadow   Provides two methods by which to create shadows without using depth maps: 2D Offset and 3D Cast.

2D Offset creates a drop-shadow effect by replicating the shape of the stroke as viewed by the camera and offsetting it in screen space. This is the least convincing shadow but may be suitable for dense strokes that lie close to a surface, such as eyebrow hair or short grass. When Fake Shadow is switched to 2D Offset, the Shadow Diffusion, Shadow Offset, and Shadow Transp. attributes become available. Shadow Diffusion controls the softness of the shadow and affects the blending of individual tube shadows. Higher values produce slightly soft results but make the shadows more cohesive. Shadow Offset sets the distance that the shadow is offset. Shadow Transp. determines the opacity of the shadow.

The 3D Cast option creates a shadow by defining an unseen, flat plane below the stroke and casting a shadow onto it. This option provides good results when the stroke itself is flat or is applied to a fairly smooth surface (see Figure 3.23 earlier in this section). 3D Cast shadows are refined by the Shadow Diffusion and Shadow Transp. attributes. Although 3D Cast shadows are relatively accurate, they have a tendency to separate from the root of the stroke.

In addition to shadow effects, Paint Effects strokes include several attributes to create self-shadowing:

Back Shadow   Darkens Paint Effects tubes that are farthest from the light. The higher the value, the darker the result.

Center Shadow   Darkens the tubes that are formed closest to the stroke path. The higher the value, the darker the result.

Depth Shadow Type   Darkens the stroke tube along its length based on the distance from a tube point to the corresponding surface or stroke path. If Depth Shadow Type is set to SurfaceDepth, the distance is measured from the tube point to the surface on which the Paint Effects stroke is drawn. If Depth Shadow Type is set to PathDist, the distance is measured from the tube point to the nearest point on the stroke path. Whereas the Depth Shadow Depth attribute defines the maximum distance that the shading effect is permitted to act within, the Depth Shadow attribute controls the resulting shadow darkness.

Shadowing with Maya Fur

The Maya Fur system grows numerous hairs over a surface. You can use depth map shadows with fur if special attributes are added to a spot light. If the special attributes are added to other light types, self-shadowing is available. In addition, you can create raytrace fur shadows with the mental ray renderer.

Creating Depth Map Fur Shadows

To create a simple fur setup and cast depth map shadows, follow these steps:

1. Create a NURBS, polygon, or subdivision surface. Switch to the Rendering menu set and choose Fur > Attach Fur Description > New. (If you don't see the Fur menu, load the Fur.mll plug-in through the Plug-In Manager.) The default fur appears on the surface. You can attach fur to any surface that has a valid UV layout. Optionally, you can adjust the look of the fur by choosing Fur > Edit Fur Description > *furDescription*n. For example, you can find attributes affecting the fur's length, width, color, curl, and randomness in the furDescription*n* Attribute Editor tab.

2. Create a primitive plane and place it below the surface so that it can catch shadows. Create and position a spot light to light the surfaces. Select Use Depth Map Shadows in the light's Attribute Editor tab. Increase Resolution to a high value, such as 2048 or 4096.

3. With the light selected, choose Fur > Fur Shadowing Attributes > Add To Selected Light. Attributes are added to the Fur Shading/Shadowing section of the light's Attribute Editor tab (see Figure 3.24). Switch the Fur Shading Type attribute to Shadow Maps. Leave the Threshold attribute set to 0. Threshold is designed to eliminate the shadows of extra-fine hairs; a hair is only included in a pixel of a depth map if it covers a percentage of the pixel greater than the Threshold value.

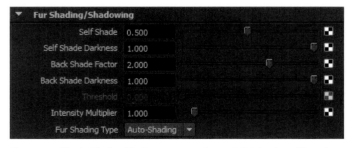

Figure 3.24 The Fur Shading/Shadowing section of a spot light's Attribute Editor tab

4. Render a test frame with the Maya Software renderer. The fur creates an appropriate shadow (see Figure 3.25). Open the Render Settings window and switch the Render Using attribute to mental ray. Render a second test frame. The shadow continues to appear. If the shadow appears grainy with mental ray, select the Use mental ray Shadow Map Overrides attribute in the Shadows subsection of the light's Attribute Editor tab and adjust the attributes within

the Shadow Map Overrides subsection. (See the section "Switching to mental ray Shadow Maps" earlier in this chapter.)

Figure 3.25 Default Fur with depth map shadows. Note that fur shadows fall across the sphere as well as the plane. This scene is included with the Chapter 3 tutorial files as `fur.ma`.

> **Note:** Maya may incorrectly place fur shadows if Auto Focus is selected in the light's Attribute Editor tab. For best results, deselect Auto Focus and enter a value in the Focus field. Maya documentation recommends that you derive the Focus value from this formula: `Cone Angle + (Penumbra Angle × 2)`.

Raytracing Fur Shadows

Maya Fur supports raytraced shadows only if the renderer is switched to mental ray. To see raytraced shadows, select Use Ray Trace Shadows in the light's Attribute Editor tab.

If Maya Software is the renderer of choice, Add To Selected Light must be applied to each spot light that is creating a shadow. You can remove the Fur Shading/ Shadowing attributes of a light by selecting the light and choosing Fur > Fur Shadowing Attributes > Remove From Selected Light. If mental ray is the renderer of choice, Add To Selected Light is not needed. If the Fur Shading/Shadowing attributes already exist, mental ray ignores them. Whereas the Maya Software renderer creates the fur as a post-process, mental ray integrates the fur directly into the scene. In general, mental ray ray-trace shadows are more accurate than Maya Software depth map shadows, which have a tendency to separate individual hair shadows from the hair bases and create diffuse self-shadowing. You can use any light type when raytracing fur shadows with mental ray. In addition, mental ray possesses the following render capabilities:

- Fur appears in reflections and refractions.
- Fur casts colored shadows.
- Fur blurs with motion.

Note: The mental ray renderer is able to integrate fur directly into the scene by treating fur in one of two ways: as hair primitives or as a volumetric mass. Hair primitives treat each hair as a polygon shape. In contrast, the volumetric mass treats the hairs as a conglomerated unit; although this method is easier to render, it cannot be used with raytracing. To choose the render method, change the Fur Shader menu in the mental ray section of the defaultFurGlobals Attribute Editor tab (you can reach this by choosing Fur > Fur Render Settings). For more information on volumetric fur limitations and settings, see the "Fur Render Settings (mental ray)" section of the Maya Help files.

Self-Shadowing Fur with Maya Software

If Fur Shading Type is switched to Auto-Shading, self-shadowing attributes become available to the Maya Software renderer (see Figure 3.24 earlier in this chapter). However, shadows of the fur cast onto other surfaces disappear. Auto-Shading is available to every light type except volume (which does not support fur shadowing). As with a spot light, the Fur Shading/Shadowing section must be added to the light by choosing Fur > Fur Shadowing Attributes > Add To Selected Light. The following attributes accompany Auto-Shading:

Self Shade   Defines the percentage of the fur hair length that is darkened. The percentage is anchored at the root. Thus, if Self Shade is 0.5, a fur hair is darkened from the root to its mid-length point. A value of 0 effectively turns the Self Shade attribute off. Self Shade Darkness controls the amount of black mixed with the fur hair's original color. A value of 0.5 equally mixes black with the fur hair color. A value of 1.0 makes the fur hair pure black.

Back Shade Factor   Artificially darkens the fur hair that lies on the surface side opposite the light source. A Back Shade Factor value of 0 creates a harsh transition from the lit side of the fur to the dark side. Values between 0 and 1.0 create a more natural falloff from the lit side to the dark side. Values above 1.0 make the falloff more gradual. A value of 0 effectively turns the Back Shade Factor attribute off. Back Shade Darkness controls the amount of black mixed with the fur hair's original color. A value of 0.5 equally mixes black with the fur hair color.

Intensity Multiplier   Serves as a multiplier for the light intensity read by the fur. Fur strongly reflects light and is thereby often rendered inappropriately bright. Reducing this attribute below 1.0 will darken the fur without affecting other objects in the scene. Intensity Multiplier functions even if Fur Shading Type is set to No Shading.

Shadowing with Maya nHair

The Maya nHair system generates a series of dynamic curves that can simulate hair, ropes, chains, and other thin, long elements. The quickest way to generate nHair in Maya is to switch to the nDynamics menu set, choose nHair > Get Hair Example, select a hair icon in the Visor window, RMB-click, and choose Import Maya File *name of hair file* from the shortcut menu. A complete scene with a polygon model and hair system is brought in. Otherwise, you can create a hair system from scratch following these steps:

1. Create a NURBS or polygon primitive. Switch to the nDynamics menu set. Choose nHair > Create Hair with default settings. An nHair system is attached. You can attach nHair to any NURBS or polygon surface that has a valid UV layout. If you would like to restrict the nHair growth to specific polygon faces, select those faces, choose nHair > Create Hair > ❑, select the At Selected Surface Points/Faces radio button in the Create Hair Options window, and click the Create Hairs button.

2. Relax the hair by playing back the Timeline from frame 1. Once the hair has fallen and has come close to rest, stop the playback. You can set the hair's current position as a new start position by selecting the nHair mass in a viewport and choosing nHair > Set Start Position > From Current. The nHair hairs automatically collide with any passive collider created through the nDynamics system. You can convert a surface into a passive collider by choosing nMesh > Create Passive Collider.

3. Create a light and select Use Depth Map Shadows. Increase the Resolution to a high value, such as 2048. Render a test frame with Maya Software. Shadows of the hair appear across the surface. Open the Render Settings window and switch the Render Using attribute to mental ray. Render a second test frame. The shadow continues to appear. If the resulting mental ray shadow appears grainy, select the Use mental ray Shadow Map Overrides attribute in the Shadows subsection of the light's Attribute Editor tab and adjust the attributes within the Shadow Map Overrides subsection. For example, increase the quality by raising Samples to 64 and give the shadow a slight softness by changing the Softness attribute to 0.001 (see Figure 3.26). (See "Switching to mental ray Shadow Maps" earlier in this chapter for additional information.)

Figure 3.26 Left: Maya nHair without shadows; Right: Maya nHair with mental ray depth map shadows. This scene is included with the Chapter 3 tutorial files as nHair.ma.

When an nHair system is created, many new nodes are included. The hair-SystemFollicles node is a group node to which all the follicle shape nodes belong as children. Follicles are small, red circles along the hair-generating surface that create individual clumps of dynamic curves. Any hair that is rendered is actually a Paint Effects tube. Hence, pfxHair, pfxHairShape, hairSystem, and hairSystemShape are included. pfxHair serves as a transform node for the hair system. pfxHairShape carries global Paint Effects attributes such as Display Quality. hairSystemShape carries a specialized set of Paint Effects attributes designed for rendering hair.

You can adjust the nHair hairs at any time by altering the attributes of the hairSystemShape node. You can access this node by selecting the nHair mass in a viewport and switching from the pfxHairShape*n* tab to the hairSystemShape*n* tab in the Attribute Editor. Within the Clump And Hair Shape section, you can change the number of hairs per clump (there is one clump per follicle), add subsegments to smooth the hairs, and adjust the hair width and clump width. Additional sections control curliness, dynamic properties, and shading qualities such as color and specularity. To change the hair length, you must interactively apply the Scale Hair Tool. To do so, select the nHair mass in a viewport, choose nHair > Scale Hair Tool, and LMB-drag left or right across the hair in a viewport. To exit the tool, return to the Select tool.

> **Note:** A specialized material, Hair Tube Shader, is designed for an nHair system that is converted from Paint Effects to polygons (you can choose Modify > Convert > Paint Effects To Polygons). The material is automatically assigned to the resulting polygons and includes specialized color ramp graphs and specular controls designed specifically for human and animal hair. The material is unique in that it ignores surface normals and instead bases its shading on the camera view and Tube Direction attribute. Because the Hair Tube Shader material is a variation of an anisotropic material, you can assign it to any surface. (For more information on the Anisotropic material, see Chapter 4, "Applying the Correct Material and 2D Texture.")

You can render nHair with raytrace shadows if the mental ray renderer is selected. Whereas the Maya Software renderer creates nHair as a postprocess, mental ray integrates the nHair directly into the scene. As such, mental ray possesses the following render capabilities:

- nHair appears in reflections and refractions.
- nHair motion blurs.

Chapter Tutorial: Creating Quality Shadows with nCloth and Paint Effects

In this tutorial, you will add nCloth and Paint Effects to the Chapter 1 interior scene (see Figure 3.27). You'll adjust the shadows of the current lights and the Paint Effects brushes to create high-quality results.

Figure 3.27 The room with the addition of an nCloth surface and Paint Effects grasses

1. In Maya, choose File > Set Project. In the Set Project window, browse for the `Project_3` directory, select the directory name, and click the Set button. This ensures that the texture bitmaps will be correctly located. Open `room_cloth.ma` from the Chapter 3 scene folder. Spend a few minutes familiarizing yourself with the model's various parts. This is the same model that was used for the Chapter 2 tutorial. It includes the positioned and adjusted lights. In addition, there is a new surface (named Cloth) in the room center that you will use for nCloth simulation. There are two cameras: persp and WorkingCamera. Use persp for rendering. Use WorkingCamera to move around the scene. For proper dynamic playback, make sure that the Playback Speed menu is set to Play Every Frame (choose Windows > Settings/Preferences > Preferences > Time Slider section).

2. Select the Cloth surface. Switch to the nDynamics menu set. Choose nMesh > Create nCloth. The surface turns pink, indicating a new nCloth node is created along with a nucleus node (nucleus nodes provide the dynamic calculations for the Maya nDynamics system). Select the ClothSupport surface directly below the Cloth surface (this is a floating beam added to catch the nCloth surface once it deforms). Choose nMesh > Create Passive Collider. Select the Floor surface and choose nMesh > Create Passive Collider. Each time a surface is converted to a passive collider, an nRigid node is created. Through the Hypergraph or Outliner, select the nRigid1 node. In the node's Attribute Editor tab, change Friction and Stickiness to 1.0. Apply the same settings to nRigid2. Extend the timeline to 300 frames. Go to frame 1 and play back. The Cloth surface, now driven by the nCloth system, drops and deforms over the floating beam (see Figure 3.28). The higher Friction and Stickiness values cause the Cloth surface to land on the beam and prevent it from eventually sliding to the ground. Stop the timeline on a frame where the Cloth has come to a rest. Choose nSolver > Initial State > Set From Current. The nCloth now starts from the current position on frame 1.

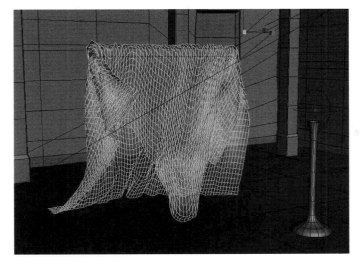

Figure 3.28 The relaxed Cloth surface, driven by an nCloth node

3. Render a test frame. The Cloth surface, as a polygonal object, is automatically shadowed. The shadows are visible on the floor below it and along the back left wall (see Figure 3.29). However, the shadows are opaque even though the assigned material (ClothMaterial) is semitransparent. To give the shadows transparency, select the LightBulb light, open its Attribute Editor tab, and select Use Ray Trace Shadows. The depth map shadows are automatically overridden. Open the render Settings window, switch to the Maya Software tab, and select the Raytracing attribute in the Raytracing Quality section. Test render. The shadows created by the Cloth surface become lighter, indicating the semitransparent quality of the shadow casting surface.

4. The raytraced shadows created by the LightBulb light remain hard-edged. To soften these, return to the Raytrace Shadow Attributes section of the light's Attribute Editor tab. Increase Light Radius to 0.25. Test render (render small regions to save time). Note that the shadow edges, particularly around the lamp base, become grainy. Incrementally increase the Shadow Rays value from 1.0 to 32, creating additional test renders along the way. The higher the value, the smoother the raytraced shadows (see Figure 3.30) but the longer the render time. Note that the shadows directly below the Cloth surface remain sharper than those on the back wall or below the lamp. This is due to the close proximity of the Cloth geometry to the floor geometry.

5. Now that raytracing is activated, you can create reflective materials. Although Maya Software materials carry a Reflectivity value of 0.5 by default, the materials in this scene have been set to 0. Open the Hypershade (choose Window > Rendering Editors > Hypershade). Double-click the FloorMaterial icon to open its Attribute Editor tab. In the Specular Shading section, change Reflectivity to 0.75, Eccentricity to 0.3, Specular Roll Off to 0.4, and Specular Color to medium gray. Test render. The floor picks up a reflection of the Cloth, lamp, walls and supports around it.

Figure 3.29 The Cloth surface is shadowed by the LightBulb light. The depth maps do not provide shadow transparency.

Figure 3.30 Left: Raytrace shadows with Shadow Rays set to 1.0 produce grainy edges around the base of the lamp; Right: Same render with Shadow Rays set to 32. The Light Radius of the point light is set to 0.25.

6.   Switch to the Rendering menu set. Select the Floor surface. Choose Paint Effects > Make Paintable. Choose Paint Effects > Get Brush. In the Visor window, navigate to the *grasses* folder. Click on the icon for the grassDryBlowing. mel brush. Close the Visor. Interactively LMB-drag the Paint Effects brush (as indicated by the pencil mouse icon) in front of one of the columns as if weeds are springing up in cracks or gaps within the concrete. Release the mouse button to end the stroke. Keep the stroke fairly short. The Paint Effects grass grows along the stroke. Note that this grass has a tendency to lie flat, as if blown by the wind. You can force the grass blades to stand upright by reducing the Path Follow value. You can find Path Follow in the Forces subsection of the grass-DryBlowing1 tab (Tubes section > Behavior subsection > Forces subsection). Feel free to experiment with other attributes within this section, all of which

affect the way in which the grass blades grow. Repeat this process in one or two other locations in front of columns or up against the walls (Figure 3.31).

Figure 3.31 Two grassDryBlowing Paint Effects strokes are painted on the floor.

7. With the first stroke selected (you can select the grassDryBlowing1 node in the Hypergraph or Outliner), go to the grassDryBlowing1 tab in the Attribute Editor. Set the Global Scale, near the top of the tab, to 2.5. Set the same Global Scale for each remaining stroke. Test render a region that covers the grass area. The grass appears at the end of the render but does not produce shadows. Go to the Shadow Effects section of the first stroke. Change the Fake Shadow menu to 3D Cast. Repeat this for the remaining strokes. Render a test frame. The grass produces shadows (because the grass blades are thin, this will be easier to see if the grass is in the foreground). If the LightBulb light employed depth map shadows instead of raytrace shadow, you would have the option to select the Cast Shadows attribute for each stroke and thereby have the grass included in the light's regular depth map.

8. At this stage, the reflection of the grass is missing from the floor reflections. In addition, the grass blades render with high contrast. To solve these problems, you can convert the Paint Effects strokes to polygons. To do so, select the first stroke and choose Modify > Convert > Paint Effects To Polygons > ❏. In the Convert Paint Effects To Polygons window, set Poly Limit to 25,000 and click the Apply button. The original Paint Effects stroke is hidden and a new polygon object takes its place. In addition, a new material is created to emulate the old Paint Effects texturing and shading. Open the Hypershade window. Open the new grassDryBlowing1Shader in the Attribute Editor. Reduce the Translucence to 0.1 and set Diffuse to 0.8 to prevent the grass from appearing overly bright. Render a test frame. The new polygon grass appears better integrated in the scene and produces reflections and cast shadows. Create a similar polygon conversion for any remaining Paint Effects strokes.

    The scene is complete! Your render should look similar to Figure 3.27 earlier in this section. If you get stuck, a finished version has been saved as `room_finished_2.ma` with the Chapter 3 tutorial files.

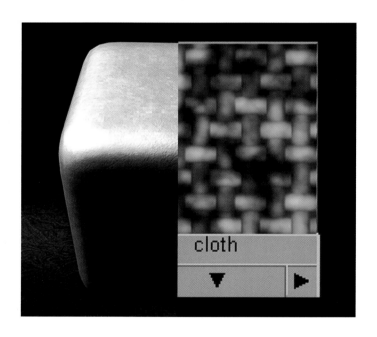

Applying the Correct Material and 2D Texture

Simply put, a material determines the look of a surface. Although it's easy enough to assign a material and a texture to a surface and produce a render, many powerful attributes and options are available to you in Autodesk® Maya®. At the same time, a rich historical legacy has determined why materials and textures work the way they do. You can map a wide range of 2D textures to materials, creating an almost infinite array of results. Simple combinations of textures and materials can lead to believable reproductions of real-world objects.

4

Chapter Contents

Theoretical underpinnings of shading models

Review of Maya materials

Review of 2D textures

Descriptions of extra texture attributes

Material and texture layering tricks

Reviewing Shading Models and Materials

A *shader* is a program used to determine the final surface quality of a 3D object. A shader uses a shading model, which is a mathematical algorithm that simulates the interaction of light with a surface. In common terms, surfaces are described as rough, smooth, shiny, or dull.

In the Maya Hypershade and Node Editor windows, a shading model is referred to as a *material* and is represented by a spherical icon. Ultimately, you can use the words *shader* and *material* interchangeably.

A shading group, on the other hand, is connected to the material as soon as it's assigned. The shading group's sole function is to associate sets of surfaces with a material so that the renderer knows which surface is assigned to which material. The shading group does not provide any definition of surface quality. If the connection between a shading group node and material is deleted, the assigned surface appears solid green in the viewport views and is skipped by the renderer (see Figure 4.1).

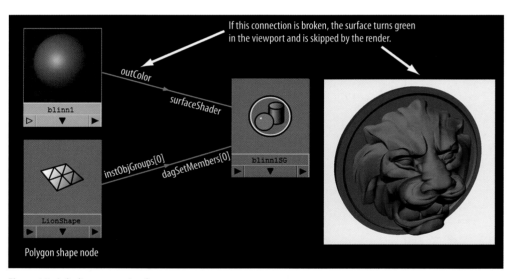

Figure 4.1 A shading group network

Lambert

The Lambert material carries common attributes: Color, Transparency, Ambient Color, Incandescence, Bump Mapping, Diffuse, Translucence, Translucence Depth, and Translucence Focus. In Maya, the Lambert node is considered a "parent" node—that is, Phong, Phong E, Blinn, and Anisotropic materials all inherit their common attributes from the Lambert material. In each case, the attributes function in an identical manner. For information on the Bump Mapping attribute, see Chapter 9, "Improving Textures through Custom UVs and Maps.")

The Lambert material in Maya uses a diffuse-reflection model in which the intensity of any given surface point is based on the angle between the surface normal and light vector. In order for the Lambert material to smoothly render across polygon faces, it applies an interpolation method. With interpolation, the intensity of any given point on a polygon face (see point C in Figure 4.2) is linearly interpolated from the intensities of the polygon's vertex normals and two edge points intersected by a scan line.

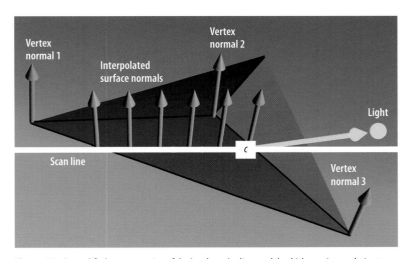

Figure 4.2 A simplified representation of the Lambert shading model, which uses interpolation to smoothly shade across polygon faces

Adjusting Diffuse, Color, Ambient Color, and Incandescence

Calculations involving diffuse reflections use Lambert's Cosine Law. This law states that the observed radiant intensity of a surface is directly proportional to the cosine of the angle between the viewer's line of sight and the surface normal. As a result, the radiant intensity of the surface, which is perceived as surface brightness, does not change with the viewing angle. Hence, a Lambertian surface is perfectly matte, does not generate highlights or specular hot spots, and is therefore referred to as diffuse. Physically, a real-world Lambertian surface has myriad surface imperfections that scatter reflected light in a random pattern. Paper, cardboard, and some woven surfaces are examples of Lambertian surfaces. The law was developed by Johann Heinrich Lambert (1728–1777), who also served as the inspiration for the Lambert material's name.

The term *diffuse* refers to that which is widely spread and not concentrated. Hence, the Diffuse attribute of the Lambert material represents the degree to which light rays are reflected in all directions. A high Diffuse value produces a bright surface. A low Diffuse value causes light rays to be absorbed and thereby makes the surface dark.

The Color attribute sets the primary color of the surface. In contrast, the Ambient Color attribute represents diffuse reflections arriving from all other surfaces in a scene. To simplify the rendering process, the diffuse reflections are assumed to be arriving from all points in the scene with equal intensities. In practical terms, Ambient Color is the color of a surface when it receives no light. A high Ambient Color value causes the object to wash out and appear flat. Low Ambient Color values may be useful for emulating translucence or subsurface scattering. High Ambient Color values may be useful for creating a "toon"-like surface.

The Incandescence attribute, on the other hand, creates the illusion that the assigned surface is emitting light. The color of the Incandescence attribute is added to the Color attribute, thus making the material appear brighter.

Note: You can use the Ambient Color and Incandescence attributes as irradiant light sources when rendering with Final Gathering. For more information, see Chapter 12, "Working with mental ray Shaders, Global Illumination, and Final Gathering."

Working with Translucence

The Translucence attribute simulates the diffuse penetration of light into a solid surface. In the real world, you can see this effect when holding a flashlight to the back of your hand. Translucence naturally occurs with hair, fur, wax, paper, leaves, and human flesh. Advanced renderers, such as mental ray®, are able to simulate translucence through subsurface scattering (see Chapter 12 for an example). The Translucence attribute in Maya, however, is a simplified system. The higher the attribute value, the more the scene's light penetrates the surface (see Figure 4.3).

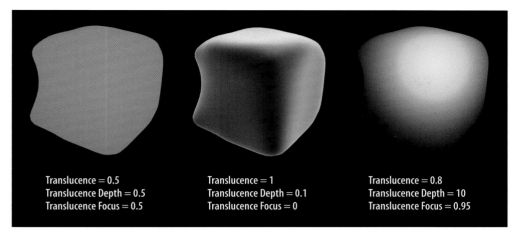

Translucence = 0.5
Translucence Depth = 0.5
Translucence Focus = 0.5

Translucence = 1
Translucence Depth = 0.1
Translucence Focus = 0

Translucence = 0.8
Translucence Depth = 10
Translucence Focus = 0.95

Figure 4.3 Different combinations of Translucence, Translucence Depth, and Translucence Focus attributes on a primitive lit from behind. This scene is included with the Chapter 4 tutorial files as `translucence.ma`.

A Translucence value of 1.0 allows 100 percent of the light to pass through the surface. A value of 0 turns the translucent effect off. Translucence Depth sets the virtual distance into the object to which the light is able to penetrate. The attribute is measured in world units and may be raised above 5. Translucence Focus controls the scattering of light through the surface. A value of 0 makes the scatter of light random and diffuse. High values focus the light into a point.

Shading with Phong

The Phong shading model uses diffuse and ambient components but also generates a specular highlight based on an arbitrary shininess. In general, specularity is the consistent reflection of light in one direction that creates a "hot spot" on a surface. With the Phong model, the position and intensity of a specular highlight is determined by reading the angle between the reflection vector and the view vector (see Figure 4.4). A vector, in this situation, is a line segment that runs between two points in 3D Cartesian space that represents direction. (For a deeper discussion of vectors and vector math, see Chapter 8, "Harnessing the Power of Math Utilities.")

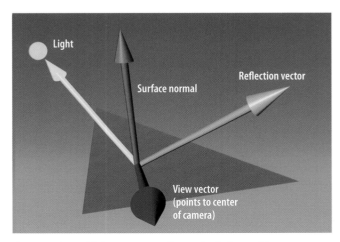

Figure 4.4 A simplified representation of a specular shading model

If the angle between the light vector and the surface normal is 60 degrees, the angle between the reflection vector and the surface normal is also 60 degrees. In this way, the reflection vector is a mirrored version of the light vector. If the angle between the reflection vector and view vector is large, the intensity of the specular highlight is either low or zero. If the angle between the reflection vector and view vector is small, the intensity of the specular highlight is high. The speed with which the specular highlight transitions from high intensity to no intensity is controlled by the Cosine Power attribute. The higher the Cosine Power value, the more rapid the falloff, and the smaller and "tighter" the highlight. (For information on specular attributes, see the next three sections.)

Ultimately, the specular highlights created by Maya materials are an artificial construct. Real-world specular highlights are reflections of intense light sources (see Figure 4.5).

TOP LEFT AND TOP RIGHT: PHOTO © BLUESKYIMAGES/DOLLAR PHOTO CLUB

Figure 4.5 Top Left: A classic specular highlight appears on an eye; Top Right: A closer look at the eye reveals that the specular highlight is the reflection of the photographer's light umbrella; Bottom Left: A glass float with a large specular highlight; Bottom Middle: With the exposure adjusted, the float's specular highlight is revealed to be the reflection of a window; Bottom Right: The window that creates the reflection.

Shading with Blinn

The Blinn shading model borrows the specular shading component from the Phong model but treats the specular calculations in a more mathematically efficient way. Instead of determining the angle between the reflection vector and view vector, Blinn determines the angle between the view vector and a vector halfway between the light vector and view vector. In practical terms, you can make the Maya Phong and Blinn materials produce nearly identical highlights (see Figure 4.6).

The Blinn material in Maya uses the Eccentricity attribute to control specular size and the Specular Roll Off attribute to control specular intensity. The Specular Color attribute determines the color of the highlight at its greatest intensity. The specular attributes of Blinn, Phong, Phong E, and Anisotropic materials are located in the Specular Shading section of the material's Attribute Editor tab.

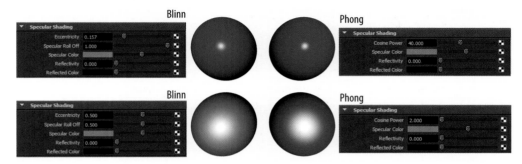

Figure 4.6 Small and large specular highlights on Blinn and Phong materials. This scene is included with the Chapter 4 tutorial files as blinn_phong.ma.

When it comes to the position of the specular highlight, both Phong and Blinn re-create Fresnel reflections, whereby the amount of light reflected from a surface depends on the angle of view (which is the opposite of diffuse reflections). That is, when the view changes, the highlight appears at a different point on the surface (see Figure 4.7).

MODEL CREATED BY PIXWATT STUDIO

Figure 4.7 Specular highlights appear at different points on the medallion as the view changes.

> **Note:** Although the Blinn and Phong materials in Maya are able to change the location of the specular highlight as the view changes, they are unable to accurately change the angle-dependent intensity of the specular highlight. A few advanced materials, such as the mental ray mia_material_x shader, alter specular reflectivity based on angle of view. This is demonstrated in Chapter 12.

Shading with Phong E

The Phong E material in Maya is a simplified variation of the Phong shading model. Phong E's specular quality is similar to both Phong and Blinn. The Roughness attribute controls the transition of the highlight core to the highlight edge. A low Roughness value will cause the highlight to fade off quickly, whereas a high Roughness value gives the highlight a diffuse taper in the style of a Blinn material. The Highlight Size attribute controls the total size of the highlight. The Whiteness attribute allows an additional color to be blended into the highlight between the colors established by the Color and Specular Color attributes.

Blinn, Phong, and Phong E highlights become distorted as they approach the edge of a surface with a high degree of curvature. In addition, Blinn, Phong, and Phong E produce elongated highlights on cylindrical objects (see Figure 4.8).

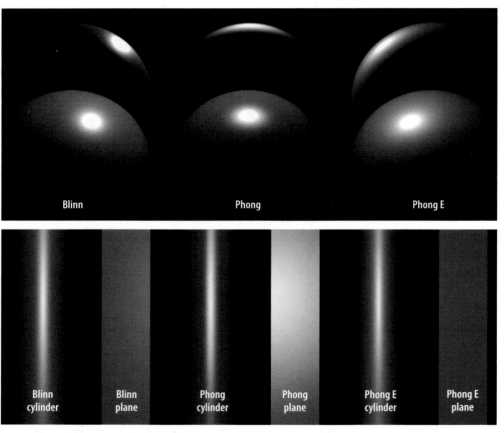

Figure 4.8 Blinn, Phong, and Phong E materials assigned to primitive spheres, cylinders, and planes. This scene is included in the Chapter 4 tutorial files as `blinn_phong_cylinders.ma`.

When comparing the material's highlights to photographs of real-world equivalents, it's apparent that the Blinn, Phong, and Phong E models are fairly realistic (see Figure 4.9). Phong and Phong E materials have a slight advantage on the edge of a spherical surface, where specular reflections naturally grow in width due to the angles of reflected light.

Figure 4.9 Left: Various cylindrical objects lit by a single overhead light; Right: A billiard ball with specular reflections of windows on its top edge.

Note: Fresnel reflections are named after Augustin-Jean Fresnel (1788–1827), who drafted theories on light propagation. The Phong shading model was created by Bui Tuong Phong in 1975. The Blinn shading model was developed in 1977 by James Blinn, who was also a pioneer of bump and environment mapping.

Shading with the Anisotropic Material

The anisotropic shading model produces stretched reflections and specular highlights. The model simulates surfaces that have microscopic grooves, channels, scratches, grains, or fibers running parallel to one another. In such a situation, specular highlights tend to be elongated and run perpendicular to the direction of the grooves. The effect occurs on choppy or rippled water, brushed, coiled, or threaded metal, velvet and like cloth, feathers, and human hair (see Figure 4.10).

Figure 4.10 Anisotropic specular highlights on water, hair, and metal

The anisotropic shading model is the opposite of isotropic shading models used by such materials as Blinn or Phong. With isotropic models, the quality of the specular highlight does not change if the assigned surface is moved or rotated. With anisotropic models, a change in the surface's translation or rotation significantly alters the resulting highlight. As a simple demonstration, two NURBS spheres are assigned to default Blinn and Anisotropic materials and are translated and rotated (see Figure 4.11).

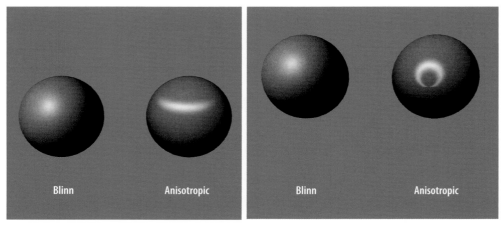

Figure 4.11 The specular highlight of an Anisotropic material changes with translation and rotation of the assigned sphere on the right. This scene is included with the Project 4 tutorial files as `anisotropic_spin.ma`. A QuickTime movie is included as `anisotropic_spin.mov`.

Working with Anisotropic Highlights

CDs, DVDs, and BluRay discs produce strong anisotropic highlights thanks to their method of manufacture—they are optical media, designed to represent information in the form of reflected light. You can simulate these highlights in Maya with the following steps, using a CD as an example:

1. Create a new Maya scene. Choose Create > NURBS Primitives > Circle with the default settings. Select the resulting circle and choose Edit > Duplicate.

2. Select the duplicated circle and reduce the scale so that it is the appropriate size for the disc's center hole. Select both circles, switch to the Surfaces menu set, and choose Surfaces > Loft.

3. Select the new surface and assign it to a new Anisotropic material. Open the material's Attribute Editor tab. Set Spread X to 100, Spread Y to 1.0, Roughness to 0.8, and Fresnel Index to 9.5.

4. Create a point light and place it above the surface. Render a test. At this point, the specular highlight is white. (If the specular highlight does not form a straight line but bows or forms a partial circle, change Spread X to 1.0 and Spread Y to 100.) To insert colors into the highlight, click the checkered Map button beside Specular Color. From the Create Render Node window, choose Ramp. Open the new ramp texture in the Attribute Editor tab. Set Interpolation to Smooth. If you are using Maya 2014, the Ramp texture runs from red to blue. If you are using Maya 2015, the texture runs from black to white. You can change the color of a ramp handle by clicking a circular handle icon, clicking the Selected Color swatch, and picking a new color in the Color Chooser window.

5. Once you've adjusted the colors, render a test. The highlight now roughly emulates the color shift of real CDs (see Figure 4.12). If the colors run in a direction opposite that of a real CD, switch the top and bottom handles of the ramp texture.

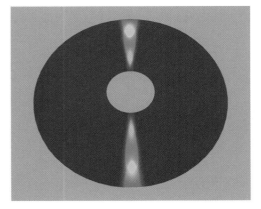

Figure 4.12 The anisotropic highlight of a CD is re-created in Maya. This scene is included with the Chapter 4 tutorial files as `anisotropic_cd.ma`.

Understanding Anisotropic Material Attributes

Anisotropic material attributes work in the following way:

Angle Determines the angle of the specular highlight.

Spread X Sets the width of the grooves in the X direction. The X direction is the U direction rotated counterclockwise by the Angle attribute.

Spread Y Sets the width of the grooves in the Y direction, which is perpendicular to the X direction. If Spread X and Spread Y are equal, the specular highlight is fairly circular.

Roughness Controls the roughness of the surface. The higher the value, the larger and the more diffuse the highlights appear.

Fresnel Index Sets the intensity of the specular highlight.

Anisotropic Reflectivity If selected, bases reflectivity on the Roughness attribute. If deselected, the standard Reflectivity attribute determines reflectivity.

For more information on reflectivity and associated raytracing, see Chapter 11, "Raytracing, mental ray, and Effects Rendering."

Shading with a Shading Map

The Shading Map material in Maya remaps the output of another material. In other words, the Shading Map discreetly replaces the colors of a material, even after the qualities of that material have been calculated. In a basic example, the Out Color attribute of a Blinn material is mapped to the Color of a Shading Map material (see Figure 4.13). The Out Color of a Ramp texture is mapped to the Shading Map Color of the Shading Map material. In turn, the Shading Map material is assigned to a polygon frog. Where the Blinn material normally shades the model with a dark color, the bottom of the Ramp is sampled. Where the Blinn normally shades the model with a light color, such as a specular highlight point, the top of the Ramp is sampled.

Shading with a Surface Shader

The Surface Shader material in Maya has no inherent shading properties. It derives its color, transparency, and glow information from arbitrary inputs mapped to its Out Color, Out Transparency, and Out Glow Color attributes. You can map attributes from materials, textures, geometry, lights, or cameras. For example, if you map the Rotate XYZ channels of a sphere to the Out Color of an assigned Surface Shader, the sphere automatically changes color as it rotates. (For information on connecting non-material nodes to materials, see Chapter 7.)

In addition, the Surface Shader material fails to take into account any light or shadow information. A surface assigned to a Surface Shader appears self-illuminated. Any texture mapped to the Out Color attribute of the Surface Shader comes through the render with all its original vibrancy intact (see Figure 4.14). This makes the Surface Shader ideal for background skies and brightly lit signs. The material is also well suited for custom cartoon materials in which shadowing and highlights are provided by a custom network and not by actual lights.

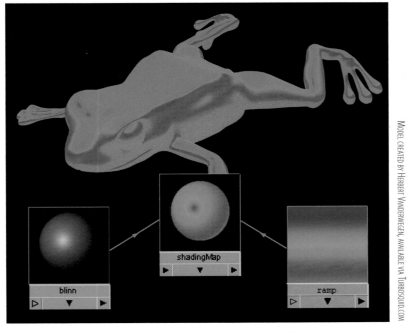

Figure 4.13 A polygon frog is assigned to a Shading Map material. A simplified version of this scene is included in the Chapter 4 tutorial files as `shading_map.ma`.

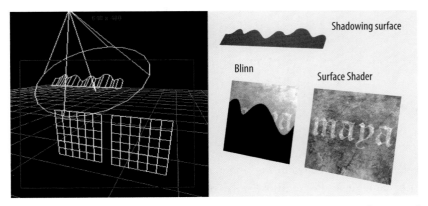

Figure 4.14 A plane assigned to a Blinn material picks up shadows and highlights, whereas a plane assigned to a Surface Shader material ignores all lighting information. This scene is included with the Chapter 4 tutorial files as `surface_shader.ma`.

Shading with Use Background

The Use Background material in Maya allows the assigned surface to pick up color from a camera's Background Color attribute or image plane. For example, in Figure 4.15 a photo of a quiet town is loaded into the default persp camera as an image plane (choose View > Image Plane through the camera's viewport menu). A NURBS plane is aligned to the perspective of the photo's street. The plane is assigned to a Use Background material. The resulting render places the shadow of a polygon craft on top of the street.

MODEL CREATED BY KONSTANTINOFF, AVAILABLE VIA TURBOSQUID.COM

Figure 4.15 The Use Background material is assigned to a primitive plane, thus placing a shadow on a photo of a street. A simplified version of this scene is included with the Chapter 4 tutorial files as use_background.ma. The image is also included in the textures folder as street.tif.

If the image plane is removed from the camera (you can delete image plane nodes in the Hypershade Cameras tab) and the polygon craft is assigned to a 100 percent transparent Lambert material, the shadow is rendered by itself and appears in the alpha channel (see Figure 4.16). This offers an excellent means to render shadows out on their own pass. If shadows are rendered separately, you can composite them back onto a static background. For more information on shadow render passes, see Chapter 13, "Color Management, HDR Workflow, and Render Passes." For more information on alpha channels, see Chapter 6.

The Use Background material also serves as an "alpha punch" that cuts holes into other objects. For this to work, the camera's Background Color attribute (found in the Environment section of the camera's Attribute Editor tab) should be set to black. For example, in Figure 4.17 three polygon gorillas stand close together, partially occluding each other. In a first render pass (see the top of Figure 4.17), a Use Background material is assigned to the center gorilla whereas the other surfaces are assigned to several Blinn materials. As a result, the center gorilla cuts a hole into the other two. As a second render pass (see the middle of Figure 4.17), the Use Background material is assigned to the two outer gorillas and the ground plane. The center gorilla is assigned to a Blinn. As a result, the two outer gorillas cut a hole into the center gorilla. When the two render passes are brought into a compositing program, they fit together perfectly (see the bottom of Figure 4.17). This works whether the objects are static or are in motion. When used in this fashion, the Use Background material allows characters and objects in a scene to be rendered separately without any worry of which object is in the front and which is in the back.

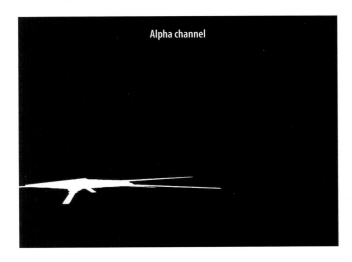

Figure 4.16 The Use Background material isolates a shadow in the alpha channel. A simplified version of this scene is included with the Chapter 4 tutorial files as `back-ground_shadow.ma`.

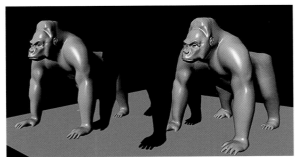

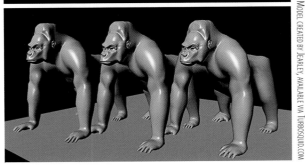

MODEL CREATED BY JEARLEY, AVAILABLE VIA TURBOSQUID.COM

Figure 4.17 The Use Background material cuts holes into the alpha of two renders. When the renders are composited back together, they fit perfectly. A simplified version of this scene is included with the Chapter 4 tutorial files as `background_alpha.ma`.

Note: Five materials—Hair Tube Shader, Ocean Shader, Ramp Shader, Bifrost Liquid Material, and Shaderfx Shader—are not discussed in this chapter. The Hair Tube Shader is designed for the Maya Hair system, which is covered briefly in Chapter 3, "Creating High-Quality Shadows." The Ocean Shader is designed specifically for fluid dynamic ocean simulations and has no other general purpose. The Ramp Shader is reviewed in Chapter 7. Bifrost Liquid Material is included with the Bifrost liquid simulation system and is reviewed in Chapter 11. The Shaderfx Shader material is designed for the ShaderFX editor. The editor allows you to create custom shaders intended for display in Viewport 2.0. The system emulates shaders provided by game engines. You can access the editor by clicking the Open ShaderFX button in the Shaderfx Shader material's Attibbrute Editor tab. For more information, see the "About ShaderFX" page on the Autodesk Knowledge Network (`knowledge.autodesk.com`).

Note: The mental ray renderer includes a large set of shaders, many of which produce results similar to the materials discussed in this chapter. In addition, many of the mental ray shaders provide advanced attributes that more accurately replicate real-world lighting situations. Nevertheless, understanding the strengths and weaknesses of standard Maya materials can help you make decisions that optimize your work flow. For example, advanced shaders generally require time-intensive rendering and may be overly complex for some projects. Chapter 12 explores mental ray shaders in more depth.

Reviewing 2D Textures

Maya 2D textures can be grouped into the following categories: cloth, water, Perlin noise, ramp, bitmap, and square. Aside from bitmaps, all these textures are generated procedurally. That is, Maya creates these textures with specialized algorithms that create repeating patterns. These textures are located in the Maya > 2D Textures section of the Hypershade and Create Render Node windows.

Applying Cloth

The Cloth texture is unique in that it generates interlaced fibers. Aside from obvious use in clothing, it can be adjusted to generate various organic patterns such as reptile scales. For example, in Figure 4.18 a Cloth texture is mapped to the Bump Mapping attribute of a Blinn material.

Figure 4.18 Left: Cloth texture is adjusted as a bump map to create scales. The Cloth's Repeat UV is set to 36, 30. Middle: The Cloth icon with a Repeat UV set to 1.0, 1.0; Right: The Cloth attributes values. This scene is included with the Chapter 4 tutorial files as `cloth_scales.ma`.

The regularity, or irregularity, of the cloth pattern is controlled by 10 attributes. Gap Color, U Color, and V Color set the color of the virtual threads. U Width and V Width determine the width of the threads in the U and V direction. U Wave and V Wave insert wave-like distortion into the cloth pattern. Randomness harshly distorts the pattern in the U and V directions. Width Spread randomly changes the thread widths. Bright Spread randomly darkens or lightens the thread colors.

Applying Water

By default, the Water texture produces overlapping wave patterns. Although the default is not particularly suited for creating realistic liquids, you can adjust the attributes to create other patterns found in nature. For example, in Figure 4.19 a Water texture is applied to a plane as a bump map and is adjusted to emulate windblown sand.

Figure 4.19 A water texture, used as a bump map, emulates patterns found on a sand dune. This scene is included with the Chapter 4 tutorial files as `water_sand.ma`.

Critical attributes of the Water texture include the following:

Number Of Waves   Sets the number of waves used to create the pattern.

Wave Time and Wave Velocity   Wave Time controls the placement of the waves. Gradually increasing the value will cause the waves to "roll" across the texture as if part of a body of water. Wave Velocity sets the speed by which the waves move if Wave Time is changed. Both attributes are designed for keyframe animation.

Wave Amplitude   Controls the height of the waves. Higher values introduce greater degree of contrast into the pattern.

Wave Frequency and Sub Wave Frequency   Wave Frequency sets the fundamental frequency of the waves. Higher values create waves that are narrower and more tightly packed. Sub Wave Frequency overlays a higher frequency onto the base waves, which makes the wave pattern more irregular.

Smoothness   Smoothness blurs the wave pattern. A higher value makes the pattern softer and less detailed. (The generated pattern is never hard-edged, even when Smoothness is turned down to 0.)

The Concentric Ripple Attributes section sets aside another 10 attributes for creating and controlling circular ripples. You can isolate the concentric ripples by setting Number Of Waves to 0.

In addition, you can use the Water texture to distort flags and other cloth-like surfaces. For example, in Figure 4.20 a Water texture is mapped to the Bump Mapping attribute of a Blinn material. The Repeat UV attribute of the Water's 2D Placement utility is kept below 1.0 in the U and V direction.

Without bump map

With bump map

Figure 4.20 A Water texture is applied to a plane as a bump map, giving the cloth texture extra dimension. This scene is included with the Chapter 4 tutorial files as `water_cloth.ma`.

Applying Perlin Noise

Perlin noise was invented by Ken Perlin in the early 1980s as a means of generating random patterns from random numbers. You can use Perlin-based 2D textures to break up surface regularity. For example, you can map a Noise texture to a material's Specular Color to make a specular highlight appear more irregular (see Figure 4.21).

Figure 4.21 Left: A Blinn assigned to a polygon barrel shows little variation in the specular highlight; Right: A Noise texture mapped to the Specular Color of the same Blinn produces a more complex result. A simplified version of this scene is included with the Chapter 4 tutorial files as `specular_noise.ma`.

In addition, you can map a Noise texture to a File texture's Color Gain to dirty up an otherwise clean bitmap. For an example, see "Combining Textures through Color Gain and Alpha Gain" later in this chapter. The Fractal texture in Maya is a more complex variation of classic 2D Perlin noise in which turbulence (the averaging of multiple scales) is added for detail. The majority of attributes are identical to the Noise texture. The attribute list for both the Noise and Fractal texture is quite long but is detailed in Chapter 5, "Applying 3D Textures and Projections." The Mountain texture, on the other hand, is a variation of Perlin noise that lacks a smoothing function. It simulates a simplified mountain range where snow occurs at a particular elevation (as viewed from above). Although it's not possible to create a realistic mountain with the Mountain texture, you can use the texture to create granular patterns. For example, in Figure 4.22 two Mountain textures are respectively mapped to the Color and Bump Mapping attributes of a Phong material, creating the illusion of green debris and scum on a floor. A Checker texture is mapped to the Snow Color of the Mountain texture connected to the Phong's Color attribute, thus providing the red and white tiles.

The Mountain texture's unique attributes follow:

Amplitude, Snow Color, and Rock Color   Amplitude sets the amount of Rock Color that appears "through" the Snow Color. A low value favors Snow Color in the coloring scheme. As demonstrated in Figure 4.22, Snow Color can be mapped with another texture. The same is true for Rock Color.

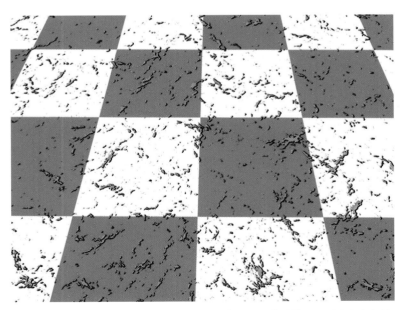

Figure 4.22 A Mountain texture creates green debris and scum on a floor. This scene is included with the Chapter 4 tutorial files as `mountain_dirt.ma`.

Boundary   Controls the raggedness of the Snow Color to Rock Color transition. A low value creates smoother transitions and favors the Snow Color. A high value creates numerous interlocking nooks and crannies.

Snow Altitude, Snow Dropoff, and Snow Slope   Snow Altitude determines the "height" at which Snow Color appears. Higher values increase the overall amount of snow. Snow Dropoff controls the rapidity at which the snow disappears at lower altitudes. The lower the Snow Dropoff value, the less snow there is. Snow Slope is the angle at which snow sticks to the virtual mountain. The higher the Snow Slope value, the more snow there is.

Applying Ramps, Bitmaps, and Square Textures

The Ramp texture allows selected colors to transition in the U or V direction. The texture carries a total of nine ramp Type attribute options and seven Interpolation attribute options, supporting a wide range of results (see Figure 4.23). Note that Maya 2015 represents the texture in the Attribute Editor as a horizontal ramp graph (as opposed to the old vertical presentation); nevertheless, the functionality remains the same as in prior versions. Ramp textures are ideal for custom shading networks and are demonstrated in more detail throughout this book.

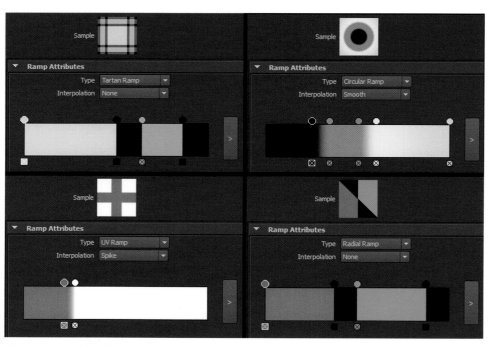

Figure 4.23 Unusual combinations of ramp types and interpolations. These textures are included with the Chapter 4 tutorial files as `ramps.ma`.

Importing custom bitmaps, whether as File, PSD File, or Movie textures, is the most powerful way to achieve realism and detail in Maya. File textures are used extensively in the custom shading networks demonstrated in Chapters 5–7. Movie textures are simply variations of File textures. Movie textures will read any movie format supported by Maya, including Windows Media Player AVI and QuickTime MOV. To use all the frames contained within the movie, you must select the Use Image Sequence attribute. Both File and Movie textures are able to accept numbered image sequences.

Note that an image sequence must carry a specific naming convention to be read correctly: *name.###.ext*, where the # signs represent the frame number—for example, `render.001.jpg`, `render.002.jpg`, and so on. See Chapter 10 for more information on naming conventions.

Square textures are generated by repeating color blocks or lines in the U and V directions. Square textures include Bulge, Grid, and Checker. The Bulge texture can be thought of as a blurry Grid texture. Both Bulge and Grid are often useful for bump mapping. If either the U Width or V Width attribute of the Grid texture is set to 0, parallel grooves are generated in one direction. The Checker texture is handy for checking UV distortions on surfaces.

Mastering Extra Map Options

Several texture attributes are often overlooked but are nonetheless quite useful. These include Filter, Filter Offset, Filter Type, Invert, and Color Remap.

Adjusting Filter and Filter Offset

By default, many Maya textures are filtered, whether they are procedural or bitmap. This is necessary to prevent aliasing problems. In general, aliasing artifacts occur when the detail contained within a texture is smaller than corresponding screen pixels. The problems are most noticeable when textures have a high degree of contrast and the camera or surface is in motion. In this situation, a moiré pattern is often formed (see Figure 4.24 for an extreme example). Although many of the anti-aliasing attributes in the Render Settings window reduce such problems (see Chapter 10), texture filtering remains a necessity of the 3D process.

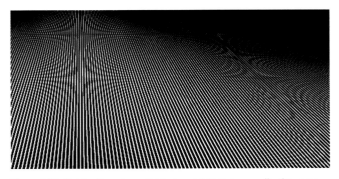

Figure 4.24 Moiré patterns formed by texture details that are smaller than corresponding screen pixels

In Maya, the filtering process is controlled by the Filter and Filter Offset attributes, found in the Effects section of the texture's Attribute Editor tab. Filter forces the renderer to employ a lesser or greater degree of filtering. In essence, filtering averages the texture pixels, thus blurring the texture. The lower the Filter value, the lesser the degree of filtering and the sharper the texture. The higher the Filter value, the greater the degree of filtering and the blurrier the texture. You can stylistically add or subtract detail from a texture by adjusting the Filter attribute. For example, in Figure 4.25 the effect of a large Filter value is a blurry Grid texture. Whereas Filter controls the degree of filtering in eye space (that is, from the view of the camera), Filter Offset controls the amount of blur in texture space. In practical terms, the Filter Offset value is added to the Filter value for an extra degree of blurring.

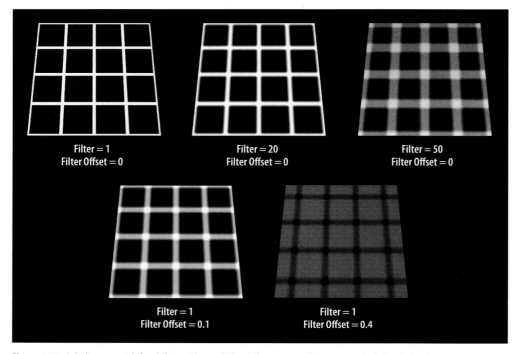

Figure 4.25 A Grid texture with five different Filter and Filter Offset settings. This scene is included with the Chapter 4 tutorial files as `grid_filter.ma`.

 Note: Cloth, Bulge, Ramp, Water, Granite, Leather, and Snow textures do not possess filtering attributes.

Choosing a Filter Type

File, Movie, and PSD File textures offer additional controls for the filtering process. You can set the Filter Type attribute, found at the top of the textures' Attribute Editor tab, to Off, Mipmap, Quadratic, Quartic, Gaussian, or Box.

Off turns off the filtering process and removes the Filter and Filter Offset attributes. Although this will speed up the render, moiré and stair-stepping artifacts will most likely appear.

Mipmap applies the mipmapping process. In this case, Maya stores averaged color values for multiple sizes of each texture. The sizes linearly decrease (for example, 512×512, 256×256, 128×128, and so on). When the renderer tackles an individual screen pixel, it determines the most appropriately sized mipmap. If the pixel falls over a distant surface, it recalls a small size. If the pixel falls over a surface in the immediate foreground, it recalls a large size. The angle between the surface and the camera is part of the equation. An oblique surface (one that is not perpendicular to the line of sight) induces a smaller mipmap, and a non-oblique surface induces a larger one. To increase the accuracy of the mipmap selection, Maya often averages a consecutive pair of mipmaps (for example, 512×512 and 256×256). Mipmap is an inexpensive option and is suitable for previews and test renders; however, it is not recommended for high-quality renders because textures may appear excessively blurry.

Gaussian shares its name with filters common to digital paint programs, such as Adobe Photoshop. Gaussian filters blur an image by convolving an array representing the original image and a second, smaller array known as a kernel. In simple terms, convolution allows the arrays to be multiplied together by "sliding" the kernel across the image array. The kernel itself contains a bell-shaped distribution of values that causes a predictable effect on different frequencies within the image. Higher frequencies equate to small details. Low frequencies equate to large image features. The end effect of a Gaussian filter is a blur that softens fine details without destroying large image features or negating edges.

Quadratic and Quartic are approximations of the Gaussian filter type that employ different bell-shaped distributions in their kernels. Both filters are optimized for speed. Quadratic offers the best balance of efficiency and quality, and is therefore the default option for Filter Type.

Box is the simplest filtering option available. Box gives equal weight to all sampled image pixels; hence, it does not preserve edges as well as other filter types.

As a Filter Types comparison, a TIFF image of a street is loaded into a File texture (see Figure 4.26). The File texture is mapped to the Out Color attribute of a Surface Shader material, which is assigned to a plane. The plane is rendered with Off, Mipmap, and Quadratic Filter Type options. The Filter attributes is temporarily set to 0 and Edge Anti-Aliasing (in the Maya Software tab of the Render Settings window) is set to Low Quality. The Off option produces the most contrast; unfortunately, the sharp edges are likely to cause stair-stepping artifacts when the camera or plane is animated. Mipmap produces a softer result while allowing the "Meat Market" sign to be fairly readable. Quadratic is very close to Mipmap; however, there is slightly more detail in the lettering. In general, Mipmap does not hold up as well as Quadratic when the camera is in motion or the textures appear at different distances.

Two extra attributes are available to File, Movie, and PSD File textures: Pre Filter and Pre Filter Radius. Pre Filter, if selected, applies additional texture-space averaging to the loaded map. The filtering occurs before any other operation is applied to the map. The higher the Pre Filter Radius value, the blurrier the image.

Note: To intentionally create a heavy blur on a texture, leave Filter set to 1.0 and raise Filter Offset by small increments (such as 0.1). Although Pre Filter also blurs the texture, its blur cannot reach the strength supplied by the Filter Offset.

Figure 4.26 Detail of a 1024×768 bitmap, loaded into a File texture and rendered with three Filter Type options. The render resolution is 1920×1080. This scene is included with the Chapter 4 tutorial files as `filter_comparison.ma`.

Shifting Color with Invert and Color Remap

The Invert check box, found in the Effects section of a texture's Attribute Editor tab, inverts the colors of the texture. The result is identical to the Reverse utility (see Chapter 8). If a color is pure white (RGB: 1.0, 1.0, 1.0), the inverted result is black (RGB: 0, 0, 0). If a color is yellow (RGB: 1.0, 1.0, 0), the inverted result is blue (RGB: 0, 0, 1.0). You can predict the results by picking an opposite side of the Maya color wheel.

The Color Remap Insert button, also found in the Effects section, attaches an RGB To HSV utility and a Ramp texture to the shading network. The new network color-shifts the original texture (see Figure 4.27). The portion of the texture that has low color values is given colors from the bottom of the Ramp (Maya 2014) or left side of the Ramp (Maya 2015). The portion of the texture that has high color values is given colors from the top or right side of the Ramp. If you change the Ramp colors, the colors of the texture automatically change. (See Chapter 6 for a demonstration of the RGB To HSV utility in a custom network.)

Figure 4.27 The result of an activated Color Remap Insert button as applied to a File texture. This scene is included with the Chapter 4 tutorial files as `color_remap.ma`.

Layering Materials and Textures

The Layered Shader material offers an easy method by which to combine two or more materials. For example, in Figure 4.28 a Blinn and a Lambert material are mapped to a Layered Shader material. The Blinn's Color is set to red with a hot specular highlight. The Lambert's Color is set to yellow and carries no specularity. The resulting material is orange (red + yellow) with a specular hot spot.

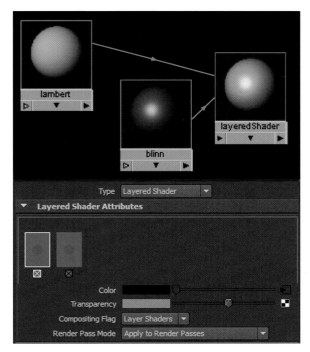

Figure 4.28 Two materials are blended with the Layered Shader material. This material is included with the Chapter 4 tutorial files as `layered_shader.ma`.

Each material mapped to a Layered Shader is represented by a purple box icon in the icon field of the Layered Shader Attributes section of the Layered Shader's Attribute Editor tab. Each mapped material receives a Transparency attribute. Note that box order is similar to Photoshop, where the leftmost box is equivalent to the highest layer. Which set of attributes is visible depends on which box icon is highlighted. You can switch between the box icons at any time by clicking them. If you hold your mouse over an icon, the name of the connected material is revealed.

Although only two materials are connected in the Figure 4.28 example, you can connect as many as you like. To connect a material, MMB-drag the material icon and drop it inside the Layered Shader Attributes field. (For other shading network connection methods, see Chapter 6.)

You can disconnect materials by clicking the small x below the corresponding box icon. By default, the Layered Shader provides a green, empty box icon before any connections are made; you can delete this after you make at least one connection. How the materials are mixed depends on each material's Transparency value. In Figure 4.28, the Blinn material, represented by the left icon, has a Transparency value set to 50 percent gray. The Lambert, represented by the right icon, has a Transparency value set to 0 percent black. The resulting Layered Shader contains a 50 percent mix of each material, producing the orange color. The specular highlight becomes more intense because the colors are added.

Adjusting Layered Shader Transparency

To choose the correct value for the various Transparency sliders in the Layered Shader material, follow these guidelines:

- The horizontal row of purple box icons is similar to a vertical stack of layers in Adobe Photoshop. The leftmost icon is equivalent to the highest layer in Photoshop, and the rightmost box is equivalent to the lowest layer.

- If the Transparency value of the first material (the one that is represented by the leftmost icon) is set to 0 percent black, the first material obscures all other materials.

- The last material mapped to the Layered Shader (represented by the rightmost icon) does not need its Transparency adjusted above 0 percent black. If the Transparency value is raised above 0 percent black, the resulting material becomes semitransparent.

Layering Textures with Layered Shader and Layered Texture

The Layered Shader material works equally well with textures. As such, the material provides the Compositing Flag attribute to determine how to output the blended items. If you are blending materials, set Compositing Flag to Layer Shaders. If you are blending textures, set Compositing Flag to Layer Texture.

The Layered Texture texture is almost identical to the Layered Shader material. (You can find Layered Texture in the Create > Maya > Other Textures section of the Hypershade, Create Render Node, and Create Node windows.) However, it prefers connections from textures and will not function with materials.

Any mapped texture receives a purple box icon. In the place of Transparency sliders, Layered Texture includes Alpha sliders. In addition, each texture connected to the Layered Texture receives a Blend Mode attribute. The Blend Mode attribute determines how each texture will combine with the texture just below it. In terms of icons, the Blend Mode attribute controls how each icon will be combined with the icon to its immediate right. A number of Blend Mode options (Add, Subtract, Multiply, Difference, Lighten, Darken, Saturate, Desaturate, and Illuminate) are identical to the equivalent layer blend modes in Adobe Photoshop and other digital-imaging programs. The None option makes the texture 100 percent opaque, preventing any lower texture (or right-hand icon) from appearing.

If an Alpha attribute is mapped with a black and white texture, the Blend Mode menu's In option cuts out the lower texture in the shape of the Alpha map; black areas become holes in the lower texture. With the same alpha map, the Out option inverts the cut. The Over option places the texture with the Alpha map on top of the lower texture as if it were a decal; black areas become holes for the upper map. For example, in Figure 4.29, two textures are blended with the Layered Texture texture. The upper map (with the left box icon) has its Alpha attribute mapped with a black and white circular ramp. This results in the upper map (an embroidered flower) being placed over the lower map (rusty metal) in a circular fashion.

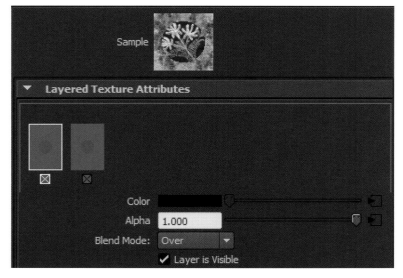

Figure 4.29 Two textures are blended together with a Layered Texture node. This texture network is included with the Chapter 4 tutorial files as `layered_texture.ma`. (After opening the file, switch to the Textures tab in the Hypershade.)

Combining Textures through Color Gain and Alpha Gain

Although the Layered Texture texture offers a great deal of control when blending separate textures, you can simply map the Color Gain attribute of a texture (found in the Color Balance section of a texture's Attribute Editor tab). Color Gain works as a scaling factor—the texture's Out Color attribute is multiplied by the Color Gain color or map. For example, in Figure 4.30 a Noise texture is mapped to the Color Gain of Cloth texture, thus dirtying it. Conversely, the Color Offset attribute works as an offset factor. Whereas Color Gain functions as a multiplier, Color Offset simply adds its value to Out Color. Thus, a black Color Offset has no effect on the texture. A 50 percent gray Color Offset will brighten the texture by adding RGB values of 0.5, 0.5, 0.5 to the texture's Out Color.

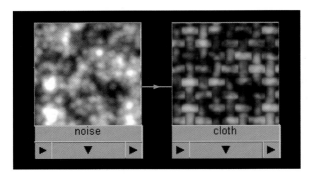

Figure 4.30 A Noise texture is mapped to the Color Gain of a Cloth texture. This material is included with the Chapter 4 tutorial files as `color_gain.ma`. (After opening the file, switch to the Textures tab in the Hypershade.)

Chapter Tutorial: Re-creating Copper with Basic Texturing Techniques

In this tutorial, you will re-create the look of copper with basic texturing techniques. You will use a generic noisy bitmap (`rusty.tif`) as a color and bump map for a Blinn material.

Copper is a "bright" metal and is highly reflective. If copper has not been polished, however, it creates a highly diffuse reflection. This is due to numerous, microscopic imperfections. Unpolished copper is therefore slightly "glowy" and has an unfocused specular highlight (see Figure 4.31).

Figure 4.31 Left: Finished 3D copper; Right: Reference photo of copper.

1. In Maya, choose File > Set Project. In the Set Project window, browse for the Project_4 directory, select the directory name, and click the Set button. This ensures that the texture bitmaps will be correctly located. Open copper.ma from the Chapter 4 scene folder. Spend a few minutes familiarizing yourself with the model's various parts.

2. Open the Hypershade window. MMB-drag a Blinn material from the Surface section of the Create tab into the work area and rename name it **Copper**. Assign Copper to the polygon cube.

3. Open Copper's Attribute Editor tab. Set the Color attribute to a semidark, reddish brown. Use Figure 4.32 as reference. Set the Ambient Color attribute to a lighter reddish brown. A high Ambient Color value replicates the bright quality of the metal. Set Diffuse to 0.7, Eccentricity to 0.49, Specular Roll Off to 0.85, and Reflectivity to 0.15. This combination of settings creates an intense specular highlight that spreads over the edge of the cube without overexposing the top face. Render a test frame. Adjust the Color and Ambient Color attributes to emulate the distinctive copper look.

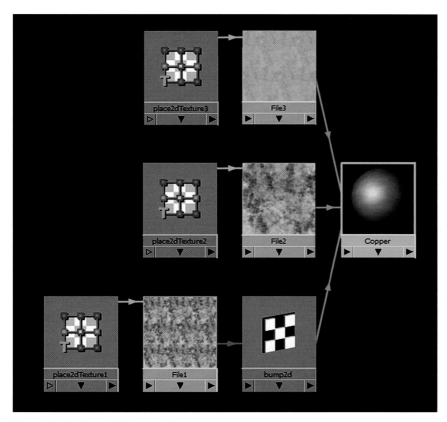

Figure 4.32 The copper shading network

4. Click the Bump Mapping attribute's checkered Map button. Click the File icon in the 2D Textures section of the Create Render Node window. The Bump 2d utility appears in the Attribute Editor. Set the Bump Depth attribute to −0.003.

5. In the work area, select the newly created File texture and rename it **File1**. Click the file browse button beside the Image Name attribute and retrieve rusty.tif from the Chapter 4 textures folder. In the work area, select the 2D Placement utility (now named place2dTexture1) connected to File1 and open its Attribute Editor tab. Set Repeat UV to 3, 3 and select Stagger. Custom UV settings ensure that the scale of the texture detail is appropriate for the model. Render a test frame.

6. Select Copper and open its Attribute Editor tab. Click the Reflected Color attribute's checkered Map button. Click the File texture icon in the Create Render Node window. The new File texture appears in the work area with a 2D Placement utility. Rename the new File texture **File2**. Click the file browse button beside the Image Name attribute and retrieve rusty.tif from the Chapter 4 textures directory. Set File2's Filter Offset to 0.005. The Filter Offset value will blur the texture and resulting simulated reflection. The strength of the reflection is controlled by Copper's Reflectivity. The simulated reflection is most noticeable in the dark front face of the cube. Render a test frame. Note that it's not necessary to match the Repeat UV values to the place2dTexture1 node; textures added with different scales make the resulting texture more complex.

7. Open Copper's Attribute Editor tab. Click the Specular Color attribute's checkered Map button. Click the File icon in the Create Render Node window. The new File texture appears in the work area with a 2D Placement utility. Rename the new File texture **File3**. Click the file browse button beside the Image Name attribute and retrieve rusty.tif from the Chapter 4 textures directory.

8. Set File3's Filter Offset to 0.005. Change the Color Gain attribute to an RGB value of 66, 62, 72. You can enter color values by clicking the Color Gain color swatch and opening the Color Chooser window (set the color space drop-down to RGB, 0 To 255). This tints the Color Gain with a washed-out lavender, which balances the red of Copper's Color and Ambient Color and creates a copper-like look. Change the Color Offset attribute to a 50 percent gray.

9. Render a test frame. If the material's color does not look correct, change Copper's Color attribute to an RGB value of 82, 44, 35 and the Ambient Color attribute to an RGB value of 116, 48, 38.

10. In the work area, select the newest 2D Placement utility (named place2dTexture3) connected to File3 and open its Attribute Editor tab. Set Repeat UV to 2, 2 and select Stagger. Render a final test. The copper material is complete! If you get stuck, a finished version is saved as `copper_finished.ma` in the Chapter 4 scene folder.

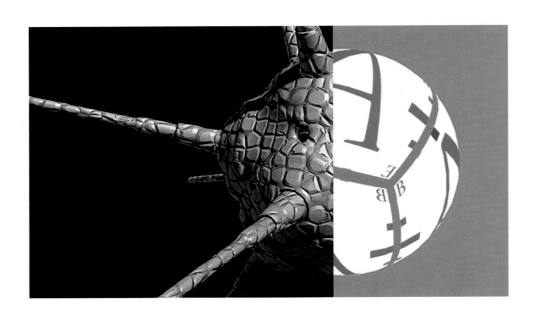

Applying 3D Textures and Projections

5

The 3D Placement utilities generated by 3D and environment textures in Autodesk® Maya® possess unique application traits. Projection utilities, on the other hand, are designed to work with 2D textures. 3D textures procedurally create a wide range of solid patterns—that is, they have height, width, and depth. In addition, you can convert 3D textures into 2D bitmaps with the Convert To File Texture tool.

Chapter Contents
Review and application of 3D textures
Attributes of 2D and 3D noise textures
Review of environment textures
Application of 2D texture Projection utilities
Strategies for positioning placement boxes and projection icons

Exploring 3D Textures

Maya 3D textures are procedural—that is, they are generated mathematically through predefined algorithms. Procedural textures are resolution-independent and do not have defined edges or borders. Procedural textures do not require external files, such as bitmap textures. As such, they may be computationally more efficient than other forms of texturing. Many of the procedural algorithms employed by Maya make use of fractal math, which defines irregular geometric shapes that have the same degree of irregularity at all scales. Thus, Maya 3D textures are suitable for many shading scenarios found in the natural world. For example, in Figure 5.1 the addition of 3D textures to a shading network distresses and dirties a clean floor and wall. This example uses Fractal, Solid Fractal, Marble, and Checker textures.

Figure 5.1 Left: Set with standard textures; Right: Same set with the addition of 3D textures to the shading networks. This scene is included with the Chapter 5 tutorial files as `dirty_set.ma`.

3D textures are grouped under the 3D Textures section of the Create tab in the Hypershade, Create Node, and Create Render Node windows. When you MMB-drag a 3D texture into the Hypershade work area or choose it through the Create Render Node or Create Node windows, a 3D Placement utility is automatically connected to the texture and named *place3dTexture*n (see Figure 5.2). The scale, translation, and rotation of the 3D Placement utility's placement box affects the way in which the texture is applied to the assigned object. If the assigned object is scaled, translated, or rotated, it picks up different portions of the texture. (The Hardware Texturing viewport mode may not show the change; however, the batch render or a Render View render reveals the correct texture placement.) By default, new placement boxes are positioned at 0, 0, 0 in world space and are $2 \times 2 \times 2$ units large. If the 3D Placement utility is deleted or its connection is broken, Maya assumes that the 3D texture sample is at its default size and position.

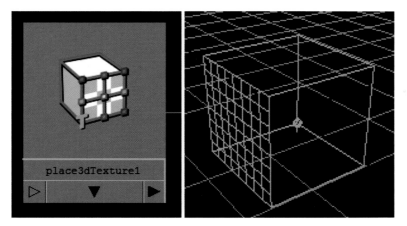

Figure 5.2 Left: 3D Placement utility; Right: Corresponding placement box.

The 3D Placement utility determines the color of each surface point by locating the point's position within the placement box. Each position derives a potentially unique color. This process is analogous to a surface dipped into a square bucket of swirled paint or a surface chiseled from a solid cube of veined stone. Should the surface sit outside the placement box, the surface continues to receive a unique piece of the 3D texture. Since 3D textures are generated procedurally, there isn't a definitive texture border at the edge of the placement box. A significant advantage of 3D textures, and the use of the 3D Placement utility, is the disregard of a surface's UV texture space. In other words, the condition of a surface's UVs does not impact the ability of a 3D texture to map smoothly across the surface.

You can divide Maya 3D textures into four categories: random, natural, granular, and abstract.

Applying Random 3D Textures

Random 3D textures follow their 2D counterparts by attempting to produce a random, infinitely repeating pattern. In this section we'll look at the Brownian, Noise and Volume Noise, Solid Fractal, and Cloud textures.

Using the Brownian Texture

The Brownian texture is based on Brownian motion, which is a mathematical model that describes the random motion of particles in a fluid dynamic system. A key element of the model is the "random walk," in which each successive step of a particle is in a completely random direction. Brownian motion was discovered by the biologist Robert Brown (1773–1858).

In general, the Brownian texture is smoother than other fractal-based textures. As such, the texture can replicate a sandy beach or similar surface. One disadvantage of the Brownian texture, however, is its tendency to produce rendering artifacts when viewed up close. For example, in Figure 5.3, a faint grid is visible on the middle plane. Note that Brownian textures, in their default state, are static. That said, you're free to animate any texture attribute over time (RMB-click over the attribute field or attribute name and choose Set Key).

Figure 5.3 Left: 2D Fractal texture applied as a bump map to left plane; Center: Brownian texture applied as a bump map to middle plane; Right: Noise texture applied as a bump map to right plane. This scene is included with the Chapter 5 tutorial files as `brownian_noise.ma`.

The Brownian texture has the following distinctive attributes:

Lacunarity　Represents the gap between various noise frequencies. A higher value creates more detail. A lower value makes the texture smoother. *Lacunarity*, as a term, refers to the size and distribution of holes appearing in a fractal.

Increment　Signifies the ratio of fractal noise used by the texture. A higher value reduces the contrast between light and dark areas.

Octaves　Sets the number of calculation iterations. A higher value creates more detail in the map.

Weight3d　Determines the internal fundamental frequency of the fractal pattern. A low value in the X, Y, or Z field causes the texture to smear in that particular direction.

Using the Volume Noise Texture

The Volume Noise texture is a 3D variation of the Noise texture, with many of the attributes shared (see Figure 5.4).

Shared attributes are described here:

Threshold and Amplitude　The Threshold value is added to the colors produced by the fractal pattern, which raises all the color values present in the pattern. If any color value exceeds 1.0, it's clamped to 1.0. The colors produced by the fractal are also multiplied by the Amplitude value. If the Amplitude value is 1.0, the texture does not change. If the Amplitude value is 0.5, all the color values are halved.

Note:　Noise and Fractal textures, at their default settings, often contain too much contrast to be useful in many situations. A quick way to reduce this contrast is to pull the Amplitude and Threshold sliders toward each other to the slider center.

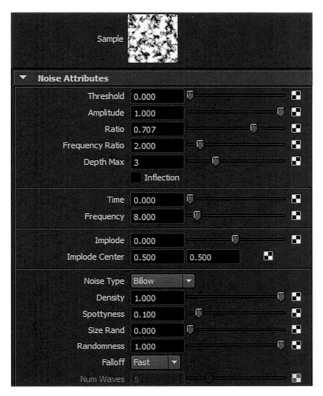

Figure 5.4 Volume Noise attributes. Many of the attributes are shared with Noise, Fractal, and Solid Fractal textures.

Noise Type   There are five types of noise (see Figure 5.5). Billow is the default and contains sharper, disc-like blobs. Billow provides additional attributes, including Density, Spottyness, Size Rand, Randomness, and Falloff. Each of these attributes controls what its name implies. Perlin Noise uses Ken Perlin's classic 2D model, which produces a fairly soft pattern. Wave produces patterns similar to the Wave texture and will undulate if Time is animated. (The Wave noise type is listed as Volume Wave with the Volume Noise texture.) Num Waves sets the number of waves used by the Wave noise type. Wispy uses classic Perlin Noise but adds smeared distortions with a second noise layer. SpaceTime is a 3D version of classic Perlin Noise. Changing the Time attribute will select different 2D "slices" of SpaceTime noise.

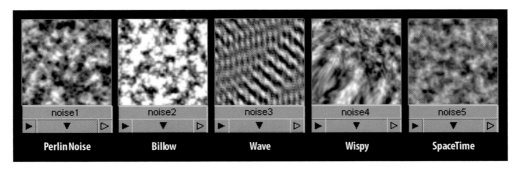

Figure 5.5 The five types of noise available to Noise and Volume Noise textures

Ratio, Depth Max, and Frequency Ratio   Ratio controls the ratio of low- to high-frequency noise. If the value is 0, only low-frequency noise is visible. The low-frequency noise creates the large black and white noise "blobs." If the Ratio value is high, multiple layers of noise with higher and higher frequencies are added to the low frequency. The number of layers added depends on the Depth Max attribute. Depth Max controls the number of iterations the texture undertakes in its calculations and therefore determines the number of potential frequency layers. The higher the Depth Max value, the more complex the resulting noise. Frequency Ratio, on the other hand, establishes the scale of the frequencies involved in the Ratio calculation. Higher values create noise with finer detail.

Inflection   If Inflection is selected, it inserts a mathematical "kink" into the noise function. In effect, this creates dark borders around various blobs of noise and injects white into the dark gaps. (Note that Inflection has no effect on the Billow noise type.)

Time   For the Noise texture, Time establishes which "slice" of the noise pattern is viewed. You can visualize the Noise texture as a 3D noise pattern from which 2D slices are retrieved. Each layer that is added with the Depth Max attribute is a slice from a noise pattern at a different frequency. The Time attribute creates a slightly different result for each Noise Type. Nevertheless, higher Time values generally move the view "through" the noise as if the viewing camera is moving deeper into the 3D pattern.

For the Volume Noise texture, Time determines the location of the three-dimensional cube sample within the noise pattern. You can see movement through the three-dimensional noise by keyframing the Time attribute. For example, in Figure 5.6 a cube is assigned to a Surface Shader material. A Volume Noise texture is mapped to the Out Color of the Surface Shader. The Noise Type attribute is set to SpaceTime. The Time attribute is animated, changing from 0 to 3 over 90 frames. Frequency Ratio is set to 1.0, Frequency is set to 4, and Scale is set to 5, 5, 5, making the pattern larger and easier to see.

Figure 5.6 Three frames from a Volume Noise texture with a keyframed Time attribute. This scene is included with the Chapter 5 tutorial files as `noise_slice.ma`. A QuickTime movie is included as `noise_slice.mov`.

Frequency   Frequency defines the fundamental frequency of the noise. A high value "zooms out" from the texture. A low value "zooms in" to the texture. A value of 0 creates a dark gray. High values add detail to the noise.

Implode and Implode Center   Implode warps the noise around a point defined by Implode Center. With the Noise texture, a high Implode value streaks the noise away from the viewer. A low value bulges the noise outward in a spherical fashion. With the Volume Noise texture, a high Implode value stretches the pattern or creates a wave-like warp depending on the Implode Center values. (If Implode Center is set to 0, 0, 0, Implode has no effect on Volume Noise.)

In addition, the Volume Noise texture has two unique attributes:

Scale   Determines the scale of the noise in the X, Y, and Z directions. You can choose different values for each axis.

Origin   Offsets the noise in the X, Y, and Z directions. In other words, the cube that cuts out a section of the 3D noise pattern is moved through the noise to a new location. The degree of change is dependent on the Noise Type.

Choosing Between Noise and Volume Noise

Whether a Volume Noise or a Noise texture should be selected depends on the nature of the object assigned to the texture's shading network. Because Volume Noise depends on the addition of a 3D Placement utility, it is not suited for an object that deforms or is in motion. The Noise texture, which is mapped directly to the surface, is restricted by the quality of the surface's UV texture space.

As a comparison, in Figure 5.7 a polygon button is given an intentionally bad UV layout (which is often the state of UVs after a model's initial construction). A Noise and Volume Noise texture is mapped to the Specular Color attribute of an assigned Blinn material. Because the button carries multiple, overlapping UV shells (groups of UV points), shell borders are noticeable as hard lines on the Noise texture version. In addition, the size of the noise "grains" is inconsistent. The Volume Noise version, by comparison, ignores the inherent UV information in favor of the 3D Placement process. Hence, the Volume Noise version renders cleanly with no shell borders.

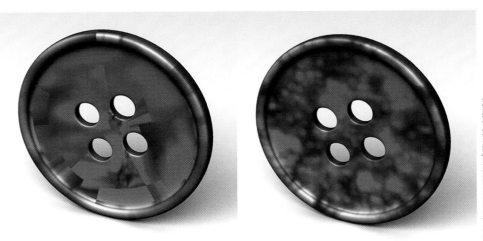

Figure 5.7   A polygon button is given a poor UV layout. When a Noise texture is mapped to the Specular Color attribute, the UV shells borders become evident (as seen on the left). When a Volume Noise texture is mapped to the Specular Color, the UV shell borders are no longer visible (as seen on the right).

To improve the quality of the Noise texture version, you must spend more time refining the UV layout. To make the Volume Noise version acceptable for animation and deformation, you must use the Convert To File Texture tool or the Transfer Maps window to create a bitmap texture that's not dependent on a projection node. (Convert To File Texture is described at the end of this chapter; the Transfer Maps window is discussed in Chapter 9, "Improving Textures through Custom UVs and Maps.") The same dilemmas occur when choosing between Fractal and Solid Fractal textures.

Using the Solid Fractal Texture

The Solid Fractal texture is a 3D variation of the Fractal texture. Both Solid Fractal and Fractal share attributes with Volume Noise and Noise. These attributes include Amplitude, Threshold, Ratio, Frequency Ratio, and Inflection. For descriptions of each attribute, see the previous section in this chapter. At the same time, Solid Fractal and Fractal share the following unique attributes:

Bias   Controls the amount of contrast in the texture. A value of −1.0 creates a solid 50 percent gray. A high value creates more contrast. If you set a Volume Fractal texture's Bias above 1.0, the texture creates rings or loops, which may be useful for creating splatters, pools, or stains (see Figure 5.8).

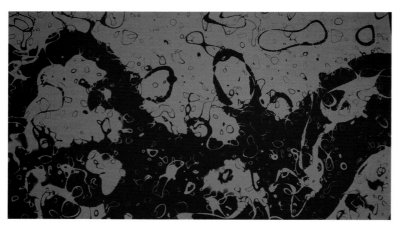

Figure 5.8   A Volume Noise texture is mapped to the Transparency of a red-brown Blinn material. The noise Bias is set to 2.5, creating loops and rings that emulate liquid splatters, pools, or stains. This scene is included with the Chapter 5 tutorial files as `fractal_stains.ma`.

Animated   If selected, makes the Time and Time Ratio attributes available. Time retrieves different "slices" of the noise. With the default settings, slight variations in the Time value make changes to the noise pattern drastic and seemingly random (equivalent to video static). However, you can control the degree of change with the Time Ratio attribute. The lower the Time Ratio value, the more gradual the change to the noise pattern. To see a truly incremental change in the noise pattern, you must raise or lower Time by less than 0.01 per frame and keep Time Ratio near 1.0.

In addition, the Fractal texture carries the Level Min and Level Max attributes. These two attributes control the number of iterations the texture undertakes in its calculations. A high Level Max value will produce finer detail in the resulting noise. Solid Fractal, on the other hand, carries the Ripples and Depth attributes. The Ripples fields, which represent Ripples X, Ripples Y, and Ripples Z attributes, create waviness in the texture in the X, Y, and Z directions. A high value in any one of the three fields causes the noise to stretch. The Depth fields, which represent Depth Min and Depth Max attributes, set the minimum and maximum number of iterations used in the Solid Fractal calculation. The higher the values, the finer the detail. The lower the values, the blurrier the texture.

Using the Cloud Texture

The Cloud texture uses Perlin and fractal noise techniques to create soft, wispy noise. Despite its name, the texture does not produce a free-floating cloud when mapped to common attributes such as Color or Specular Color. However, if you map the texture to a material's Transparency, you can make a surface appear cloud-like. To create a cloud in a sky, follow these steps:

1. Create a NURBS sphere. Scale the sphere in one direction so that it becomes elongated.

2. Open the Hypershade window. MMB-drag a Lambert material into the work area. Assign the Lambert to the sphere.

3. Open the Lambert's Attribute Editor tab. Change the Color attribute to a suitable cloud color. Click the Transparency checkered Map button and choose the Cloud texture from the Create Render Node window.

4. With the Cloud texture open in the Attribute Editor, change Color1 and Color2 to 100 percent white. In the Effects section, select Invert. This ensures that the edges, and not the sphere's center, are transparent. Render a test frame. The sphere looks like a puff of smoke.

5. In the perspective viewport, choose View > Camera Attribute Editor. The camera's Attribute Editor tab opens. In the Environment section, change Background Color to a more suitable sky color. Render a test frame.

6. Open the Cloud texture's Attribute Editor tab. To prevent the edges of the sphere from appearing too opaque or too black, incrementally raise the Edge Thresh attribute value. This erodes the cloud's edges so that a spherical outline can no longer be seen. Render a series of tests to check this. If the cloud appears too granular or noisy, lower the Ratio attribute slightly. This makes the noise pattern blurrier.

7. Open the Lambert's Attribute Editor tab. Slowly raise the Ambient Color until the majority of dark spots on the cloud disappear.

8. Return to the Cloud texture's Attribute Editor tab. Incrementally raise the Color Offset attribute in the Color Balance section. This thins the cloud and makes it appear wispier (see Figure 5.9).

Figure 5.9 A Cloud texture creates a free-floating cloud when mapped to the Transparency of a Lambert assigned to an elongated sphere. This scene is included with the Chapter 5 tutorial files as `cloud.ma`.

The Cloud texture attributes are described here:

Color1 and Color2   Mixed to create the noise pattern.

Edge Thresh and Center Thresh   Control the density of the noise. Low Edge Thresh values create a denser noise pattern along the edges of the 3D Placement box by biasing Color2. High Center Thresh values create a less dense noise pattern at the center of the placement box by biasing Color1. If both Edge Thresh and Center Thresh are low, Color2 is favored in the pattern.

Contrast   Fine-tunes the color mixture. If the Contrast value is 0, the colors are averaged across the entire texture. If the value is 1.0, the colors maintain a harder separation.

Soft Edges   When selected, creates a more gradual transition between Color1 and Color2. This attribute also reduces the amount of contrast and allows more detail to survive.

Transp Range   Controls the rapidity with which the colors transition between each other and become opaque. A low value creates a harsher transition. A high value creates a subtler, tapered transition.

Amplitude, Depth, Ripples, and Ratio function in a manner similar to those carried by Solid Fractal (see the previous section).

Applying Natural Textures

Natural textures attempt to create specific patterns visible in the natural world. These include the Marble, Wood, Leather, and Snow textures.

Using Marble

The Marble texture creates a stone-like pattern that includes virtual mineral veins. The Marble texture isn't designed to match a specific marble type, nor is the texture capable of replicating a realistic marble by itself. However, if the Marble texture is combined with other 2D and 3D textures, it becomes more convincing.

As an example, in Figure 5.10 a Marble texture is mapped to the Color of a Blinn material, which in turn is assigned to a cube. When the marble is used by itself, it betrays its procedural origin. When Leather, Noise, Fractal, and Cloud textures are mapped to the Color Gain, Color Offset, Vein Color, and Filler Color attributes of the Marble texture as well as the Bump Mapping attribute of the Blinn, the results become more complex. This technique of combining procedural textures makes any single procedural texture more believable.

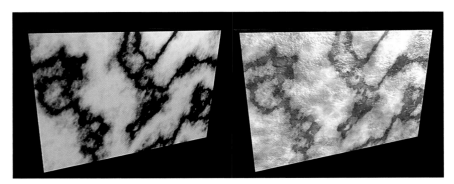

Figure 5.10 Left: Marble texture; Right: Marble texture with other procedural textures mapped to various attributes. This scene is included with the Chapter 5 tutorial files as `marble.ma`.

The Marble texture attributes are described here:

Filler Color and Vein Color   Filler Color sets the color of the stone's bulk. Vein Color determines the color of the thin veins.

Vein Width   Sets the width of the veins. If the value is high, the veins become large spots.

Diffusion   Controls the color mixture of the stone. Low values produce a high level of contrast between the Filler Color and Vein Color. High values allow the Vein Color to spread and mix into the Filler Color.

Contrast   Increases or decreases the amount of contrast set by Diffusion. A Contrast value of 1.0 is equal to a Diffusion value of 0.

Amplitude   Controls the complexity of the veins. Higher values create thinner veins with more kinks. You can raise the Amplitude value above the default maximum of 1.5. (You can raise most attribute sliders in Maya above their default maximum by entering a higher value into their numeric fields.)

Ratio, Depth, and Ripples function in a manner similar to the Cloud and Solid Fractal textures (see the previous sections).

Using Wood

The Wood texture replicates the rings found in a cross-section of a tree trunk or a branch. The Wood texture is not well suited for realistic wood. However, the texture can create convincing painted or stained wood when applied as a low-intensity bump map. For example, in Figure 5.11 a Wood texture is mapped to the Bump Mapping attribute of a Blinn material, which in turn is assigned to a flattened polygon cube.

Figure 5.11 A Wood texture applied to a cube as a bump map. This scene is included with the Chapter 5 tutorial files as wood.ma.

The Wood texture attributes are described here:

Vein Color and Filler Color   Vein Color establishes the color of the rings. Filler Color sets the color of the wood between rings.

Vein Spread   Determines how far the Vein Color will bleed into the Filler Color. A Vein Spread value of 0 will remove the Vein Color from the texture (with the exception of extremely thin ring lines).

Layer Size   "Zooms" in and out of the pattern. Higher values create fewer rings.

Randomness and Age   Randomness varies the width of each ring. When raised, Age adds more rings.

Grain Color and Grain Contrast   These attributes control the color and intensity of "grains" within the wood. These appear as tiny dots throughout the wood.

Grain Spacing and Center   Grain Spacing sets the distance between individual grain dots. Center determines where the circular heart of the wood is in the U and V directions.

The patterns created by the wood rings are controlled by a set of attributes in the Noise Attributes section of the Wood texture's Attribute Editor tab. Amplitude X sets the strength of noise function in the X direction. Amplitude Y does the same for the Y direction. When the 3D Placement box is at its default position, X direction corresponds with the world X axis and Y direction corresponds with the Y axis. The Ratio, Depth, and Ripples attributes are identical to those of the Solid Fractal, Cloud, and Marble textures (see the previous sections).

Using Leather

Although the Leather texture is not designed to create realistic animal hide, it can create interesting organic and cellular patterns (see Figure 5.12).

The Leather attributes are described here:

Cell Color and Crease Color   Cell Color sets the color of the circular cells. Crease Color sets the color found between the cells.

Cell Size and Density   Cell Size determines the size of individual cells. Density determines how closely the cells are packed together. High values create less empty space between the cells and thus less color provided by Crease Color.

Spottyness, Randomness, and Threshold   Spottyness randomly kills off cells. High values create larger areas colored by the Crease Color. Randomness varies the pattern of cells. Low values make the distance between cells and the cell size more consistent. Threshold controls the intensity of the cell growth. High values increase the intensity of the Cell Color.

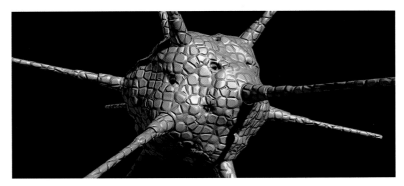

Figure 5.12 A Leather texture, with default settings, applied as a color and bump map to an assigned Blinn material

Using Snow

The Snow texture places virtual snow on the areas of a surface that point toward the positive Y axis and do not possess too great a slope. The Snow texture works in conjunction with bump and displacement maps. For example, in Figure 5.13 a Fractal texture is used as a displacement map on a primitive plane. The Snow texture is mapped to the Color attribute of the Blinn connected to the displacement. As a result, all the parts of the surface that point upward are colored white. (Note that displacement maps are render-intensive; for more information on bump and displacement mapping, see Chapter 9.)

Figure 5.13 A Snow texture colors the peaks of a displaced plane. This scene is included with the Chapter 5 tutorial files as `snow_displace.ma`.

You can adjust the Snow texture to emulate fallen dust, dirt, or other debris. For example, in Figure 5.14 a Snow texture is mapped to the Color attribute of a Blinn, which is assigned to a plate and bowl. A Mountain texture is mapped to the Snow Color attribute of the Snow texture, producing white bits of debris instead of solid snow. The Threshold attribute of the Snow texture is set to 0.75, causing the debris to appear only on surface faces whose normals lie roughly between 0 and 22 degrees off the Y axis.

MODEL COURTESY OF KEVIN ELMER

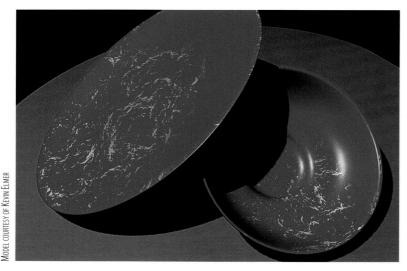

Figure 5.14 A Snow texture creates a debris-like effect over a pair of dishes. This scene is included with the Chapter 5 tutorial files as `dish_debris.ma`.

The Snow texture attributes are described here:

Snow Color and Surface Color   Snow Color sets the color of the virtual snow. Surface Color sets the color of the surface where the snow does not stick. (Surface Color is set to blue in the Figure 5.14 scene file.) You can map these attributes with another texture for more realism.

Threshold   Whether or not snow sticks to a surface face is determined by the Threshold attribute. A value of 0.5 allows the snow to stick to any surface point whose surface normal lies roughly between 0 and 45 degrees off the positive Y axis. A value of 0 allows the snow to stick to any surface point whose surface normal lies roughly between 0 and 90 degrees off the positive Y axis. For example, a value of 0 would cause the snow to appear on the top half of a sphere.

Depth Decay and Thickness   Depth Decay controls the transition from snow to lack of snow. High values make the transition fairly hard, and low values make the transition tapered and soft. A Depth Decay value of 0 removes the snow completely. Thickness determines the thickness of the virtual snow. High values make the snow more opaque.

The positive Y axis used by the Snow texture is defined by the Snow texture's 3D Placement box and not the world axis. If the box is left at its default position, the positive Y axis runs "up" in world space. However, if the box is rotated, the positive Y axis used by the Snow texture changes. When viewing the 3D Placement box, remember that the Y axis runs in the same direction as the small "tail" on the corner diamond icon (see Figure 5.2 earlier in this chapter and Figure 5.29 in the section "Positioning 3D Placement and Projection Icons").

Applying Granular Textures

Granular textures employ noise as grains or dots. These include Rock and Granite textures.

Using the Rock Texture

The Rock texture is similar to the Mountain texture in that it creates a hard-edged pattern (see Figure 5.15). Both textures may be useful for emulating rough surfaces, whether they are inorganic like stone or organic like animal skin. Although Figure 5.15 displays an intense bump map, you can lower the bump intensity and make the textures appear more subtle (bump maps are discussed in Chapter 9).

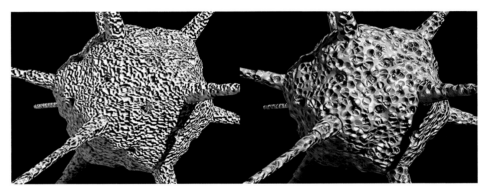

Figure 5.15 Left: Default Rock texture applied as color and bump; Right: Default Granite texture applied as color and bump.

Mix Ratio sets the ratio of Color 1 to Color 2. If the Mix Ratio value is below 0.5, Color 2 becomes the grain color. If the Mix Ratio value is above 0.5, Color 1 becomes the grain color. Grain Size controls the size of the individual grains. Diffusion controls the hardness of the grain edges. Higher values blur the grains. If you increase the Grain Size and Diffusion values, you can create a stylized tile (see Figure 5.16). Keep in mind that you can adjust any procedural texture in Maya to create a wide range of results—it's not necessary to stick with the default settings and default pattern.

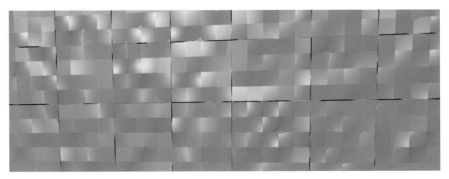

Figure 5.16 Rock texture with raised Grain Size and Diffusion values applied as a bump map. This scene is included with the Chapter 5 tutorial files as `rock_tiles.ma`.

Using the Granite Texture

The Granite texture is similar to the Leather texture in that it creates a series of colored, semicircular cells. At the same time, you can adjust the Granite texture to produce abstract patterns (see Figure 5.17).

Figure 5.17 The Granite texture is adjusted to produce an abstract pattern. This scene is included with the Chapter 5 tutorial files as `granite_pattern.ma`.

The Granite texture attributes are described here:

Color 1, Color 2, Color 3, and Filler Color   The texture combines three sets of cells, the color of which is determined by Color 1, Color 2, and Color 3. Filler Color sets the color of the space between cells.

Cell Size, Density, and Mix Ratio   Cell Size determines the size of individual cells. Density controls the intensity of the cell color. High Density values reduce the amount of empty space between cells and therefore decrease the amount of Filler Color visible. Mix Ratio controls the visible ratio of the three cell colors. A value of 0 prevents the use of Color 2 and Color 3 cells. Values between 0.001 and 0.5 create a relatively equal mix of all three cell colors. Values closer to 1.0 favor Color 1 and Color 3.

Spottyness and Randomness function in a manner similar to the Leather texture (see "Using Leather" earlier in this chapter).

Applying Abstract Textures

Abstract textures are not intended to replicate any real-world object. Nevertheless, they offer an interesting alternative to other textures. Stucco and Crater textures fall into this category.

Using the Stucco Texture

The Stucco texture mixes two colors, Channel 1 and Channel 2. The Shaker attribute determines the ratio of the two colors. A high value biases Channel 1. A low value biases Channel 2.

Two Stucco attributes, Normal Depth and Normal Melt, do not function unless the Out Normal attribute of the texture is connected to the Normal Camera attribute of a material. Since this requires a custom connection, the following steps are recommended:

1. Open the Hypershade window. MMB-drag a Blinn material into the work area. Assign the Blinn to a primitive.

2. MMB-drag a Stucco texture into the work area and drop it on top of the Blinn. The Connect Input Of menu opens. Choose Color from the menu. A connection line appears between the Stucco and Blinn icons. Note that the Stucco icon is named stucco1 and the Blinn icon is named blinn1.

3. MMB-drag the stucco1 icon on top of the blinn1 icon a second time. The Connect Input Of menu opens; choose Other from the menu. The Connection Editor window opens.

4. In the left column, click Out Normal so that it becomes italicized and highlighted. Out Normal is at the very end of the list. In the right column, click Normal Camera so that it becomes italicized and highlighted. Close the Connection Editor. This connection has the effect of turning the Stucco texture into a bump map without the need for a Bump 2d or Bump 3d utility. In fact, the Bump Mapping attribute of blinn1 lists stucco1 as its connection. Close the Hypershade and render a test frame. An example render is included in the next section.

The Normal Depth attribute, in the Stucco texture's Normal Options section, controls the depth of the bump. The Normal Melt attribute controls the smoothness of the bump. Low Normal Melt values create a rough bump with small detail, and high values create a smooth bump with large features. For information on standard bump mapping, see Chapter 9.

Using Crater

The Crater texture functions in a manner similar to the Stucco texture but adds extra attributes (see Figure 5.18).

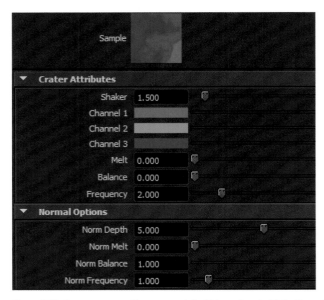

Figure 5.18 Crater texture attributes, several of which are shared with the Stucco texture

The Crater attributes are described here:

Channel 1, Channel 2, Channel 3 The Crater texture mixes three colors defined by Channel 1, Channel 2, and Channel 3.

Shaker, Melt, and Balance The Shaker attribute controls the mixture. Shaker values below 0.1 favor Channel 1. Values from 0.1 to 0.5 favor Channel 1 and Channel 2. Values above 0.5 mix all three colors. When the value is raised above 2.0, the detail is reduced in scale and Channel 3 is favored. Melt controls the smoothness of the resulting pattern. Low values introduce a greater number of kinks into the threads of color. Balance controls the ratio of the three colors. As the Balance value gets higher, a greater portion of the Channel 2 color is added to the mixture.

Norm Depth, Norm Melt, Norm Balance, and Norm Frequency The Out Normal attribute of the Crater texture must be connected to the Normal Camera attribute of a material for the Norm Depth, Norm Melt, Norm Balance, and Norm Frequency attributes to work. Norm Balance controls the ratio between high and low points on the resulting bump. High values reduce the number of deep pits created by the bump mapping process. Norm Frequency controls the noise frequency used to generate the bump. High values create finer bump detail and introduce a greater variation between high and low points. Norm Depth is the same as the Stucco texture's Normal Depth whereas Norm Melt is the same as the Stucco texture's Normal Melt (see the previous section).

Frequency controls the scale of detail created by the color mix. High values create a finer, more convoluted pattern. Frequency is similar to the Frequency Ratio attribute of the Noise, Volume Noise, Fractal, and Solid Fractal textures.

Although the default Crater and Stucco textures are quite vivid and match few surfaces in the real world, you can easily adjust their attributes to create a more complex result (see Figure 5.19).

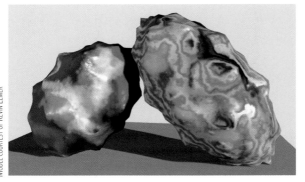

Figure 5.19 The Stucco texture (left) and Crater texture (right) applied with custom attribute settings. This scene is included with the Chapter 5 tutorial files as `crater_stucco_custom.ma`. A version with default texture settings is included as `crater_stucco.ma`.

Applying Environment Textures

Environment textures, found in the Maya > Env Textures section in the Create tab of the Hypershade, Create Node, and or Create Render Node windows, are designed to surround an object or enclose an entire scene.

Environment textures require a unique rendering process. In the process, a reflection vector is derived from the camera eye vector and the surface normal of a rendered surface point (see Figure 5.20). (The angle of reflection is equal to the angle of incidence created by the camera eye vector.) Where the reflection vector strikes a placement sphere (or cube), the pixels of the texture mapped to the sphere are noted. The noted pixels are consequently used in the color calculation of the surface point. Environment textures were developed as an inexpensive way to simulate reflections.

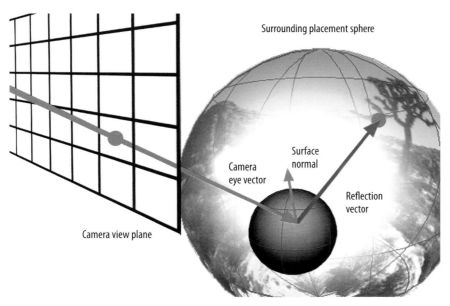

Figure 5.20 A simplified representation of the environment texture process

With Maya, you can successfully simulate reflections by mapping an environment texture to the Reflected Color attribute of a material. As such, the Maya Software or mental ray® raytracing option is not required and the render becomes more efficient. For example, in Figure 5.21 the materials assigned to a polygon car's glass, chrome, and paint have an Env Sphere texture mapped to their Reflected Color. A bitmap photo of a desert landscape is mapped to the Env Sphere's Image. As a result, a simulated reflection appears in appropriate places. Environment textures are not limited to the Reflected Color attribute, however. Any attribute is fair game. For example, an environment texture mapped to a material's Color applies the color of the Image bitmap through the camera eye vector and reflection vector process.

Figure 5.21 A car's reflections are provided by an Env Sphere texture. A simplified version of the scene is included with the Chapter 5 tutorial files as `car_env_sphere.ma`.

When you MMB-drag an environment texture into the Hypershade work area or choose it through the Create Render Node or Create Node windows, a 3D Placement utility is automatically connected to the texture node. This utility creates the placement sphere or cube that appears in the viewport view. Each of the five environment texture types creates a unique placement sphere or cube with specialized attributes. Although the 3D Placement utility node created for an environment texture looks similar to the 3D Placement utility node created for a 3D texture, the utilities are not identical. The 3D Placement used for a 3D texture defines the volume in which a surface point is plotted in the X, Y, and Z directions to determine a color. The 3D Placement used for an environment texture employs camera eye and reflection vectors.

Working with Env Sphere and Env Cube

The Env Sphere texture simulates an environment by applying a map to the inner surface of an infinite sphere. You can map any texture to the Env Sphere's Image attribute. The placement icon created for the Env Sphere texture is drawn as a full circle and a half circle enclosed by two planes (see Figure 5.22). The translation and scale of the placement icon does not affect the application of the Env Sphere texture. However, the rotation of the icon will change the texture placement. The Env Sphere texture carries two unique attributes: Shear UV and Flip. Shear UV twists the mapped texture in the U and V directions (producing a barber pole effect). Flip swaps the U direction with the V direction, thus turning the mapped texture 90 degrees. Since the Env Sphere texture is based on a spherical placement, the mapped texture is pinched at the top and bottom pole.

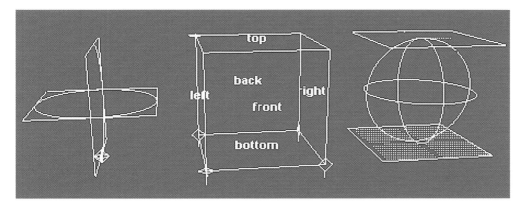

Figure 5.22 Left: Env Sphere placement icon; Middle: Env Cube placement icon; Right: Env Chrome placement icon.

The Env Cube texture maps six textures to the six sides of a cube placement icon (see Figure 5.22). The scale and translation of the icon affects the application of the texture unless the Env Cube's Infinite Size attribute is selected. In either situation, the rotation of the icon changes the texture placement. The six attributes to which you can map six textures are intuitively named Right, Left, Top, Bottom, Front, and Back. The Env Cube texture is ideal for simulating an interior room.

Adjusting Env Chrome

The Env Chrome texture creates stylized chrome with a procedural ground plane and sky. The placement icon is differentiated by a top and bottom plane (see Figure 5.22 in the previous section). Env Chrome has an extremely long list of attributes. Nevertheless, to make the texture more realistic, I suggest the following guidelines:

- Turn off the light boxes in the virtual sky by reducing Light Width and Light Depth to 0.
- Turn off the dark grid on the virtual floor by reducing the Grid Width and Grid Depth, in the Grid Placement section, to 0.
- Map more realistic textures to Sky Color, Zenith Color, Horizon Color, and Floor Color. Use the same texture for Sky Color and Zenith Color as the two attributes determine the color of the virtual sky. Use the same texture for Horizon Color and Floor Color as the two attributes determine the color of the virtual ground plane.

After you turn off the virtual light boxes and grid, you can use the Env Chrome texture to create a simulated reflection with a distinct ground plane and sky (see Figure 5.23).

Figure 5.23 An Env Chrome texture is mapped to the color of a Blinn material, creating a simulated reflection on the surface of the sphere. This scene is included with the Chapter 5 tutorial files as `chrome_custom.ma`.

Note: The Env Sky texture creates a procedural ground and sky, complete with a virtual sun. The placement icon is a half sphere attached to a plane. The attribute list for the Env Sky texture is as long as the Env Chrome texture. Fortunately, the attributes are intuitively named and fairly straightforward.

The Env Ball texture is designed for High Dynamic Range Image (HDRI) rendering techniques, which are explored in Chapter 13, "Color Management, HDR Workflow, and Render Passes."

2D Texture Projection Options

You can apply any 2D texture in three ways:

Normal The "normal" method maps the texture directly to the surface with tiling controlled by the 2D Placement utility, which is connected automatically. This is the default method.

As Stencil As Stencil creates a shading network with a Stencil utility. For a demonstration, see Chapter 8, "Harnessing the Power of Math Utilities."

As Projection This method creates a Projection utility in addition to a 3D Placement utility and a 2D Placement utility.

To create a 2D texture as a projection, RMB-click over a texture icon in the Hypershade, Create Node, or Create Render Node windows and choose Create As Projection (Figure 5.24). Note that the Create Texture option uses the normal method of mapping. The As Stencil option is also available through this menu.

Projected 2D textures suffer the same pitfalls as 3D textures. If the assigned surface or the Projection icon is moved, the surface picks up a different portion of the texture. If the Projection icon, or the 3D Placement icon, is smaller than the surface, the texture is repeated across the surface. One way to avoid these problems is to convert the texture through the Convert To File Texture tool. This is demonstrated at the end of this chapter.

Figure 5.24 A Fractal texture is created as a projection with the Create As Projection option. You can access this option by RMB-clicking over the texture in the Create Hypershade, Create Node, or Create Render Node windows.

Differentiating 2D Projection Types

By default, when the As Projection option is selected, the Out Color attribute of the texture is connected to the Image attribute of the Projection utility. The Projection utility defines the style and coverage of the projection. The 3D Placement utility, in this scenario, stores the transform information of the Projection utility and provides the interactive projection icon. During a render, a projection ray is shot out from each pixel of the projected texture in a direction defined by the 3D Placement utility. If a projection ray strikes a surface, the pixel of the ray is noted and thereafter used in the color calculation of the struck surface point. To relate the 3D Placement utility to the Projection utility, the World Inverse Matrix attribute of the 3D Placement utility is connected to the Placement Matrix attribute of the Projection utility. (For more information on Maya matrices, see Chapter 7, "Automating a Scene with Sampler Nodes.")

By default, the Projection utility creates a Planar projection. The utility provides a total of nine projection styles. You can switch between these styles by changing the Proj Type attribute in the Projection utility's Attribute Editor tab. The projection styles follow:

Off Disables the projection. The texture connected to the Projection utility is ignored.

Planar Places the texture on a projection plane. Its main disadvantage is its inability to match complex shapes. For example, in Figure 5.25 a Planar projection appears correct on a plane but streaks through a cube, sphere, and torus.

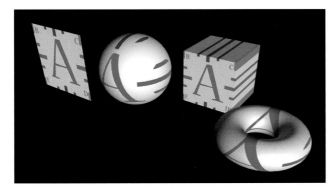

Figure 5.25 Planar projections mapped to various primitive surfaces. This scene is included with the Chapter 5 tutorial files as `proj_plane.ma`.

Spherical Places the texture inside a projection sphere. By default, the sphere is incomplete and covers only 180 degrees along the U direction and 90 degrees along the V direction. This creates a projection shape similar to a piece of paper pressed against one side of a ball. Whatever section of the assigned surface is not covered by the projection receives a repeated portion of the texture. You can create complete coverage of the projection sphere by raising the Projection's U Angle attribute to 360 and V Angle attribute to 180. Regardless of the U Angle and V Angle values, "pinched poles" appear. That is, the upper edge of the texture is pinched into a single point, as is the lower. For example, in Figure 5.26 a Checker texture is mapped to a Surface Shader material as a Spherical projection.

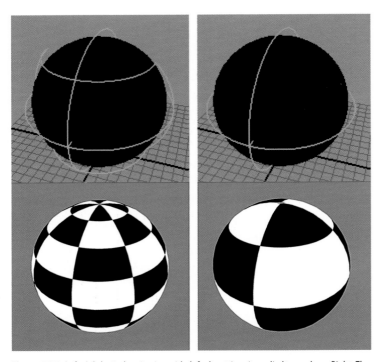

Figure 5.26 Left: A Spherical projection with default settings is applied to a sphere; Right: The Spherical projection's U Angle is set to 360 and its V Angle is set to 180. This scene is included with the Chapter 5 tutorial files as `proj_spherical.ma`.

Note: Although always visible, a Projection utility's V Angle attribute is functional only for a Spherical projection type. U Angle is functional only for Spherical and Cylindrical projections.

Ball Places the texture inside a projection sphere. The projection pinches the texture at only one pole. A real-world equivalent is a blanket draped over a ball with the blanket's four corners twisted together at one spot. The pole is indicated by the diamond-shaped UV origin symbol on the projection icon (see Figure 5.27).

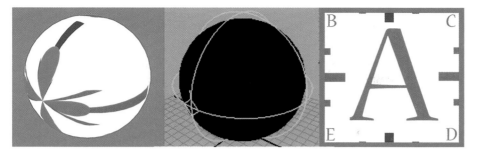

Figure 5.27 Left: A Ball projection is applied to a sphere; Middle: The Ball projection icon; Right: The test bitmap. This scene is included with the Chapter 5 tutorial files as `proj_ball.ma`.

Cylindrical   Places the texture inside a cylinder. The left and right edges of the texture will meet if the projection's U Angle is set to 360 degrees. The Cylindrical type creates two pinched poles at the top and bottom of the projection.

Cubic   Places a texture onto the six faces of a cube.

Concentric   Randomly selects vertical slices from the texture and projects them in a concentric pattern.

TriPlanar   Projects the texture along three planes based on the surface normal of the object that is affected.

Perspective   Projects the texture from the view of a camera (see Figure 5.28). For this to work, you must select a camera from a drop-down list provided by the Link To Camera attribute (found in the Camera Projection Attributes section of the Projection utility's Attribute Editor tab). The projection icon takes the form of a camera frustum but is not aligned to the linked camera in 3D space. Nevertheless, the texture is projected from the view of the linked camera.

Figure 5.28 A Perspective projection applied to a series of spheres. This scene is included with the Chapter 5 tutorial files as `proj_persp.ma`.

Positioning 3D Placement and Projection Icons

There are several approaches you can take when positioning the 3D Placement box icons created for 3D textures, which are listed here:

- If a surface is already assigned to the material to which the 3D Placement utility belongs, click the Fit To Group BBox button in the 3D Texture Placement Attributes section of the 3D Placement utility's Attribute Editor tab. This snaps the placement box to the bounding box of the surface.

- If you need to translate, scale, or rotate the 3D Placement icon, select the place3dTexture icon in the Hypershade window. You can also click the Interactive Placement button found in the 3D Placement utility's Attribute Editor tab. The Interactive Placement button selects the icon and displays an interactive translate, rotate, and scale handle.

- When a 2D texture is created with the Create As Projection option, a 3D Placement utility supplies the transformation information for the Projection node. Therefore, you can apply the same approaches when positioning in the Projection icon. In addition, the Projection node supplies its own Interactive Placement and Fit To BBox buttons that function in the same way as the same-named 3D Placement buttons.

Projection icons indicate the employed UV orientation. For example, a Planar projection icon features a diamond-shaped symbol at one corner (see Figure 5.29). This represents the 0, 0 origin in UV texture space. (For more information on UV texture space, see Chapter 9.) Using the origin symbol as a reference, you can orient the icon and predict the resulting render. For example, if a Planar projection icon is viewed from a front viewport view and the origin symbol is at the bottom-left corner, V runs down to up and U runs left to right, matching a texture's icon in the Hypershade window.

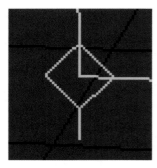

Figure 5.29 The UV origin symbol of a projection icon

Spherical, Cylindrical, Ball, TriPlanar, and Cubic projection icons also carry an origin symbol. For Ball projections, the diamond shape represents the point where all four corners of the texture converge. TriPlanar projections carry three origin symbols, one at the corner of each plane. Each plane is identical to a Planar projection. Cubic projections carry six symbols, although three of them overlap at one corner. Concentric projections carry no symbols, since standard UV interpretation does not apply.

Applying the Convert To File Texture Tool

The Convert To File Texture tool allows you to convert projected 2D textures, as well as 2D and 3D procedural textures, into permanent, flattened bitmaps. This prevents the projected texture from "swimming" as the surface deforms or moves relative to the projection utility.

To apply the tool, follow these steps:

1. Select a material that has a projected or procedural texture assigned to one or more of its attributes. Shift+click the surface to which the material is assigned.

2. Choose Edit > Convert To File Texture (Maya Software) > ❏ from the Hypershade window menu. The Convert To File Texture Options window opens.

3. The X Resolution and Y Resolution attributes determine the size of each bitmap written out. Choose appropriate sizes and specify a File Format value. Then click the Convert And Close button.

For each projected 2D texture, procedural 2D texture, and procedural 3D texture mapped to the material, a bitmap is written to the following location with the following name:

project_directory\sourceImages*texture_name-surface_name.format*

At the same time, the original material is duplicated with the original shading network structure. In place of the projected and procedural textures, however, File textures are provided with the new bitmaps preloaded. The new material is automatically assigned to the surface. When compared side by side, the converted bitmap surface is virtually identical to the original when the X and Y Resolutions are kept fairly high (see Figure 5.30). Once the converted bitmaps are applied to the surface through the duplicated material, you can delete the original material. Thereafter, you can animate or deform the surface; the textures will not slide.

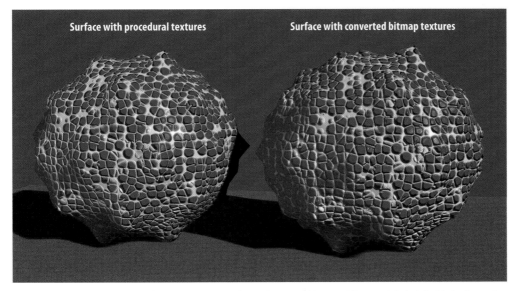

Figure 5.30 Procedurally mapped surface compared to surface with converted bitmaps. This scene is included with the Chapter 5 tutorial files as `convert.ma`.

Note: Oddly enough, the Convert To File Texture tool also converts all nonprocedural bitmaps. This offers the advantage of locking in any custom UV settings. In addition, any bitmap mapped to a single channel attribute, such as Transparency or Diffuse, is converted to grayscale. The original bitmaps are not harmed.

The Convert To File Texture tool will not work if the surface is assigned to the default Lambert material or if the surface is connected to more than one shading group. In general, the default Lambert material should not be used in the texturing process.

The Convert To File Texture tool carries additional attributes for fine-tuning. Anti-Alias, if selected, anti-aliases the bitmap. Background Mode controls the background color used in the conversion. Fill Texture Seams, when selected, extends the color of any UV shell past the edge of the shell boundary; this prevents black lines from forming at the boundaries when the surface is rendered. Bake Shading Group Lighting, Bake Shadows, and Bake Transparency, when selected, add their namesake elements to the converted bitmap. Double Sided must be selected for Bake Shadows to function correctly. UV Range allows the custom selection of a non-0-to-1.0 range. (It's also possible to bake lighting information through the Transfer Maps window, which is discussed in Chapter 9.)

Chapter Tutorial: Creating Skin with Procedural Textures

In this tutorial, you will texture a character's head using nothing more than 2D and 3D procedural textures (see Figure 5.31). Although custom bitmaps and mental ray subsurface scatter shaders generally create the highest level of realism, the proper use of procedural textures can save a significant amount of time. This is particularly true for those productions that use characters that are stylized and do not require 100 percent realism. (For an example of subsurface scatter shader use, see Chapter 12.)

1. Open head.ma from the Chapter 5 tutorial scenes folder. This file contains a polygon head.

2. Open the Hypershade window. MMB-drag a new Blinn material into the work area. Assign the Blinn to the head. Open the Blinn's Attribute Editor tab. Change the Color attribute to a flesh color of your choice. Change the Ambient Color to a dark red. This will give the surface a subtle, skin-like glow in the shadows. The Ambient Color slider should not be more than ⅛ of the slider length from the left side. For example, an RGB value of 38, 0, 0 on a 1.0-to-255 scale works fairly well. If the Ambient Color is too strong, the surface will look washed out and flat.

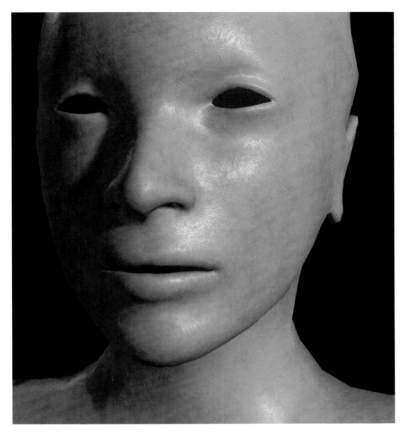

Figure 5.31 A skin material created with 2D and 3D procedural textures

3. To properly judge the results, create several lights. Follow either the 2- or 3-point lighting techniques discussed in Chapter 1, "Understanding Lighting and Color." Render a series of tests until the lighting is satisfactory.

4. Open the Blinn's Attribute Editor tab. Click the Specular Color checkered Map button and choose a Fractal texture from the Create Render Node window. Double-click the place2dTexture1 icon in the work area, which opens its Attribute Editor tab. (See Figure 5.32 for the final shading network layout.) Set Repeat UV to 45, 45 and select Stagger. This reduces and randomizes the scale of the fractal pattern so that it can emulate pores.

5. Open the Blinn's Attribute Editor tab. Adjust the Eccentricity and Specular Roll Off attributes. Correct values depend on the lighting of the scene. The goal is to create a strong specular highlight without losing the detail provided by the Fractal texture. Be careful not to raise the Eccentricity value too high; doing so will spread out the highlight and make the skin look dull.

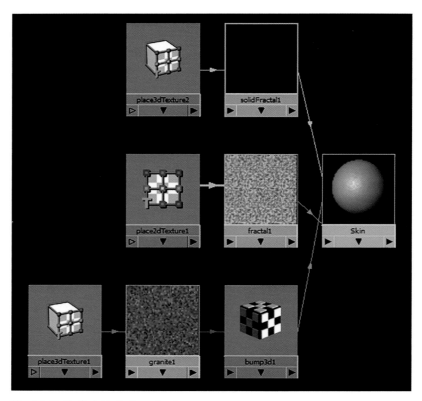

Figure 5.32 The final skin shading network

6. In the work area, double-click the Fractal icon (named fractal1), which opens its Attribute Editor tab. Reduce the Amplitude value and raise the Threshold value slightly. This reduces the amount of contrast in the fractal pattern and makes its effect subtler. Tint the Color Gain attribute a pale blue. This inserts a color other than red into the material and helps make the skin color more varied.

7. Open the Blinn's Attribute Editor tab. Click the Bump Mapping checkered Map button. Choose a Granite texture from the Create Render Node window. In the work area, double-click the bump3d1 icon, which opens its Attribute Editor tab. Change Bump Depth to 0.01. Open the attached place3dTexture1 node in the Attribute Editor. Change the Scale to 2, 2, 2 to increase the size of the procedural pattern. Render a test. The Granite texture provides a subtle bumpiness/fuzziness to the parts of the skin that do not have specular highlights.

8. Return to the Blinn's Attribute Editor tab. Click the Incandescence checkered Map button and choose a Solid Fractal texture from the Create Render Node window. In the work area, double-click the Solid Fractal icon (named solid-Fractal1), which opens its Attribute Editor tab. Change the Ratio value to 1.0 and the Frequency Ratio value to 4. Change Color Gain to a dark purple (for example, 17, 14, 26 in RGB). Open the attached place3dTexture2 node in the Attribute Editor. Change the Scale to 2, 2, 2 to increase the size of the fractal pattern. Render a test frame. The Solid Fractal texture introduces variation within the basic skin color. If the result is too bright or the color is not quite right, adjust the Color Gain and render additional tests.

The skin material is complete! Your render should look similar to Figure 5.31. If you decide to apply this material to a character that moves or deforms, you can use the Convert To File Texture tool to change the 3D procedural textures into bitmaps. If you get stuck with this tutorial, a finished version is included as `head_finished.ma` in the Chapter 5 tutorial `scenes` folder.

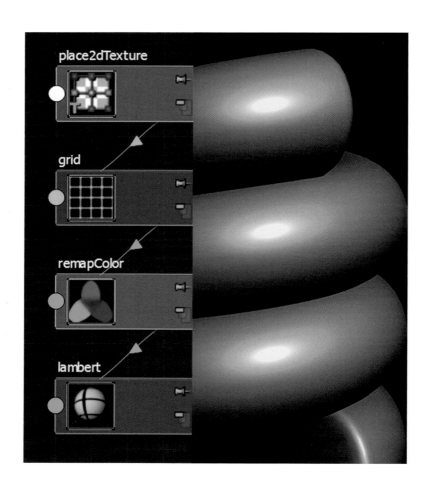

Creating Custom Connections and Applying Color Utilities

Creating custom shading networks is a powerful way to texture and render with Autodesk® Maya®. You can connect hundreds of material, texture, geometry, light, and camera attributes through the Hypershade and Node Editor windows for unique results. In addition, you can apply specialized color utilities that can customize the hue, saturation, value, gamma, and contrast of any input and output.

Chapter Contents
A review of the Hypershade and Node Editor workflow
Multiple approaches for creating connections
Tips for keeping node networks organized
Practical applications of each color utility

A Closer Look at Nodes

A fundamental concept in working with networks and their connections is the node. Technically speaking, a *node* is a construct that holds specific information plus any actions associated with that information. A node might be a curve, surface geometry, material, texture, light, camera, joint, IK handle, and so on. Any box that appears in the Hypergraph, Node Editor, or Hypershade window is a node. (For the difference between transform and shape nodes, see Chapter 7, "Automating a Scene with Sampler Nodes.")

A node's information is organized into specific *attributes*. If an attribute can be animated, it's called a *channel* (and appears in the Channel Box). For example, the Scale X of a sphere is a channel. Some attributes carry multiple channels, such as X, Y, Z or Red, Green, Blue, whereas others carry a single channel. With a single channel, the attribute name and the channel name are one and the same. For example, the Diffuse attribute carries a single channel, which is also named *Diffuse*.

Every node, attribute, and channel in Maya has two variations of its name: a long name and short name. The long name separates multiple words and capitalizes each word. You'll see the long names used for material, texture, and utility nodes in the Hypershade, Create Node, and Create Render Node window Create tabs. You'll see long names used for attributes and channels in the Attribute Editor and Channel Box.

In contrast, you'll see short names used for node names in the Hypershade and Node Editor (unless you rename them). You'll also see short names used for node connections in the Connection Editor and within connection label boxes (both are discussed later in this chapter). Short names remove spaces between words and alter the capitalization. For example, *Specular Color* is the long name of an attribute whereas *specularColor* is the short name for the same attribute. Although long names are easier to read through the graphic interface in Maya, short names are more efficient for MEL scripting and are thus used at the programming level.

Hypershade vs. Node Editor

The Node Editor is a recent addition to Maya. It combines the functionality of the Hypershade, Connection Editor, and Hypergraph: Connections window. Although we've used the Hypershade to discuss materials and textures thus far, we will begin using the Node Editor more heavily through the remainder of this book. Nevertheless, you'll also find tips and techniques for using the Hypershade and Connection Editor for creating custom shading networks throughout this chapter. Keep in mind that any shading network you create in the Node Editor can be created in the Hypershade, and vice versa. You can access the Hypershade by choosing Window > Rendering Editors > Hypershade. You can access the Node Editor by choosing Window > Node Editor.

Creating and Exporting Nodes

Create new nodes at any time by clicking a node icon in the Create tab of the Hypershade or Create Render Node window. You access the Create Render Node window by clicking the checkered Map button beside an attribute in the Attribute Editor. You can also launch the Create Node window by RMB-clicking in an empty area of the Node Editor and choosing Create Node from the marking menu. The Create Node window is identical to the Create Render Node window. You can MMB-drag nodes from the Create tab into the Hypershade work area or the Node Editor.

You can copy, export, and import shading networks through the Hypershade menu. To copy individual nodes, choose Edit > Duplicate > Without Network. To copy entire shading networks, choose Edit > Duplicate > Shading Network. You can export shading networks by choosing File > Export Selected Network. You can save the network in any of the supported file formats. Bring networks back into the Maya scene by choosing File > Import from the Hypershade menu.

Assigning Materials

To assign a material to a surface, MMB-drag the material node from the Hypershade or Node Editor to the surface geometry in a viewport view. Alternatively, you can select the geometry, RMB-click over a material node in the Hypershade or Node Editor, and choose Assign Material To Selection (Hypershade) or Assign Material To Viewport Selection (Node Editor) from the marking menu.

Reading Node Connections

You can connect attributes and channels in an almost endless fashion. A series of connected nodes is a *node network*. If the network is designed for rendering, it's called a *shading network*. Any node connected to any other node is considered *upstream* or *downstream*. An upstream node is one that outputs information, and a downstream node is one that receives or inputs information. The node icons show whether an upstream or downstream connection exists.

Hypershade node icons display small arrows along their bottom edge. If the bottom-left arrow is solid, the node is downstream of another node. If the bottom-right arrow is solid, the node is upstream of another node. If either arrow is hollow, a connection does not exist in the direction in which the hollow arrow points (see Figure 6.1).

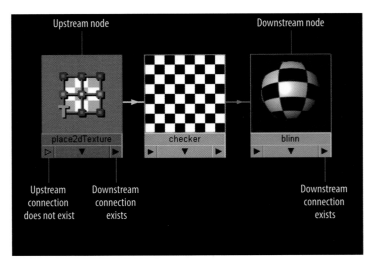

Figure 6.1 Hypershade upstream and downstream node connections

The Node Editor simplifies the connection display by including distinct input and output dots (Figure 6.2). The left-hand dot is the input port. The right-hand dot is the output port. Connections flow downstream into the input port and out of the output port.

Figure 6.2 A shading network displayed in the Node Editor

The node connection lines also indicate the flow of information, where the direction the line arrow points indicates a flow of information toward the downstream/input node. Hence, in Figures 6.1 and 6.2, the information is flowing left to right, from the place2dTexture node to the checker node, and from the checker node to the blinn node. Any node can output multiple channels. Whereas older versions of Maya show each and every channel with a separate connection line, Maya 2014 and 2015 represent multiple channel connections for a single attribute with a single orange connection line. Hence, in Figures 6.1 and 6.2 you can see multiple connections between the place2dTexture node and the checker node.

Creating Custom Connections

You can create custom connections through the Node Editor, Hypershade work area, or Connection Editor.

Making Connections in the Node Editor

Each node displayed in the Node Editor has three viewing modes: Hide Attributes, Show Connected Attributes, and Show Primary Attributes. You can switch between modes on an individual node by clicking the view mode button on the node box. This appears as a series of nested rectangles at the box's lower-right corner (see Figure 6.3). You can also click the buttons along the toolbar with the same names (see Figure 6.4 in the next section).

The Hide Attributes mode simply displays the node box. Show Connected Attributes displays only those attributes and channels that have connections. Show Primary Attributes displays all the primary attributes and channels. (This is the list you see by default in the Connection Editor.) If an attribute carries multiple channels, the channels are initially hidden. You can reveal the channels by clicking the small + symbol beside the attribute name. Note that individual channel connection lines are revealed when Show Connected Attributes or Show Primary Attributes is selected.

To make a connection in the Node Editor, click the output dot beside an attribute or channel name and LMB-drag the attached connection line and drop it on top of an input dot beside an attribute or channel name. In the Node Editor, input dots are on the left and output dots are on the right. Note that you must match attribute type. For example, vector attributes must be connected to vector attributes. The Node Editor helps to ensure this by graying out invalid connections. (The concept of attribute types is discussed more thoroughly in the "Using the Connection Editor" section later in this chapter.) Note that you can also LMB-click the main output dot on the node box and choose an attribute from the resulting menu list. If you choose Other from the menu, a full list of available attributes is listed in a separate Output Selection window.

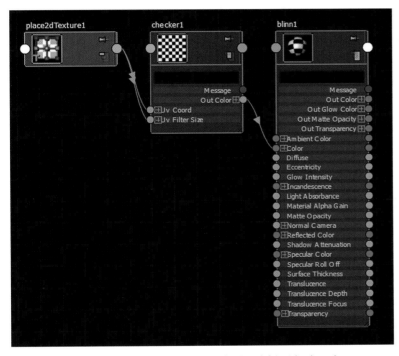

Figure 6.3 Three nodes use three different viewing modes. From left to right, the nodes are set to Hide Attributes, Show Connected Attributes, and Show Primary Attributes.

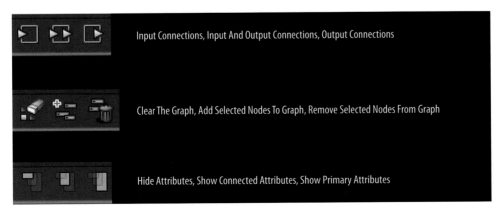

Figure 6.4 Useful buttons on the Node Editor toolbar

Node Editor Tips

Here are additional guidelines for viewing and clearing nodes in the Node Editor:

- You're free to move any node by LMB-dragging it.
- To view a node in the Node Editor, MMB-drag it from another window, such as the Hypershade or Hypergraph: Hierarchy.
- Optionally, you can select a piece of geometry, a light, or camera in a viewport view and click the Add Selected Nodes To Graph button (see Figure 6.4). By default, a shape node and transform node are displayed for each item you select in a viewport (see Chapter 7 for more information on these nodes).
- To clear the Node Editor view, click the Clear The Graph button in the toolbar (see Figure 6.4).
- You can use Alt/Opt+MMB to scroll the view or Alt/Opt+RMB to zoom in or out.
- To better see the output of a texture node, RMB-click over the node and choose Test Texture from the marking menu. This renders the output through the Render View window.
- To view the node network connected to a selected node, click the Input Connections, Input And Output Connections, or Output Connections button (see Figure 6.4). Input Connections shows all the upstream nodes. Output Connections shows all the downstream nodes. Input And Output Connections shows both directions. Keep in mind that many nodes of a node network are not initially displayed.
- To hide a selected node, select it and click the Remove Selected Nodes From Graph button (see Figure 6.4).
- You can delete a connection line by selecting it (so that it turns yellow) and then pressing the Delete key.

Employing Drag and Drop in the Hypershade

The Hypershade offers its own unique approach to making custom connections. Dragging and dropping one node on top of another using the MMB automatically opens the Connect Input Of menu (see Figure 6.5). The default attribute (usually Color) of the output (upstream) node is automatically used for the connection. The Connect Input Of menu makes no distinction between vector and single attributes. If a Connect Input Of menu selection is made that confuses the program, the Connection Editor automatically opens. The attributes listed by the Connect Input Of menu are incomplete (although they are the most common and often the most useful). To see the full list, choose Other to open the Connection Editor. Dragging and dropping one node on top of another using the MMB while pressing Shift opens the Connection Editor immediately. (The Connection Editor is discussed later in this chapter.)

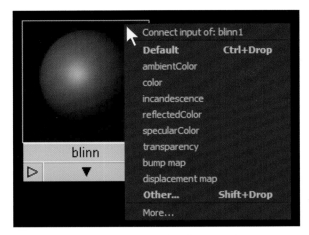

Figure 6.5 The Connect Input Of menu for a Blinn material

Dragging and dropping one node on top of another using the MMB while pressing Ctrl/Cmd instantly makes a connection. In this situation, the default attribute for both nodes is used. For instance, the default input attribute of a Blinn material is Color. The default input attribute of a Bump 2d node is Bump Value. If the two nodes involved in the connection are not a standard pair, Maya will not be able to make a decision. For example, dragging one texture on top of another texture with the MMB and Ctrl/Cmd forces Maya to open the Connection Editor.

You can also MMB-drag nodes from the Hypershade window to the Attribute Editor. An outlined box appears around any valid attribute when the mouse arrow hovers over it (see Figure 6.6). Releasing the mouse button over an attribute automatically creates a connection. In this case, it's best to double-click the downstream node first to open the node's Attribute Editor tab, and then MMB-drag the upstream node without having actually selected it. Note that Maya chooses the default channel for the upstream/output node. Of course, clicking the standard checkered Map button on an Attribute Editor tab opens the Create Render Node window and creates a connection once a material, texture, or utility is selected.

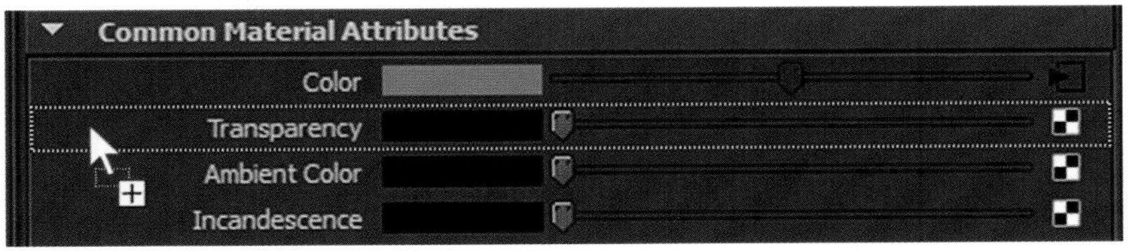

Figure 6.6 A node MMB-dragged to the Attribute Editor. The outlined box around the attribute signifies a potentially valid connection.

RMB-clicking the bottom-right corner of a node in the Hypershade opens the Connect Output Of menu (see Figure 6.7). Vector attributes are represented by an arrow on the right side; you can choose either the vector attribute or any single channel. Once an attribute is chosen, a connection line attaches itself to the mouse arrow. When you click another node, the Connect Input Of menu opens. After you choose an input attribute, the connection is made.

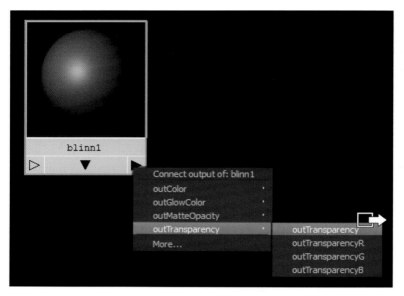

Figure 6.7 RMB-clicking the bottom-right corner of a node in the Hypershade opens the Connect Output Of menu.

Hypershade Tips

Here are additional guidelines for viewing and clearing in the Hypershade:

- You're free to move any node by LMB-dragging it.

- You can use Alt/Opt+MMB to scroll the view in the work area or Alt/Opt+RMB to zoom in or out.

- To clear the work area of all nodes, RMB-click in the work area and choose Graph > Clear Graph from the menu. This operation is nondestructive; the work area is a temporary place to examine and create connections.

- You can delete a connection line by selecting it (so that it turns yellow) and pressing the Delete key.

- Choose Edit > Delete Unused Nodes from the Hypershade menu to delete any node that is not assigned to geometry or that is not part of an assigned shading network.

The nodes you want to work with may not be present in the work area. You can include one or more nodes in the following ways:

- MMB-drag a selected node icon from the node tabs (Materials, Textures, Utilities, and so on) to the work area.

- RMB-click over the node icon in one of the node tabs and choose Graph Network from the marking menu. This offers the advantage of displaying *all* of the upstream nodes connected to the one you've chosen.

- To view the node network connected to a selected node, click the Input Connections, Input And Output Connections, or Output Connections button. These use the same symbols as those in the Node Editor (see Figure 6.4 earlier in this chapter). Input Connections shows all the upstream nodes. Output Connections shows all the downstream nodes. Input And Output Connections shows both directions. Keep in mind that many nodes of a node network are not initially displayed.

Node Names and Connection Labels

You can display the input and output channels of a connection in the Hypershade or Node Editor by hovering the mouse over a connection line. For example, when examining the Hypershade connection in Figure 6.8, checker1.outColor appears on the left side of a label box, whereas blinn1.color appears on the right side of the label box.

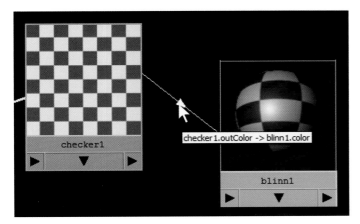

Figure 6.8 A connection label is displayed in the Hypershade.

The box uses the following naming convention:

`node_name.channel_name`

Internally, Maya uses this naming convention for all connections. You must use this convention when including attribute and channel names in expressions, as well as MEL and Python scripts.

The label box always uses short names and is formatted consistently, regardless of the way nodes are arranged. The output (upstream) attribute is displayed to the left of the box arrow, whereas the input (downstream) attribute is displayed to the right of the box arrow.

Some nodes carry subchannels. For example, a Remap Value node carries an input channel with the long name *Color[0] Color Color Red*. With this example, the subchannel is Color Color Red. The same short name is *color[0].color_ColorR*. Note that there is a period between *color[0]* and *color,* which indicates the transition from the channel to the subchannel. The label box would display this channel as *remapValue.color[0].color_ColorR*. Subchannels are often necessary for complex nodes that include ramp graphs.

If you hover your mouse over an orange connection line, which represents multiple connections, all the connections are listed with the input and output channels. (Output channels often carry an *out* prefix and therefore appear on the left side, or output side, of the box.)

Using the Connection Editor

You can open the Connection Editor by choosing Window > General Editors > Connection Editor. The window also opens when making certain connections in the Hypershade (see the "Employing Drag and Drop in the Hypershade" section earlier in this chapter). The Connection Editor is divided into two sections. By default, the left side contains outputs (on the upstream side of a connection) and the right side contains inputs (on the downstream side of a connection). A single node can be displayed on each side. To load a selected material, texture, surface, or any other Maya node, click the Reload Left or Reload Right button.

To make a connection, select an attribute on the left and an attribute on the right. After a connection is made, the names of the attributes become italicized. A number of attributes are grouped into sets of three, as represented by the plus sign (see Figure 6.9). This grouping is a type of vector. (See Chapter 8, "Harnessing the Power of Math Utilities," for a discussion of vectors.) It occurs most commonly with the Color attribute, which is composed of Red, Green, and Blue channels, but it also applies to color-driven attributes such as Transparency and Incandescence. You can reveal the individual channels of any given vector attribute by clicking the + plus sign.

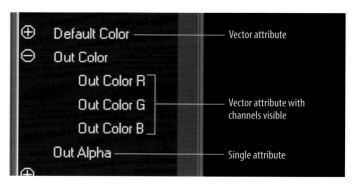

Figure 6.9 Vector attributes and a single attribute in the Connection Editor

Other attributes, such as Translate or Normal Camera, represent a spatial vector with X, Y, and Z coordinates. Any vector attribute can be connected to any other vector attribute. However, a vector attribute cannot be connected to a single attribute. Nevertheless, a single attribute can be connected to any single channel of the vector (see Figure 6.10). If any attribute is dimmed out, it cannot be keyed and is thereby off-limits for a custom connection.

Color, the most common attribute, is predictably named Color on the input (downstream) side of a node. However, it is named Out Color on the output (upstream) side. Similarly, there are Out Glow Color, Out Alpha, and Out Transparency attributes. See the next section for a discussion of Out Alpha and Out Transparency.

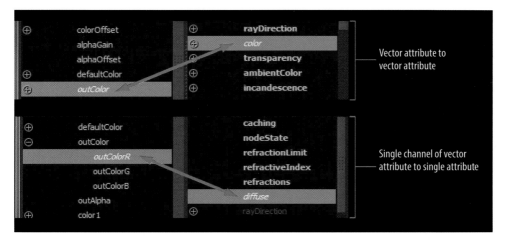

Figure 6.10 Vector and single attribute connections

A Note on Alpha and Transparency

An alpha channel carries opacity information and determines whether a pixel is transparent, semitransparent, or opaque. The opacity information is used by compositing programs, such as Adobe After Effects or The Foundry Nuke, to determine how multiple layers are combined.

You can render images with an alpha channel in Maya. The empty space is converted to transparent alpha, whereas geometry assigned to an opaque material is assigned opaque alpha. Many (but not all) image formats support alpha channels. The supporting formats include Maya IFF, OpenEXR, PNG, RLA, Targa, TIFF, and PSD. Rendering with alpha is discussed in more detail in Chapter 10, "Prepping for Successful Renders."

Additionally, you can use alpha channels as part of the texturing process. In fact, as illustrated in Figure 6.11 you can use a bitmap with an alpha channel to define the transparency of a material. To do so, load a bitmap with an alpha channel into a File texture, and connect the Out Transparency attribute of the File texture to the Transparency attribute of a material. If you are using Maya 2015, you can simply MMB-drag a File node and drop it on top of a material node and choose Default from the Connect Input Of menu. Maya detects the color channels and alpha channel of the bitmap loaded into the File texture and makes two connections: Out Color to Color and Out Transparency to Transparency.

The Out Alpha attribute, on the other hand, is used commonly as a grayscale version of a texture. A Bump 2d node, for example, connects Out Alpha to its own Bump Value attribute by default. (See Chapter 9, "Improving Textures through Custom UVs and Maps," for a discussion of bump mapping.) Out Alpha and similar single-channel attributes are sometimes referred to as *scalar*, meaning that they possess only magnitude.

Figure 6.11 The alpha channel of a TIFF bitmap provides transparency to the material. As a result, a logo is cut out of a plane. This example is included with the Chapter 6 tutorial files as `transparency.ma`.

Organizing Nodes and Networks

Shading networks can become complex in the Hypershade and Node Editor window. Hence, they are often difficult to work with unless you take steps to organize all the various nodes.

Filling Bins in the Hypershade

Hypershade *bins* are containers for nodes; the contents of only one bin can be seen in the tab area at any given time. By default, there is one Master Bin. To create a new bin, click the Create Empty Bin button (the leftmost button above the Master Bin—see Figure 6.12). To assign a node to a bin, MMB-drag-and-drop the node from the tab area onto the bin icon. You can also select the node, RMB-click over the bin icon, and choose Add Selected from the menu. You can remove a node from a bin by choosing Remove Selected from the same menu. If necessary, a node can be assigned to multiple bins. (The entire shading network that is connected to a node will be added to any bins that the node has been assigned to.) By default, all nodes belong to the Master Bin. To see the contents of a bin in the right-hand node tabs, click the bin name. You can assign any node, including lights and utilities, to a bin.

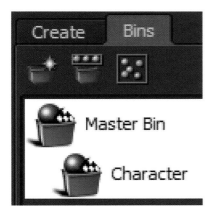

Figure 6.12 The Bins tab of the Hypershade window. A custom bin, named *Character*, sits below the Master Bin.

Creating Containers in the Hypershade and Node Editor

Containers are specialized node groupings. A container is represented by a thick, rounded edge in the Hypershade (see Figure 6.13). In the Node Editor, the container is simply given the name container*n*.

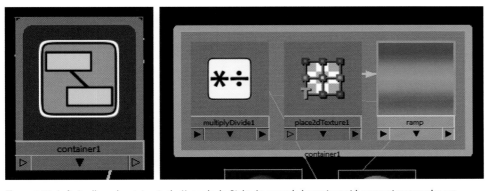

Figure 6.13 Left: A collapsed container in the Hypershade; Right: An expanded container with connections to nodes not included in the container.

For texturing, you can use containers as a method of organization. For example, you can select all the nodes that make up a shading network and convert them to a container using the Hypershade. Follow these steps:

1. Select the shading network nodes in the work area.

2. RMB-click one of the nodes and choose Create Asset From Selected. The nodes are collapsed into a single container.

3. To view the original nodes, double-click the container edge. To hide the original nodes in the Hypershade, double-click the edge again.

If only a portion of a network is converted to a container, connections run from the nodes within the container to nodes outside the container. If you move the nodes that belong to a container while the container is expanded, the container automatically resizes itself. You can rename a container by opening it in the Attribute Editor tab and changing the name in the Container field. To remove selected nodes from a container, RMB-click a selected node and choose Remove Selected Nodes From Asset.

To create a container in the Node Editor, follow these steps:

1. Select the shading network nodes.

2. RMB-click one of the nodes and choose Create Asset From Viewport Selection. The editor creates a new container node; however, it does not hide the original nodes. Nevertheless, you can hide the original nodes by selecting them and clicking the Remove Selected Nodes From Graph button.

If only a portion of a network is converted to a container, connections run from the nodes within the container to nodes outside the container. However, these are initially hidden. You can display them by selecting the container and clicking the Input And Output Connections button. If you want to display nodes that are part of the container group, it's easiest to double-click the container edge within the Hypershade work area.

Shifting Colors

A number of utility nodes in Maya are designed to shift colors. These utilities can convert color spaces, remap color ranges, adjust brightness and contrast, and even read the luminance of a surface within a scene. You can find utility nodes in the Maya > Utilities section of the Create > Maya tab in the Hypershade, Create Render Node, or Create Node window.

> ### Examining Shading Networks
>
> The figures throughout the remainder of this chapter use the Node Editor to display shading networks. Feel free to use either the Node Editor or the Hypershade to examine the downloaded project files.
>
> Some of the project files contain shading networks but no geometry or lights. To examine the shading networks, follow these steps:
>
> 1. Open the Hypershade and the Node Editor windows. Position them side by side.
>
> 2. In the Materials tab of the Hypershade, RMB-click over the material of interest and choose Graph Network from the marking menu. This displays the shading network attached to the material in the work area.
>
> 3. If you'd like to examine the network in the Node Editor, select all the nodes of the network in the Hypershade work area and MMB-drag them into the Node Editor. Alternatively, you can click the Add Selected Nodes To Graph button in the Node Editor.

Converting RGB to HSV

The Rgb To Hsv utility converts an RGB Red/Green/Blue vector into a HSV Hue/Saturation/Value vector. The Hsv To Rgb utility does the opposite.

In Maya, Red, Green, and Blue channels have a numeric range of 0 to 1.0. In HSV color space, Hue corresponds to a pure color and has a range of 0 to 360. Saturation, which represents the amount of white mixed into a color, has a range of 0 to 1.0. Value, which represents the amount of black mixed into a color, also has a range of 0 to 1.0.

If you are working with a color swatch attached to an attribute, you can display the color values in an 8-bit, 0-to-255 range by clicking the color swatch to open the Color Chooser window and changing the color space menu, at the lower right, to RGB, 0 To 255. You can display color values in HSV color space by changing the color space menu to HSV.

The Rgb To Hsv and Hsv To Rgb utilities allow calculations to stay in HSV color space. In addition, the Hsv To Rgb utility can serve as a color "dial." For example, in Figure 6.14 a bitmap is tinted different colors as the timeline plays forward.

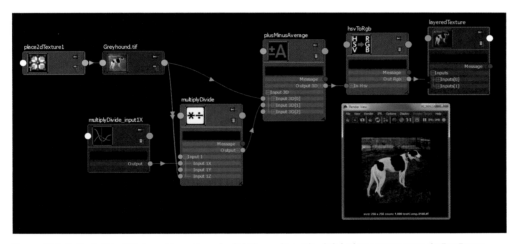

Figure 6.14 An Hsv To Rgb utility is used to create a color dial. The resulting color shift for frame 100 is seen in the Test Texture render located at the bottom right of the figure. This scene is included with the Chapter 6 tutorial files as `hsvtorgb.ma`.

The Hsv To Rgb node provides three input channels for hue, saturation, and value: In Hsv R, In Hsv G, and In Hsv B. These are vector channels carried by the In Hsv attribute. The Hsv To Rgb node provides three output channels for red, green, and blue: Out Rgb R, Out Rgb B, and Out Rgb G. The Rgb To Hsv node swaps the input and output channels so that RGB is on the input side and HSV is on the output side. In the network shown in Figure 6.14, a multiplyDivide node serves as a color dial controller. The multiplyDivide node's Input 1X attribute determines the outgoing hue. Input 1X is animated with keyframes so that the value changes from 0 to 359. This creates a complete clockwise revolution of the HSV color wheel (which is a counterclockwise spin on the RGB color wheel). The plusMinusAverage node averages the hue value provided by the multiplyDivide node and the Out Color R channel value of the `Greyhound.tif` bitmap texture (which is loaded into a File texture node that is labeled with the bitmap name). In this way, the final texture is not washed out or completely overtaken by the new hue value. The Out Alpha of the File node determines the saturation of the final texture as it is connected to the Input 1Y of the multiplyDivide node. The Out Alpha also determines the value (brightness) of the final texture as it is connected to the Input 1Z of the multiplyDivide node.

You can trace the HSV values from the multipleDivide node through the plus-MinusAverage node to the hsvToRgb node by looking at the input channel positions. For example, the hue value is established by the multiplyDivide node's Input 1X. Input 1X is in the first position of the vector attribute (it's the first listed channel). This value is passed to the plusMinusAverage node's first sub-channel input attached to Input 3D[1] (which is labeled Input 3Dx). Finally, the value is sent to the hsvToRgb node's In Hsv R channel.

Converting RGB to Luminance

The Luminance utility converts RGB values into luminous values. In Maya, a luminous value signifies the apparent brightness of a color as seen by the human eye. The Luminance utility's Out Value attribute outputs a scalar (single-channel) version of the Value input. For example, in Figure 6.15 the Out Color of a File texture node is connected to the Value of a luminance node.

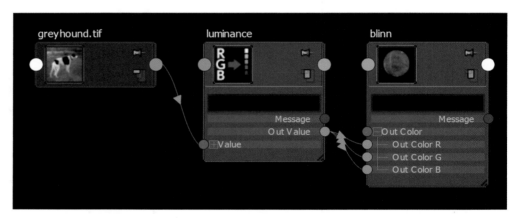

Figure 6.15 The Luminance utility converts RGB values into luminous values that are represented as grayscale shades. This material is included with the Chapter 6 tutorial files as `luminance.ma`.

The Out Value of the luminance node is connected to the Color R, Color G, and Color B of a blinn material node. The result is a grayscale version of the original bitmap. The Out Value attribute varies from the common Out Alpha attribute in that it biases the green channel. Colors are not perceived equally by the human brain; hence, the Luminance utility uses the following formula:

```
Out Color = (0.3 × Red) + (0.59 × Green) + (0.11 × Blue)
```

Blending Colors and Other Values

The Blend Colors utility blends two colors or textures together using a third color or texture as a control. The Blend Colors formula is as follows:

```
Out Color = (Color1 × Blender) + (Color2 × (1 - Blender))
```

If the Blender attribute is 1.0, Color 1 is the resulting output. If Blender is 0, Color 2 is the resulting output. If Blender is 0.5, an equal percentage of Color 1 and Color 2 are added.

In Figure 6.16, the Blend Colors utility is used to create a logo stenciled onto a wall. logo_mask.tif is loaded as a File texture. The Out Alpha of the File node is connected to the Blender of a blendColors node. wall.tif is brought in as a second File texture. The Out Color of the second File node is connected to Color 1 of the blendColors node. logo_color.tif is brought in as a third File texture. The Out Color of the third File node is connected to Color 2 of the blendColors node. The Output of the blendColors node is finally connected to the Color of a blinn material node. The raggedness of the logo is generated by logo_mask.tif, which determines where Color 1 and Color 2 are visible based on its values. (For a discussion on the Stencil utility, which can provide results similar to this example, see Chapter 8.)

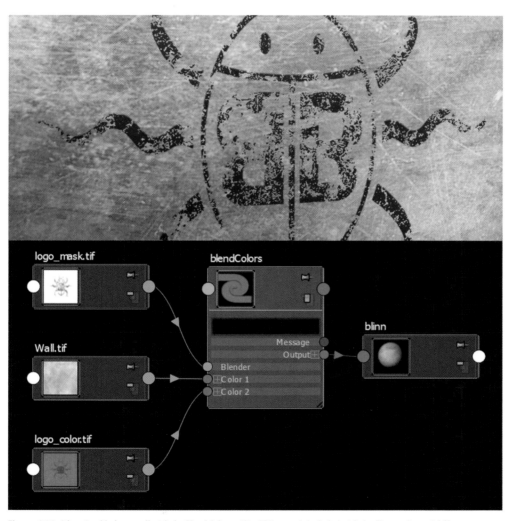

Figure 6.16 A logo is added to a wall with the Blend Colors utility. This scene is included with the Chapter 6 tutorial files as blend_colors.ma.

Remapping Color

The Remap Color utility allows the adjustment of a color attribute through the use of interactive ramp graph (also referred to as gradient). Technically speaking, a ramp graph is a graphic representation of the transition between two colors. The far-left side of a graph represents the output color value that will be given to the lowest values of the input color. The far-right side of the graph represents the output color value that will be given to the highest values of the input color. With the default upward slope, 0 is given 0, 0.5 is given 0.5, and 1.0 is given 1.0, and thus there is no change.

The simplest way to see the Remap Color utility functioning is to reverse the ramp graph slopes for the Color R, Color G, and Color B inputs (these are labeled Red, Green, and Blue in the Attribute Editor). In Figure 6.17, the Out Color of a grid texture node is connected to the Color of a remapColor node. The Out Color of the remapColor node is connected to the Color of a lambert material node. When the slope direction is reversed on each graph, the whites become black (RGB: 1.0, 1.0, 1.0 to 0, 0, 0) and the blacks become white (0, 0, 0 to 1.0, 1.0, 1.0).

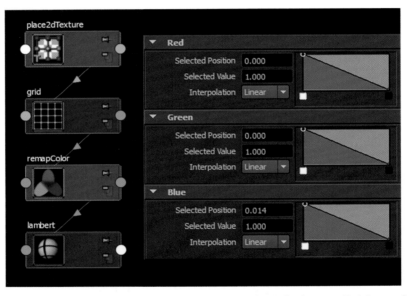

Figure 6.17 Left: A Grid texture is inverted with a Remap Color utility; Right: The inverted Red, Green, and Blue graphs. This material is included with the Chapter 6 tutorial files as `remap_invert.ma`.

In Figure 6.18, a Noise texture is used. The Red graph is reversed and given a plateau by inserting an additional handle. Any part of the Noise texture that has a red value of 0.5 or less receives the maximum amount of red. Any part of the Noise texture that has a red value greater than 0.5 receives less red, allowing the green and blue to triumph and thus produce a cyan color.

You can insert additional handles into any of the three ramp graphs by clicking in the dark gray area. You can move any handle up/down and left/right by LMB-dragging. Any handle can be deleted by clicking its X box. You can change the transition from handle to handle by switching the graph's Interpolation attribute from Linear to Smooth, Spline, or None.

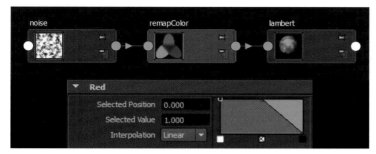

Figure 6.18 White is shifted to cyan with a Remap Color utility. This material is included with the Chapter 6 tutorial files as `remap_red.ma`.

Remapping HSV

The Remap Hsv utility works in the same fashion as the Remap Color utility. Instead of offering Red, Green, and Blue ramp graphs, however, it carries Hue, Saturation, and Value graphs. By separating Hue from Value, it's possible to isolate very narrow sections of a texture or material.

In Figure 6.19, the specular highlight of a Blinn material is given an artificial chromatic aberration. Optically, chromatic aberration is the inability of a lens to focus various color wavelengths on the same focal plane. This artifact often appears in both traditional and digital color photography and is referred to as "purple fringing."

Figure 6.19 Top: The specular highlight of a Blinn is given an artificial chromatic aberration, seen as a purple fringe, with a Remap Hsv utility; Bottom: The highlight seen on an assigned sphere. This scene is included with the Chapter 6 tutorial files as `remap_hsv.ma`.

To achieve the purple fringe on the highlight, the Out Color of a blinn material node, named blinnBase, is connected to the Color of a remapHsv node. The Out Color of remapHsv is connected to the Specular Color of a second blinn material node named blinnHighlight. The blinnHighlight is given 100% Transparency, causing the specular highlight to show up by itself. The Out Color of blinnHighlight is connected to the Color of a remapColor node. The Out Color of remapColor is connected to the Inputs[1] Color of a layeredShader material node. The Out Color of blinnBase is connected to the Inputs[0] Color of the layeredShader node. Thus, the diffuse color and default specular highlight of blinnBase is combined with the isolated purplish, specular highlight created by the remapHsv, blinnHighlight, and remapColor nodes.

By adjusting the remapHsv Value graph, we keep a narrow sliver of the blinnBase specular highlight, creating a ring-like shape (see Figure 6.20). This is visible on the icon of blinnHighlight. The remapColor node tints the pulled highlight a purplish color.

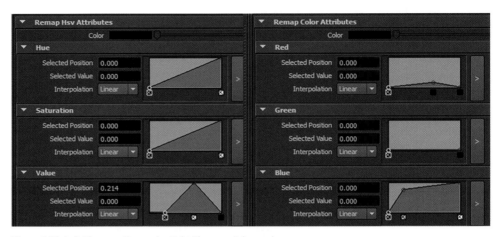

Figure 6.20 Left: The remapHsv graphs; Right: The remapColor graphs.

Remapping Value

Although the Remap Value utility controls color through two ramp graphs, its basic functionality is different from those of the Remap Color and Remap Hsv utilities. Remap Value provides a single-channel Value graph that can be used by itself.

As shown in Figure 6.21, the Remap Value utility also provides a Color ramp graph. This ramp functions in a manner similiar to the ramp of a Ramp texture. The ramp is controlled by the Input Value attribute—that is, if a texture mapped to the Input Value attribute provides the color black, the left side of the Color ramp is sampled. If a texture mapped to the Input Value attribute provides the color white, the right side of the Color ramp is sampled. Hence, the Remap Value utility supports an additional method of blending two sources together.

For example, in Figure 6.22, maya.tif is brought in as a File texture. The Out Color of the File texture node is connected to Color[0] Color _Color of a remapValue node. This connection attaches the File node to a handle within the Color ramp (see Figure 6.22). The Out Color of a crater texture node is connected to Color[1] Color _Color of the remapValue node. This connection attaches the crater node to a second Color ramp handle. The handles are arranged so that the File node handle is at the far right of the ramp and the crater node handle is at the far left. The Out Alpha of a fractal texture node is connected to Input Value of the remapValue node. Thus, the fractal node becomes a controller for the Color ramp. Black spots within the fractal cause the remapValue node to select color from the crater node. White spots within the fractal cause the remapValue node to select color from the File node. Gray spots cause the remapValue node to average the File and crater together to determine a color. The Out Color of the remapValue node is finally connected to the Color of the lambert material node, which in turn is assigned to a plane. In the end, the lambert node color is a mixture of the crater and `maya.tif` based on the pattern provided by the fractal.

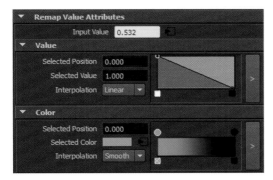

Figure 6.21: Adjusted Value ramp graph and Color ramp of the Remap Value utility. Note that the first handle of the Color ramp and the Input Value attribute show that they are mapped with the right-facing upstream arrows.

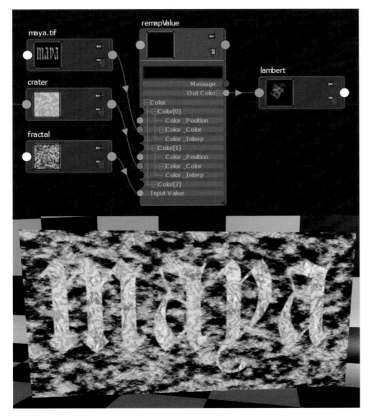

Figure 6.22 Two textures are blended together with a Remap Value utility. This scene is included with the Chapter 6 tutorial files as `remap_value.ma`.

Smearing Colors

The Smear utility allows one texture to be distorted by another. If Smear is combined with a Ramp texture, it creates a stylized vision effect that might be appropriate for an alien, a monster, or a robot.

In Figure 6.23 an image sequence is loaded into a File texture. The Use Image Sequence attribute is selected so that the images are automatically loaded as the time-line moves forward. This produces the expression1 node, which in turn is connected to the universal time1 node (see Figure 6.23). The Out Color of the File node is connected to the In Rgb of a smear node. The Out U of the smear node is connected to the Offset U of the place2dTexture node of a ramp texture node. The Out V of the smear node is also connected to the Offset V of the place2dTexture node of the ramp node. The Out Color of the ramp node is finally connected to the Out Color of a surfaceShader material node, which is assigned to a primitive plane. UV-based attributes, such as Out UV and Offset UV, carry two channels.

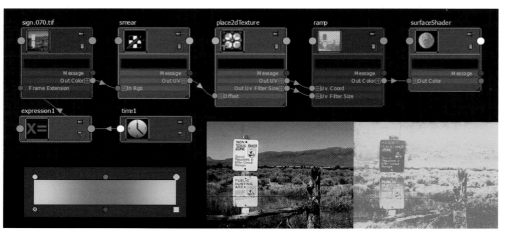

Figure 6.23 An image sequence and a Ramp texture are combined with the Smear utility. This scene is included with the Chapter 6 tutorial files as smear.ma. A QuickTime movie is included as smear.mov.

The ramp has three handles: one red and two orange. The higher the values are in the image sequence, the farther the smear node "pulls" the ramp to the left in the V direction. For example, if a bitmap provides a pixel with RGB values 0.5, 0.5, 0.5, the ramp is pulled left so that the right rests at the center of the ramp field. If a bitmap provides a pixel with RGB values 0.9, 0.9, 0.9, the ramp is pulled left so that the right rests one tenth of the distance from the left side of the ramp field. When the ramp is called upon by the surfaceShader material, every pixel of the ramp is offset in the V direction by a unique amount. Hence, the ramp appears as a colored version of the original video. Internally, the Smear utility converts the input RGB to HSV. New UV coordinates are generated by plotting values on an HSV color wheel.

Correcting Gamma and Adjusting Contrast

Gamma correction is the adjustment of an image to compensate for human sensitivity to darker value ranges. Without gamma correction, images may appear inappropriately dark or washed-out on a monitor. Operating systems apply gamma correction through color profiles. (The internal color profile management in Maya is discussed in Chapter 13, "Color Management, HDR Workflow, and Render Passes"; general color correction and monitor calibration is discussed in Chapter 1, "Understanding Lighting and Color.") The most common gamma correction is expressed as 2.2. Gamma correction is applied to the image with the following standard formula:

```
new pixel value = image pixel value ^ (1.0 / gamma value)
```

Thus, if an image pixel has a value of 0.5, 0.5, 0.5 and the gamma value is set to 2.2, the new pixel value, which is sent to the monitor, is roughly 0.73, 0.73, 0.73.

The Gamma Correct utility also applies the standard gamma formula to a specific input:

```
Out Value = Value ^ (1.0 / Gamma)
```

As such, the Gamma Correct utility adjusts the values of the Value input and outputs the result through the Out Value. As a general rule, the higher the Gamma attribute values are, the more washed out the mid-range values become. High- and low-range values (white whites and black blacks) are affected to a lesser degree. Hence, the Gamma Correct utility offers a means to adjust the distribution of tones of an input, such as a texture.

On the other hand, the Contrast utility does exactly what its name implies. The higher the Contrast attribute value of the Contrast utility, the whiter the whites and the blacker the blacks become. The lower the Contrast attribute value, the more the colors converge toward each other. The Bias attribute sets the midpoint of the contrast adjustment. Higher Bias values move the midpoint upward, which creates greater contrast and causes more of the input to become dark.

Clamping Values

The Clamp utility is designed to keep a value within a particular range. If a value is too low or too high, this utility "clamps" it. Table 6.1 shows what happens to Input R values if Min R is set to 0.3 and Max R is set to 1.0.

▷ **Table 6.1** Clamped output values resulting from different input values

inputR	0	0.2	0.8	1.1	4.5	9
outputR	0.3	0.3	0.8	1.0	1.0	1.0

In this example, if the Input R value is less than 0.3, the Output R value is 0.3. If Input R is greater than 1.0, Output R is 1.0. If Input R is between 0.3 and 1.0, Output R is the same value.

The Clamp utility has three inputs and three output channels (Input R, Input G, Input B, Output R, Output G, and Output B); you can connect single attributes or channels to any of these. Otherwise, you can connect vector attributes directly to Input or Output. In a similar fashion, Min and Max, which set the clamp range, are vector attributes that carry three channels each (Min R, Min G, Min B, Max R, Max G, and Max B). You can enter negative or positive values into the Min and Max fields.

A Note on Sliders and Superwhite

In Maya, many sliders that include numeric fields can readjust themselves. For example, a Diffuse attribute slider normally runs from 0 to 1.0. However, if you enter 2 in the field, the slider automatically readjusts itself to run between 0 and 4.

For the Diffuse attribute, higher values result in a predictably brighter surface. Other sliders, when pushed past their default range, do not display a perceptible change. Nevertheless, any value above 1.0 on the 0-to-1.0 scale is considered *superwhite*. The superwhite values are used in color calculations as is; however, any resulting superwhite values cannot be displayed on a standard 8-bit monitor.

Along these lines, any Maya color channel can exceed the standard bounds of 0 to 1.0. Although it's not possible to do this directly through the Attribute Editor, you can enter extra-high values into the fields of the Color Chooser window. To do so, follow these steps:

1. In an Attribute Editor tab, click the color swatch of an attribute. The Color Chooser window opens.

2. Choose either RGB or HSV from the color space drop-down menu. If you choose RGB, enter a value into the Red, Green, or Blue field. There is no practical limit to the size of the number you enter. If you choose HSV, enter a value into the Value field. Move your mouse away from the window to close it.

 Note: Maya supports high-dynamic range (HDR) image formats, which are able to store superwhite values. See Chapter 13 for details.

Chapter Tutorial: Creating a Custom Iridescent Material in the Node Editor

In this tutorial, you will create a custom material that emulates iridescence (see Figure 6.24). Iridescence is the property of a material that causes a surface to change colors based on the viewing angle. This is often the result of several semitransparent layers creating *thin-film interference*, where light is reflected back at slightly different wavelengths producing different hues. This effect is often seen in soap bubbles, sea shells, and insect wings. We'll use the Node Editor to create the shading network.

1. Create a new Maya scene. Choose Window > Node Editor.

2. In the editor, RMB-click and choose Create Node. The Create Node window opens. Click the Blinn icon twice to create two new Blinn materials. Click the Lambert icon once to create one new Lambert material. Close the Create Node window.

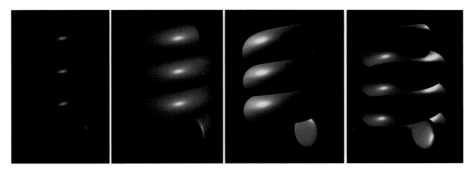

Figure 6.24 Four renders with a custom material that emulates iridescence. Note how the purple portion of the surface appears wherever the surface is bright but is not strictly centered under the specular highlight. The first two renders, counting from the left, use different light intensities. The third render uses a different light angle. The rightmost render uses two lights placed at new locations.

3. A new shading group node is attached to each material. These are named after the material and follow the naming convention *materialNumber*SG. Shift-click the shading group nodes and click the Remove Selected Nodes From Graph button. The nodes are hidden but are not destroyed. (If the material nodes become hidden, you can LMB+drag them from the Hypershade back into the Node Editor.)

4. RMB-click and choose Create Node once again. In the Create Node window, switch to the Maya > Utilities section in the Create tab. Click on the Blend Colors icon and the Remap Colors icon once. Close the window.

5. Rename the first Blinn material **Orange**. You can rename a node in the Node Editor by double-clicking the node name above the box icon and typing the new name. Rename the Lambert material **Green**. Rename the second Blinn material **Combined**. Shift-click all the nodes and click the Show Primary Attributes button. This expands the node boxes and reveals the various input and outputs you can use to connect the nodes. Arrange the nodes side by side, using Figure 6.25 as a guide.

6. LMB-click the Out Color output dot of the Orange material and drag the connection line to the Color 1 input dot of the blendColors node. When you release the mouse button, the connection is made.

7. LMB-click the Out Color output dot on the Green material and drag the connection line to the Color input dot of the remapColor node. LMB-click the Out Color output dot of the remapColor node and drag the connection line to the Color 2 input dot of the blendColors node. LMB-click the Output dot of the blendColors node and drag the connection line to the Color input dot of the Combined material node.

8. The connections for the shading network are complete. To simplify the view, select all the nodes and click the Show Connected Attributes button. This hides all the unconnected inputs and outputs. Feel free to rearrange the nodes to make them easier to read (see Figure 6.26).

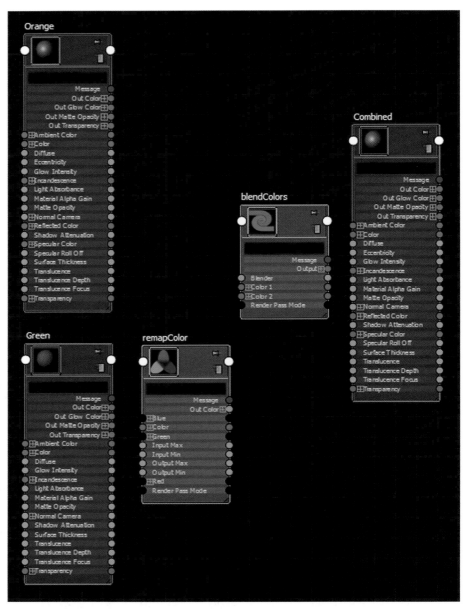

Figure 6.25 Three materials, a Blend Color utility, and a Remap Color utility are added to the scene. The primary attributes of each are displayed.

9. At this point, the Green and Orange materials are blended together by the blendColors node. The result is mapped to the Color of the Combined material. Because we are blending materials, and not textures, the net shading model from each material is used. This takes into account basic material shading formulas. This is one method of creating a material whose colors are dependent on the angles between the scene lights and the assigned surface (and not simply the brightness). Although this is not strictly a view-dependent situation, it does emulate a surface whose colors are dependent on the surroundings and are not

fixed. Nevertheless, to make the Combined material interesting, we need to adjust the Orange and Green materials so they are not default gray.

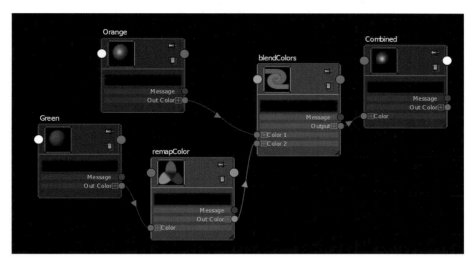

Figure 6.26 The connected nodes

10. Open the Green material in the Attribute Editor by double-clicking its icon. Change the Ambient Color to a medium green. Normally, a high Ambient Color would wash out the material. Nevertheless, because we're blending this material with another and running it through a remapColor node, we can apply high values. Using the Ambient Color attribute will give the final materials a flat, greenish sheen along partially lit areas.

11. Open the Orange material in the Attribute Editor. Change Color to a medium red. Change Eccentricity to 0.3, Specular Roll Off to 1.0, and Specular Color to orange. This creates a red-orange material with a medium-sized specular highlight.

12. Open the Combined material in the Attribute Editor. Change the Eccentricity to 0.1, Specular Roll Off to 0.7, and Specular Color to yellow. This places a smaller, more intense specular highlight over the more diffuse highlight generated by the Orange material.

13. Open the blendColors node in the Attribute Editor. Experiment with the Blender value. Note how the two materials mix together. The colors are not simply averaged. Instead, the resulting colors are based on the surface lighting, as seen in the thumbnail for the combined material. The final version of this tutorial uses a Blender value of 0.5, which gives each material equal weight.

14. Open the remapColor node in the Attribute Editor. Insert a new point into the center of the Green ramp graph. Adjust the graph to form a pyramid shape (see Figure 6.27). The center of the Combined material shifts toward purple. Experiment with different graph shapes. The Remap Color utility offers an interactive way to shift colors.

Figure 6.27 The adjusted Green ramp graph of the remapColor node

15. Create a primitive piece of geometry or import a pre-existing model. Assign the Combined material to the geometry by selecting it, RMB-clicking over the Combined node, and choosing Assign Material To Viewport Selection. Create a new directional light. Test render. Rotate the light and re-render. Note how the colors are dependent on the lighting. Adjust the light Intensity. The brighter the surface, the more intense the purplish core becomes (see Figure 6.24 at the beginning of this section). The darker the surface, the greener the surface becomes. Although you can tint the specular highlight of a standard Blinn material, it cannot create the same degree of change in the surface color as the light changes. Feel free to add additional lights and create additional test renders.

16. The custom material is complete! Your renders should look similar to Figure 6.24. View the shading network in the Hypershade as a comparison to the Node Editor layout (see Figure 6.28). If you get stuck, a finished version of the material is saved as `iridescence.ma` with the Chapter 6 tutorial files.

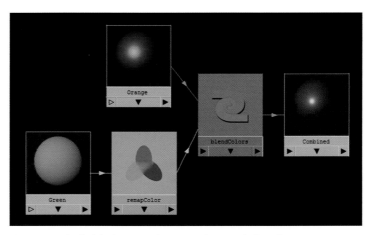

Figure 6.28 The final shading network, as seen in the Hypershade work area

Automating a Scene with Sampler Nodes

Sampler utilities automate a render. They can evaluate every surface point for every frame and return unique values that other nodes can use. The values may indicate the relationship of surface normals to lights or cameras, or they may include transformation matrices that store object position, rotation, and scale. At the same time, the Autodesk® Maya® program lets you connect cameras, lights, and geometry to materials and textures for unique shading networks.

7

Chapter Contents
Review of the Ramp Shader material and coordinate spaces
Practical applications of sampler utilities
Review of software-rendered particles
Connecting materials to nonmaterial nodes

Coordinate Spaces and DAG Hierarchies

Creating custom shading networks often requires the use of different coordinate spaces, as well as specific portions of Maya DAG (Directed Acyclic Graph) hierarchies such as shape and transform nodes. The next two sections review these elements.

Common Coordinate Spaces

3D programs such as Maya employ a number of coordinate spaces. The term *coordinate space* signifies a system that uses coordinates to establish a position. When applying materials and textures or creating custom shading networks, you'll encounter the following types of space:

Object Space A polygon surface is defined by the position of its vertices relative to its center. By default, the center is at 0, 0, 0 in object space (sometimes called *model space*). A NURBS spline has its origin point at 0, 0, 0 in object space. The axes of a surface in object space are rotated with the surface.

UV Texture Space To determine the color of a particular pixel when rendering a surface assigned to a material that uses a texture map, the renderer maps the XY values of the texture to the surface's UV texture space. Unique UV values are carried by each surface vertex (assuming the UV texture space is properly prepared). Hence, each pixel in the texture map is associated with a unique UV coordinate and a unique surface location. UV texture space is examined in more detail in Chapter 9, "Improving Textures through Custom UVs and Maps."

World Space World space represents the virtual "world" in which the animator manipulates objects. A surface is moved, rotated, and scaled in this space. To do this, the vertex positions defined in object space must be converted to positions in world space through a world matrix. A matrix is a table of values, generally laid out in rows and columns. (Matrices are explored further in Chapter 8, "Harnessing the Power of Math Utilities.")

Camera Space World space must be transformed into camera space (sometimes called *view space*) in order to appear as if it is viewed from a particular position. In the camera space in Maya, the camera is at 0, 0, 0 with an "up" vector of 0, 1.0, 0 (positive Y) while looking down the negative Z axis.

Screen Space Three-dimensional camera space must be "flattened" so that it can be seen in 2D screen space on a monitor.

Working with DAG Hierarchies

In Maya, cameras, lights, and surfaces are represented by two nodes: a transform node and a shape node. For example, *spotlight* is a transform node that carries all the light's transform information (Translate, Rotate, Scale), and *spotLightShape* is a shape node that possesses all the nontransform light attributes (Intensity, Cone Angle, and so on). As for geometry, *nurbsSphere* is the transform node, and *nurbsSphereShape* is the shape node.

Transform and shape nodes are also known as DAG objects. Directed Acyclic Graphing is a hierarchical system in which objects are defined relative to the transformations of their parent objects. *Acyclic* is a term from graphing theory that means the graph is not a closed loop. At the same time, Maya uses a dependency graph system, which simply supports a collection of nodes connected together. Technically, DAG objects are dependency graph nodes. However, not all dependency graph nodes are DAG objects, since dependency graph nodes can be cyclic and do not need the parent/child relationship.

Note: Every shape node must have one transform node as a parent. A transform node cannot have more than one shape node as a child, although it can have multiple transform nodes as children. A shape node is considered a "leaf level" node and cannot have any node as a child. To view the transform and shape nodes of an object, select the object and open the Node Editor or Hypergraph: Connections window. The transform node tab also appears to the left of the shape node tab in the Attribute Editor.

The worldMatrix[0] attribute, used in the example shading networks in this book, includes the [0] to indicate the index position within an array that stores the attribute. World Matrix is an "instanced attribute," meaning that it can be used at different positions within a DAG hierarchy. For examples of the World Matrix attribute, see Chapter 8.

Employing Samplers

The following utility nodes serve as scene samplers:

- Sampler Info
- Light Info
- Surface Info
- Curve Info
- Distance Between
- Angle Between
- Particle Sampler
- Surface Luminance

The utilities automatically sample object transforms, particle transforms, or surface and curve subcomponent information throughout the duration of an animation. You can find these nodes in the Maya > Utilities section of the Create tab of the Hypershade, Create Node, or Create Render Node window. Before I discuss the Sampler Info and Light Info utilities, however, a look at the Ramp Shader material and a review of coordinate space is warranted.

A Review of the Ramp Shader Material

The Ramp Shader material has a Color Input attribute that has Light Angle, Facing Angle, Brightness, and Normalized Brightness options (see Figure 7.1).

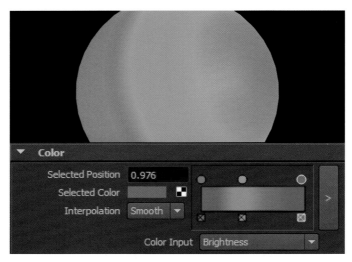

Figure 7.1 Bottom: The Selected Color ramp and Color Input attribute of a Ramp Shader material; Top: The resulting material assigned to a primitive sphere lit from screen right. To see a larger version of the ramp, click the large > button to the ramp's right. This scene is included with the Chapter 7 tutorial files as `ramp_shader.ma`.

The Color Input attribute allows the Ramp Shader to sample different points along the Selected Color ramp based on feedback from the environment. With Light Angle, the material compares the angle of the surface normal to the direction of the light. If the angle between the two is small, a high value is returned and the right side of the ramp is sampled. If the angle between the two is large, a small value is returned and the left side of the ramp is sampled. On a technical level, the surface normal vector and the light direction vector are put through a dot product calculation, producing the cosine of the angle between the two vectors. For a deeper discussion of vectors and vector math, see Chapter 8.

This technique is also used for the Facing Angle option, whereby the angle of the surface normal is compared to the camera (view) direction. The Brightness option, on the other hand, calculates the luminous intensity of a surface point. If the surface receives the maximum amount of light, the right side of the ramp is sampled. If the surface receives a moderate amount of light, the middle of the ramp is sampled. The ramp runs from 0 to 1.0 from left to right. The Light Angle, Facing Angle, and Brightness calculations are normalized to fit to that scale.

The disadvantage of the Ramp Shader is its inflexibility. Although you can change the colors of each ramp handle through its Selected Color swatch, the Facing Angle, Light Angle, and Brightness calculations cannot be fine-tuned. Sampler Info, Light Info, and Surface Luminance utilities solve this problem by functioning as separate nodes. The Sampler Info utility replaces the Facing Angle option. The Light Info utility replaces the Light Angle option. The Surface Luminance utility replaces the Brightness option. Although the Normalized Brightness option normalizes all the light intensities in the scene, its basic function is identical to Brightness and can be replicated with the Surface Luminance utility in a custom shading network. Most important, the Sampler Info, Light Info, and Surface Luminance utilities provide a wide array of supplementary attributes.

Using Sampler Info

Many surfaces, including clear-coat car paints, produce Fresnel reflections (see Chapter 4, "Applying the Correct Material and 2D Texture"). In this situation, the intensity of a reflection or specular highlight varies with the angle of view. To create this effect, you can use the Facing Ratio attribute of a Sampler Info utility. For example, in Figure 7.2 a polygon car is lit with default lighting. The persp camera's Background Color attribute is set to a light blue. Raytracing is selected in the Render Settings window so that the background color is picked up as a reflection. The car body is assigned to a Blinn material named CarPaint. CarPaint's Color is set to black. CarPaint's Diffuse and Eccentricity are set to 0. Reflectivity is set to 0.3. Specular Roll Off is increased to an artificially high value of 5. These settings leave the paint a deep black with highlights derived solely from reflections.

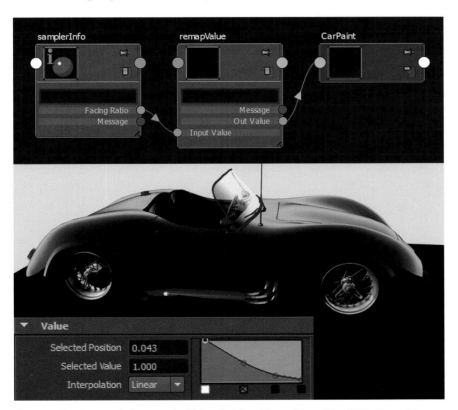

Figure 7.2 Top: A custom shading network with Sampler Info and Remap Color utilities; Middle: The resulting reflection changes intensity over a surface of a car model; Bottom: The reversed and sloped Value gradient of the remapValue node. A simplified version of this scene is included with the Chapter 7 tutorial files as paint.ma.

As for the custom shading network, the Facing Ratio of the samplerInfo node is connected to the Input Value of a remapValue node. The Out Value of the remapValue node is connected to the Specular Color R, Specular Color G, and Specular Color B of the CarPaint node. If a surface point faces away from the camera (such as one on the top of the hood), it receives a low Facing Ratio value. This low value is increased, however, by the reversed Value ramp slope of the remapValue node. Conversely, if the Facing Ratio value is high (from the door or fender), the ramp lowers it. Thus, the top of the hood receives the most reflection and the doors and fenders receive the least. Additional handles are inserted into the Value ramp in order to increase the rapidity of the reflection falloff. The handles are all set to Spline to give the ramp a smooth shape. With this network, the Color ramp of the remapValue node is not used. The shading network works equally well with the Maya Software or mental ray® renderer.

Using Light Info

The Light Info utility retrieves directional and positional information from a light connected to it. The utility can function like the Light Angle option of the Ramp Shader material, but it's more flexible. Two examples of the utility's use follow.

Creating Falloff for Directional and Ambient Lights

Directional and ambient lights do not decay naturally, nor do they possess a Decay Rate attribute. However, you can employ a Light Info, Reverse, and Set Range utility to overcome this. For example, in Figure 7.3 a directional light has an extremely short throw despite its proximity to a nearby primitive plane.

For this to work, the World Matrix[0] of the light's transform node is connected to the World Matrix of a lightInfo node. The Sample Distance of the lightInfo node is connected to the Input X of a reverse node. The Sample Distance attribute returns a value that represents the distance from the connected light to the surface point being rendered. A Reverse utility inverts the input with the following formula: Output = 1 − Input. Hence, at this stage of the network, the distance value is turned into a negative range of values, such as −3 to 0.

The Output X of the reverse node is connected to the Value X of a setRange node, which has the following settings:

Min = 0

Max = 10

Old Min = −5

Old Max = 0

Old Min and Old Max set the range of values accepted by the node. Values outside this range are ignored and are essentially converted to 0. Surviving values are remapped to the Min and Max range. The Out Value X of the setRange node is connected to the Intensity of the directionalLightShape node. Hence, the light Intensity falls between 0 and 10 within the distance range of −5 to 0 (5 units from the light). To extend the light's throw, change the Old Min value to a larger negative number, such as −10. To raise the light intensity where the light is permitted to illuminate, raise the Max value. This network functions equally well for ambient lights; in such a case, the falloff becomes radial.

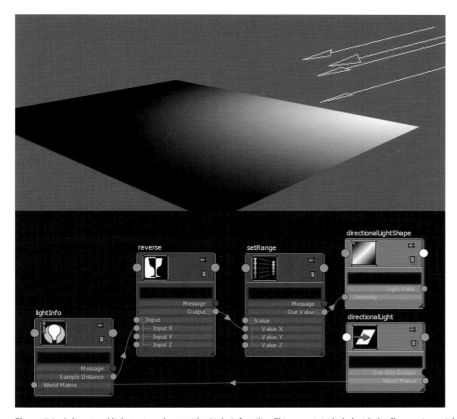

Figure 7.3 A directional light is given decay with a Light Info utility. This scene is included with the Chapter 4 tutorial files as `directional_decay.ma`. Notice that there is no connection line between the light's transform node and shape node.

For more information on the Reverse and Set Range utilities, see Chapter 8. For instructions on connecting nonmaterial nodes to shading networks, see the section "Tying Into Nonmaterial Nodes" later in this chapter.

> **Note:** You can give a Maya light a negative Intensity value, such as –1.0. This causes the light to negate other lights in the scene. Wherever the negative light strikes an object, it reduces the net effect of other lights in proportion to its Intensity. That said, this does not happen if the light is connected to a shading network similar to the one described in this section. Instead, the negative Intensity value is clamped to 0.

Deriving Color from a Spatial Vector

In a second example of the Light Info utility, a camera is connected in order to retrieve world space directional information. This information is then used to control the color of an "in camera" display.

For example, in Figure 7.4, the World Matrix[0] of the default camera's persp-Shape node is connected to the World Matrix of a lightInfo node. The camera's World Matrix[0] is also connected to the matrix of a vectorProduct node. The Light Direction of the lightInfo node is connected to the Input 1 of the vectorProduct node as well.

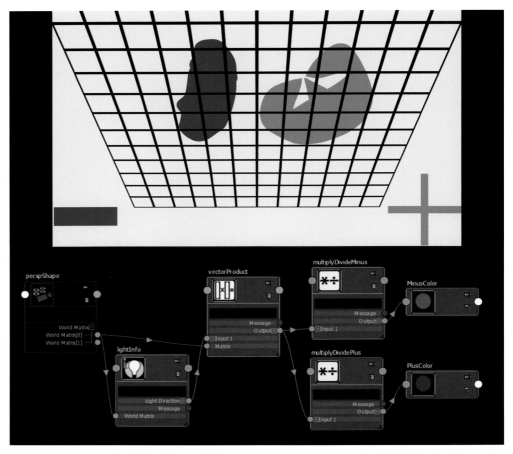

Figure 7.4 An "in camera" display that indicates which direction a camera is pointing is created with a Light Info utility. This scene is included with the Chapter 7 tutorial files as `camera_display.ma`. A QuickTime movie is included as `camera_display.mov`.

The Vector Product utility is designed to perform mathematical operations on two vectors. A vector is the quantity of an attribute that has direction as well as magnitude. (See Chapter 8 for information on vectors.) In addition, it can multiply a vector by a matrix. This function allows the Vector Product utility to convert a vector in one coordinate space to a second coordinate space. With this scene, the vectorProduct node's Operation attribute is set to Vector Matrix Product, which undertakes this task. Because the World Matrix[0] of the camera is used as the input matrix, the output of the vectorProduct node is the camera direction vector in world space. The output vector runs between –1.0, –1.0, –1.0 and 1.0, 1.0, 1.0 in X, Y, and Z.

Note: If Light Direction is connected directly to either multiplyDivide node, the network will not function. Instead, the minus sign will remain blue regardless of camera rotation. This indicates that the lightInfo node outputs a camera-space 0, 0, 1.0 vector, which means the camera lens is pointing down the negative Z axis with no rotation in X or Y.

The output of the vectorProduct node is connected to the Input 1 attributes of two multiplyDivide utility nodes, named *multiplyDividePlus* and *multiplyDivideMinus*. Both nodes have their Operation set to Multiply. The multiplyDividePlus node has its Input 2 set to –1.0, –1.0, –1.0, guaranteeing that it produces a negative value. The multiplyDivideMinus node has its Input2 left at 1.0, 1.0, 1.0. Last, the output of each multiplyDivide node is connected to the Out Color of two different surface shader material nodes. The PlusColor material is assigned to a plus sign created as a text primitive. The MinusColor material is assigned to a minus sign. Both signs are placed near the bottom of the camera and parented to the camera itself. As the camera is rotated, the colors of the symbols change in correspondence to the direction the camera points. (If the colors are not visible with Hardware Texturing selected, you will have to render a test frame.) As with the axis display found in the viewport views, red corresponds to X, green corresponds to Y, and blue corresponds to Z.

Hence, if the camera points in the positive X direction, the plus sign becomes red. If the camera points in the negative X direction, the minus sign becomes red. Table 7.1 reveals what happens mathematically when the camera is given other rotations.

Table 7.1 Colors resulting from different camera rotations

Camera rotation	vectorProduct output	MinusColor RGB (output × 1.0, 1.0, 1.0)	PlusColor RGB (output × –1.0, –1.0, –1.0)
0, 0, 0 (default state with lens pointing toward negative Z)	0, 0, 1.0	0, 0, 1.0 (bright blue)	0, 0, 0 (black)
45, –45, 0 (lens pointing toward positive X and positive Y)	–0.5, –0.7, 0.5	0, 0, 0.5 (blue)	0.5, 0.7, 0 (yellow-green)
–90, 0, 0 (lens pointing straight down in Y)	0, 1.0, 0	0, 1.0, 0 (bright green)	0, 0, 0 (black)

Any RGB value less than 0 is clamped to 0 by the renderer (negative color values are rendered black). You can use this coloring technique on any object (as can be seen by the two primitive shapes in the camera's view). In addition, you can connect any object that possesses a World Matrix attribute—such as a camera, light, or NURBS surface—to the Light Info and Vector Product utilities so that its direction can be derived in this fashion.

Texturing Particles with the Particle Sampler Utility

The Particle Sampler utility has the unique ability to graft a UV texture space onto a particle mass. Before I suggest specific applications, however, let's take a quick look at particle texturing.

Particle Refresher

With more recent versions of Maya, there are two particle systems: Dynamics particles and nDynamics nParticles. Although much of the functionality is shared by the two systems, nParticles derive their dynamic properties through the more advanced nDynamics system. Hence, this book's examples make use of nParticle simulations. Nevertheless, you can apply similar texturing techniques to Dynamics particles.

In Maya, particles and nParticles are either hardware- or software-rendered. This chapter focuses on software-rendered particles because they accept standard materials. The three software-rendered particle types are Blobby Surface, Cloud, and Tube. Their software-rendering capability is symbolized by the *(s/w)* beside the particle name in the Particle Render Type drop-down menu, which is found in the Render Attributes section (particles) or Shading section (nParticles) of the particle or nParticle shape node Attribute Editor tab (see Figure 7.5). Although Cloud particles are excellent for smoke, Blobby Surface particles can replicate a wide range of liquid and semi-liquid materials. You can render software particles and nParticles with Maya Software and mental ray renderers.

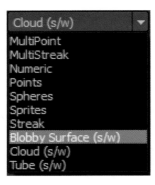

Figure 7.5 The Particle Render Type drop-down menu. The menu is identical for particle and nParticle nodes.

Assigning Materials to Particles

When you create a new particle node through the Dynamics system (by choosing, for example, Dynamics menu set > Particles > Create Emitter), the node is connected automatically to the default lambert1 surface material and the default particleCloud1 volumetric material through the default initialParticleSE shading group node. If you switch the Particle Render Type to Blobby Surface, the particles function as solid surfaces and pick up their surface quality from lambert1. Optionally, you can assign the Blobby Surface particle node to any standard material. If you switch Particle Render Type to Tube, the particle surface quality is picked up from the particleCloud1 material. If necessary, you can create new Particle Cloud materials through the Maya > Volumetric section of the Create tab of the Hypershade, Create Node, or Create Render Node window. By default, a new scene is given the particleCloud1 material.

If you switch Particle Render Type to Cloud, the particle surface quality is picked up from the particleCloud1 material. That said, you can "mix" the surface material and volumetric material together. The mix is controlled by the Surface Shading attribute, located in the Render Attributes section of the particle shape node Attribute Editor tab. If Surface Shading is set to 0, the network uses the volumetric material and ignores the surface material. If Surface Shading is set to 1.0, the network uses the surface material and ignores the volumetric material. In-between values mix the qualities of both materials. The volumetric Particle Cloud material distinguishes itself by creating a feathery-edged cloud of color in the center of each particle.

> **Note:** Whenever you change a particle, nParticle, or emitter attribute value, it's important to play back the simulation from the first frame of the timeline to see an accurate result. In addition, make sure that Playback Speed is set to Play Every Frame. You can find Playback Speed in the Time Slider section of the Preferences window (Window > Settings/Preferences > Preferences).

Assigning Materials to nParticles

When you create a new nParticle node (for example, by choosing nDynamics menu set > Create nParticles > Create Emitter), you have the option to apply one of five presets: Points, Balls, Cloud, Thick Cloud, or Water (Figure 7.6).

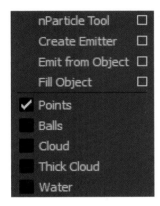

Figure 7.6 The nParticle presets list. You must select a preset before creating an nParticle node through one of the create options at the top of the Create nParticles menu.

Each of the presets creates a unique set of nParticle settings as well as unique material assignments. The resulting particle types, assigned surface materials, and assigned volumetric materials are listed in Table 7.2.

▷ **Table 7.2** nParticle presets

Preset	Particle render type	Assigned surface material	Assigned volumetric material
Points	Points	Blinn (npPointsBlinn)	Particle Cloud (npPointsVolume)
Balls	Blobby Surface	Blinn (npBallsBlinn)	Particle Cloud (npBallsVolume)
Cloud	Cloud	Blinn (npCloudBlinn)	Particle Cloud (npCloudVolume)
Thick Cloud	Cloud	Blinn (npThickCloudBlinn)	Fluid Shape (npThickCloudFluid)
Water	Blobby Surface	Blinn (npWaterBlinn)	Particle Cloud (npWaterVolume)

Much like Dynamics particles, Cloud nParticles allow you to mix the surface and volumetric material qualities by adjusting the Surface Shading attribute (located in the Shading section of the nParticle shape node's Attribute Editor tab). For information about texturing Cloud and Blobby Surface nParticles, see the next two sections.

The Thick Cloud preset is unlike the other presets in that it uses a fluid dynamics Fluid Shape node to give the nParticle a volumetric surface quality. The Thick Cloud preset is briefly discussed in the section "Working with the Thick Cloud Preset" later in this chapter.

Introduction to "Life" Attributes and the Particle Sampler Node

The Particle Cloud material provides "Life" attributes that can have different values over time based on the age of individual particles or nParticles.

If you create a Dynamics particle node, you are free to map Life Color, Life Transparency, or Life Incandescence. To do so, click one of the Life attribute's checkered map buttons. Although you can choose any texture, the attribute only uses an averaged pixel value in the V direction. Hence, a Ramp texture is commonly used for this purpose. With Maya 2015, the Ramp texture's graph runs left to right, with 0 in V located at the left and 1.0 in V located at the right. (Maya 2014 uses a vertical graph with 0 in V at the bottom.). The lifespan of a particle or nParticle is determined by the Lifespan Mode menu, found in the Lifespan Attributes and Lifespan sections of the particle or nParticle shape node (see Figure 7.7).

Figure 7.7 The drop-down menu of a nParticle shape node's Lifespan Mode attribute

The Lifespan Mode has four settings, which are described here:

Live Forever   Particles do not die. They are given values from the bottom of any Life texture.

Constant   Particles live n number of seconds, where n is set by the nearby Lifespan attribute. The particle transitions through the entire Life texture before dying.

Random Range   Each particle lives a random length based on the Lifespan Random attribute value. The following formula is used: Lifespan + or − (Lifespan Random / 2). For example, if Lifespan is 4 and Lifespan Random is 2, a particle may live between 3 and 5 seconds. The Life attributes use the mean (average) particle lifespan to assign values.

lifespanPP Only   This option uses an expression established by the Lifespan PP attribute in the Per Particle (Array) Attributes section of the particle or nParticle shape node. By default, there is no expression created for Lifespan PP for particles or nParticles. Thus, you are free to create your own. That said, nParticle Ball, Cloud, Thick Cloud, and Water presets create Radius PP, Opacity PP, and RGB PP expressions. For information on per-particle attributes, see Chapter 8.

If you create an nParticle node, the Life Color, Life Transparency, and Life Incandescence attributes of the assigned Particle Cloud node are premapped. In addition, the Color, Transparency, and Incandescence attributes of the assigned Blinn are converted to "Life" attributes by mapping them to a Particle Sampler node (named particleSamplerInfo*n*). See Figure 7.8 for a sample network. Notice that there is no connection line between the particleSamplerInfo1 and nParticleShape1 nodes. The nucleus1 node provides the scene with nDynamics simulation information. The time1 node provides all other nodes with timeline frame values.

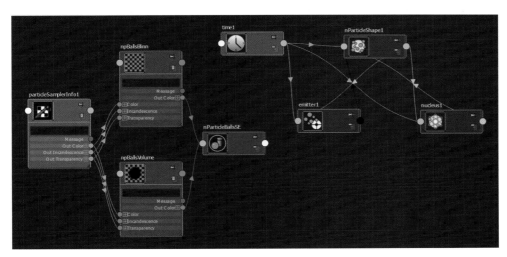

Figure 7.8 The shading network created for the Balls nParticle preset

Particle Sampler utility nodes serve as "go between" nodes by passing particle and nParticle information—such as world position, radius, and age—to material nodes assigned to the particle or nParticle shape node. (If you manually map a Life attribute for a Dynamics particle node, a Particle Sampler node is added automatically to the network.) nParticle shading networks differ from particle networks in that they do not require an additional texture, such as a Ramp. Instead, nParticle shape nodes carry their own, internal color ramps for this purpose. These ramps are included in the Shading > Opacity Scale, Color, and Incandescence subsections (see Figure 7.9).

The color ramps function in the same manner as ramps included by other texture nodes. However, the way in which nParticle qualities are associated with the ramps is controlled by the associated Input and Input Max attributes. The Input menu has the following options:

Constant   The far-right of the ramp (the 1.0 position) is used for all nParticles, regardless of age.

Age   The left of the ramp equates to nParticle birth and the right of the ramp equates to nParticle death.

Normalized Age   The age of an nParticle is mapped within the full lifespan age range, as determined by the attributes within the Lifespan section. The left of the ramp is used for a young nParticle, and the right of the ramp is used for an old nParticle.

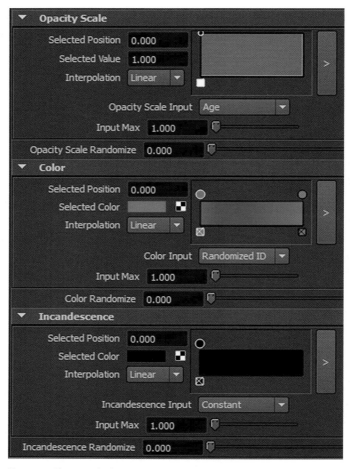

Figure 7.9 The internal color ramps of an nParticle shape node

Speed   Fast-moving nParticles are given values from the right of the ramp and slow-moving nParticles are given values from the left of the ramp.

Acceleration   The greater the change in nParticle speed over time, the greater the ramp position value. The ramp positions run from 0 on the left to the Max Input value on the right.

Particle ID   Uses the unique ID number of each nParticle to choose a ramp position. To see this option work, adjust the associated Input Max attribute. For example, with the default nParticles Balls preset, change the Color Input Max to 5 to see the nParticles transition from red to blue as more and more nParticles are born.

Randomized ID   Works like the Particle ID option but scrambles the results by randomizing ramp positions.

Radius   Attaches the ramp position to the nParticle radii. If the radii are not varied through the Radius Scale ramp, the right of the ramp is sampled. The Radius Scale ramp is located in the Particle Size > Radius Scale subsection of the nParticle shape node Attribute Editor tab. To vary the radii, alter the ramp curve so that it does not have a consistent value of 1.0. The way in which the ramp is associated with the radii is determined by its own Input menu. (The Radius Scale ramp values are multiplied against the Radius value in the Particle Size section.)

If you change any of the ramps or change the Input and Input Max values, be sure to return to the first frame of the timeline and play back before rendering to see an accurate result.

Texturing Blobby Surface Particles

When a Blobby Surface particle or nParticle node is assigned to a material that employs a texture, it picks up that texture. The texture is mapped to each particle or nParticle as if it's a sphere with pinched poles at the top and bottom. The texture appears even if the Threshold attribute is raised above 0 and the Blobby Surface particles begin to stick together, as is the case with the checkered nParticles in Figure 7.10. The Threshold attribute is located in the Render Attributes section (particles) or Shading section (nParticles) of the particle or nParticle shape node Attribute Editor tab. Threshold is designed to form more cohesive particle masses that can emulate water, mud, and so on.

Figure 7.10 One Blobby Surface nParticle node is assigned to a Phong material with a Checker texture. A second node is assigned to a Phong with an iris bitmap. This scene is included with the Chapter 7 tutorial files as `particle_eye.ma`.

Using the Particle Sampler Node in a Custom Network

You can manually add a Particle Sampler node to a network to graft new UV information onto a mass of particles or nParticles. For example, in Figure 7.11 the word "Maya" appears on an nParticle mass. The nParticle node is assigned to a Blinn material. The Blinn material's Color is mapped by a File texture (labeled *Maya.tif*). A bitmap with the word "Maya" is loaded into the bitmap. However, in place of the standard 2D Placement node, a Multiply Divide utility and a Particle Sampler node are connected to the File node (see Figure 7.11).

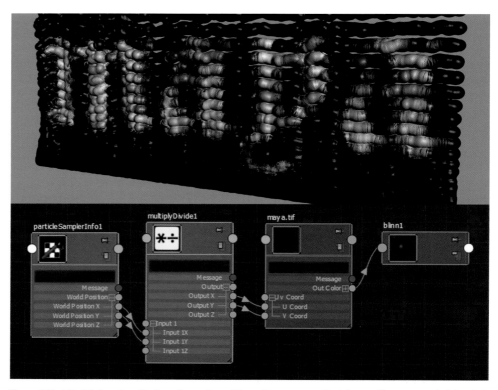

Figure 7.11 A Particle Sampler utility is used to graft new UV coordinates onto an nParticle mass. This scene is included with the Chapter 7 tutorial files as `particle_word.ma`.

The World Position X and World Position Y of the particleSampler1 node are connected to the Input 1X and Input 1Y of the multiplyDivide1 node. The multiplyDivide1 node's Operation is set to Multiply. The Input 2X is set to 0.095 and Input 2Y is set to 0.25. These values are multiplied by each nParticle's current position X, Y for the current frame. The results are kept between 0 and 1.0 to maintain a valid UV position. For example, if an nParticle has an X, Y world position of 2, 3 for frame 1, the multiplyDivide node outputs 0.19, 0.75 (2×0.095, 3×0.25). The Input 2X and Input 2Y values were derived by dividing 1.0 by the world width and world height of the nParticle mass.

The Output X of the multiplyDivide1 node is connected to the U Coord of the File node. Output Y of the multiplyDivide1 node is connected to V Coord. Thus, each nParticle receives a unique part of the bitmap based on its current X, Y location. As for the nParticle simulation, an Emit From Object emitter emits from a narrow polygon plane. The Gravity of the nucleus1 node is reversed by changing the Gravity Direction to 0, 1.0, 0 (positive Y). The Lifespan Mode menu of the nParticle node is set to Constant and Lifespan is set to 0.9, causing the nParticles to die after reaching 4 units in Y. nParticle Threshold is set to 0.5, which makes the nParticles shrink and stick together.

The Particle Sampler utility can also control various per-particle attributes. For a discussion of this feature and the Array Mapper utility, see Chapter 8.

Working with the Thick Cloud Preset

The Thick Cloud preset offers a way to generate puffy, cloud-like smoke. However, the resulting shading network requires adjustment after the preset is applied.

When you create an nParticle node with the Thick Cloud preset, it connects a Fluid Shape node as a volumetric material. The Fluid Shape node uses a fluid dynamic simulation to render cloud-like "blobs" within each nParticle. By default, the nParticle node's Surface Shading attribute is set to 0, which means that the connected surface material, a Blinn, is ignored.

Brief guidelines for adjusting the Thick Cloud preset follow:

Lifespan   By default, nParticles live forever. Change the Lifespan Mode menu to Constant or Random Range so they die off within a specified number of seconds or within a time range. This allows you to take advantage of age-driven shading qualities.

Particle Count   If the nParticles appear separated, increase the emitter's Rate (Particles Per Sec). Always play back from frame 1 after adjusting emitter and particle attributes.

Size   By default, all the nParticles are the same size. To better blend the nParticles so they look like a mass of smoke, increase the Radius Scale Randomize value and/or adjust Radius Scale ramp. These attributes are multiplied against the Radius value to determine the final nParticle size. Overlapping nParticles creates a more solid mass.

Noise   By default, each nParticle receives the full extent of the Fluid Shape node's built-in noise texture. This makes the particles appear identical. To prevent this, follow these steps:

1. Delete the connection between the Fluid Shape Transparency attribute and the Particle Sampler node by RMB-clicking the attribute name in the Attribute Editor and choosing Break Connection from the menu. Transparency is located in the Shading section of the Fluid Shape node.

2. Click the checkered Map button beside Transparency and choose a 3D noise texture, such as Solid Fractal, in the Create Render Node window. The 3D noise supplies opacity variation across the entire nParticle mass without creating a repeating pattern.

3. Adjust the position and scale of the 3D Placement box, fine-tune the 3D texture attribute values, and test render until the roughness or softness of the nParticle mass is acceptable.

Lighting   The fluid created by the Fluid Shape node reacts to scene lights by default and self-shadows. You can adjust the built-in lighting and shadowing attributes through the Lighting section of the Fluid Shape node.

Fluid-Driven Qualities Although a Particle Sampler node is connected through the Thick Cloud preset, it's not used for age-driven attributes. Instead, it connects the nParticle with the Fluid Shape's built-in ramps that control color, incandescence, and opacity of the fluid. The ramps are driven by fluid properties such as Density and Temperature. To make these ramps function, you must add fluid properties to the system using the Contents Method section. For example, you can change the Contents Method's Density menu to Gradient and change the Incandescence ramp's Incandescence Input to Density. With these settings, each nParticle uses the incandescence ramp. The dense areas of the nParticles use the right side of the ramp, and the less-dense edges use the left side of the ramp.

Age-Driven Qualities To use age-driven attributes directly, adjust the ramps within the nParticle shape node's Shading section. For example, in Figure 7.12, the Color and Incandescence ramps are adjusted so that the nParticles are bright yellow and orange shortly after their birth and slowly darken to gray and black toward their death. In addition, the other adjustments listed in this section are applied (with the exception of the fluid-driven ramps).

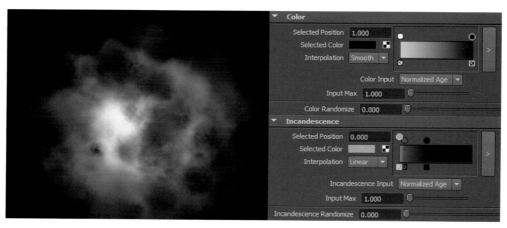

Figure 7.12 Left: An nParticle simulation, using the Thick Cloud preset, is adjusted to take advantage of age-driven qualities and to form a cohesive, smoke-like mass; Right: The adjusted Color and Incandescence ramps off the nParticle shape node. This scene is included with the Chapter 7 tutorial files as `thick_cloud.ma`.

Tying Into Nonmaterial Nodes

Custom connections are not limited to materials, textures, and geometry transform nodes. Any node that you can access in the Hypershade or Node Editor is fair game. You can make connections between attributes as long as the attribute types match (vector to vector, single channel to single channel, and so on).

If you are using the Hypershade, you can drag nonmaterial and nontexture nodes into the work area by MMB-dragging from the node tabs above or by MMB-dragging a node from the Hypergraph: Connections, Hypergraph: Hierarchy, or Outliner windows. You can also select an object in a viewport and choose Graph >

Add Selected To Graph from the Hypershade menu. The Node Editor supports the same MMB-dragging functionality. You can add selected objects by clicking the Add Selected Nodes To Graph button. You can MMB-drag back and forth between the Node Editor and the Hypershade.

Using Measurement Utilities

Maya provides several utilities designed to take measurements within the scene. These include Surface Info, Curve Info, Angle Between, and Distance Between.

Surface Info provides information about NURBS surface control vertices and knots (edit points). It is designed for use with expressions or MEL scripting. For example, the following MEL lines connect a NURBS sphere shape node to a Surface Info node and then query the node to produce the position of each knot:

```
connectAttr nurbsSphere1.worldSpace surfaceInfo1.inputSurface;

getAttr surfaceInfo1.controlPoints["*"];

// Result:  0.199917 -1 -0.199917 . . . /
```

Curve Info is similar to Surface Info in that it queries control points and knots of a NURBS curve.

Angle Between determines the angle between two inputs and outputs a vector that represents this. For example, in Figure 7.13, the rotational values of two NURBS spheres are connected to an angleBetween node. The angleBetween node can be queried with the following MEL line:

```
getAttr angleBetween1.axisAngle.axis
```

This results in the following message, which is the angle expressed as a vector:

```
// Result: -0.264846 -0.141527 -0.953848 //
```

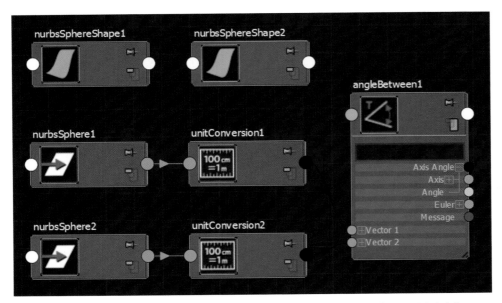

Figure 7.13 An Angle Between node determines the vector angle between two rotated spheres. This scene is included as `angle_between.ma` with the Chapter 7 tutorial files.

Note the appearance of two Unit Conversion nodes to this network. Maya adds these automatically whenever attributes with dissimilar units of measure are connected. With this scene, the Euler rotational values of the NURBS shape nodes must be converted to vector values. In Maya, the Euler values are expressed in degrees in XYZ whereas vectors are expressed as values from 0 to 1.0 in XYZ. Euler refers to Leonhard Euler, who developed a means to represent an object's orientation with three angular values.

The Distance Between utility does exactly what its name implies: it returns a value that represents the distance between any two objects. You can automatically create this utility by choosing Create > Measure Tools > Distance Tool and clicking in two different locations in any viewport view. Two locators are placed in the scene, and the distance is measured between them by a Distance Between utility. The distance value is displayed on a line drawn between the two locators. Although this method is convenient, it is possible to connect a Distance Between utility to a custom shading network manually, as you'll see in the next section.

Adding Distance Between to a Custom Network

In Figure 7.14 the color of two primitive polygon shapes changes from blue to red as they approach each other. This is made feasible by the connection of a Distance Between utility. (To see the color change in a viewport without rendering, use Viewport 2.0.)

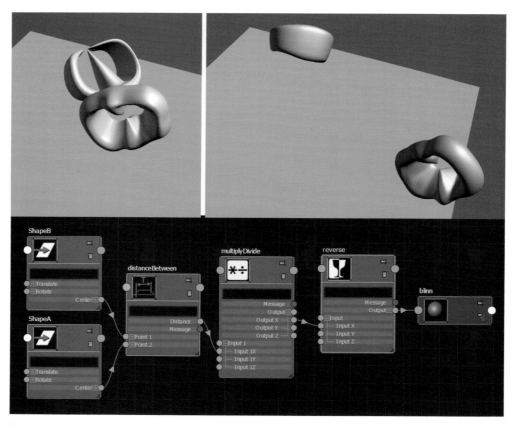

Figure 7.14 The colors of two abstract shapes are controlled by a Distance Between utility. This scene is included with the Chapter 7 tutorial files as distance.ma. A QuickTime movie is included as distance.mov.

In this shading network, the Center attribute of ShapeA's transform node is connected to Point 2 of a distanceBetween node. The Center of ShapeB's transform node is connected to Point 1 of the distanceBetween node (the Translate attribute does not work with this network). The Distance attribute of the distanceBetween node is connected to the Input 1X of a multiplyDivide node. Distance outputs a value that represents the world distance between Point 1 and Point 2. The Input 2X attribute of the multiplyDivide node is set to 0.05, guaranteeing that the result will be well below 1.0 even when the shapes travel a significant distance apart. The Output X of the multiplyDivide node is connected to the Input X of a reverse node. This ensures that the shapes will become redder as they approach each other and not vice versa. Last, the Output of the reverse node is connected to the Color of a blinn material node. The Input Y and Input Z attributes of the reverse node are set to 0.5 because they have no inputs. This creates the green-blue color when the Output X of the multiplyDivide node, which controls the Input X of the reverse node, provides a low value.

Chapter Tutorial: Building a Custom Crosshatch Shader

During a render, the Surface Luminance utility automatically reads the luminance of every single rendered point on the surface assigned to a material that is part of the same shading network. That is, the utility can determine the total amount of light a point on a polygon face receives and outputs a value from 0 to 1.0 representing this. As part of this tutorial, you'll create a custom crosshatch material that uses the Surface Luminance node (see Figure 7.15).

Figure 7.15 A crosshatch material is created with a standard Ramp texture and a Surface Luminance utility.

Follow these steps:

1. Open the Node Editor window. RMB-click and choose Create Node. In the Create Node window, click on the icons for a Surface Shader material, Ramp texture, and Surface Luminance utility (listed as Surf. Luminance). Close the Create Node window.

2. Shift-click the new ramp1, surfaceShader1, and surfaceLuminance1 nodes and click the Show Primary Attributes button to reveal each node's inputs and outputs. Feel free to rearrange the nodes. You can also hide an unwanted node, such as the shading group node, by selecting the node and clicking the Remove Selected Nodes From Graph button.

3. Select the ramp1 node, RMB-click over the node icon, and choose Show All Attributes to reveal the full attribute list. Connect the Out Value of surfaceLuminance1 to Color Entry List[0] Position of the ramp1 node. You will need to expand Color Entry List and Color Entry List[0] to see the Position subchannel. The Color EntryList[n] Position subchannel controls the V-direction position of a color handle in a ramp texture. Refer to Figure 7.16 for the final shading network. (If you choose to make these connections with the Hypershade and Connection Editor, choose Right Display > Show Hidden from the Connection Editor window to show any hidden channels on the input node.)

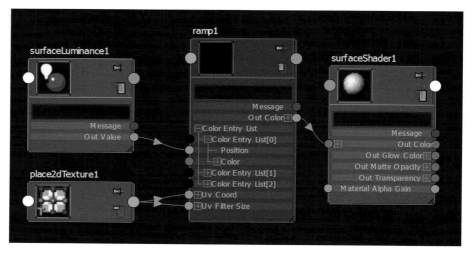

Figure 7.16 The final shading network for the crosshatch material

4. Connect the Out Color of ramp1 to the Out Color of surfaceShader1. Note that you must drag the connection line to the Out Color dot on the right side of the surfaceShader1 node icon.

5. Open the ramp1 node in the Attribute Editor. Set the Type attribute to UV Ramp. This allows the pattern to repeat on the surface vertically and horizontally. Set Interpolation to None to give the rendered lines a hard edge. Set the Noise attribute to 0.1 and Noise Freq to 0.05 to give the rendered lines some squiggle.

6. If you are using Maya 2014, delete the middle ramp handle by clicking on its x. Change the color of the low handle (Maya 2014) or left handle (Maya 2015) to black. Change the top handle (Maya 2014) or right handle (Maya 2015) to white. Pull the white handle down (2014) or left (2015) to the same spot as the black handle (see Figure 7.17).

7. Open the place2dTexture1 node connected to ramp1. Set Repeat UV to 50, 50. Higher repeat values will produce finer lines. Change Rotate UV to 45 to angle the rendered pattern.

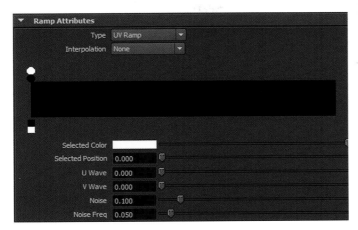

Figure 7.17 The adjusted ramp, as seen in Maya 2015

8. Assign surfaceShader1 to a piece of geometry. Render a test. Set lights in the scene and render additional tests. Wherever the surface is dark, the crosshatch lines become thick. Wherever the surface is bright, the crosshatch lines become thin. With this scene, the surfaceLuminance1 node drives the black ramp handle up and down (2014) or left and right (2015) based on how much light a surface point receives. If a surface point receives the maximum amount of light, the Out Value of the surfaceLuminance1 node is 1.0, which forces the black handle up to the top/right of the ramp (leaving the entire ramp field white). If a surface point receives a little light, the Out Value is a lower value, which allows the black handle to stay low/left, thus creating a mix of black and white within the ramp color field. You can adjust the size the hatch lines by altering the place2dTexture1 node's Repeat UV values.

The custom material is complete! If you get stuck, a sample scene is saved as `crosshatch.ma` with the Chapter 7 tutorial files.

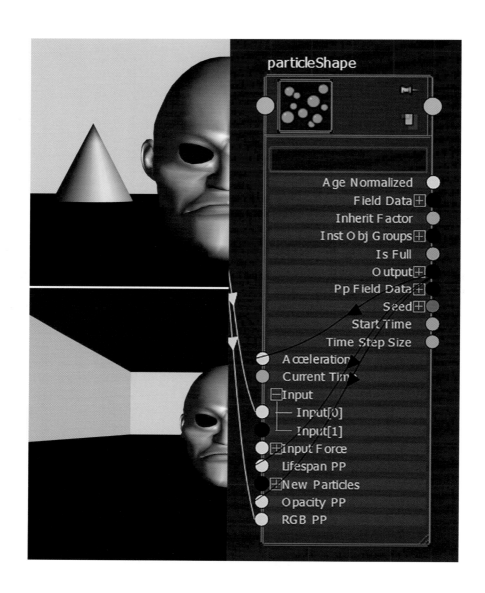

Harnessing the Power of Math Utilities

8

Math utilities refine outputs and emulate complex mathematics. Switch utilities let you create numerous texture variations with a single material. With the Array Mapper and Particle Sampler utilities in the Autodesk® Maya® program, you can control a particle's material and movement on a per-particle basis. You can also create unique effects with Stencil and Optical FX utilities.

Chapter Contents

Practical applications of each math utility
A general approach to using per-particle attributes
The functionality of the Array Mapper and Particle Sampler utilities
Uses for the Stencil and Optical FX utilities
The purposes of various scene nodes

Math Utilities

The values provided by various attributes in Maya are often unusable in a custom shading network. The numbers may be too large, too small, or negative when they need to be positive. Hence, Maya provides a host of math utilities designed to massage values into a usable form. The utilities vary from simple operations (Reverse, Multiply Divide, and Plus Minus Average) to advanced (Array Mapper, Vector Product, and others). There are also switch utilities, which provide the means to texture large groups of objects with a limited number of materials.

Reversing Input

The Reverse utility simply reverses an input. The following math occurs:

```
Output = 1.0 - Input
```

Thus, an input of 1.0 produces 0 and an input of 0 produces 1.0. At the same time, the Reverse utility will make larger numbers negative or positive. For example, an input of 100 produces –99 and an input of –100 produces 101. Only an input of 0.5 leads to an unchanged output.

For example, in Figure 8.1 the Specular Roll Off of a Blinn material is driven by its Transparency value. The Transparency attribute is connected to the Input of a reverse node. The Output X of the reverse node is connected back to the Specular Roll Off of the blinn node. Without this network, a specular highlight of the Blinn material remains visible even if its Transparency value is turned up to the maximum of 1.0. With this network, the specular highlight fades as the transparency decreases. For example, if Transparency is 0.75, the Specular Roll Off is reduced to 0.25 (1.0 – 0.75 via the reverse node).

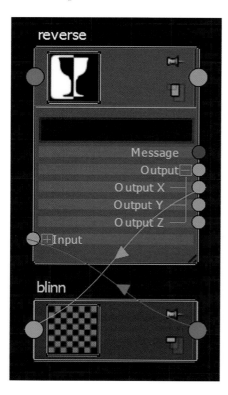

Figure 8.1 The Specular Roll Off of a Blinn material is driven by its Transparency attribute with the aid of a Reverse utility. This scene is included with the Chapter 8 tutorial files as reverse.ma. Note that you can display the connection lines in front of the node icons in the Node Editor by LMB-clicking a connected node.

For an additional example of the Reverse utility used in a custom network, see the "Creating Falloff for Directional and Ambient Lights" section in Chapter 7, "Automating a Scene with Sampler Nodes."

Multiplying and Dividing

The Multiply Divide utility applies mathematical operations to one or two inputs (see Figure 8.2). The Operation menu determines if multiplication, division, or a power function is applied. If there are no inputs, you can enter values in any of the Input 1 and Input 2 vector fields. As is the standard throughout Maya, the left field is X, the middle field is Y, and the right field is Z.

Figure 8.2 The Operation and Input attributes of a Multiply Divide node. With this example, a connection is made to Input 2X while values are entered by hand for Input 1X, Input 1Y, and Input 2Y.

The utility uses the following logic:

```
Input 1X / Input 2X, Input 1Y / Input 2Y, Input 1Z / Input 2Z
Input 1X * Input 2X, Input 1Y * Input 2Y, Input 1Z * Input 2Z
Input 1X ^ Input 2X, Input 1Y ^ Input 2Y, Input 1Z ^ Input 2Z
```

If the utility's Operation attribute is set to Multiply, the input order makes no difference. If the utility's Operation is set to Divide or Power, however, the input order is critical, as in this example:

```
10 / 2 = 5 while 2 / 10 = 0.2
10 ^ 2 = 100 while 2 ^ 10 = 1024
```

For an example of Multiply Divide utilities used in a custom network, see the "Deriving Color from a Spatial Vector" section in Chapter 7.

> **Note:** For simple multiplication, you can use the Mult Double Linear utility. The node accepts two inputs, Input 1 and Input 2, and outputs the result through its Output channel.

Adding, Subtracting, and Averaging Values

The Plus Minus Average utility supports addition (sum), subtraction, and average operations, as set by its Operation menu. It operates on single, double, and vector inputs. Single-channel connections are listed in the Input 1D section of the utility's Attribute Editor tab; double and vector connections are listed in the Input 2D and Input 3D sections (see Figure 8.3.) Note that the Plus Minus Average utility is listed as +|– Average in the Maya > Utilities section.

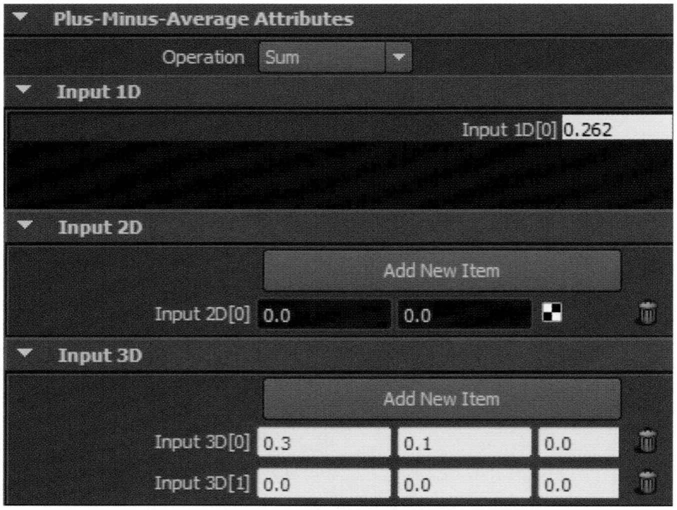

Figure 8.3 A Plus Minus Average utility with one single-channel and two vector inputs. Although a double-channel input is added, no connection has been made to it, as is indicated by the dark field color.

The utility provides Add New Item buttons in the Input 2D and Input 3D sections. When you click one of these buttons, a new set of input fields is added to the appropriate section. The input fields are not connected to a node, which allows you to enter values by hand. However, you can choose to make a custom connection to the new input.

When creating custom connections in the Hypershade or Node Editor, you can connect single-channel attributes to Input 1D [*n*] of the Plus Minus Average node. You can connect double attributes, such as UV Coord, to Input 2D [*n*]. You can connect vector attributes, such as Out Color, to Input 3D [*n*]. *n* represents the order with which attributes have been connected, with the [0] position being the first. There is no limit to the number of attributes that may be connected.

In Figure 8.4, the Translate X attributes of four primitive polygon shape transform nodes are connected to Input 1D [*n*] of a plusMinusAverage node with the node's Operation set to Average. To illustrate the resulting averaged X position, the Output 1D of the plusMinusAverage node is connected to the Translate X of a locator.

To see this custom network, follow these steps:

1. Open the `plus_simple.ma` file from the Chapter 8 tutorial directory. Open the Hypershade window and switch to the Utilities tab.

2. MMB-drag plusMinusAverage1 into the Hypershade work area or Node Editor.

3. With plusMinusAverage1 selected, click the Input And Output Connections button. The network becomes visible.

The locator position represents the result of the following math:

```
Output 1D = (shape1.tx + shape2.tx + shape3.tx + shape4.tx) / 4
```

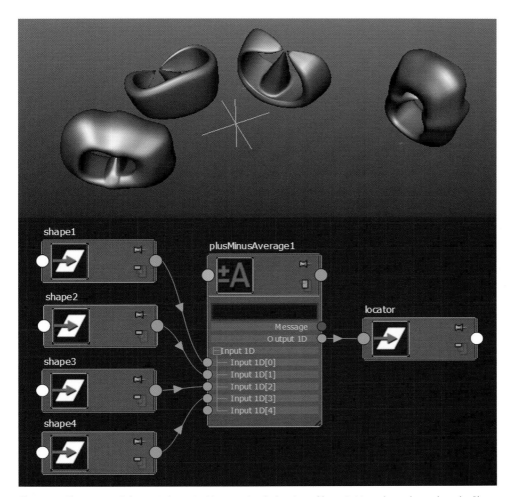

Figure 8.4 The position of a locator is determined by averaging the locations of four primitive polygon shapes through a Plus Minus Average utility. This scene is included with the Chapter 8 tutorial files as `plus_simple.ma`.

If the Operation menu is set to Sum or Subtract, the following math is performed:

```
Output 1D = shape1.tx + shape2.tx + shape3.tx + shape4.tx
Output 1D = shape1.tx − shape2.tx − shape3.tx − shape4.tx
```

You can apply the Average operation to color attributes as well. In the same example, the Out Color attributes of four textures are connected to the Input 3D [n] of a second plusMinusAverage node, as shown in Figure 8.5. The utility's Output 3D is connected to the Color attribute of a Blinn material node, which is assigned to all four shapes. The following happens to the red channel of an individual pixel:

```
Output 3D = (water.colorR + ramp.colorR + mountain.colorR + bulge.colorR ) / 4
```

> **Note:** For simple addition, you can use the Add Double Linear utility. The node accepts two inputs, Input 1 and Input 2, and outputs the sum through its Output channel. For an example of its use, see the tutorial at the end of this chapter.

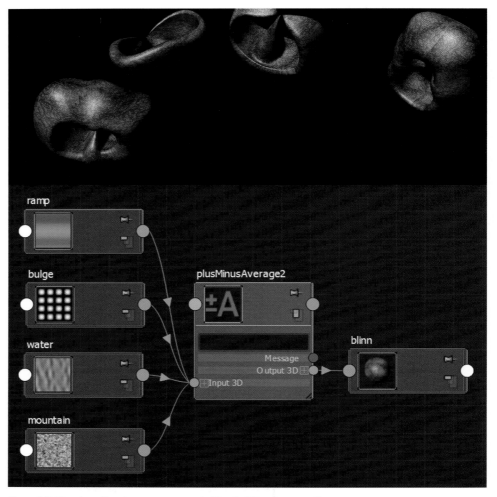

Figure 8.5 The colors of four textures are averaged with a Plus Minus Average utility.

Using Expressions

Maya expressions offer the most efficient and powerful way to incorporate math calculations into a custom shading network. Although a discussion of expressions is beyond the scope of this book, here are a few items to keep in mind:

Create New Expression RMB-clicking an attribute field in the Attribute Editor and choosing Create New Expression from the shortcut menu opens the Expression Editor window. The attribute that was chosen is highlighted in Expression Editor's Attributes list. After a valid expression is created and the Create button is clicked, an Expression node and appropriate connections are created (see Figure 8.6). The attribute field, as seen in the Attribute Editor, turns purple to indicate the connection to an expression. If the Expression node is not immediately visible in the Hypershade work area or Node Editor, click the Input And Output Connections button.

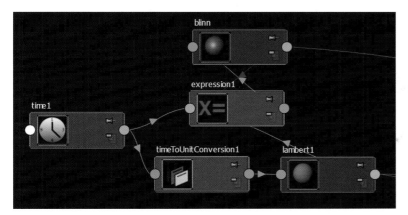

Figure 8.6 An expression node, a universal time1 node, and a timeToUnitConversion node are visible in a network.

Time   A master Time node (time1) is automatically connected to each Expression node and is undeletable. This node manages the flow of time for the Maya timeline. You can connect the time1 node's Out Time to any single attribute of any node. However, a Time To Unit Conversion node is inserted along the connection (see Figure 8.6), thus allowing the timeline frame range to be scaled to fit within the standard 0-to-1.0 range of most material and texture attributes.

Nodes and Channels   You can reference any channel of any node in an expression. The naming convention follows the formula *node.channel*. If a node carries multiple channel positions, as is the case with the Plus Minus Average utility, the convention follows *node.channel*[n].

Functions   For a list of Maya math, vector, array, and other functions available to expressions, choose the Insert Functions menu of the Expression Editor window.

Changing the Range of a Value

The Set Range utility maps one range of values to a second range of values. This is useful for conforming one range to another when the ranges are significantly different. The underlying math for the utility follows:

```
Out Value = Min + (((Value - Old Min)/(Old Max - Old Min)) * (Max - Min))
```

As an example illustrated by Table 8.1, five different Value X inputs are processed by a Set Range utility, resulting in new Out Value X outputs. For this example, Old Min X of the utility is set to –100, Old Max X is set to 100, Min X is set to 0, and Max X is set to 1.0.

▷ **Table 8.1** The result of various Value X inputs applied to a Set Range utility

Value X	−200	−50	0	75	100
Out Value X	0	0.250	0.5	0.875	1.0

The mid-range value of the Old Min X to Old Max X range (–100 to 100) is changed to the mid-range value of the new Min X to Max X range (0 to 1.0). Thus, a Value X input of 0 becomes an Out Value X output of 0.5. Any Value X input that is less than Old Min X is clamped to the Old Min X value before it is mapped to the Min X to Max X range. Thus, a Value X input of –200 is clamped to –100, producing an Out Value X of 0. Any Value X input that is greater than Old Max X is clamped to the Old Max X value.

For an example of the Set Range utility used in a custom network, see the "Creating Falloff for Directional and Ambient Lights" section in Chapter 7.

Mapping Per-Particle Attributes

The Array Mapper utility is designed to control per-particle attributes on particle or nParticle nodes. The attributes can affect particle size, dynamic behavior, color, and opacity. (An *array* is an ordered list of values.) The Particle Sampler utility, on the other hand, serves as a go-between, retrieving attribute information from a particle shape node and passing it on to a material assigned to the software-rendered particles. These nodes work with Maya Software, mental ray®, and Maya Hardware renderers.

Creating an Array Mapper Network with the RGB PP Attribute

The simplest way to see the Array Mapper utility work is to create an RGB PP attribute for hardware-rendered particles or nParticles. Because the process is a little unusual, I recommend you use the following steps with an nParticle node:

1. Create a new scene. Switch to the nDynamics menu set and choose nParticles > Create nParticles > Points. Choose nParticles > Create nParticles > Create Emitter. Increase the duration of the timeline so that the particle simulation has time to develop. For example, set the timeline range to 100 frames.
    Play back the timeline. Select the resulting cloud of nParticles.

2. Open the Attribute Editor tab for a selected particle shape node (nParticleShape1) and expand the Lifespan section. Set the Lifespan Mode value to either Constant or Random Range and choose a Lifespan length (measured in seconds).

3. Click the Color button in the Add Dynamic Attributes section. The Particle Color window opens. Select the Add Per Particle Attribute option and click the Add Attribute button. This adds an RGB PP attribute to the list in the Per Particle (Array) Attributes section (see Figure 8.7).

4. RMB-click the field next to RGB PP and choose Create Ramp from the shortcut menu. An Array Mapper utility and a Ramp texture are automatically connected to the particle shape node (see Figure 8.8). If you are using Maya 2014, the ramp has the traditional red/green/blue colors. If you are using Maya 2015, the ramp is black and white. You are free to change the ramp colors.

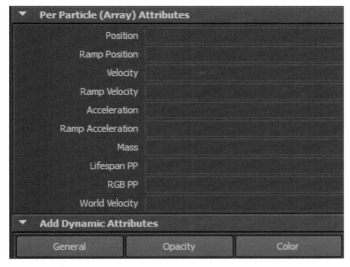

Figure 8.7 The Per Particle (Array) Attributes and Add Dynamics Attributes sections of a particle shape node's Attribute Editor tab. Note the addition of the RGB PP attribute.

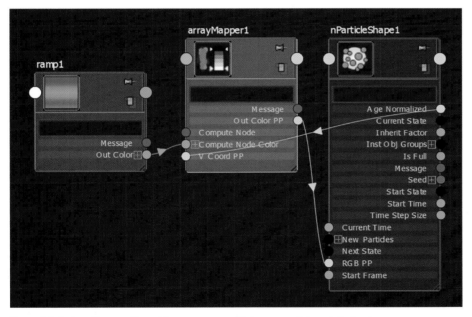

Figure 8.8 An Array Mapper utility and Ramp texture are added to a network through the Create Ramp option available to the RGB PP attribute (as seen in Maya 2014).

5. The nParticles pick up the color of the ramp over their lifespan. To render the nParticles, open the Render View window, change the renderer menu to Maya Hardware or Maya Hardware 2.0, and click the Render The Current Frame button. Feel free to move the camera closer, reduce the Lifespan value, or adjust emitter attributes to more easily see the color change. (See Chapter 10, "Prepping for Successful Renders," for more information on hardware rendering.)

Creating a Custom Array Mapper Network

You can manually connect the Array Mapper utility (found in the Maya > Utilities section of the Create tab section of the Hypershade, Create Node, and Create Render Node windows).

For the Array Mapper to become functional when using a Ramp texture to supply the particle color, the following connections are necessary (outputs are on the left and inputs are on the right):

ramp.outColor to arrayMapper.computeNodeColor

ramp.message to arrayMapper.computeNode

arrayMapper.outColorPP to particleshape.rgbPP

particleShape.ageNormalized to arrayMapper.vCoordPP

The Min Value and Max Value attributes of the Array Mapper utility serve as a clamp for the Out Color PP and Out Value PP attributes (Out Value PP is the single-channel version of Out Color PP). You can replace the ramp texture with other types of textures, but the results will be unpredictable.

In addition to RGB PP, a number of other per-particle attributes are available, including Incandescence PP, Radius PP, and Opacity PP. You can add Opacity PP by clicking the Opacity button in the Add Dynamic Attributes section of the particle shape's Attribute Editor tab. You can add other PP attributes by clicking the General button in the Add Dynamics Attributes section and choosing the Particle tab of the Add Attribute (see Figure 8.9). In addition to the PP attributes, the Particle tab carries a long list of more esoteric attributes, any of which can be used for per-particle operations through an expression.

Figure 8.9 The Particle tab of the Add Attribute window. Only a small portion of the available PP attributes are shown.

As an example of a custom network, in Figure 8.10 a single Array Mapper utility drives the color, opacity, and acceleration of a point particle node. Note that the process for using per-particle attributes is identical for Dynamics particles and nDynamics nParticles.

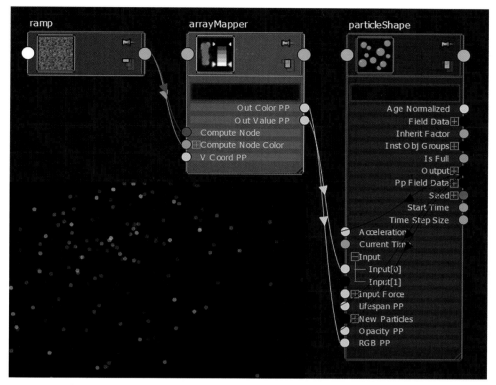

Figure 8.10 A point particle node receives its color, opacity, and acceleration from an Array Mapper utility. This scene is included with the Chapter 8 tutorial files as `array_point.ma`. A QuickTime movie is included as `array_point.mov`.

To view the shading network, follow these steps:

1. Open the `array_point.ma` file from the Chapter 8 tutorial directory. Open the Hypershade window and switch to the Textures tab.

2. MMB-drag the ramp node into the Hypershade work area or the Node Editor.

3. With the ramp node selected, click the Input And Output Connections button. The network becomes visible.

With this network, the Noise attribute of the connected ramp node is set to 1.0 and its Noise Freq attribute is set to 50, which creates a random pattern throughout the ramp. Although RGB PP receives its color directly from the Out Color PP of the ramp node, an expression controls the particle node's opacity, acceleration, and lifespan. The expression follows:

```
particleShape.opacityPP=arrayMapper.outValuePP;
particleShape.acceleration=arrayMapper.outValuePP*-500;
particleShape.lifespanPP=rand(1,3);
```

To view the expression, follow these steps:

1. Choose Window > Animation Editors > Expression Editor.

2. Choose Select Filter > By Expression Name from the Expression Editor menu. Click the word *particleShape* in the Expressions field.

3. Switch the Particle attribute to Creation. The expression code is revealed in the text field at the bottom of the window.

In the first line of the expression, Out Value PP of the arrayMapper node drives Opacity PP. In the second line of the expression, Out Value PP drives the particle's acceleration attribute. The acceleration attribute controls the rate of velocity change on a per-particle basis (although it's not listed as a "PP"). You can see the effect of the variable acceleration if the particle count is reduced to a low number. Some particles move rapidly, whereas others fall very slowly. The Out Value PP is multiplied by −500, which makes the acceleration more rapid and changes the particles' direction to the negative X, Y, and Z direction. The ability to use Out Value PP as an input for multiple particle attributes eliminates the need for additional arrayMapper and ramp nodes.

In the third line of the expression, the particle lifespan is assigned a random number from 1.0 to 3 with the rand() function. The Out Value PP attribute is automatically connected to Input[0] of the arrayMapper node; this represents the use of Out Value PP in an expression. When an expression is created for a per-particle attribute, the expression is carried by the particle shape node and no separate expression node is generated.

Note: RMB-clicking an attribute field in the Per Particle (Array) Attributes section of a particle shape node's Attribute Editor tab provides the Creation Expression option in a shortcut menu. Creation Expression opens the Expression Editor and lists the particle shape and its numerous channels in the editor's Attributes list. Using the Creation Expression option is also a quick way to access preexisting per-particle expressions.

Creation expressions are executed at the start time of an animation. They are not executed as the animation plays. When using particles or nParticles, a creation expression is applied once per particle at the frame in which the particle is born. In contrast, a runtime expression executes at each frame during playback. A runtime expression is useful when values need to change constantly over the life of an animation. You can create a runtime expression by RMB-clicking an attribute field in the Per Particle (Array) Attributes section of a particle or nParticle shape node's Attribute Editor tab and choosing either Runtime Expression Before Dynamics or Runtime Expression After Dynamics.

Employing the Particle Sampler Utility

The Array Mapper utility will not work with software-rendered particles—*unless* it is used in conjunction with a Particle Sampler utility. For example, in Figure 8.11 a Particle Sampler utility is added to a prior network. The Particle Render Type of the particle shape node is switched to Blobby Surface. The particle node is assigned to a blinn material node. The Noise value of the original ramp texture node is reduced and the ramp colors are adjusted. The Rate (Particles/Sec) value of the particle node is reduced for easier viewing. A directional light is added to the scene.

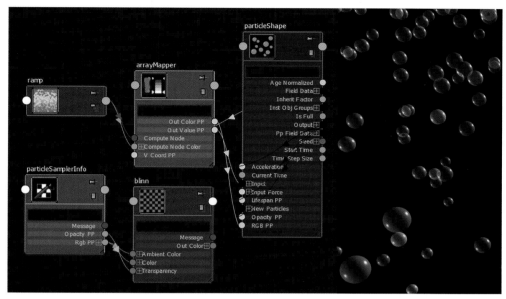

Figure 8.11 A Blobby Surface particle node receives its color, opacity, and acceleration through Array Mapper and Particle Sampler utilities. Note that there is no visible connection between the particleSampler node and the particleShape node. This scene is included with the Chapter 8 tutorial files as `array_blobby.ma`. A QuickTime movie is included as `array_blobby.mov`.

Aside from these adjustments, all the old network connections and the old expression are intact. In addition, the RGB PP of a Particle Sampler node (named particleSamplerInfo) is connected to the Color and the Ambient Color of the blinn node. The Opacity PP of the particleSamplerInfo node is also connected to the Transparency R, Transparency G, and Transparency B of the blinn node. The end result is a color distribution, opacity, lifespan, and acceleration roughly identical to Figure 8.10 but with a software-rendered particle node.

The Particle Sampler utility carries a long list of read-only attributes. These attributes remotely read attribute information from the particle or nParticle shape node that is assigned to the material. (For this to work, the material must share the shading network with the Particle Sampler utility.) The attributes are intuitively named (for example, particleSamplerInfo.rgbPP remotely reads particleShape.rgbPP). You can connect these attributes to any attribute of a material that may prove useful.

Note: You can change various per-particle attributes, such as Lifespan PP and Opacity PP, in the Particles tab of the Component Editor (Window > General Editors > Component Editor). Select particle nodes in a viewport by clicking the Select By Object Type: Select Dynamic Objects button in the Status Line toolbar. Select particles individually by clicking Select By Component Type: Select Point Components in the Status Line toolbar.

Note: Not all per-particle attributes will work with all particle render types. For example, Radius PP will work only with Blobby Surface, Cloud, and Sphere particles. For a detailed attribute list, see "List of Particle Attributes" in the Maya Help files.

Working with Vectors and Matrices

Vectors are useful for determining direction within Maya. Matrices, on the other hand, are an intrinsic part of 3D and are necessary for converting various coordinate spaces. Comparing the direction of lights, cameras, and surface components within different coordinate spaces can provide information useful for custom shading networks. Before I discuss such networks, however, a review of vector math, the Vector Product utility, and Maya matrices is warranted.

Understanding Vector Math

In the mathematical realm, a vector is the quantity of an attribute that has direction as well as magnitude. For example, wind can be represented by a vector because it has direction and speed (where speed is the magnitude).

In Maya, there are several variations of vectors. Vector attributes are simply a related group of three floating-point numbers. Color is stored as a vector attribute (R, G, B). At the same time, Maya vector attributes are used for transforms in 3D space. For example, the translation of an object is represented as a vector attribute (X, Y, Z).

A second variation of a Maya vector is used to determine direction. That is, a particular point in space (X, Y, Z) has a measurable distance from the origin (0, 0, 0) and a specific angle relative to the origin. In this case, the distance serves as the vector magnitude and the angle is the vector direction. A number of specialized attributes provide this style of vector (which can be loosely described as a "spatial vector"). A more detailed description of commonly used spatial vectors follows:

Normal Camera and Surface Normal   The Normal Camera attribute is provided by the Sampler Info utility and material nodes. It represents the surface normal of the point being sampled in camera space. A surface normal is a vector that points directly away from the surface (and at a right angle to the surface). In general, surface normals are normalized so that their length (that is, their magnitude) is 1.0.

Ray Direction   The Ray Direction attribute is provided by the Sampler Info utility and material nodes. It's a vector that runs from the surface point being sampled to the camera in camera space.

Facing Ratio   The Facing Ratio attribute is uniquely provided by the Sampler Info utility and is the cosine of the angle between Ray Direction and Normal Camera. (A *cosine* is the trigonometric function often defined as the ratio of the length of the adjacent side to that of the hypotenuse in a right triangle.) The Facing Ratio is clamped between 0 and 1.0. A value of 0 indicates that the surface normal is pointing away from the camera. A value of 1.0 indicates that the surface normal is pointing toward the camera.

Light Direction The Light Direction attribute is provided by the Light Info utility and is a vector that represents the direction in which a light, camera, or other input node is pointing in world space. Lights also have a built-in Light Direction attribute (found in the Light Data section of the light shape node's Connection Editor attribute list). However, the Light Direction attribute of a light is in camera space.

Using the Vector Product Utility

The Vector Product utility accepts any vector attribute, whether it is a color, a transform, or a spatial vector. You can set the utility's Operation attribute to one of four modes:

Dot Product Dot Product multiplies two vectors together and returns a value that represents the angle between them. Its output may be written as

```
Output = (a*d) + (b*e) + (c*f)
```

The first input vector is (a, b, c) and is connected to Input 1 of the utility. The second input vector is (d, e, f) and is connected to Input 2 of the utility. The output is a single value. If Normalize Output is selected, the output is the actual cosine and will run between −1.0 and 1.0. A value of −1.0 signifies that the vectors point in opposite directions, 0 signifies that the vectors are at right angles to each other, and 1.0 signifies that the vectors point in the same direction. When the Operation attribute is set to Dot Product, Output X, Output Y, and Output Z attributes are the same value.

Cross Product Cross Product generates a third vector from two input vectors. The new vector will be at a right angle (perpendicular) to the input vectors.

Vector Matrix Product and Point Matrix Product Vector Matrix Product converts the coordinate space of a vector. This becomes useful when input vectors are in different coordinate spaces, such as camera and world. For conversion to work, the utility requires the connection of a transform matrix to its Matrix attribute. Maya transform nodes carry Xform Matrix and World Matrix attributes. Xform Matrix carries world coordinates. However, Xform Matrix ignores transforms from upstream nodes (parent nodes). Thus, the space Xform Matrix operates in may be considered *local space*. In contrast, World Matrix stores the net transformations of the node and all of its parent nodes in world space. For an example of a shading network using Xform Matrix, see the "Converting Camera Space to World Space" section later in this chapter. The vector that requires conversion is connected to the Input 1 attribute. The Point Matrix Product operation offers the same space conversion but operates on a point (an XYZ position).

An Overview of Maya Matrices

Maya uses a 4 × 4 matrix for transformations (see Figure 8.12). The position of an object is stored in the first three numbers of the last row. The object's scale is stored as a diagonal from the upper left. The object's rotation is indirectly stored within the first three vertical and horizontal positions from the upper-left corner (the rotation values are stored as sine and cosine values). When an object is created, or has the Freeze Transformations tool applied to it, its transform matrix is an *identity matrix*. An identity matrix is one that produces no change when it is multiplied by a second transform matrix. In other words, an object with an identity matrix has no translation, rotation, or increased/decreased scale.

$$\begin{bmatrix} sx & 0 & 0 & 0 \\ 0 & sy & 0 & 0 \\ 0 & 0 & sz & 0 \\ tx & ty & tz & 1 \end{bmatrix}$$

Figure 8.12 The 4 × 4 transformation matrix in Maya

Note: Maya provides the Add Matrix, Weighted Add Matrix, and Mult Matrix utility nodes for adding and multiplying two or more matrices to produce a single matrix result. These nodes accept 4 × 4 matrix inputs. Weighted Add Matrix differs from Add Matrix in that it accepts a Weight In value for each matrix to bias one matrix over the other. Maya also provides the Four By Four Matrix node, which allows you to construct a 4 × 4 matrix by entering values into its 16 In (input) fields. The In fields are ordered so that the first row is numbered 0 to 3, the second row is numbered 10 to 13, and so on. In addition, the Transpose Matrix node is included for transposing a single input matrix (transposing converts matrix rows into columns or vice versa). These matrix nodes may be useful for constructing custom color filters or custom space and transform conversions.

Converting Camera Space to World Space

As an example of camera space to world space conversion, in Figure 8.13 the Xform Matrix of a polygon cube is used to convert a Normal Camera vector of a Sampler Info utility into a world space vector. The results are illustrated by applying the resulting vector to the color of a material.

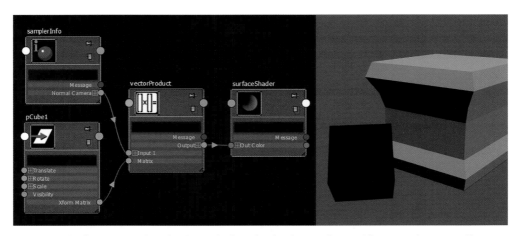

Figure 8.13 The Xform Matrix attribute of a polygon cube drives the color of a material. Here, pCube1 is rotated −45, −45, 0. This scene is included with the Chapter 8 tutorial files as `xform_matrix.ma`. A QuickTime movie is included as `xform_matrix.mov`.

The Xform Matrix of the pCube1 transform node is connected to the Matrix of a vectorProduct node. (pCube1 is the small gray cube in Figure 8.13.) The Normal Camera of a samplerInfo node is connected to the Input 1 of the vectorProduct node. The vectorProduct Operation menu is set to Vector Matrix Product. The output of the vectorProduct node is connected directly to the Out Color of a surfaceShader material node, which is assigned to a second, larger polygon cube (pCube2). Note that there is no direct connection between the samplerInfo node and the pCube2 shape node. The Sampler Info utility samples any surface that is assigned to the shading network to which the utility is connected.

As a result of the custom connections, the faces of the larger shape that point toward the camera render blue *until* pCube1 is rotated. This is a result of the Normal Camera attribute existing in camera space. A normal that points directly toward the camera always has a vector of 0, 0, 1.0. At the same time, while pCube1 is at its rest position, its Xform Matrix is an identity matrix and has no effect on the normalCamera value. Thus, the values 0, 0, 1.0 are passed to Out Color of the surfaceShader node.

When pCube1 is rotated, the Normal Camera value is multiplied by the new Xform Matrix. Hence, the camera space vector is converted to a world space vector. The world space vector is then used for pCube2's color values. For example, if pCube1 is rotated −45, −45, 0 (as is seen in Figure 8.13), a medium green-blue results on the faces of pCube2 that point toward the camera. The resulting math is illustrated in Figure 8.14.

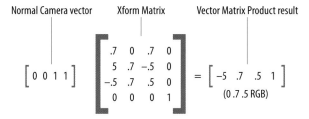

Figure 8.14 A matrix calculation based on pCube1's rotation of −45, −45, 0. The matrix numbers have been rounded off for easier viewing.

This network functions in the same way if you connect World Matrix[0] of pCube1 to the Matrix of the vectorProduct node. This is due to the fact that pCube1 does not have a parent node. Thus, the world space of World Matrix[0] is identical to the local space of Xform Matrix.

When representing the 4 × 4 matrix calculation, as we do in Figure 8.14, the extra number 1.0 at the right side of the Normal Camera vector (and at the bottom-right corner of the Xform Matrix) is necessary for this type of math operation; however, these numbers do not change as the corresponding objects go through various transformations.

Note: You can retrieve the current World Matrix[0] value of a node by typing `getAttr name_of_node.worldMatrix[0];` in the Script Editor.

Note: Maya 2015 adds a series of utility nodes with the "Quat" prefix. These are designed to manipulate quaternion values, which are often used to interpolate rotational values in 3D space. Maya supports two forms of rotation interpolations: Euler and quaternion. Euler rotations are calculated using three angles, representing rotations about the X, Y, and Z axes. With Euler systems, there is a rotate order; by default, the rotation order in Maya is XYZ (other systems may use ZXY or other variants). In contrast, quaternions store the overall orientation of an object instead of three distinct axis rotations. You can choose the method of interpolating rotations by choosing Windows > Settings/Preference > Preferences and going to the Settings > Animation > Rotation Interpolation section. For more information about the advantages and disadvantages of each rotational system, visit the "Animated Rotation in Maya" Help files or at the Autodesk Knowledge Network (`knowledge.autodesk.com`).

Testing a Condition

The Condition utility functions like a programming `If Else` statement. `If Else` statements are supported by Maya expressions and are written as follows:

```
if ($test < 10){
    print "This Is True";
} else {
    print "This Is False";
}
```

If the $test variable is less than 10, Maya prints "This Is True" on the command line. The `If Else` statement serves as a switch of sorts, choosing one of several possible outcomes depending on the input. The function of the Condition utility, when written in the style of an `If Else` statement, looks like this:

```
if (First Term  Operation  Second Term){
    Color If True;
} else {
    Color If False;
}
```

First Term and Second Term attributes each accept a single input or value, whereas the Color If True and Color If False attributes accept vector values or inputs. The Operation attribute has six options: Equal, Not Equal, Greater Than, Less Than, Greater Or Equal, and Less Or Equal.

With the Condition utility, you can apply two different textures to a single surface, a task that is difficult to do otherwise. By default, all surfaces in Maya are double-sided but only carry a single UV texture space. Hence, a plane receives the same texture on the top and bottom. You can avoid this, however, with the shading network illustrated by Figure 8.15.

The Flipped Normal of a samplerInfo node is connected to First Term of a condition node. The Flipped Normal attribute indicates the side of the surface that is renderable. If the attribute's value is 1.0, then the "flipped," or secondary, side is sampled. If the value is 0, the nonflipped, or primary, side is sampled. The nonflipped side is the side that is visible when the Double Sided attribute of the surface shape node is deselected (this is located in the Render Stats section of the Attribute Editor tab).

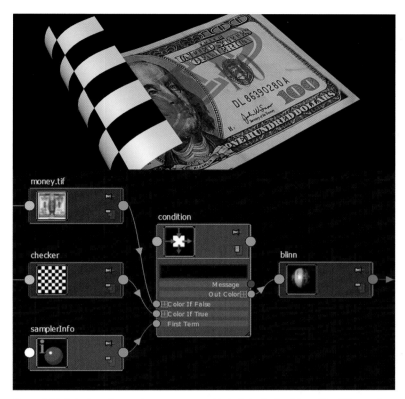

Figure 8.15 A single surface receives two textures with the help of a Condition utility. This scene is included with the Chapter 8 tutorial files as `condition_flipped.ma`.

Returning to the network, the Out Color of a checker texture node is connected to the Color If True of the condition node. The Out Color of a file texture node is connected to the Color If False attribute of the same condition node. A bitmap image of a hundred dollar bill is loaded into the file texture node. The condition's Second Term is set to 1.0 and Operation is set to Equal. Last, the Out Color of the condition node is connected to the color of a blinn material node. Thus, the flipped side of a primitive plane receives the Checker texture because the Flipped Normal value of 1.0 equals the Second Term value of 1.0. The nonflipped side receives the money texture because the Flipped Normal value of 0 does not equal the Second term value of 1.0.

Switching Outputs

Switch utilities provide multiple outputs from a single node—that is, they switch between different values in order to create different results among the geometry assigned to their shading network.

Employing a Triple Switch

You can use the following steps to employ a Triple Switch within a custom network:

1. Choose an RGB attribute of a material, such as Color, and click its checkered Map button. Choose a Triple Switch from the Maya > Utilities section of the Create Render Node window.

2. Assign the material to two or more surfaces.

3. Open the Attribute Editor tab for the new tripleShadingSwitch node. Click the Add Surfaces button. All the surfaces assigned to the material appear in the list.

4. RMB-click the first surface name in the Switch Attributes list and choose Map from the shortcut menu. The Create Render Node window opens. Choose a texture. The Out Color attribute of the texture node (for example, stucco.out-Color) appears in the In Triple column of the Switch Attributes list. This represents a connection to the node's Input[*n*].In Triple subchannel. You can connect an unlimited number of inputs to Input[*n*].In Triple, with each connection receiving a higher *n* number. Repeat this process for each of the remaining surfaces in the Switch Attributes list. Note that the Inst Obj Groups[*n*] attribute of each geometry shape node is connected automatically to the Input[*n*].In Shape of the tripleShadingSwitch node.

5. Render a test. Each surface picks up the texture listed in the corresponding In Triple field. Figure 8.16 shows an example scene that uses two surfaces and two textures.

Figure 8.16 Color is controlled by a Triple Switch utility. A simplified version of this scene is included with the Chapter 8 tutorial files as `triple_switch.ma`.

Although these steps apply the Triple Switch to a material, you can apply the same process to nonmaterial nodes. That said, Triple Switches are designed for vector values and are best suited for any attribute that uses RGB colors or XYZ coordinates.

Using Single, Double, and Quad Switches

Single Switch utilities are designed for scalar values and are best suited for such attributes as Diffuse, Eccentricity, Reflectivity, Bump Value, and so on. The steps listed in the prior section are equally applicable when using a Single Switch utility. The Single Switch utility automatically chooses the Out Alpha attribute when a texture is chosen via the Map option. In this case, the Out Alpha of each texture connects to the Input[*n*].In Single subchannel.

Double switches are designed for paired or double attributes. This makes the utility well suited for controlling UVs. For example, in Figure 8.17 a Cloth texture receives standard UV coordinates from a default place2dTexture node. The Repeat UV values, however, are supplied by a Double Switch utility. In this example, the Repeat UV attributes of three additional place2dTexture nodes are connected to the Input[*n*].In Double attributes of a doubleShadingSwitch node. place2dTexture1 has a Repeat UV value of 5, 5. place2dTexture2 has a Repeat UV value of 25, 25, and place2dTexture3 has a Repeat UV value of 50, 50. This shading network offers the ability to adjust UVs on multiple objects without affecting the base texture or necessitating the duplication of the entire shading network.

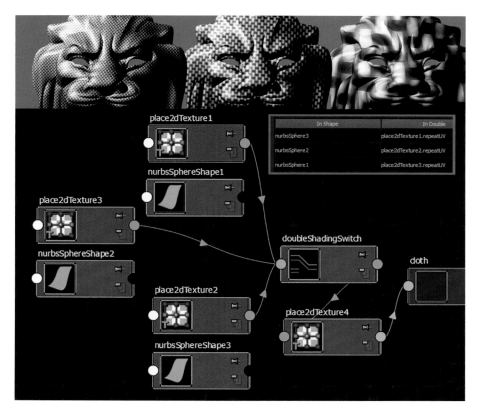

Figure 8.17 Repeat UV is controlled by a Double Switch utility. A simplified version of this scene is included with the Chapter 8 tutorial files as `double_switch.ma`.

The Quad Switch utility is suited for handling a vector attribute and a single attribute simultaneously. For example, in Figure 8.18 the Out Triple attribute of the quadShadingSwitch node is connected to the Color of a blinn material node. The Out Single attribute of the quadShadingSwitch node is connected the Diffuse of the same blinn. To split the switch's output in such a way, it is necessary to use the Connection Editor or the Node Editor. The Color attributes of three additional blinn nodes are connected to the Input[n].In Triple subchannels of the quadShadingSwitch node. The Diffuse attributes of the blinn nodes are also connected to the Input[n].In Single subchannels of the quadShadingSwitch node. Each of the three blinn nodes has the Out Color of a different texture connected to its Color and Diffuse attributes.

Note that the vector and single attributes *do not* need to correspond with each other. For example you can connect blinn2's Color to Input[0].In Triple and blinn2's Diffuse to Input[4].In Single. This ability to mix and match outputs and inputs allows for a great diversity of results. Hence, the Quad Switch provides the flexibility necessary to texture crowds, flocks, and swarms. Although such custom connections function properly, they do not appear in the Switch Attributes list of the switch's Attribute Editor tab.

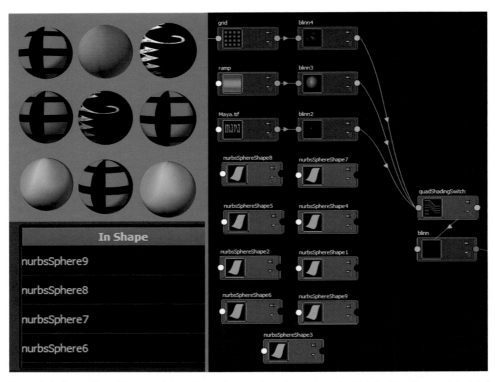

Figure 8.18 Three different Blinn materials are dispersed among nine spheres using a Quad Switch utility. This scene is included with the Chapter 8 tutorial files as quad_switch.ma.

Using Esoteric Utilities and Scene Nodes

Several utilities and nodes fail to fit into any specific category. For example, the Stencil utility provides an alternative method of blending maps together and the Optical FX utility creates postprocess glows, halos, and flares. Although scene nodes (those automatically generated by Maya) are not particularly flexible, they provide critical services in a 3D scene.

Stenciling Color

When mapping a texture, you have the option to apply it with the As Stencil option. To do so, click a checkered Map button beside an attribute in the Attribute Editor, RMB-click over a texture icon in the Create Render Node window, and choose As Stencil from the drop-down menu. If a texture is chosen through As Stencil, the new texture automatically receives a Stencil utility and two 2d Placement utilities. The Stencil utility stencils the new texture on top of the material color. For example, in Figure 8.19 a red logo is applied to a wall map with this technique. Although the Stencil utility produces results similar to the Blend Colors utility (see Chapter 6, "Creating Custom Connections and Applying Color Utilities"), its methodology is fairly different.

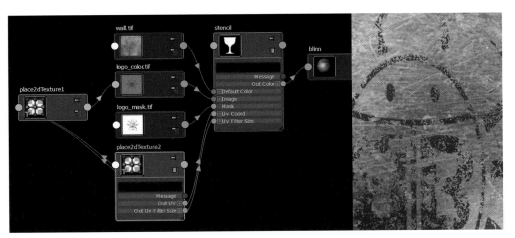

Figure 8.19 A logo is applied to a wall with a Stencil utility. This scene is included with the Chapter 8 tutorial files as `stencil.ma`.

In the example shading network, a red logo bitmap is loaded into a File texture labeled logo_color.tif. The Out Color of logo_color.tif is connected to Image of a stencil node. Standard UV connections run from the first place2dTexture node to logo_color.tif. The second place2dTexture node is connected to the stencil node with similar (albeit fewer) standard UV connections. The Out UV of the stencil's place2dTexture node is connected to the UV Coord of logo_color.tif's place2dTexture node. The Out UV Filter Size of the stencil's place2dTexture node is also connected to the UV Filter Size of logo_color.tif's place2dTexture node.

Normally, this minimal set of connections causes the logo_color.tif texture to completely overtake the blinn node's color. To avoid this, the Out Alpha of a second file texture node, logo_color.tif, is connected to the Mask of the stencil node. The Mask attribute controls where the new texture shows over the material color. In this case, a black and white bitmap is loaded into the logo_mask.tif node. Where the mask bitmap is white, the material color shows through; where the bitmap is black, the red logo is rendered.

At this point, the material color that is revealed by the Mask attribute is the solid color of the material's Color attribute. To bypass this, the Out Color of a third file texture node, labeled wall.tif, is connected to the Default Color of the stencil node. A bitmap photo of a wall is loaded into the wall.tif node. (If the wall.tif node were connected directly to the Color attribute of the blinn node it would not be visible.)

Applying Optical FX

The Optical FX utility (found in the Maya > Glow section of the Create Render Node, Create Node, and Hypershade windows) is automatically created whenever Light Glow is applied to a directional, area, or spot light. The utility controls the look of the glow, halo, or lens flare. (For a discussion of this and other fog effects, see Chapter 2, "Applying the Correct Maya Light Type.")

You can "graft" the Optical FX utility onto a surface. For example, in Figure 8.20 the World Matrix[0] attribute of a polygon lightbulb shape node is connected to the Light World Mat matrix input of an opticalFX node. This connection ensures that the optical effect occurs in the center of the lightbulb regardless of the lightbulb's position.

The color of the blinn node is connected to the Light Color of the opticalFX node. The blinn Color attribute is set to gold, which is picked up by the opticalFX glow. (The lightbulb surface is also assigned to the blinn node.) Last, the Ignore Light attribute of the opticalFX node is selected; this informs the program that no light is present. The result is a glow that follows the lightbulb wherever it goes. Unfortunately, since the opticalFX node creates a postprocess effect, the size of the glow does not change. However, you can animate the Glow Spread and Halo Spread attributes of the opticalFX node. Postprocess effects appear after the render has completed; hence, if the render is interrupted, the effect does not appear.

Understanding Scene Nodes

Render Partition, Default Light Set, and Light Linker nodes sit the farthest downstream in any shading network (see Figure 8.21). In addition, Maya provides a Layer

Manager node and Default Layer nodes. If animation is created, an animation curve node is created automatically for each animated channel.

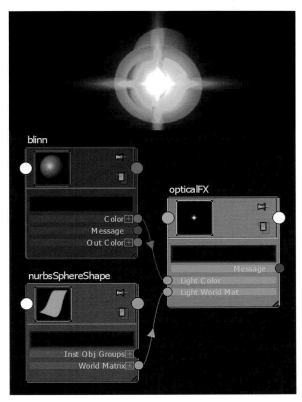

Figure 8.20 An Optical FX utility is attached to a lightbulb model, thereby creating a traveling glow. A simplified version of this scene is included with the Chapter 8 tutorial files as `optical_bulb.ma`. A QuickTime movie is included as `optical_bulb.mov`.

The Render Partition utility defines which shading group nodes are called upon during a render. The Default Light Set utility carries a list of lights that illuminate all objects within a scene. The Inst Obj Groups[0] attribute of each light's transform shape node is connected automatically to the Dag Set Members[0] attribute of the defaultLightSet node. If you deselect the Illuminates By Default attribute in a light's Attribute Editor tab, the connection is removed until the attribute is once again selected.

The Message of the defaultLightSet node is connected automatically to Link[*n*]. Light and Shadow Link[*n*].Shadow Light subchannels of the lightLinker utility node. The Light Linker utility defines the relationship between lights and objects. If a light is connected through to defaultLightSet node to the Link[*n*].Light subchannel, the light illuminates all shading groups connected to the lightLinker node. If a light is connected through the defaultLightSet node to the Shadow Link[*n*].Shadow Light attribute, then the light creates shadows for all shading groups connected to the lightLinker node. All shading group nodes are connected automatically to the light-Linker node. However, if you manually delete the connections, the shading group and the shading group's materials are ignored by the lights in the scene.

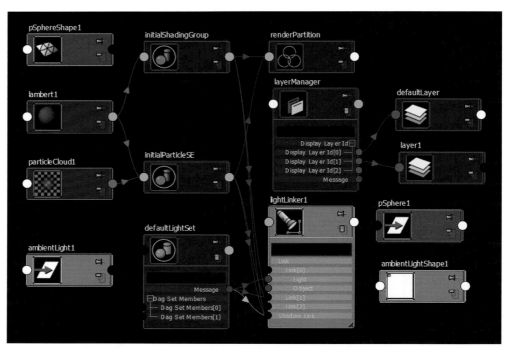

Figure 8.21 A simple scene containing a single polygon sphere, ambient light, and custom layer nevertheless includes a number of additional scene nodes. Many of these nodes are hidden by default, but can be located by clicking the Input And Output Connections button several times with all the visible nodes selected.

The Light Linker utility also stores broken links between lights, shadows, and surfaces. If a light link is broken through the Lighting/Shading > Break Light Links tool, a connection is made between the Message attribute of the surface shape node and the Ignore[n].Object Ignored subchannel of the lightLinker node. A connection is also made between the Message of the light shape node and Ignore[n].Light Ignored subchannel of the lightLinker node. If the Lighting/Shading > Make Light Links tool is applied, the connections are removed. Similar connections are made between the surface and light shape node's Message and the lightLinker node when the Break Shadow Links tool is applied.

If a light is linked or unlinked in the Relationship Editor, the connections are identical to those made with the Make Light Links and Break Light Links tools. For more information on the Relationship Editor, Make Light Links, and Break Light Links, see Chapter 2.

The Layer Manager node keeps a list of existing layers; it also keeps track of which layer is currently visible. A node is also created for each layer, including the Default Layer. Custom layers are connected to any transform node that belongs to the layer.

If animation exists in a scene, an animation curve node is created for each animated channel. If you open a curve node in the Attribute Editor, a Keys table lists the location of keyframes in time, the stored keyframe values, and the type of incoming and outgoing tangent types (see Figure 8.22).

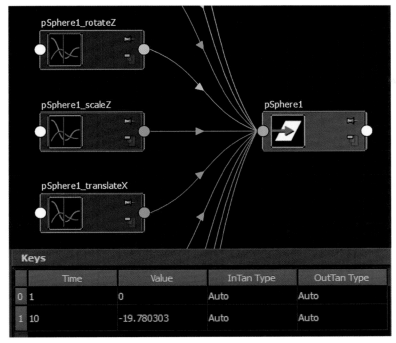

Figure 8.22 Top: Animation curve nodes for animated transform channels; Bottom: The Keys table for the Rotate Z channel showing two keyframes.

> **Note:** The Frame Cache utility is designed to retrieve the value of an animation curve at a particular frame. You can connect an animated attribute to its Stream input. The curve value is output by the Varying channel, with the frame number defined by the Vary Time attribute. You can also transfer the animation curve to another object by connecting the Frame Cache node's Past or Future channel to a transform channel. To offset the curve in time, you must use MEL scripting and include a time offset within brackets, such as `frameCache.past[6]`.

Chapter Tutorial: Creating a Zoom-Dolly by Connecting Nonmaterial Attributes

Alfred Hitchcock introduced a famous zoom-dolly camera move in the film *Vertigo* (1958). Steven Spielberg later popularized the same motion in *Jaws* (1978). As shown in Figure 8.23, if a camera zooms out while simultaneously dollying forward, the background distorts over time. This is caused by the optical characteristics of the camera lens. Telephoto lenses (for example, 300 mm) flatten a scene, but wide lenses (for example, 24 mm) give a scene more depth. It's possible to change the focal length of a zoom lens with a twist of the hand (for example, 200 mm to 50 mm).

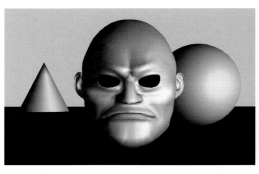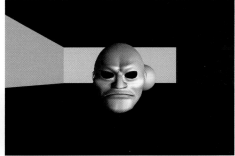

Figure 8.23 A Hitchcock zoom-dolly is created by connecting a camera's translation to its focal length. The result is a lens distortion that changes as the camera moves. A QuickTime movie of the final scene is included as `hitchcock.mov` with the Chapter 8 tutorial files..

You can automate the Hitchcock zoom-dolly with custom connections, which we'll create in this tutorial. You can follow these steps:

1. Open the `hitchcock.ma` file from the Chapter 8 `scenes` directory. Examine the scene. There is a primitive set, as well as two cameras. We'll use the HitchCam camera to create the dolly-zoom.

2. Select the HitchCam camera. Open the Node Editor. Click the Add Selected Nodes To Graph button. Select the HitchCam node and choose Edit > Group > ❑ from the main Maya menu. In the Group Options window, select the Group Pivot Center radio button and click the Group button. A new group node, Group1, appears. Rename the new node **HitchCamGroup**. Note that there is no apparent connection between the group and camera nodes in the Node Editor. However, the hierarchy connection exists when viewed in the Hypergraph or Outliner windows. Because the Center radio button was selected, the pivot point appears at the base of the camera icon lens.

3. In the Node Editor, RMB-click and choose Create Node. In the Create Node window, select the Multiply Divide utility. Select all the visible nodes and click the Show Primary Attributes button. Connect the Translate Z attribute of the HitchCamGroup node to the Input 1X of the multiplyDivide node. Connect the Output X of the multiplyDivide node to the Focal Length of the HitchCamShape node. This creates a one-to-one relationship between the camera Z position and the lens size (in millimeters). However, because the new group node has a Z position of 0, the Focal Length becomes 0, and the view suddenly becomes distorted (as if the objects are far away).

4. In the Node Editor, RMB-click and choose Create Node. In the Create Node window, select the Add Double Linear utility. Delete the connection line between the HitchCamGroup and multiplyDivide nodes. Connect Translate Z of HitchCamGroup to Input 1 of the addDoubleLinear node (LMB-drag the connection line from Translate Z to the left input dot on the addDoubleLinear node, choose Other from the drop-down menu, and select Input 1 in the Input Selection window). Connect the Output of addDoubleLinear to Input 1X of multiplyDivide. Use Figure 8.24 as a reference. After the connections are made, select the visible nodes and click Show Connected Attributes button. the Open the addDoubleLinear node in the Attribute Editor. Enter **10** in Input 2. This adds 10 to the current Z position and ensures that the camera has a nonzero value at frame 1.

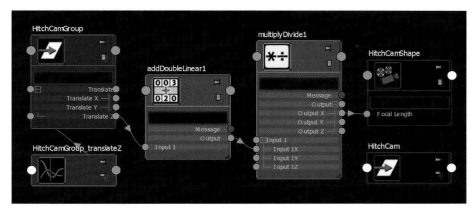

Figure 8.24 The final custom network. The animation curve node is added automatically after Translate Z is keyframed.

5. Note that the camera view remains distorted. Open the multiplyDivide node in the Attribute Editor. Change Input 2X to 10. This increases the resulting Focal Length by ten times and prevents the Focal Length from remaining excessively small. The Focal Length becomes 100 mm and the view returns to normal.

6. Select the HitchCamGroup node by itself. While on frame 1, key Translate Z with its current value. To key one channel, open the Channel Editor, RMB-click over the channel name, and choose Key Selected from the menu.

7. Go to frame 60. With the HitchCamGroup node selected, interactively move the camera along the Z axis so that it sits closer to the face and set. Note that the face and set stretches as you do this. This is caused by the change in Focal Length value. Similar distortion happens with real-world zoom lenses. With this scene, the lower the Output X value, the smaller the value of the Focal Length and the "wider" the lens; the larger the Output X value, the larger the value of the Focal Length and the "longer" and more "zoomed-in" the lens. This creates an inverse relationship, which emulates the Hitchcock zoom-dolly discussed at the start of this section.

8. While on frame 60, key the Translate Z while the camera is close to the face. For example, set a key while the HitchCamGroup sits at 0, 0, −8. (If the camera passes 0, 0, −10 and Output X becomes negative, the Focal Length becomes negative, which turns the geometry inside-out; this is not recommended.) Play back the timeline to see the lens distortion over time (see Figure 8.23 at the start of this section). Note that the dolly motion of the camera does not distort the view; however, the dolly does ensure that the head maintains the same portion of the frame *despite* the distortion created by the focal length change.

   The tutorial is complete! If you get stuck, a finished version is saved as `hitchcock_finished.ma` with the Chapter 8 tutorial files.

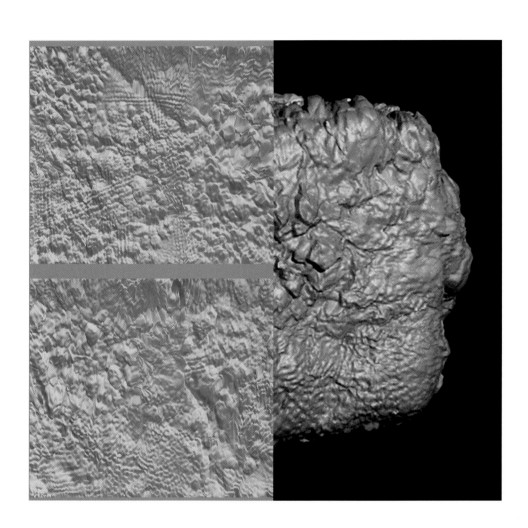

Improving Textures with Custom UV Layouts and Maps

Although the Hypershade and Node Editor windows in the Autodesk® Maya® program provide numerous ways to prepare materials, several important techniques outside these windows are worth a look. Preparing proper UVs for any model is a critical step in the texturing process. Using the 3D Paint tool is an efficient way to prepare custom bitmaps. The support of the Photoshop PSD format in Maya allows the use of layers. At the same time, the proper use of bump and displacement maps can add realism to a render. Lastly, the Transfer Maps tools allow you to generate maps based on geometry comparison.

Chapter Contents

UV approaches for NURBS and polygon surfaces
Workflow for the 3D Paint tool
Support of the Photoshop PSD format
Intricacies of bump and displacement maps
The Transfer Maps tool

Preparing UV Texture Space

The NURBS and polygon surfaces employed in the examples featured in previous chapters carry UV texture spaces that are satisfactory for their corresponding renders. For a render to be successful, the UV texture space of a surface must avoid undue stretching, pinching, or overlapping.

Although the modeling steps necessary to create high-quality UVs are numerous and far beyond the scope of this book, a few important concepts and techniques are worth reviewing.

To display the UV texture space of a selected surface, choose Window > UV Texture Editor. By default, U runs from left to right; V runs from bottom to top. In the UV Texture Editor, the upper-right portion of the grid represents the full 0-to-1.0 UV texture space. If a face sits outside this area, it will receive a repeated portion of a texture (that is, the texture is *tiled*).

Note: *UV texture space* is a coordinate space that relates the pixels of a texture to points on a surface. UV points represent the location of a polygon's vertices within UV texture space; you can transform UV points of a polygon surface in the UV Texture Editor. Groups of connected UV points are known as *UV shells* or *UV islands*. *UVs*, *UV layout*, and *UV map* are loose terms that describe the current state of UV points in a particular UV texture space.

Working with NURBS Surfaces

NURBS surfaces automatically receive UV texture information when they are created. 0, 0 in UV texture space occurs at the origin box of the surface. The two vertices appearing closest to the origin box are represented by a tiny U and V, indicating the U and V direction (see Figure 9.1). Although you can examine the UV layout of a NURBS surface in the UV Texture Editor, you cannot manipulate the UV points.

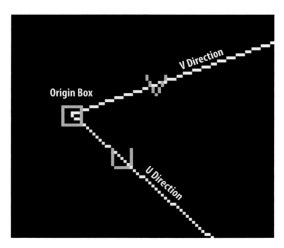

Figure 9.1 The origin box and UV vertices of a NURBS surface

Fixing NURBS Texture Stretch

In general, NURBS surfaces are ready to texture as soon as they're created. Nevertheless, NURBS are prone to texture stretching if the surfaces are not properly constructed. Stretching may occur for any of the following reasons:

- The distribution of surface isoparms is uneven due to unevenly spaced curves at the point of surface creation.

- The Open/Close Surfaces or Attach Surfaces tool is applied to the surface.

- Some control vertices are moved manually a significant distance from their neighboring control vertices.

Although you can rebuild a UV-stretched surface in various ways by using surface modeling tools, you can temporarily fix texture stretching by selecting the Fix Texture Warp attribute in the Texture Map section of a NURBS surface's Attribute Editor tab (see Figure 9.2). In this situation, the renderer ignores the inherent UV information of the surface and applies a new, nonpermanent chord length parameterization. The Grid Div Per Span U and Grid Div Per Span V attributes set the density of a virtual grid that is placed over the surface to calculate the new UV texture space. Although the default value of 4 works in most situations, you can increase the value for greater accuracy. This fix is supported by the Maya Software and mental ray® renderers but will not work with the Hardware Texturing option in a viewport view.

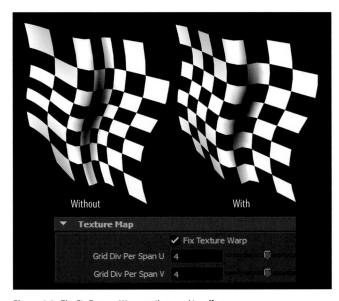

Figure 9.2 The Fix Texture Warp attribute and its effect

Aligning NURBS Surfaces

If you want to create a complex model with NURBS modeling tools, multiple surfaces are necessary. In this situation, it is important to align the UVs in such a way that they are easily interpreted. One technique employed professionally involves a global alignment of all the surfaces, where the U and V directions of each surface in a scene match. You can check the current U and V alignment by selecting the surfaces in question and choosing Display > NURBS > Surface Origins. An axis is superimposed on the selected surfaces with a red line indicating the U direction, a green line indicating the V direction, and a blue line indicating the surface normal (see Figure 9.3). Note that the 0, 0 of the UV texture space occurs where the U, V, and normal lines meet.

Figure 9.3 The Surface Origins tool displays U, V, and normal directions on a NURBS torus. U runs around the tube circumference and V runs along the length of the tube.

If the UVs of a particular surface are not aligned, you can choose Surfaces menu set > Edit NURBS > Reverse Surface Direction > ❑. In the Reverse Surface Direction Options window, you can choose to reverse the U direction or the V direction. You can also reverse both directions or swap the U and V axes. Because the U direction, V direction, and surface normal are linked, any choice you make affects all three of these axes. For example, reversing the U direction causes the normal to be reversed, because Maya uses "right-handed" coordinate space, which relates the U, V, and normal direction. You can relate this space to your own right hand, where the thumb points toward positive Z, the middle finger points toward positive Y, and the index finger points toward positive X (see Figure 9.4). This relationship does not change and is consistent across all surfaces. All surfaces in Maya are double-sided by default. If the Double Sided attribute is deselected in the Render Stats section of the surface's Attribute Editor tab, the UV-to-normal relationship is easier to see when shading is activated for the viewport. By default, surface normals are perpendicular to the surface face and indicate the primary side of the surface that is shaded when the surface is single-sided.

Reviewing Polygon UV Options

Although NURBS surfaces are ready to render with their default UVs, polygon surfaces often need a great deal of adjustment. The use of primitives is the exception since the primitive's inherent UVs are orderly (see the top of Figure 9.5). As soon as various polygon modeling tools are applied to a primitive, however, the resulting UV texture space is cluttered and unusable. For example, at the bottom of Figure 9.5, a pig model sports a tangled UV layout with numerous overlapping faces.

Right-handed Cartesian space   UV texture space

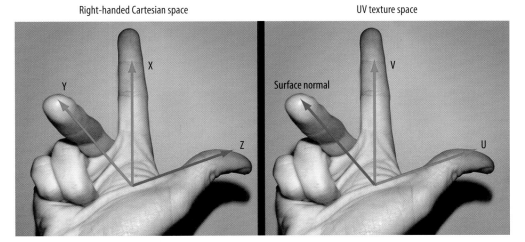

Figure 9.4 The right-handed system for Cartesian space and UV texture space

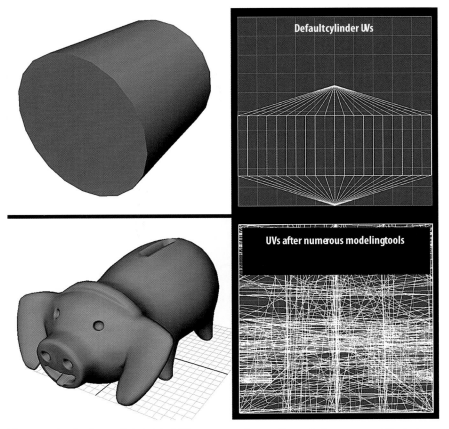

Figure 9.5 Top: A polygon cylinder's default UV texture space; Bottom: The result of numerous modeling tools.

Here are some approaches to creating an orderly UV texture space for polygon surfaces:

Maya Projection Tools   With the Create UVs menu, Maya provides several UV projection tools (see Figure 9.6). The tools allow you to determine interactively how the 2D texture space is mapped to a 3D surface. For example, the Create UVs > Planar Mapping tool creates a planar projection. UV coordinates within the 2D planar projection are traced, in a straight line, from the projection to the surface; the surface point that is struck receives the new UV coordinate. Although UV projections are suitable for simple, mostly flat, polygon surfaces, they fail to produce good results for any surface that is convoluted or complex.

For example, projecting new a UV layout for a human character in one step creates an unusable UV layout. (Although the Automatic Mapping tool prevents UV overlapping, it creates myriad small UV shells.) The workaround for a complex model is to create UV projections for individual parts. For example, can use the Cylindrical Mapping tool to project each arm, then each leg, then the torso, and finally the head. As such, this method is time-consuming and still produces multiple UV shells that may need additional adjustment.

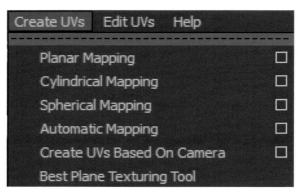

Figure 9.6 The projection tools within the Create UVs menu. The menu is accessible from the Polygons menu set.

Maya UV Manipulation Tools   Maya also provides a long list of UV manipulation tools through the Polygons menu set > Edit UVs menu or the Polygons menu with the UV Texture Editor. These tools allow you to transform UV points or UV shells and split or sew UV edges. They allow you to fine-tune the shape of UV shells, rearrange UV shell layouts, prevent overlapping UV faces through unfolding or relaxation, sew together separate UV shells, and create new UV shells by splitting edges. In addition, you can manipulate UV components directly in the UV Texture Editor. For example, you can RMB-click in the editor, choose UV from the marking menu, draw a selection marquee around UV points, and either move, scale, or rotate the points by using the standard transform tools (Figure 9.7). You can also move entire UV shells by choosing Tool > Move UV Shell Tool.

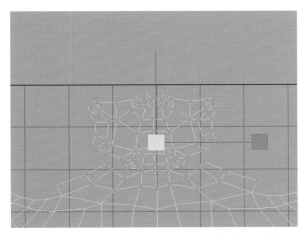

Figure 9.7 Selected UV points are scaled with the Scale tool in the UV Texture Editor.

Pelt-Mapping Tools Pelt-mapping tools use various techniques to unwrap and relax UV points so that large, continuous "pelts" are created. The pelts appear similar to animal pelts produced by hunters when skinning an animal (see Figure 9.8). UV pelts offer the advantage of producing a minimum number of UV border edges. A large number of border edges may make texture painting more difficult or may produce artifacts if texture colors aren't consistent across two halves of split and separated UV edges. (When a UV edge is split, it forms two separate edges that may be moved apart.) UV pelting tools come in the form of stand-alone programs, such as Roadkill or headus UVLayout, or plug-ins available in Maya. Generally, the programs offer interactive means to select UV edges, split those edges, and thus form UV borders. They also offer means to select UV edges, merge those edges, and thus reduce the overall size of the shell's UV border or borders. Aside from the advantage of minimizing the number of UV shells, pelt mapping redistributes UV points to minimize potential texture stretching.

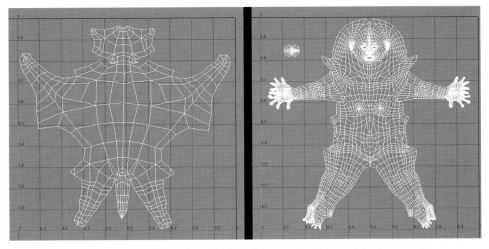

Figure 9.8 Left: Pelt-mapped low-resolution dog model; Right: Pelt-mapped medium-resolution human model.

Ptex Texturing Ptex texturing does away with traditional UV layouts by converting the UV space to a specialized texel (texture element) system. The texels allow each geometry face to carry its own discrete texture with an independent resolution within a single Ptex file. As such, only one Ptex file is required per channel per model. For example, a single diffuse Ptex file is needed to color a model. Ptex may be applied to a surface with a limited number of steps and therefore is much more efficient to set up. Although Maya 2015 reads Ptex textures (see the next section), it cannot produce them. Hence, it's necessary to import geometry that already carries a Ptex layout. For example, you can convert a surface to Ptex in Autodesk® Mudbox® and then import an OBJ or FBX file into Maya. Although Ptex is easy to set up and provides advantages when rendering (such as resolution independence across the faces), it is difficult to directly manipulate Ptex maps. For example, you cannot open Ptex files in Adobe Photoshop. Even if converted, the Ptex layout appears as a random series of UV "bricks" (see Figure 9.9). In contrast, manipulating a map that belongs to standard UV layout in Photoshop is fairly easy. Hence, 3D paint tools are often used to create and adjust Ptex maps. For example, the native 3D paint tools found within Mudbox are easily used in conjunction with Ptex.

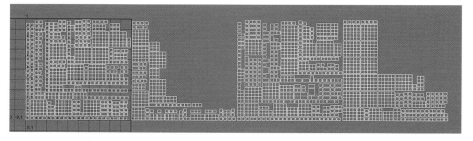

Figure 9.9 A Ptex layout for a character model, as seen in the UV Texture Editor. Ptex layouts often extend outside the 0-to-1.0 area.

Rendering Ptex Textures in Maya 2015

With Maya 2015 and the mental ray renderer, you can render geometry with a Ptex layout. To set up a Ptex shading network and create a test render, follow these basic steps:

1. Import geometry with a Ptex layout into a new Maya 2015 scene. An example model is included as `Ptex.obj` in the Chapter 9 `scenes` directory.

2. Assign a new material, such as Blinn, to the geometry. Map any Ptex bitmaps to the appropriate attributes. For example, map the color Ptex bitmap to the Color attribute of the Blinn. A sample color Ptex map is included as `PtexColor.ptx` in the Chapter 9 `textures` directory. A standard File texture is able to read the Ptex file format, which is generated by a program such as

Mudbox or The Foundry's MARI. However, the File thumbnail remains black after you load the Ptex file. As of this writing, Maya is unable to preview Ptex bitmaps within the Hypershade or Node Editor windows.

3. Switch to the mental ray renderer and render a test frame. The Ptex texture appears as any other texture. The border edges of the Ptex "bricks" are not visible (Figure 9.10). However, if you open the surface in the UV Texture Editor, you can see the unique Ptex layout (see Figure 9.9 in the previous section). To soften the surface, select it and choose Polygons menu set > Normals > Soften Edge.

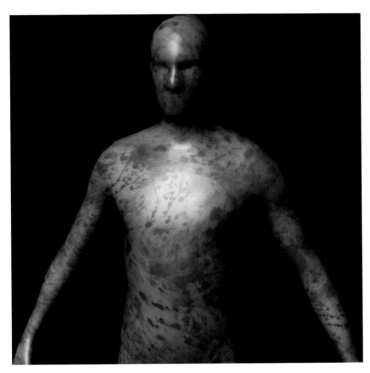

Figure 9.10 A primitive character model with a Ptex layout is rendered in Maya 2015. Despite the brick-like Ptex layout, no border edges are visible when the noisy color Ptex map is rendered. This scene is included with the Chapter 9 tutorial files as `ptex.ma`.

Using the 3D Paint Tool

With the 3D Paint tool, you can paint texture maps in a viewport with a virtual paint brush. In addition, you can rough in bitmaps in preparation for painting the final texture map in Adobe Photoshop or a similar paint program.

Because the workflow required by the 3D Paint tool is fairly esoteric, I'll show you the basic steps:

1. Select a NURBS or polygon surface. (Polygon surfaces must have non-overlapping UVs that fit within a normalized UV range of 0 to 1.0.) Assign a new material to the surface.

2. Select the surface again, switch to the Rendering menu set, and choose Texturing > 3D Paint Tool > ❏. The options for the 3D Paint tool appear in the Tool Settings panel. In the File Textures section, choose a setting from the Attribute To Paint drop-down (see Figure 9.11). Although Color is the default, you can paint Transparency, Incandescence, and many other material attributes. Click the Assign/Edit Textures button. In the Assign/Edit File Textures window, choose Size X, Size Y, and Image Format values for the bitmap that will be written. Click the Assign/Edit Textures button at the bottom of the window. The window closes and a File texture is mapped automatically to the appropriate attribute of the material assigned to the surface. Note that the surface must be assigned to a material other than the default lambert1 material.

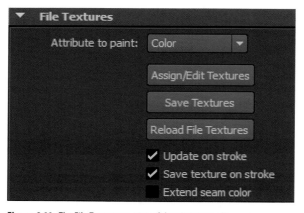

Figure 9.11 The File Textures section of the 3D Paint tool's panel

3. To adjust the brush radius, change the Radius(U) value in the Brush section of the Tool Settings panel. You can also interactively change the brush radius by pressing the B key and LMB-dragging left or right in the viewport. The brush is visible as a crosshair within a circle as the mouse pointer crosses the surface. Choose a brush style by clicking one of the Artisan brush icons. Select a Color value and an Opacity value (in the Color section). LMB-click and drag the mouse over the surface. A paint stroke appears as long as Smooth Shade All and Hardware Texturing are selected in the viewport's Shading menu.

Note: If you use a pressure-sensitive stylus and tablet, Radius(U) signifies the brush's upper size limit and Radius(L) signifies the brush's lower size limit. If you use a mouse, Radius(L) is ignored.

4. You can change the brush Radius(U), Color, and Opacity values as often as necessary. Two additional Artisan brush options—Erase and Clone—are available in the Paint Operations section (see Figure 9.12). Erase removes old

paint strokes and leaves the material's original color. Clone functions in the same manner as a clone brush in a digital paint program. To choose a clone source, click the Set Clone Source button and then click the surface. There are two options for the Clone Brush Mode: Dynamic and Static. Dynamic allows the clone source to move with the brush (the standard Photoshop method). Static fixes the clone source and allows the same sampled area to be painted over and over. In addition, you can set Blend Mode to Lighten, Darken, Multiply, Screen, or Overlay. These modes are similar to those found in Adobe Photoshop.

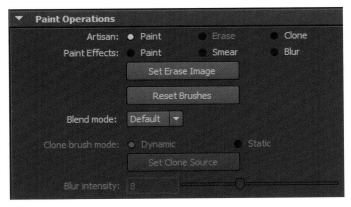

Figure 9.12 The Paint Operations section of the 3D Paint tool's panel

5. To permanently save the painting, click the Save Textures button (see Figure 9.11 earlier in this section). A bitmap is written out in the size and image format specified in step 2. In addition, the File texture lists a path that points to a default Maya location, as in this example:

   ```
   3dPaintTextures\scene_name\sphere_color.iff
   ```

   You can move the resulting bitmap to a different location and reload it into the File texture if necessary. If Save Texture On Stroke is selected, the texture is saved automatically at the end of each stroke. If the Update On Stroke is selected, the material icon constantly updates. The Extend Seam Color option extends the paint color at the UV shell borders to prevent seams from appearing on the surface during the render.

6. You can paint multiple textures on a single surface. To create a new texture, choose a different texture type from the Attribute To Paint drop-down menu (see Figure 9.11 earlier) and set the options in the Assign/Edit File Textures window. Only one texture is visible on the surface at a time. To return to a previously edited texture, simply choose the appropriate attribute from the Attribute To Paint drop-down menu. If the texture is not visible immediately, click the

surface with the brush. Click the Save Textures button to save all the textures at once.

Note: To fill a surface with a single solid color, click the Flood Paint button. The color is set by the Color attribute in the Flood section of the 3D Paint tool's panel.

It's possible to paint across multiple surfaces simultaneously, even when the surfaces are dissimilar (for example, polygons mixed with NURBS surfaces). If multiple surfaces are selected when Assign/Edit Textures is applied, Maya automatically creates a Triple Switch utility (see Chapter 8, "Harnessing the Power of Math Utilities," for a description). In turn, the Triple Switch utility is connected to a series of File textures that correspond to each surface.

PSD Support

Maya supports the Adobe Photoshop PSD file format. The PSD File texture in Maya supports the creation of PSD networks in which multiple textures are stored in one file. This offers the advantage of reducing the number of individual textures required for a Maya scene. In addition, it simplifies the workflow when you're altering or updating the texture maps in Photoshop. To achieve this, follow these steps:

1. Create a material and assign it to a NURBS or polygon surface. Apply various textures to the material's Color, Specular Color, Transparency, Diffuse, or other attributes. You can use any 2D or 3D texture, whether they are bitmaps or procedural.

2. Select the surface, switch to the Rendering menu set, and choose Texturing > Create PSD Network to open the Create PSD Network Options window, as shown in Figure 9.13.

3. Enter a filename and path into the Image Name field and specify an image size in the Size X and Size Y fields. If you prefer that Maya provide a snapshot of the UV texture space in the resulting PSD file, check Include UV Snapshot.

4. Choose attributes from the Attributes column and select the right-arrow button (between the Attributes and Selected Attributes columns) to list the selected attributes in the Selected Attributes column (see Figure 9.13). You can choose any combination of attributes (even those with no texture assigned).

5. By default, all procedural textures listed in the Selected Attributes column are converted to a File texture. You can set the options for the conversion by clicking the Convert To File Texture Options button.

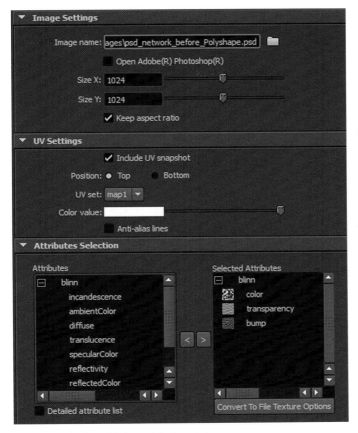

Figure 9.13 The Create PSD Network Options window

6. Click the Create button in the Create PSD Network Options window. Any attribute that is listed in the Selected Attributes column has its old texture node replaced by a PSD File texture node that is named after the material and texture (for example, PSD_blinn_transparency). An example network is illustrated in Figure 9.14. If an attribute had no texture mapped to it but was nevertheless listed in the Selected Attributes column, an empty layer is set aside in the resulting PSD file. Each PSD File node's Link To Layer Set attribute is set to the appropriate group name for a connection to the matching attribute. For example, if a texture was originally mapped to the Color attribute of a Blinn, the old texture node is disconnected and replaced by a PSD File node with its Link To Layer Set attribute set to blinn.color. Each layer in the PSD file is grouped—by itself. The Link To Layer Set recognizes only group names and *not* layer names. You can manually create a group in Photoshop by selecting a layer in the Layers panel and choosing New Group From Layers from the panel menu.

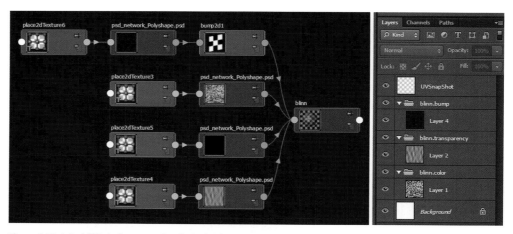

Figure 9.14 Left: A PSD shading network in the Node Editor; Right: The matching PSD file revealed in the Adobe Photoshop CC Layers panel. The scene before the application of Create PSD Network is included with the Chapter 9 tutorial files as `psd_network_before.ma`. The scene after the application of Create PSD Network is included as `psd_network_after.ma`. The resulting PSD file is included as `psd_network_Polyshape.psd`.

You can edit the resulting PSD file in Photoshop. If you make changes and save the file, choose Texturing > Update PSD Networks to ensure that Maya recognizes the changes. You can revise an existing network at any point by selecting the surface and choosing Texturing > Edit PSD Network. At this point, you can add and remove attributes from the Selected Attributes column of the Edit PSD Network Options window. If you remove an attribute, the layer is automatically deleted and the connection to the corresponding psdFileTex node is broken.

Bump, Normal, and Displacement Mapping

Bump, normal, and displacement mapping can add an extra level of detail to any material. Each has its own unique strengths, weaknesses, and application. Although the Maya Displacement shader can be difficult to adjust, the Height Field utility provides a rough preview in a workspace view.

Bump Mapping

Bump maps perturb normals along the interior of a surface at the point of render. They do not, however, affect the outer edges. Nevertheless, the bump effect can easily sell the idea that a surface is rough. When you use a texture as a bump map, middle-gray (0.5, 0.5, 0.5) has no effect. High values cause peaks and low values cause valleys. To set the intensity of a bump map, you can adjust the value of the Bump Depth attribute of the Bump 2d or Bump 3d utility. Bump Depth accepts negative numbers, thus inverting the peaks and valleys. In general, the default Bump Depth value of 1.0 creates a bump that is too strong and should be adjusted.

The simplest way to add a bump map is to click the Bump Mapping checkered Map button in a material's Attribute Editor tab. In this case, a Bump 2d or a Bump 3d utility is automatically connected to the shading network. The Bump 2d utility is designed for standard 2d textures such as File, Checker, or Ramp. The Bump 3d utility is designed for 3d textures such as Brownian, Cloud, or Solid Fractal.

If necessary, you can make the bump mapping connections by hand in the Hypershade or Node Editor windows. Connect the Out Normal of the Bump 2d or Bump 3d node to the Normal Camera of the material node. Connect the Out Alpha of the texture to the Bump Value of the Bump 2d or Bump 3d node. If the Out Color of the texture is already connected to another attribute of the material, you can continue to connect the texture's Out Alpha to the Bump Value (see Figure 9.15). In this way, only a single place2dTexture node need be adjusted.

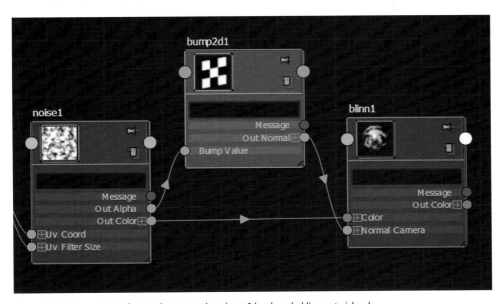

Figure 9.15 A texture is simultaneously connected to a bump2d node and a blinn material node.

Bump maps are extremely efficient to render. In fact, bump maps are as convincing as displacement maps in many situations. For example, if a bump map is applied to a surface that sits against a cluttered background, the smooth edges of the surface are difficult to perceive (see Figure 9.16). Motion blur, shadows, and other 3D phenomena also help disguise the bump map's limitations.

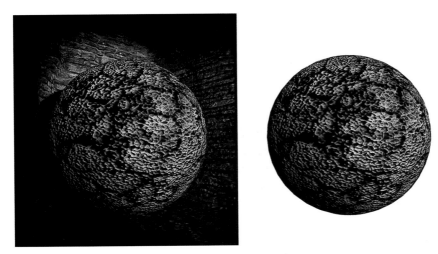

Figure 9.16 A bump-mapped surface against two different backgrounds

Normal Mapping

Normal mapping is similar to bump mapping in that it perturbs surface normals at the time of rendering. Although it makes the interior of a surface appear bumpy, it does not affect the surface's silhouette. Normals maps are often generated by comparing a high-resolution surface to a low-resolution version of the same surface. Hence, normal maps create the illusion of high resolution while maintaining a "light" (low-resolution) model. For this reason, normal maps are commonly used in the gaming industry. You can generate normal maps with Maya (demonstrated later in this chapter) or other programs such as Pixologic Zbrush, Mudbox, or xNormal.

Maya supports two styles of normal maps: tangent space and object space. Tangent space is the local coordinate space of a vertex that is described by a tangent vector, a binormal vector, and the surface normal. The tangent vector is aligned with the surface's U direction. The binormal vector is aligned with the surface's V direction. Tangent space normal maps take on purple-to-blue hues because the surface normals have vectors of 0, 0, 1.0 in tangent space. In contrast, object space normal maps take on rainbow-like color (see Figure 9.17). This occurs because each surface normal points in a unique XYZ direction in object space. Object space normal maps are suitable only for surfaces that *do not* undergo animation or deformation. Due to the limitations of object space maps, tangent space maps are more commonly used.

The steps to apply a normal map are identical to applying a bump map (see the previous section). However, you must set the Bump 2d or Bump 3d node's Use As menu to Tangent Space Normals or Object Space Normals.

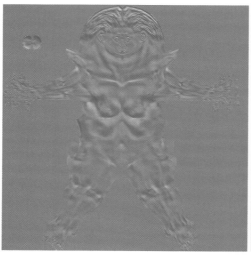 

Figure 9.17 Left: Tangent space normal map for a character; Right: Object space normal map for the same character.

Displacement Mapping

Displacement maps distort geometry at the point of render. That is, the assigned surface is tessellated and the resulting vertices are translated a distance based on the source texture. The maps are grayscale, with brighter pixels creating the greatest distortion and black creating no change to the surface (see Figure 9.27 at the end of the chapter for an example). Although displacement maps are more processor intensive, they are more realistic than bump maps. Thus, displacement maps provide the following advantages:

- The surface's silhouette is displaced.
- Displaced detail casts and receives shadows.
- A displacement map can create surface features far more detailed than any other common modeling techniques within Maya.

Setting Up a Displacement Network

You cannot create a displacement map shading network through standard material connections in Maya. Instead, you must connect a Displacement Shader to a shading group node. Follow these steps:

1. Select a material node in the Node Editor window and open its Attribute Editor tab. Click the Input And Output Connections button. The Shading Group node appears (its name ends with *SG*). Open the Shading Group node in the Attribute Editor.

2. Click the Displacement Mat. checkered Map button in the Shading Group Attributes section. Choose a texture from the Create Render Node window. A displacementShader node is created. The Displacement of the displacementShader is connected to the Displacement Shader of the Shading Group node (see Figure 9.18). The Out Alpha of the texture is connected to the Displacement of the displacementShader node. The displacementShader's input and output attribute names are identical. Render a test frame.

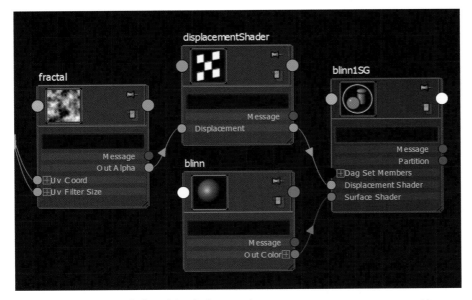

Figure 9.18 A Displacement Shader node in a shading network

Adjusting the Displacement Mapping

Other aspects of a displacement map can be controlled through the Displacement Map section of the assigned surface's Attribute Editor tab or the displacement texture's Color Balance section.

The surface's Displacement Map section (see Figure 9.19) includes controls for altering surface tessellation, which occurs at the point of render but does not permanently alter the surface.

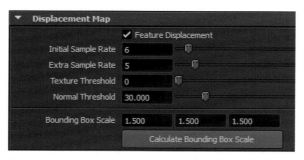

Figure 9.19 The Displacement Map section of a surface's Attribute Editor tab

The following attributes are particularly useful:

Feature Displacement   Toggles on or off feature-based displacement. If selected, the Displacement Shader tessellates the assigned surface only in those areas where displaced features occur. If deselected, the Displacement Shader adds no additional tessellation; in this case, detail contained within the displacement map may be lost if the surface does not have sufficient subdivisions. Maya attempts to make up for the loss of detail inherent with non-feature-based displacement by simultaneously treating the displacement map as a bump map. The use of Feature Displacement is almost always advantageous as it produces superior results. Nevertheless, if the inherent resolution of the surface is too low, the subdivision of the Feature Displacement process may not be sufficient enough to produce high-quality results.

Initial Sample Rate and Extra Sample Rate   Initial Sample Rate determines the size of a sampling grid laid over each polygon triangle. The grid is used to determine whether the triangle should be tessellated. Tessellation is deemed necessary if the contrast between neighboring texture pixels is sufficient. Extra Sample Rate adds additional sampling. In effect, Extra Sample Rate further subdivides the sampling grid applied by Initial Sample Rate. When setting Initial Sample Rate and Extra Sample Rate, use these guidelines:

- If the surface is highly subdivided, a low Initial Sample Rate is usually satisfactory.

- If the surface is sparsely subdivided and contains large polygon faces, the Initial Sample Rate should be large. Even so, increase the Initial Sample Rate slowly while rendering tests.

- Displacement maps with fine detail and/or a great deal of contrast often necessitate high Initial Sample Rate values.

- If the displacement requires sharp corners or strongly defined transitions between no displacement and high displacement, you should incrementally raise the Extra Sample Rate value. That said, start with an Extra Sample Rate of 0.

Texture Threshold   Eliminates unneeded vertices and aims to reduce noise within the displacement. The Texture Threshold value is a percentage of the maximum height variation within the displacement. Any vertex whose difference in height from neighboring vertices is below the Texture Threshold value is removed. The default value of 0 leaves this feature off. When raising the value, do so incrementally. If possible, eliminate any fine noise in the texture map before applying it as a displacement (for example, soften or blur the texture in Photoshop).

Normal Threshold   Controls the "softness" of the resulting displacement. This attribute's functionality is identical to that of the Set Normal Angle tool (which you can access by switching to the Polygons menu set and choosing Normals > Set Normal Angle). If the angle between two adjacent triangles is less than the Normal Threshold value, the triangles are rendered smoothly. If not, the triangles are rendered with a sharp edge between them.

Bounding Box Scale   Sets the size of the bounding box used to contain a displacement. If a displacement appears cut off at the peaks or carries other render flaws, gradually increase the X, Y, and Z values. The default values of 1.5, 1.5, 1.5 are adequate for most displacements. Large Bounding Box Scale values increase memory usage. The Calculate Bounding Box Scale button estimates an appropriate bounding box size based on the shading network and world scale of the assigned surface.

You can adjust the strength of a displacement by altering the Alpha Gain and Alpha Offset values of the texture map used for the displacement. Alpha Gain, found in the texture's Color Balance section, is a multiplier that's applied to the texture's Out Alpha attribute. The Alpha Gain default value is 1.0, which has no effect on the Out Alpha value. An Alpha Gain value of 0 removes the displacement completely. An Alpha Gain value of −1.0 reverses the displacement. In contrast, Alpha Offset is an offset factor for the texture's Out Alpha. The Alpha Offset value is added to the Out Alpha value, thus increasing the intensity of the displacement. A negative Alpha Offset reduces the displacement intensity. You can use any combination of Alpha Gain and Alpha Offset values to adjust the displacement.

> **Note:** Environment textures, which require 3D Placement utilities, are not recommended for use as displacement maps. The resulting calculations will be inaccurate.

Note: The mental ray Approximation Editor (choose Window > Rendering Editors > mental ray > Approximation Editor) provides a means to further subdivide a surface for displacement during the render. To apply this tool, select the displaced surface and click the Create button in the Displacement Tessellation section of the editor. A mentalrayDisplaceApprox node is created. The node provides various means to subdivide the surface through its Attribute Editor tab (you can reach this by clicking the Edit button in the Displacement Tessellation section of the editor). The mentalrayDisplaceApprox node differs from the mentalraySubdivApprox node (which you can also create in the editor) in that it also takes into account details within the displacement texture to determine subdivision density. The mentalrayDisplaceApprox node works on NURBS and polygon surfaces, whereas the mentalraySubdivApprox node only works with polygon surfaces. The mentalraySubdivApprox node is often useful for smoothing out a non-displaced polygon surface. You can create a mentalraySubdivApprox node by selecting the surface and clicking the Create button in the Subdivisions section of the mental ray Approximation Editor window.

Using the Height Field Utility to Preview Displacements

The Height Field utility previews displacements in a viewport. When a texture node is connected to the utility, it creates a plane at 0, 0, 0 and displaces it with the displacement shading network. Although the Height Field utility provides only a rough approximation of the displacement, it can aid in the adjustment of the displacement shading network.

To add a Height Field utility to a displacement network, follow these steps:

1. Using the Node Editor, RMB-click and choose Create Node. Select the Height Field utility from the Maya > Utilities section of the Create Node window. A heightField node and Transform node are added to the scene.

2. Connect the Out Alpha channel of the texture used as a displacement to the Displacement channel of the heightField node. A Height Field plane appears in the viewport and previews the displacement (Figure 9.20).

3. To increase the preview quality, open the heightField node in the Attribute Editor and raise the Resolution value. For an example shading network, see Figure 9.21.

The Height Field plane cannot be rendered; however, it can be repositioned. The Height Scale attribute of the Height Field utility controls the scale of the previewed displacement (but does not alter the rendered displacement). If Height Scale is left at 1.0, the previewed displacement matches the render of the actual Displacement Shader (see Figure 9.20).

Note: The Displacement Shader node can accept 3D textures. As such, you can connect the texture's Out Color to the Vector Displacement of the Displacement Shader node. You can interpret the vector values in world, object, or tangent space, as determined by the Displacement Shader node's Vector Space menu. When you are using a 3D texture, I recommend using the mental ray renderer to produce accurate results.

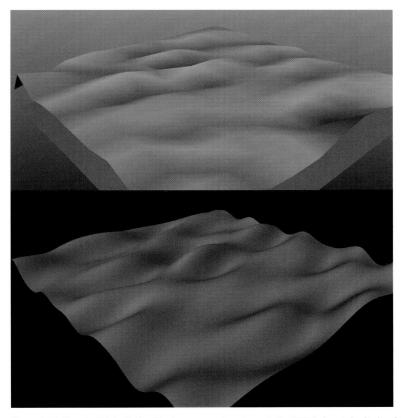

Figure 9.20 Top: The Height Field utility plane, as seen in a viewport. The NURBS plane to be displaced sits below it. Bottom: Render of displaced NURBS plane. The plane's Normal Threshold attribute is set to 180. This scene is included with the Chapter 9 tutorial files as `displacement.ma`.

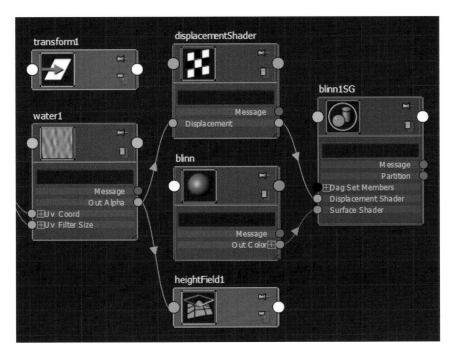

Figure 9.21 The Height Field utility in a shading network

Creating Textures with the Transfer Maps Tool

The Transfer Maps tool can create normal maps and displacement maps by comparing surfaces. This section describes the creation of normal maps; the creation of displacement maps with the Transfer Maps tool is demonstrated in the tutorial at the end of this chapter.

In addition, Transfer Maps can bake lighting and texturing information.

Normal Mapping

To create a normal map with the Transfer Maps tool, follow these steps:

1. Create a new scene. Build a high- and a low-resolution version of a single-surface polygon model. An example file, which includes a simple high- and low-resolution surface, is included as `high_low.ma` with the Chapter 9 tutorial files. The low-resolution surface carries a mere 384 faces, whereas the high-resolution surface carries 392,216 faces.

2. Transform the high- and low-resolution surfaces to 0, 0, 0 in world space. They should overlap.

3. Select the low-resolution surface, switch to the Rendering menu set, and choose Lighting/Shading > Transfer Maps. The low-resolution surface is listed automatically in the Target Meshes section of the Transfer Maps window.

4. Switch the Display drop-down menu in the Target Meshes section to Envelope. Activate Smooth Shade All for the viewport you are working in. The search envelope assigned to the low-resolution surface appears red. The search envelope is a "cage" in which the Transfer Maps tool searches for source surfaces during the normal mapping process. Initially, the search envelope is the same size as the low-resolution surface. To scale the search envelope, increase the Search Envelope (%) attribute slider, also in the Target Meshes section. The search envelope should surround the high-resolution surface (Figure 9.22).

5. Expand the Source Meshes section of the window. By default, All Other Meshes is listed under the Name attribute. This means that the tool will evaluate all non-target meshes it encounters within the search envelope. To specify the high-resolution surface as a source surface, select the high-resolution surface and click the Add Selected button. The name of the high-resolution surface appears under the Name attribute (see Figure 9.23).

6. Click the Normal button (represented by the dimpled ball). Choose a destination for the normal map by clicking the file browse button beside the Normal Map attribute. Choose a file format. Normal maps can be written in any of the standard Maya image formats. Choose Map Height and Map Width values in the Maya Common Output section. Click the Bake And Close button at the bottom of the window.

Figure 9.22 The red envelope of a low-res mesh is scaled up to surround the high-res mesh, which appears as the bumpy surface in the center.

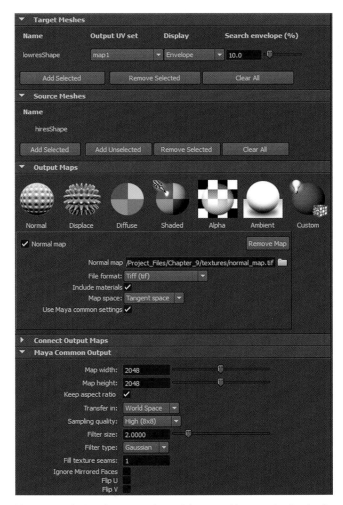

Figure 9.23 The Transfer Maps window with low-res and hi-res meshes listed and the Search Envelope (%) set to 10

7. At this point, the Transfer Maps tool creates a new material, assigns it to the low-resolution surface, and loads the newly written normal map into a connected bump2d node. The Use As attribute of the bump2d node is set to Tangent Space Normals. To see the result, move the low-resolution surface away from the high-resolution surface and render a test. (You can also preview the result of a normal or bump map in a viewport by choosing the Viewport 2.0 renderer.) The result should be similar to Figure 9.24. Use the mental ray renderer to produce a more accurate render of the normal map. Note that the reproduction is relatively accurate within the interior of the low-resolution surface (particularly when the normal map resolution is high), but the normal map is unable to affect the surface edges.

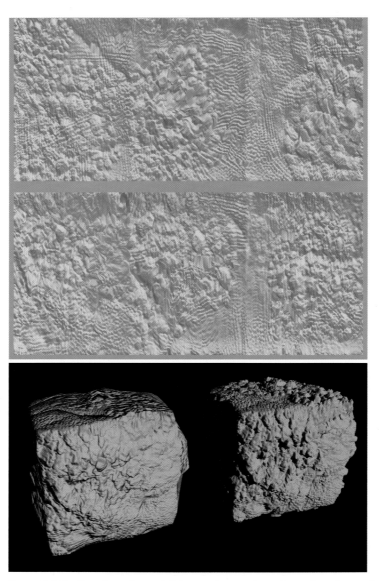

Figure 9.24 Top: Normal map; Bottom-Left: Low-resolution surface with normal map; Bottom-Right: High-resolution surface. The mental ray renderer is used. This scene is included with the Chapter 9 tutorial files as `normal_final.ma`. The normal map is included as `normal_map.tif`.

To improve the quality of the normal mapping process, you can adjust additional attributes:

Sampling Quality   Located in the Maya Common Output section, Sampling Quality sets the number of samples taken for each pixel of the normal map. This serves as a subpixel sampling system. The higher the values, the more accurate the resulting normal map.

Transfer In   Located in the Maya Common Output section, Transfer In determines which space the normal map calculations are carried out in. If Transfer In is set to the default World Space, the target and source surfaces can be different sizes. However, they must be positioned at the same world location. If Transfer In is set to Object Space, target and source surfaces can be moved apart; however, the Freeze Transformation tool should be applied while they are positioned at the same world location. If Transfer In is set to UV Space, the surfaces can be dissimilar (different shapes or different proportions); however, the surfaces must carry valid UVs for this option to work.

Map Space   You can choose a tangent space map or object space map with this menu, which is located in the Output Maps section.

Baking Lighting and Shading Information

You can "bake" lighting, texture, and shadow information with the Transfer Maps tool. In this situation, a textured and lit source creates a color bitmap for a target surface. This is useful for converting procedural maps to bitmap textures or "freezing" lighting information so that the lights and/or shadows are no longer necessary. Such a conversion may be useful for speeding up renders. Similar baking is often used in the gaming industry to make the real-time simulations more efficient.

The Transfer Maps tool provides two attributes to choose from for this operation: Diffuse Color Map and Lit And Shaded Color Map. Diffuse Color Map captures a source surface's color without regard to lighting or shadows. Lit And Shaded Color Map captures all of the source surface's information, including specular highlights, bump maps, ambient color textures, and so on (see Figure 9.25). You can map the resulting color bitmap to the low-resolution surface to reduce render times (by avoiding bump mapping, shadow casting, and the like). The use of Diffuse Color Map and Lit And Shaded Color Map attributes is identical to the creation of a displacement map or normal map. The Diffuse Color Map is activated with the Diffuse button, and the Lit And Shaded Color Map is activated with the Shaded button.

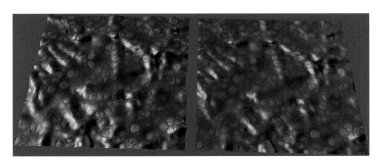

Figure 9.25 Left: A high-resolution surface assigned to a Blinn material that uses a Leather texture for its color and bump; Right: A flat, low-resolution surface given the same detail with a Transfer Maps baked texture. This scene and map are included with the Chapter 9 tutorial files as lit.ma and lit_map.tga.

Chapter Tutorial: Generating and Rendering a Displacement Map with the Transfer Maps Tool

In this tutorial, you will create a displacement map with the Transfer Maps tool and render it with the mental ray renderer (see Figure 9.26).

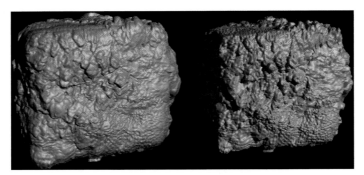

Figure 9.26 A 300-face low-resolution surface (left) is made to emulate a 300,000 face high-resolution surface (right) with the aid of a displacement map.

1. Open the `high_low.ma` file from the Chapter 9 tutorial directory. Create a test render to compare the low-resolution surface with the high-resolution surface. Whereas the low-resolution cube appears smooth, the high-resolution is full of intricate detail and convolutions. Assign the high-resolution surface to a new Blinn material. Assign the low-resolution surface to a second Blinn material.

2. Move the high-resolution surface back to 0, 0, 0 using the Channel Box. With the low-resolution surface selected, choose Rendering > Lighting/Shading > Transfer Maps. The low-resolution surface is listed in the Target Meshes section of the Transfer Maps window. Select the high-resolution surface and click the Add Selected button in the Source Meshes section. Change the Display menu to Envelope and Search Envelope (%) to 10. This displays the search envelope and enlarges it to surround the high-resolution detail. This process is similar to creating a normal map, which is illustrated in the section "Normal Mapping" earlier in this chapter.

3. Click the Displace button (this has a spiked ball icon). In the Output Maps section, change the File Format menu to Tiff. Click the file browse button beside the Displacement Map field and choose a destination for the displacement map to be written out.

4. In the Maya Common Output section, change Map Width and Map Height to 2048. Leave Transfer In set to World Space. Change the Sampling Quality to Medium (4x4). Set the Filter Size to 2. Higher Sampling Quality settings increase the map accuracy but slows the map calculation considerably. Raising the Filter Size slightly softens the map and prevents high-frequency noise from appearing.

5. Switch the Connect Maps To attribute, found in the Connect Output Maps section, to Assigned Shader. This connects to the new displacement map to the currently assigned material. Click the Bake And Close button at the bottom of the window.

6. When the Transfer Maps window completes the map and closes, a displacement shading network is connected automatically to the assigned material and the new displacement map is loaded into a new File texture. The displacement is grayscale with brighter portions representing the greatest distortions to the surface (see Figure 9.27). For a description of the displacement network, see the section "Displacement Mapping" earlier in this chapter. Move the high-resolution surface away from the low-resolution surface.

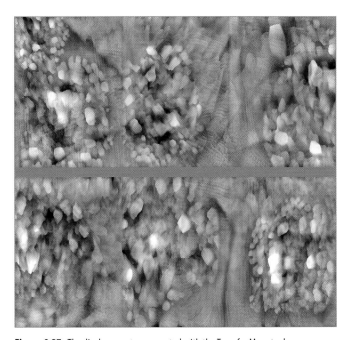

Figure 9.27 The displacement map created with the Transfer Maps tool

Because of the intricacy of the resulting displacement map and the small number of polygon faces on the low-resolution model, the resulting render can take a significant amount of time. To make the render more efficient for testing, open the Attribute Editor node for the lowresShape node, expand the Displacement Map section, and lower Initial Sample Rate to 2 and Extra Sample Rate to 1.0. Test render with mental ray. Continue to incrementally raise Initial Sample Rate and Extra Sample Rate and test render to compare the results. Render regions to save time.

7. The initial displacement is similar to the high-resolution surface, although the peaks are not as high. Open the new file node in the Attribute Editor. In the Color Balance section, set Alpha Gain to 1.5 and Alpha Offset to 0. (The Transfer Maps tool sets the initial values for Color Gain and Color Offset.) Re-render. Note that higher Alpha Gain values tend to "puff" up the surface.

8. You can continue to fine-tune the result of the displacement by adjusting attributes in the Displacement Mapping section of the low-resolution surface. See the "Adjusting the Displacement Mapping" section earlier in this chapter for more details. The tutorial is complete! Your render should look similar to Figure 9.26 at the start of this section. If you get stuck, a final version is included as `displacement_final.ma` with the Chapter 9 tutorial files.

Prepping for Successful Renders

Although rendering is the final step of an Autodesk® Maya® 3D project, it is often given less attention than it needs. The correct choice of aspect ratios, pixel ratios, frame rates, focal lengths, and film backs at the earliest stage of animation can ensure that the project progresses smoothly. At the same time, careful selection of anti-aliasing, image format, resolution size, depth of field, and motion blur settings will guarantee a successful render. Time-saving techniques, including scene cleanup and command-line rendering, will help you finish projects more efficiently.

10

Chapter Contents

Selecting aspect ratios and frame rates
Choosing film backs and focal lengths
Recommended render settings
Command-line rendering
Preparing scene files for rendering
Selecting image formats and resolutions
Creating efficient depth of field and motion blur

Determining Critical Project Settings

Aspect ratios, frame rates, and film backs are important elements of any animation project and should therefore be selected early in the production process. Although you can change the aspect ratio at any time, such a change can lead to poor compositions. Selecting a different film back midway through a project can also lead to drastic composition changes and interfere with live-action footage matching. Switching frame rates can lead to improperly timed motion and broken lip sync. Camera focal lengths, although less critical than aspect ratios, frame rates, and film backs, should nonetheless be selected early in the animation process.

Deciphering Aspect Ratios

The aspect ratio of an image is its displayed width divided by its displayed height. Aspect ratios are commonly represented as x:y (for example, 4:3) or x (for example, 1.33), whereby x is the width and y is the height. Figure 10.1 illustrates common aspect ratios.

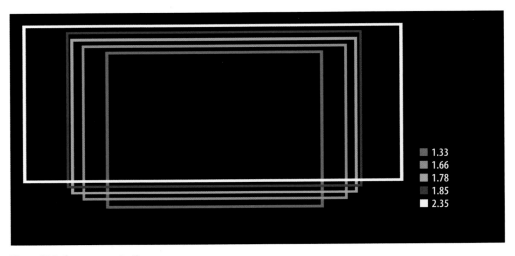

Figure 10.1 Common aspect ratios

Common aspect ratios are described here:

16:9 (1.78)   The aspect ratio of HDTV, which uses two resolutions—1280×720 and 1920×1080.

4:3 (1.33)   The standard definition television (SDTV) aspect ratio, whose roots can be traced to silent 35 mm motion pictures. SDTV is an analog broadcast standard and has thus fallen into disuse with the advent of digital HDTV. Nevertheless, the 4:3 aspect ratio continues to be used to broadcast predigital content. To display a 4:3 show on an HDTV set, the video is either horizontally stretched or letterboxed (solid-colored bars are placed on either side). A common SDTV resolution is 640×480, which remains the default render resolution in Maya.

1.66   A masked variation of the 1.37 Academy motion picture format originally developed by Paramount Studios in 1953. A mask is an aperture plate placed behind a projector lens with a cutout "window" that allows only a portion of the film image to reach the screen.

1.85   Standard, nondigital theatrical widescreen in the United States and United Kingdom. Much like 1.66, 1.85 was developed as a method to mask 1.37 in the early 1950s.

2.35   The aspect ratio of Cinemascope that was developed by 20th Century Fox in the early 1950s. Cinemascope is an anamorphic motion picture format that requires special camera and projector lenses to squeeze and restrength the image for proper viewing. If the anamorphic projector lens is missing, the image appears excessively tall and skinny.

> **Note:**   *Letterboxing* adds solid-colored bars to the top/bottom or left/right of broadcast or projected video when the aspect ratio of the source material doesn't match the aspect ratio of the broadcast format. For example, 1.33, 1.66, and 1.85 aspect ratios must be letterboxed when broadcast on HDTV. An alternative solution requires horizontal stretching, which degrades the source material. Any source that is wider than the broadcast format, such as a 2.35 film on HDTV, must be scaled down horizontally and vertically or *panned and scanned*. With pan and scan, the source height is fit to the broadcast height and the source is electronically panned left and right to reveal missing parts of the frame.

> **Note:**   Lens flares, a common artifact of motion picture cameras, are by no means consistent. 2.35 anamorphic flares, for example, produce thin solid lines across the width of the frame, while 1.66 and 1.85 flares produce the more commonly recognized bright spots.

> **Note:**   Several predigital video formats made use of nonsquare pixels. The resulting footage requires stretching to display the video with a proper aspect ratio. Maya supports custom pixel aspect ratios (PARs) through the Pixel Aspect Ratio attribute within the Render Settings window. However, I recommend leaving this attribute set to 1.0 because nonsquare pixels are rarely used in contemporary video production. Rendering nonsquare pixels also leads to quality loss because the pixels must be stretched at a later step, such as editing or compositing.

Maya Camera Types

As a quick review, Maya offers five types of cameras.

One-node, two-node, and three-node camera attributes are identical. What differs is the number of nodes in their hierarchies. Two- and three-node cameras offer additional "handles" (an "aim" used for pointing the lens and an "up" for tilting the camera body) that ease or aid camera animation. One-node cameras are created with the Create > Cameras > Camera tool. Two-node cameras are created with the Camera And Aim tool. Three-node cameras are created with the Camera Aim And Up tool.

In addition, recent versions of Maya offer stereoscopic camera setups. These include the Create > Cameras > Stereo Camera rig and Multi Stereo Rig. The Stereo Camera rig features a pair of one-node cameras joined by a group node. The cameras are designed to render left-eye and right-eye views. The group node is actually a third, central one-node camera that carries all the basic camera attributes (see the next section). The attribute values are passed to the left- and right-eye cameras via expressions. Stereoscopic adjustments are included in the Stereo, Stereo Adjustments, and Stereo Display Controls sections. The most critical stereo attribute is Interaxial Separation, which sets the distance between left- and right-eye cameras and ultimately determines where objects appear when viewed in a stereoscopic setting (such as a theater). To see a left- or right-eye view, you can choose Panels > Stereo > stereoCamera Rig > stereoCameraLeft or stereoCameraRight from a viewport menu.

The Multi Stereo Rig expands the stereo complexity by adding additional cameras to cover near-, mid-, and far-range regions of the scene. For information on rendering stereo rigs, see the section "Mastering Render Settings" later in this chapter.

Selecting a Film Back

In Maya, a camera's virtual optical properties are defined in the Film Back section of the camera's Attribute Editor tab (see Figure 10.2). The most important attribute in this section is Film Gate. In a real-world motion picture camera, a film gate is a plate with a rectangular opening that sits behind the lens and in front of the film stock. The gate controls the exposure of the film by allowing only one frame at a time to be struck by light. Commonly used cameras have distinct lens and film gate setups with specific physical properties. These properties cause light to strike the film in a distinct way. The Film Gate attribute's drop-down menu provides a selection of common motion picture cameras. When one of these camera presets is selected, the Camera Aperture, Film Aspect Ratio, and Lens Squeeze Ratio attributes automatically update. A description of these attributes follows:

Camera Aperture A "dummy" attribute that carries the Horizontal Film Aperture (the left field) and Vertical Film Aperture (the right field), which set the width and height of the virtual film gate, respectively. With Maya 2014, the camera Aperture measurement is in world inches. Maya 2015 includes two Camera Aperture attributes—one for inches and one for mm. If you change an inch field, the corresponding mm field changes, and vice versa.

Figure 10.2 The Camera Attributes and Film Back sections of a camera's Attribute Editor tab, as seen in Maya 2015

Film Aspect Ratio Sets the width-to-height ratio of Camera Aperture. As you change the value, the Horizontal Film Aperture and Angle Of View fields automatically update.

Lens Squeeze Ratio Sets the amount of horizontal squeeze created by a lens. Cinemascope anamorphic lenses require a Lens Squeeze Ratio value of 2. Most lenses do not require a special Lens Squeeze Ratio value and can be left at 1.0.

Note: *Film back* refers to the plate that holds the film against the film gate. With 3D animation software, the term has come to represent the general qualities of the film gate. In contrast, a real-world camera aperture is the articulated diaphragm that opens or closes to control the amount of light striking the film.

Note: Maya 2015 includes the Frustum Display Controls section, which allows you to turn on viewport icons for the frustum (the pyramidal shaped area-of-view of the camera) and the near and far clipping planes. Objects or surface components closer than the Near Clip Plane value and farther than the Far Clip Plane value are ignored by the viewports and renderers. If an object is "cut off" in a viewport and fails to fully render, adjust the Near Clip Plane and Far Clip Plane values so that a larger region is visible.

In contrast, digital video cameras do not have traditional film gates. Their light-gathering CCD or CMOS sensors, however, serve the same basic function. When matching a video camera in Maya, you can derive approximate inch values for Horizontal Camera Aperture and Vertical Camera Aperture. For example, a Canon 5D camera possesses a 35.8 × 23.9 mm CMOS sensor. This equates to 1.409 × 0.94 inches. However, the full sensor has an aspect ratio of roughly 1.5. Thus, when recording 1.78 video, only a portion of the sensor is used. To maintain a 1.78 aspect ratio film back in Maya, you can set the Horizontal Camera Aperture to 1.409 and the Vertical Camera Aperture to 0.79 (which is 1.409 / 1.78). Sensor specifications for such calculations are generally available from the video camera manufacturers.

If an animation represents an abstract, fanciful, or imaginary scene, you can leave the Film Gate attribute set to the default User. For exaggerated camera effects, you can also enter custom numbers into any of the attributes in the Film Back section. However, if an animation is intended to replicate or fit into preexisting live-action motion picture or video footage, the Film Gate and associated attributes should be carefully selected.

Displaying Gates

As you choose an aspect ratio and a film back for an animation project, you should use the camera's various gates. Choosing View > Camera Settings > Resolution Gate through the viewport menu displays the Resolution Gate frame in the perspective view. The Resolution Gate represents the maximum render area (see Figure 10.3). It's a good practice to display the Resolution Gate for the rendering camera as soon as a new Maya scene is created; this prevents the accidental cropping or misframing of the subject.

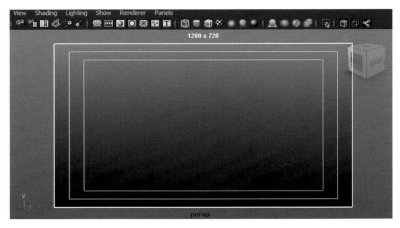

Figure 10.3 Resolution Gate with Safe Action (middle box) and Safe Title (inner box) toggled on

The renderer ignores anything outside the Resolution Gate. For extra security, you can toggle on Safe Action and Safe Title gates by choosing View > Camera Settings > Safe Action and View > Camera Settings > Safe Title. Because the average television set (whether SDTV or HDTV) cuts off a portion of the frame between the Resolution Gate and the Safe Action gate, keep critical animation within the Safe Action gate. Keep critical text and titles within the Safe Title gate.

The Resolution Gate aspect ratio, determined by the Device Aspect Ratio attribute of the Render Settings window, may be different from the Film Aspect Ratio value. (See the section "Mastering Render Settings" later in this chapter for more information on Device Aspect Ratio.) Hence, you can use the Fit Resolution Gate attribute, in the Film Back section of the camera's attribute Editor tab, to adjust the result. The Fit Resolution Gate menu contains the following options:

Fill   Scales the Film Gate so that it covers the entire Resolution Gate. Depending on the render resolution, a portion of the Film Gate may be lost outside the Resolution Gate. This option may be useful when adding an image plane that is not the same aspect ratio as the render resolution.

Horizontal or Vertical   The Film Gate is scaled in one direction so that it matches the Resolution Gate's dimension in that direction.

Overscan   The Film Gate is stretched to fit within the Resolution Gate so that no part is left unrendered.

Selecting a Focal Length

Focal length is the distance from the optical center of a lens to its focal point (the point at which the light rays are focused). After specific shots are determined within an animation project, it's wise to select specific focal lengths. Motion picture and television productions regularly change focal lengths (and even the entire lens) from shot to shot. Different focal lengths can have a significant impact on camera placement, composition, and object distortion. (See Chapter 8, "Harnessing the Power of Math Utilities," for a demonstration.) Focal length is controlled in the Camera Attributes section of the camera's Attribute Editor tab, which includes Angle Of View, Focal Length, and Camera Scale attributes (see Figure 10.2 earlier in this chapter):

Angle Of View   A measurement of the angular extent visible through the camera. If this attribute is changed, the Focal Length attribute automatically updates. Because the formula used by Angle Of View is a nonintuitive (2 * arctan ((frame or sensor width / 2) / focal length), it is more convenient to set the Focal Length attribute.

Focal Length   Sets the focal length of a camera lens as measured in millimeters. Common real-world focal lengths include 20 mm, 35 mm, 50 mm, and 135 mm (see Figure 10.4).

Camera Scale   Scales the Focal Length attribute as if the entire virtual camera mechanism were resized. Objects will appear twice as far away if this attribute is set to 2 and twice as close if this attribute is set to 0.5. Note that scaling the camera icon does not affect the camera's view.

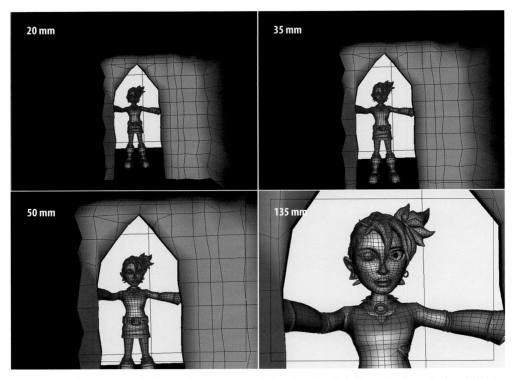

Figure 10.4 Clockwise, from top left: 20 mm, 35 mm, 135 mm, and 50 mm focal lengths in Maya with a 35 mm Academy Film Gate

Selecting Frame Rates

A proper frame rate is critical for smooth animation. A frame rate determines the number of individual frames per second (fps). It's best to choose a frame rate before beginning an animation. Although you can change the frame rate midway through a project, existing animation curves will be scaled. This may lead to animation that is too fast or too slow. In addition, changing the frame rate may lead to fractional keyframes, where the keyframes fall on non-whole numbers, such as 5.25.

Maya supports the most common frame rates, including 24, 25, and 30 fps. To set the rate, choose Window > Setting/Preferences > Preferences, switch to the Settings section, and choose an option from the Time attribute's drop-down menu. The frame rate you choose should match your output medium. Descriptions of the common frame rates follow:

24 fps The standard frame rate of predigital motion picture film. This is the default frame rate for Maya.

25 fps The standard frame rate of PAL and SECAM video, which are analog broadcast standards outside North American and Japan.

30 fps The standard frame rate of analog NTSC video, the North American predigital standard. 30 fps is a simplification of the more technically accurate 29.97 fps.

The 24, 25, and 30 fps frames rates are supported by the HDTV standard. Two variations of the HDTV frame rates exist: interlaced and progressive. Interlacing breaks each frame into two fields and is a legacy of analog television broadcast. Progressive frames are whole frames where no interlacing is applied. Frames rendered from Maya are progressive by default. Progressive frames are preferable for animation and visual effects projects, because the frames are not degraded by the interlaced frame-splitting.

One problematic area of postproduction is frame rate conversion. A conversion is necessary when the frame rate of a source doesn't match the frame rate of the broadcast or projection. For example, broadcasting a 24 fps video to a 30 fps television means that six frames must be repeated or otherwise generated for each second. If a 30 fps video is broadcast on a 25 fps television, five frames must be discarded for each second. To avoid conversion difficulties, determine the primary presentation format of your animation project. If an animation is destined for multiple outlets at multiple points around the globe, conversion artifacts should be expected. Although postproduction processes exist to convert between frame rates electronically or digitally, the result is never as smooth as the original.

> **Note:** To accurately gauge an animation when using the timeline's playback controls, switch the Playback Speed attribute to Real-Time. You can find Playback Speed in the Timeline section of the Preferences window (choose Window > Setting/Preferences > Preferences). When examining dynamic simulations, set Playback Speed to Play Every Frame (otherwise, the dynamic calculation becomes inaccurate). You can also examine animation outside the timeline by creating a Playblast movie. To do so, choose Window > Playblast. With a Playblast, the selected viewport is played back and captured with the system graphics card. The resulting movie is played with the system movie player, such as Windows Media Player.

Mastering Render Settings

Default render settings are rarely suitable for a project and should be adjusted. The settings are divided into common attributes and those that are renderer-specific. You can access the settings through Window > Rendering Editors > Render Settings or by clicking the Display Render Settings button in the Status Bar.

Working with the Common Tab

The majority of Render Settings window attributes are intuitive and easy to use. However, several of them are worth a closer look. The Common tab includes the Frame Padding, Renderable Camera, Alpha Channel (Mask), Depth Channel (Z Depth), Resolution, Resolution Units, Device Aspect Ratio, and Pixel Aspect Ratio attributes (see Figure 10.5). These attributes are described in this section.

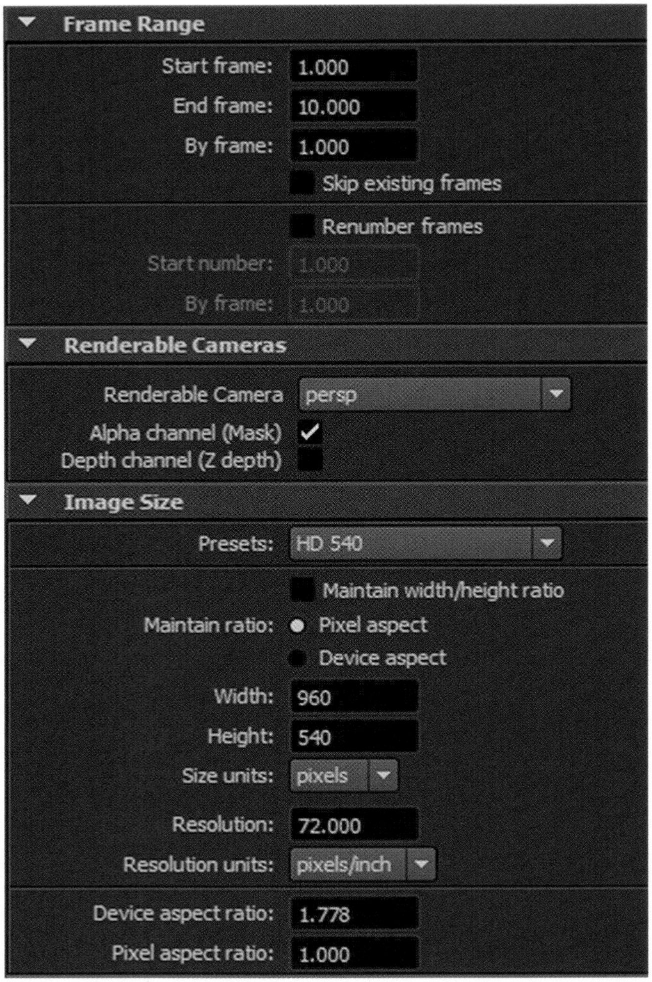

Figure 10.5 The Frame Range, Renderable Cameras, and Image Size sections of the Common tab in the Render Settings window

Frame Padding Ensures that each filename carries the same number of numeric placeholders. Many compositing programs, such as Adobe After Effects, expect specific frame numbering conventions. For example, the following naming convention may cause a problem:

```
Test.1.jpg
Test.5.jpg
Test.10.jpg
Test.100.jpg
```

However, if the Frame Padding attribute is set to 3, the images will be named in a universally understood manner:

```
Test.001.jpg
Test.005.jpg
Test.010.jpg
Test.100.jpg
```

Renderable Camera This menu lists cameras that are available for batch rendering. If there is more than one perspective camera in a scene, you can select a favored camera by changing the menu. If you wish to render more than one camera, switch the Renderable Camera menu to Add Renderable Camera. This adds an additional Renderable Camera menu, which you can change to any secondary camera, including orthographic cameras. Using this method, you can render left- and right-eye views of stereo camera rigs. If you need to remove a Renderable Camera menu, click the Make This Camera Non Renderable trash-can button.

Alpha Channel (Mask) Toggles on the alpha channel for select image formats (Maya IFF, TIFF, Targa, OpenEXR, and others). Alpha represents the opacity of objects in a scene. Alpha is stored as a scalar (grayscale) value in the fourth channel (the *A* in RGBA). In Maya, white alpha indicates opaque objects and black alpha indicates empty space. You can view the alpha channel in the Render View window by clicking the Display Alpha Channel button. Common compositing programs automatically read the Maya alpha channel.

> **Note:** When rendering, Maya pre-multiplies alpha and RGB color values. When importing a Maya image sequence into a compositing program, it's generally wise to interpret the imported alpha channel as "pre-multiplied." This step ensures that the semitransparent object edges are properly interpreted. Pre-multiplication is used for mathematical efficiency when compositing.

Depth Channel (Z Depth) Toggles on the depth channel for select image formats (Maya IFF, RLA, OpenEXR, and others). With TIFF, Targa, and SGI images, the attribute causes the depth channel to be written out as a separate file with a *_depth* suffix. Depth channels represent the distance between the camera and objects in the scene. Depth channels (sometimes referred to as Z-depth buffers) are employed by compositing programs to determine object occlusion. For example, a depth channel might be used to properly place 2D fog "into" a rendered 3D scene or to create a depth-of-field effect as part of the compositing process. In another variation, Maya depth map shadows are depth channel maps from the view of the light (see Chapter 3, "Creating High-Quality Shadows"). You can view the depth channel of an image file by choosing File > View Image, browsing for the file, and clicking the Z Buffer button in the FCheck window (see Figure 10.6). Like alpha channels, depth channels are scalar.

Resolution and Resolution Units For video and film, the image size is determined solely by the Width and Height attributes. For projects destined for print, however, the Resolution attribute is added to determine pixels per inch. For example, many print jobs require 300 pixels per inch. You can thus set the Resolution attribute to 300 and the Resolution Units attribute to Pixels/Inch.

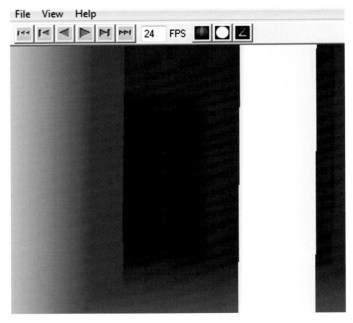

Figure 10.6 A depth channel viewed in FCheck

Device Aspect Ratio and Pixel Aspect Ratio   Device Aspect Ratio defines the aspect ratio of rendered images based on the following formula:

$$\text{Device Aspect Ratio} = \text{Image Aspect Ratio} \times \text{Pixel Aspect Ratio}$$

Unless Pixel Aspect Ratio is set to a non-1.0, nonsquare value, Device Aspect Ratio is identical to the image aspect ratio. For information on pixel aspect ratios, see the note in the "Deciphering Aspect Ratios" section earlier in this chapter.

Maya includes common resolution presets through the Presets menu. When manually setting the Width and Height values, you can select the Maintain Width/ Height attribute to maintain the current image aspect ratio. Avoid selecting the Device Aspect radio button when changing the Width and Height values—otherwise, you'll alter the current Pixel Aspect Ratio value.

Render-specific attributes reside in the Maya Software, Maya Hardware, Maya Hardware 2.0, and Maya Vector tabs. (See Chapter 11, "Raytracing with Maya Software and mental ray," for a discussion of mental ray® attributes.)

Prepping Maya Software Renders

The Maya Software renderer is a general-purpose renderer that is suitable for many projects. Critical attributes, found in the Maya Software tab of the Render Settings window, include Edge Anti-Aliasing, Shading, and Max Shading. Important sections include Multi-Pixel Filtering and Contrast Threshold (see Figure 10.7). The attributes and sections are described here.

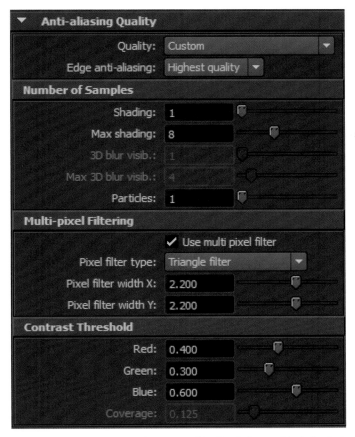

Figure 10.7 The Anti-Aliasing Quality sections of the Maya Software tab in the Render Settings window

Edge Anti-Aliasing   Anti-aliasing is an inescapable necessity of 3D and other computer graphics. Because of the physical limitations of computer monitors and television screens (which possess a limited number of display pixels), normally smooth edges become "jaggy" or "stair-stepped." The anti-aliasing process uses a subpixel sampling technique that computes multiple sample points within a single pixel and assigns the averaged sample values to that pixel. Although Maya offers various anti-aliasing presets through the Edge Anti-Aliasing menu, such as Low Quality or Highest Quality, you can tailor the anti-aliasing by entering values into the Shading and Max Shading attribute fields.

Shading   Sets the minimum number of subpixel samples taken within a pixel during the anti-aliasing process. If set to 1.0, each pixel is sampled once. If set to 4, each pixel is sampled four times. The number of subpixel samples is not permitted to exceed the Max Shading value.

Max Shading   Sets the maximum number of subpixel samples taken within a pixel during the adaptive shading pass of the anti-aliasing process. This is in effect only when the Edge Anti-Aliasing attribute is set to Highest Quality. Whether or not the Max Shading value is applied is dependent on Contrast Threshold attribute, which controls the adaptive shading pass.

Contrast Threshold   This section controls the adaptive shading pass of the anti-aliasing process. The Edge Anti-Aliasing attribute must be set to Highest Quality for the Contrast Threshold section to be available. Contrast Threshold tests for pixels whose contrast with neighboring pixels exceeds the Red, Green, or Blue attribute threshold values. For these pixels, additional subpixel sampling is undertaken. In this case, Max Shading sets the maximum number of permitted samples. Choosing different presets through the Quality menu alters settings in the Contrast Threshold and Multi-Pixel Filtering sections.

Multi-Pixel Filtering   Multi-pixel filtering is designed to blend neighboring pixels into a coherent mass. Such filtering helps to prevent common aliasing artifacts. In particular, multi-pixel filtering can improve renders destined for low-resolution or interlaced video. However, multi-pixel filtering may not be necessary for renders destined for motion picture film or high-resolution, progressive-frame HDTV. You have the option to deselect the Use Multi Pixel Filter check box. You can also reduce the intensity of the filtering by reducing the Pixel Filter Width X and Pixel Filter Width Y values.

If Use Multi Pixel Filter is selected, you can choose between five filter styles from the Pixel Filter Type drop-down menu. Box Filter and Triangle Filter are mathematically simple filters that create a higher degree of softening. Quadratic B-Spline and Gaussian Filter are sophisticated filters that soften while maintaining some edge sharpness. Plug-in Filter allows you to write a custom filter in the Maya plug-in language. The Gaussian Filter option is suitable for most projects.

Using Maya Hardware Renderers

Recent versions of Maya include three hardware renderers: Maya Hardware Buffer, Maya Hardware, and Maya Hardware 2.0. Hardware renderers are dependent on the rendering abilities of the operating system graphics card.

The Maya Hardware Buffer is available via the Window > Rendering Editors menu. The buffer serves as a hardware-based counterpart to the Render View window and is useful for test-rendering hardware-rendered particles and nParticles (those particle types that lack the *s/w* suffix). You can render the current frame by opening the buffer window and choosing Render > Test Render from the buffer menu (see Figure 10.8).

To access basic quality settings, choose Render > Attributes from the buffer menu. The quality settings are limited, controlling line (edge) quality and simple shading quality. Nevertheless, the buffer offers various means to generate alpha, which varies from copying color channel information to the on-board alpha capabilities of the system graphic card. You can choose an alpha type through the Alpha Source menu of the Attribute Editor tab (named defaultHardwareRenderGlobals). You can also use the buffer to render an image sequence. Choose Render > Render Sequence through the buffer menu. The buffer renders each frame to the screen, takes a screen snapshot of each frame, and saves each snapshot to the project images directory. You can use the FCheck window (File > View Sequence) to load and play back image sequences.

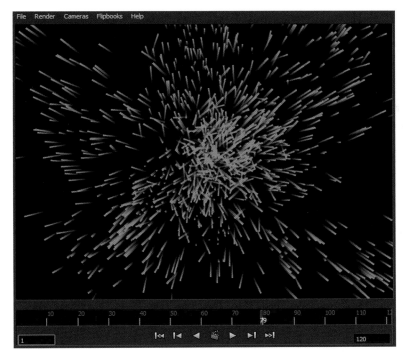

Figure 10.8 A Multi-Streak nParticle simulation is test-rendered in the Hardware Render Buffer window.

The Maya Hardware and Maya Hardware 2.0 renderers are available through the Render Using menu of the Render Settings window. Of the two renderers, Maya Hardware 2.0 offers more sophistication with the support of texture baking, ambient occlusion, motion blur, and anti-aliasing. For a demonstration of the Maya Hardware 2.0 renderer, see the tutorial at the end of this chapter.

Prepping Maya Vector Renders

The Maya Vector renderer can create stylized cartoon and wireframe renders (see Figure 10.9). Although the majority of its options (found in the Maya Vector tab of the Render Settings window) are straightforward, a few warrant a more detailed description.

Figure 10.9 Left to Right: Maya Vector renders with Single Color and Entire Mesh, Single Color and Outlines, and Four Color

Curve Tolerance Determines the smoothness of a NURBS or subdivision surface edge. A value of 0 leaves the edge faceted (as if the surface was converted to a polygon). The maximum value of 15 smoothes the surface to such an extent that it becomes slightly distorted. The Curve Tolerance attribute has no effect on polygon surfaces.

Detail Level and Detail Level Preset Detail Level controls the accuracy of the Vector renderer. A high value improves the quality but slows the render significantly. Detail Level Preset, if set to Automatic, overrides the Detail Level attribute. You can also set the Detail Level Preset to standard quality settings, which include Low, Medium, and High. If Detail Level Preset is set to Low, small polygons are combined with adjacent polygons, thus reducing any fine detail.

Fill Style Controls the solid color that appears on the surface of rendered objects. The Single Color radio button (see Figure 10.10), when selected, creates a solid color based on the surface material. The Average Color option also creates a single color based on the material but includes shading based on the scene lighting. Two Color and Four Color add additional solid colors based on the material color and scene lighting. The Full Color radio button tints each individual polygon face with a solid color based on the surface material and scene lighting. Finally, the Mesh Gradient and Area Gradient radio buttons apply color gradients based on material color and scene lighting. Mesh Gradient and Area Gradient are supported by the SWF format. (See the section "Selecting Image Formats" later in this chapter.) In addition, you can toggle on or off Shadows, Highlights, and Reflections in this section; these options are not radio buttons.

Figure 10.10 The Fill Options and Edge Options sections of the Maya Vector tab

Include Edges When selected, creates edge lines. The Edge Weight Preset attribute controls the thickness of the line. If the Edge Style attribute is set to Outlines, a line is created at the outer edge of each surface. If the Edge Style attribute is set to Entire Mesh, a line is drawn along each and every polygon edge. In this case, all polygon faces render as triangles. In addition, NURBS surfaces receive lines derived from the tessellation process. (As an alternative, you can use mental ray contour shaders; these are discussed in Chapter 12, "Working with mental ray Shaders, Global Illumination, and Final Gathering.")

A Note on IPR

Thus far, the Render View window has been used for test renders. You have the option to switch the window to Interactive Photorealistic Rendering (IPR) mode, which automatically updates the selected region whenever there is a texturing, lighting, or camera placement change.

To switch on IPR, choose IPR > IPR Render > *view* from the Render View menu, click the Render Region (Maya Software) button, and draw a region box over the area of the scene you wish to update. Note that IPR is designed to work with Maya Software. To turn off IPR, click the Render Current Frame button. Whether or not you use IPR, it is generally more efficient to test small regions as you make adjustments to texturing and lighting.

Rendering with the Command Line

You can launch a batch render with the Maya Software or mental ray renderer from the Microsoft Windows Command Prompt, the Macintosh OS X's Terminal window, or the shell window of a Linux system. It is not necessary to run the Maya interface; therefore, this method uses less memory. To achieve this, a Maya scene need only be saved in advance. The scene may be saved as a Maya binary file, with the .mb extension, or as a Maya ASCII text file, with the .ma extension. (*ASCII* stands for American Standard Code for Information Interchange and is a character-encoding scheme.) At that point, follow these steps:

1. Launch the Command Prompt (Windows), the Terminal window (OS X), or appropriate Linux shell window.

2. Switch to the directory in which the Maya scene file resides. For example, in Windows the command might be:

   ```
   cd c:\3d\maya\projects
   ```

3. Launch the software renderer by entering the following command:

   ```
   render file_name
   ```

The Maya Software renderer proceeds using the settings contained within the Render Settings window when the file was saved. You can interrupt the renderer at any time by pressing Ctrl/Cmd+C in the Command Prompt or Terminal window. You can simultaneously launch multiple renders in separate Command Prompt, Terminal, or shell windows; the renders evenly divide the available CPU cycles.

If you prefer to render with mental ray, you must enter this:

```
render -r mr file_name
```

The -r or -renderer flag specifies the renderer used. You can override the file's render settings by using various flags. For example, you can force the renderer to render frames 5 to 10 with the following line:

```
render file_name -s 5 -e 10
```

To display the lengthy list of render flags, open Help with the following line (see Figure 10.11):

```
render -h
```

```
Command Prompt                                                    _|□|×|

Specific options for renderer "default": Maya software renderer

General purpose flags:
  -rd path                    Directory in which to store image files
  -im filename                Image file output name
  -fnc int                    File Name Convention: any of name, name.ext, ... See the

                Render Settings window to find available options. Use namec and
                namec.ext for Multi Frame Concatenated formats. As a shortcut,
                numbers 1, 2, ... can also be used
  -of string                  Output image file format. See the Render Settings window

                to find available formats

  -s float                    Starting frame for an animation sequence
  -e float                    End frame for an animation sequence
  -b float                    By frame (or step) for an animation sequence
  -pad int                    Number of digits in the output image frame file name
        extension
```

Figure 10.11   A portion of render Help, as shown in the Command Prompt window

The ability to launch the command-line renderer from any directory relies on the proper setup of a system environment variable. If the variable is not present, you must launch the render from the directory where the command is installed. The location varies per system:

Windows:

```
C:\Program Files\Autodesk\Maya_version\bin
```

Mac OS X:

```
/Applications/Autodesk/Maya_version/Maya.app/Contents/bin/
```

Linux:

```
/usr/autodesk/Maya_version/bin
```

For more detailed information on the command-line renderer, see the "Render from the Command Line" page in the Maya Help files or at the Autodesk Knowledge Network (knowledge.autodesk.com).

Note: A number of external programs are designed to manage Maya batch renders. These include Shoran Software RenderPal, Brave Rabbit Pipeline, Uberware Smedge, and Thinkbox Software Deadline. Render management is cost- and time-effective for complex or lengthy projects that involve a large number of scenes, shots, elements, or participating animators. In addition, cloud-based render farm services have become available to professional and amateur 3D animators alike. These include Render Rocket, Rayvision, RebusFarm, and numerous other services. Cloud-based render farms offer the advantage of high-power systems, where you can spread renders over myriad CPUs.

Organizing the Render

Rendering is the final step of the animation process, yet it requires the same attention to detail as any other aspect of 3D to be successful. Creating clean scene files and establishing appropriate paths to bitmaps are important steps.

Cleaning Up

The speed of any given Maya render depends on the quality of the scene file. If a scene file contains unnecessary construction history, broken nodes, and unneeded geometry, the render will suffer. A quick solution to this problem is to choose File > Optimize Scene Size. By default, Optimize Scene Size deletes unused curves, unassigned materials, orphaned group nodes (those without children), and empty layers. By opening the Optimize Scene Size Options window, you can optimize specific categories by selecting or deselecting the category buttons (see Figure 10.12). Use caution when dealing with complex scenes since it is possible to unintentionally delete critical components of character rigs and other advanced setups.

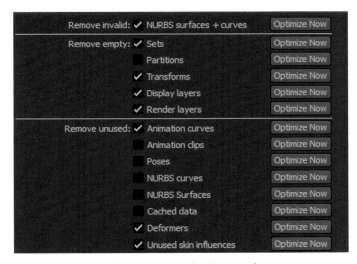

Figure 10.12 A portion of the Optimize Scene Size Options window

If you are unable to determine why a particular scene is rendering slowly, from the Rendering menu set choose Render > Run Render Diagnostics. The Script Editor opens and displays suggestions for optimizing the scene in question (see Figure 10.13). Although these suggestions can be quite helpful, they are by no means mandatory.

During the modeling process, it is also important to choose Edit > Delete By Type > History when construction history is no longer needed. If construction history remains on a rigged character, for example, the render time can be significantly increased.

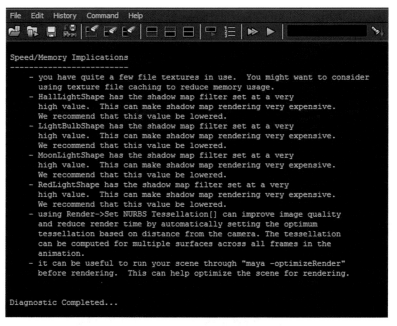

Figure 10.13 A sample render diagnostics message displayed in the Script Editor window

Recovering Lost Bitmaps

Maya binary and ASCII scene files contain all the elements required for a render—except actual bitmaps. Instead, paths pointing to bitmaps are hard-coded in a Maya file. For example, as shown at the top of Figure 10.14, a Maya ASCII file contains the following line:

```
settAttr ".ftn" -type "string" "C:/3D/logo.tif";
```

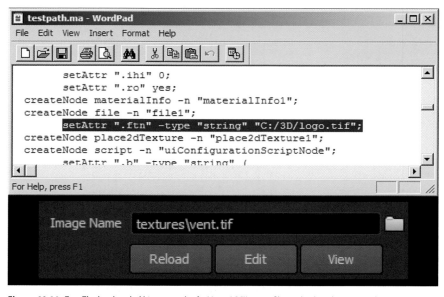

Figure 10.14 Top: The hard-coded bitmap path of a Maya ASCII scene file, as displayed in a text editor; Bottom: A truncated path listed by the Image Name attribute of a File texture.

Thus, if the Maya file in question is moved between computers with different drive letters or directory structures, logo.tif will be "lost." In this case, the Hypershade and Node Editor windows display a black icon for bitmaps that are missing. This holds true even if the project directory has been set through File > Project > Set. If a project is set, Maya displays a truncated path in the File texture's Image Name field (see the bottom of Figure 10.14).

If a limited number of bitmaps are missing, you can go to the associated File textures and reload the bitmaps by using the Folder button beside Image Name. Otherwise, you can fix this problem by editing a Maya ASCII version of the file, which is simply text. Using the Find and Replace All function of Microsoft Windows WordPad or an equivalent text editor, replace c:/ with d:/ or any other appropriate path. In a similar fashion, you can edit Maya binary files; however, a hexadecimal editor is required. It's also possible to write or run MEL and Python scripts that automatically update or change bitmap paths in an open scene file. You can find example scripts at such websites as www.creativecrash.com.

Selecting Image Formats

Maya Software, Hardware, and Vector renderers can output 32 different image formats. You can select the format by switching the Image Format attribute in the Render Settings window. Although any of the formats can be used successfully in the right circumstances, the following formats are commonly used:

AVI (.avi**) and QuickTime(**.mov**)**   On Microsoft Windows systems, Windows Media Player AVI movies are an available format. By default, Maya renders AVI files with no compression. However, you can choose other compression schemes by clicking the Compression button that appears just below the Image Format attribute. Although AVIs are convenient for short tests, they are not suitable for most renders. If a batch render fails or is intentionally interrupted, the AVI file is permanently lost. In addition, individual AVI frames cannot be checked as the render progresses. Conversely, the QuickTime format is available on systems running Macintosh OS X. QuickTime suffers from the same drawbacks as AVI.

> **Note:**   Maya Software, Maya Hardware, Maya Vector, and mental ray renderers are unable to support all 32 image formats. For a detailed list of which renderer supports what format, see the "Supported Image Formats (Rendering)" page in the Maya Help files or at the Autodesk Knowledge Network (knowledge.autodesk.com).

> **Note:**   Some image formats are supported through the addition of a plug-in. If a format is missing from the list, choose Window > Settings/Preferences > Plug-Manager and load the associated plug-in. For example, OpenEXRLoader.mll loads OpenEXR.

OpenEXR (.exr**)**   Developed by Industrial Light & Magic, the format supports an arbitrary number of custom channels with support for 16-bit half-floating point and 32-bit full-floating point architecture. (See Chapter 13, "Color Management, HDR Work Flow, and Render Passes." for more information about floating-point formats.) OpenEXR files can carry alpha, Z-depth, and other specialized channels such as motion vector. You must use mental ray to render OpenEXR files. OpenEXR is used widely in the visual effects industry.

Targa (.tga**)**   Developed by Truevision in the mid-1980s, this remains a robust and reliable image format. Targas can store an alpha channel and are readable by the majority of digital image and compositing programs. Targa file sizes are relatively large, which is perhaps their main disadvantage. An average 720×540 Targa might take up 1.1 megabytes, while the same size JPEG with a 75 percent quality setting will be a mere 60 kilobytes. Not all Targa formats are supported by Maya.

TIFF (.tif**)**   TIFF stands for Tagged Image File Format and is another popular format developed in the mid-1980s. TIFFs can store alpha and are similar in size to Targas. The TIFF format has numerous variations and compression schemes, however, which are inconsistently interpreted by various graphics programs. In fact, the mental ray renderer in Maya may return an error when unsupported TIFF variations are encountered as File textures. (Should this happen, convert the image to another format.) By default, Maya TIFFs are compressed with TIFF 6.0 compression.

Maya IFF (.iff**)**   This is a native format created by Alias, the original developer of Maya. Although the FCheck program in Maya and various Adobe products read the IFF format, some digital imaging programs are unable to interpret them. Maya IFF files can carry alpha, Z-depth, and motion vector channels.

PSD and PSD Layered (.psd**)**   These are the standard Photoshop image formats. If PSD Layered is chosen, the background color is placed on a Photoshop locked background and the objects are placed on a separate layer with transparency surrounding them. As such, no alpha channel is provided (even if it is selected in the Render Settings window).

PNG (.png**) and JPEG (**.jpg**)**   PNG stands for Portable Network Graphics. PNG files store transparency but do not carry a standard alpha channel. The PNG format offers the advantage of small file sizes through aggressive compression as compared to larger formats such as Targa or TIFF. JPEG stands for Joint Photographic Experts Group and is one of the most popular image formats in the world. The main weakness of this format is the lossy quality of its compression. The JPEG format may be suitable for tests but should not be used for final output.

Macromedia Flash (.swf**)**   SWF is a vector image format. All the frames of a Macromedia Flash render are contained within a single file. You must use the Maya Vector renderer to output this format.

RLA (.rla**) and SGI (**.sgi**)**   RLA is a legacy Wavefront image format that can store alpha and Z-depth channels. SGI is a legacy Silicon Graphics image format that supports an alpha channel.

Creating Depth of Field

Depth of field is the range of distances that encompass objects that appear acceptably sharp. Because of the optical characteristics of real-world lenses and the physical qualities of the atmosphere, photography and videography rarely produce images that are 100 percent in focus. In contrast, 3D renders are always in perfect focus unless depth of field is used. You can activate the depth of field in Maya by selecting the Depth Of Field attribute in the Depth Of Field section of the camera's Attribute Editor tab (see Figure 10.15).

Figure 10.15 Top: The Depth Of Field section of a camera's Attribute Editor tab; Bottom: Depth of field in action. This scene is included with the Chapter 10 tutorial files as `depth_of_field.ma`.

The depth of field can be difficult to set up at times. The following process is therefore recommended:

1. Measure the distance between the camera lens and subject by choosing Create > Measure Tools > Distance Tool (see Figure 10.16). For an accurate reading, place the Distance Tool's first locator at the base of the camera icon lens.

Select the Depth Of Field attribute. Enter the resulting distance into the Focus Distance attribute field.

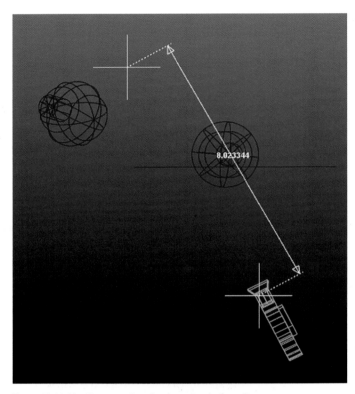

Figure 10.16 The Distance tool used to determine the focus distance

2. Set the F Stop attribute to the slider maximum of 64. The higher the F Stop value, the greater the depth of field. This will make the depth of field adjustments easier at the start.

3. Render a test frame. Incrementally reduce the F Stop value and re-render. When the depth of field appears satisfactory, leave the F Stop value as is.

4. For fine-tuning, increase or decrease the Focus Region Scale attribute by small increments. The Focus Region Scale attribute is a multiplier of the depth of field effect.

Note: The F Stop attribute roughly approximates the f-stop of real-world cameras. *F-stop* is a number that represents the ratio between the diameter of the lens aperture and the focal length of the lens. F-stops are scaled by an approximate factor of 1.4 (for example, f/1.4, f/2, f/2.8, and so on). Each increased f-stop halves the open area of the aperture, halves the amount of light striking the film, and increases the depth of field. The f-stop isn't the only factor to influence depth of field, however. Depth of field is inversely proportional to the focal length of the lens and directly proportional to the distance from the camera to the subject. Note that the Maya Camera Aperture attribute has no relationship to the Maya F Stop attribute (in contrast to real-world camera apertures and F-stops).

Applying Motion Blur

Motion blur is a streaking of objects in motion as captured by motion picture, film, or video mediums. The effect is an artifact of the time required to chemically expose film stock or electronically process light through a video CCD or CMOS chip. If an object moves 1 foot during the 1/60 of a second required by a camera to create one frame, the motion blur appears 1 foot in length on that frame. Motion blur is also perceived by the human eye when the motion is rapid. Although the human brain processes information continuously and does not perceive "frames" per se, rapid motion is seen as blurry through various physiological and psychological mechanisms (the exact nature of which continues to be studied and contended).

You can toggle on the Motion Blur attribute in the Motion Blur section of the Maya Software tab in the Render Settings window. (Chapter 11 discusses mental ray motion blur.) The Motion Blur Type attribute has two options—2D and 3D (see Figure 10.17).

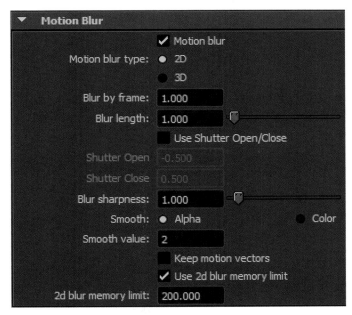

Figure 10.17 The Motion Blur section of the Maya Software tab

2D motion blur applies a postprocess blur to the rendered image. The blur is laid between the object's blur start and blur end position in a linear fashion. Hence, the blur is not realistic for objects spinning, weaving, or making rapid changes in direction (see Figure 10.18). Nevertheless, 2D motion blur is efficient and convincing for many animations (and the default settings work quite well).

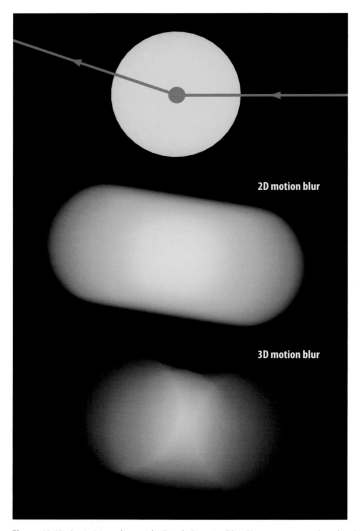

Figure 10.18 A primitive sphere with 2D and 3D motion blur. (Arrows represent the sphere's motion vector.)

3D motion blur, on the other hand, samples the moving object at multiple points along its path (see Figure 10.18). 3D motion blur is more accurate than 2D motion blur, but it's more time consuming. Unless the anti-aliasing quality is set fairly high, 3D motion blur suffers from graininess.

Note: The 3D Blur Visib and Max 3D Blur Visib attributes (found in the Number Of Samples section of the Maya Software tab) control the number of subpixel samples used to determine if blurred objects are occluding each other.

The Blur By Frame attribute controls the time range within which the blur for one frame is calculated. The following formula is used:

```
Time Offset = ((Shutter Angle / 360) * Blur By Frame) / 2
```

The Shutter Angle attribute, found in the Special Effects section of the camera's Attribute Editor tab, emulates the shutter of a motion picture camera, which is a spinning metal disk that sits between the lens and the film gate. Shutters have a pie-shaped cut that allows light to strike the film. The cut is measured in degrees. The default 144 degree Shutter Angle value is equivalent to a standard motion picture camera that ultimately exposes a frame of film for 1/60th of a second. The larger the Shutter Angle value, the longer the exposure and the lengthier the motion blur streak. Other common shutter angles are 150 and 180.

> **Note:** You can derive the exposure duration of a frame by employing the following formula: 1 / ((360 / Shutter Angle) × frames per second).

If the Blur By Frame attribute is set to 1.0 and the Shutter Angle value is 144, Maya performs the following math:

```
((144 / 360) * 1) / 2 = 0.2
```

Thus, Maya looks backward in time 0.2 frames to determine the object's blur start position and forward in time 0.2 frames to determine an object's blur end position. The blur is thereby streaked between the object's blur start and blur end. This effect is clearly visible when an object makes a hard turn and 3D motion blur is used (see Figure 10.18 earlier in this section).

If you increase the Blur By Frame attribute, Maya goes back further in time and forward further in time to calculate the blur. For example, if Blur By Frame is set to 4, the following math occurs:

```
((144 / 360) * 4) / 2 = 0.8
```

If 2D motion blur is activated, the Blur Length attribute serves as a multiplier for the Blur By Frame attribute. 2D motion blur provides several additional attributes:

Blur Sharpness Controls the sharpness of the postprocess blur. Low values increase the blur feathering and thus increase the length of the blur streak. High values reduce the blur feathering and thus shorten the length of the blur streak.

Smooth Helps reduce artifacts created in high-contrast situations. For example, if a dark object passes in front of a bright object or background, a dark ring may appear along the edge of the blur streak. Switching Smooth from Alpha to Color eliminates this error but continues to produce a high-quality alpha channel.

Smooth Value Controls the amount of blur applied to the edges of the motion blur streak. Use caution when raising this value above 2, as it may cause static objects to become blurred along their edges.

Keep Motion Vectors If selected, Maya stores the motion vectors but does not apply the blur. This feature is only supported by the Maya IFF image format. You can import the Maya IFF files into a compositing program such as The

Foundry's Nuke and use the vector information to create a motion blur during the compositing stage.

Use 2D Blur Memory Limit If selected, places a cap on the amount of memory the blur operation is allowed to use. The number of megabytes is set by the 2D Blur Memory Limit attribute. If a motion blur render fails, try raising the 2D Blur Memory Limit.

Note: Video cameras do not employ physical shutters. Instead, the CCD or CMOS chips are programmed to take a light sample at a fixed length of time. This length is referred to as shutter speed and can vary from 1/4 to 1/2000 of a second. Shutter speed also indicates the exposure time of still film cameras.

Working with the Render Layer Editor

With the Render Layer Editor, Maya provides a means to break up a render. Instead of rendering a shot as single image sequence or movie that contains all the scene's objects, you can render multiple sequences or movies that contain subsets of objects. This is useful for optimizing a render in the following ways:

- Rendering objects separately decreases the render times of individual frames.
- You can re-render specific objects without re-rendering *all* the objects.
- If objects are rendered separately, you are free to adjust them separately in a compositing program. For example, you can apply special color grading or add additional effects, such as blurs.
- When using render layers, you can assign special overrides. Thus, layers can use unique renderers, render settings, or material assignments.

For example, if you have a shot that contains two characters, a surrounding set, and an effects simulation, you can set up four render layers: character A, character B, set, and effects simulation.

Note: Render layers and render passes refer to two different types of renders. Render layers allow you to separate objects whereas render passes allow you to separate the shading components of a single object. Render passes are detailed in Chapter 13.

Setting Up Render Layers

The Render Layer Editor is located in the central tab at the bottom of the Channel Box (see Figure 10.19). You can reveal the Channel Box by clicking the right-hand Channel Box/Layer Editor tab.

By default, a Maya scene carries one layer, named *masterLayer*. All objects, including geometry, lights, camera, and projections, are included automatically on this layer.

Figure 10.19 The Render Layer Editor tab with default masterLayer and one new layer, renamed *newLayer*

You can create a new layer by selecting one or more objects and choosing Layers > Create Layer From Selected from the Render Layer menu. You can also click the Create New Layer And Assign Selected Objects button at the right side of the editor. When a new layer is created, it's added to the top of the Render Layer outline. You can rename the layer by double-clicking the layer name and typing the new name. To display the contents of the layer in the viewports, click the layer name so the layer is highlighted with a blue bar.

When an object is assigned to a layer, it still exists on the masterLayer. However, you are free to choose what objects are assigned to any additional layers. You can assign a selected object to a pre-existing layer by RMB-clicking over the layer name and choosing Add Selected Objects, Conversely, you can remove objects by choosing Remove Selected Objects.

Keep in mind that you'll need to add lights to layers so that objects on those layers are properly illuminated.

Rendering Render Layers

When more than one render layer exists, you can choose how to render them. Whether or not a render layer is renderable is controlled by the Renderable button beside each layer. This carries a small clapboard icon. If the icon has a green check mark, the layer renders; if the icon caries a red x, it does not. For example, as seen in Figure 10.19 in the previous section, the masterLayer is not renderable, whereas newLayer is renderable.

If you render with the Render View window, only the topmost renderable layer will render. However, you can force the Render View to render all the renderable layers with these steps:

1. In the Render Layer editor, choose Options > Render All Layers so that the Render All Layers check box is selected.

2. Choose Options > Render All Layers > ❑. In the Render All Layers Options window, select the Keep Layers radio button. Click the Apply And Close button.

3. In the Render View, click the Render The Current Frame button. Each render layer is rendered. When the render is complete, the topmost render layer is

displayed. In addition, a scroll bar is added to the bottom of the window. You can LMB-drag the bar to the right to display the other rendered layers, one at a time.

If you batch render, the render follows the Render Layer Editor settings. Each renderable layer is rendered to its own directory folder within the project's images directory. There are options for compositing the layers into a single image or storing the layers in a single Photoshop PSD file. These options are discussed in Chapter 12.

Creating Render Overrides

You can create unique render settings for each render layer. By default, the settings associated with the masterLayer are passed to other layers. However, you can selectively create render overrides for particular attributes on specific layers. This is useful for optimizing renders by choosing unique renderers or unique attribute values for each layer. For example, if only one layer requires raytracing, you can disable raytracing for the other layers to speed up the overall render time.

To create a render override, follow these steps:

1. Go to the Render Layer Editor and click the Controls button beside a new layer (a layer other than masterLayer). The button icon includes a small clapboard with two small circles and is directly to the left of the layer name (see Figure 10.20). The Render Settings window opens. All the attribute settings are inherited from the masterLayer.

Figure 10.20 The Render Layer Editor with two custom layers. Layer1 has a render override, as is indicated by the red dash on its Controls icon.

2. Go to an attribute, such as Render Using, and RMB-click over the attribute name. Select Create Layer Override from the menu that appears. The attribute name turns orange, indicating an override (see Figure 10.21). Change the attribute value. For example, change the Render Using value to mental ray. The layer now carries a unique attribute value that differs from the masterLayer and any other layer that does not have an override in place.

Figure 10.21 The Render Using attribute is given a render override, as is indicated by the orange front color. The settings affect layer1, as is indicated by the Render Layer menu.

3. If you wish to remove the override, RMB-click over the attribute name and choose Remove Layer Override. The attribute name loses the orange color and the attribute value returns to the value of the masterLayer.

When render overrides exist, you are free to change any of the settings of the masterLayer. You can see the masterLayer settings by clicking the Controls button beside the masterLayer name. You can also choose to display the settings for a particular layer by changing the Render Layer menu at the top of the Render Settings window. Note that the masterLayer includes tabs for all the renderers after a layer override is created for the Render Using attribute. You can create an override for any attribute visible within the Render Settings window.

Additional functionality of the Render Layer Editor, which includes mental ray render pass management, material overrides, and in-program compositing, is discussed in Chapter 13.

Chapter Tutorial: Test Rendering with Maya Hardware 2.0

Test rendering is an intrinsic part of the texturing and lighting process in Maya. To make the testing efficient, you can render regions in the Render View, switch to IPR, and batch render with low-quality settings. Another solution requires the use of Maya Hardware 2.0 renderer, which may speed up rendering by tapping into the on-board power of the system graphics card. To create and fine-tune a Maya Hardware 2.0 render, follow these steps:

1. Open the alien.ma scene file from the Chapter 10 tutorial directory. The scene features a work-in-progress alien model with textures and a shadow-casting light.

2. Open the Render Settings window. Note that the renderer is set to mental ray to properly render the included normal map. The resolution is set to 1920×1080. Hardware-rendering a large resolution image generally proves quicker than rendering the same image with mental ray. Go to frame 5.

3. Open the Render View window. Render the Persp camera. Choose File > Keep Image In Render View from the Render View menu. Change the Select Renderer menu to Maya Hardware 2.0. Render the Persp camera. (Hardware 2.0 does not support render regions.) The entire rendered frame appears almost instantly (the exact length of time depends on your graphics card). Upon completion, move the Render View's lower scroll bar back and forth to compare the hardware and mental ray renders (see Figure 10.22). The hardware render includes all the shading qualities of the mental ray renderer. Nevertheless, variations may exist in specular highlight intensity and normal map bumping. With this particular model, the normal map is adding all the grooves and seams to the spacesuit.

4. Go to the Render Settings window. Switch to the Maya Hardware 2.0 tab. To further optimize the render, select the Clamp Texture Resolution check box and lower the Max Texture Resolution to 64. Click the Reload All Texture button.

Test render. The textures become simplified. The hardware renderer bakes all the textures as part of the rendering process. Large bitmap textures are reduced in size. Standard Maya procedural textures are converted to bitmaps. This creates greater efficiency when rendering multiple frames and re-rendering one frame multiple times. By setting a clamp on the textures, you can choose a maximum size for each baked texture. Raise the Max Texture Resolution to 512. Re-render. Most of the texture detail returns.

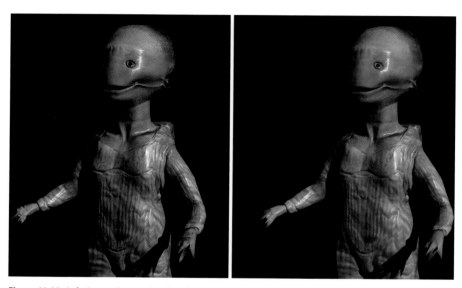

Figure 10.22 Left: A mental ray render of an alien model with a shadowed light and normal map bump; Right: Same render with the Hardware 2.0 renderer.

5. Choose File > Remove All Images From Render View from the Render View menu. Change the Select Renderer menu to mental ray. Open the Render Settings window. In the mental ray Quality tab, go to the Motion Blur section. Change the Motion Blur menu to Full. In the Render View, choose File > Keep Image In Render View. Run a test render.

6. Change the Select Renderer menu to Maya Hardware 2.0. Expand the Motion Blur section of the Maya Hardware 2.0 tab and select the Enable check box. Test render. Motion blur appears (see Figure 10.23). To remove graininess, change the Sample Count menu to a higher value, such as 10, and re-render. The blur is smoothed. Compare the mental ray render to the hardware render. The quality of the blur is fairly consistent between renderers, although the hardware render tends to create harder edges. To better match the blur trail length of the hardware render, raise the Shutter Open Fraction to 0.4. Click the Display Alpha Channel button. Alpha is displayed with the appropriate motion blur trail.

The tutorial is complete! Feel free to compare the Maya Software, mental ray, and Maya Hardware 2.0 renderers with Maya scenes included with the tutorial files. Note that the Maya Hardware 2.0 renderer does not support advanced rendering features, such as mental ray Final Gather, and places limitations on some of the light types, such as area lights. Because the Maya Hardware 2.0 renderer is dependent on the system graphics card, you may find that another renderer, such as Maya Software, is faster or more useful for gauging test renders.

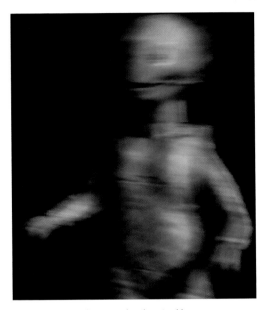

Figure 10.23 Hardware-rendered motion blur

Raytracing, mental ray, and Effects Rendering

In Autodesk® Maya® software, reflections, refractions, and chromatic aberrations are important qualities of materials such as water and glass. The Maya Software and mental ray® renderers provide these qualities through the raytracing process. Although the two renderers share many attributes, mental ray offers many advanced features. In particular, mental ray provides greater flexibility when rendering shadows and motion blur.

11

Chapter Contents
Raytracing with the Maya Software renderer
Creating reflections, refractions, and chromatic aberrations
mental ray quality, shadow, motion blur, and raytracing settings
Problem-solving raytracing errors
Rendering effects systems, including Fluid Effects and Bifröst

Maya Software vs. mental ray

By default, Maya renders with the Maya Software renderer. You can switch to the Maya Hardware, Maya Hardware 2.0, Maya Vector, or mental ray renderer by changing the Render Using attribute in the Render Settings window. Although the hardware and vector renderers are designed for specialized rendering situations, mental ray can easily handle renders normally tackled by Maya Software. As such, the comparative advantages of the Maya Software and mental ray renderers may not be immediately obvious. To help you make the choice between them, I've included a short list for each:

Maya Software

- Renders rapidly while providing attributes for high-quality anti-aliasing (Chapter 10).
- Offers relatively few attributes and is thus easy to set up (Chapter 10).

mental ray

- Includes Maya Fur and the nHair system in reflections and refractions (Chapter 3).
- Renders bump maps and normal maps with greater accuracy (Chapter 9).
- Is able to motion blur shadows (this chapter).
- Is able to impart transparency to depth map shadows (this chapter).
- Provides Global Illumination, Caustics, Final Gathering, importons, and irradiance particle rendering options. These options are able to incorporate light bounce and color bleed (Chapter 12).
- Utilizes Maya materials as well as a long list of mental ray shaders (Chapter 12).

Although mental ray's list of advantages is quite long, Maya Software is perfectly suitable for many renders. The trick is to become familiar with both systems so that you can make appropriate decisions at render time.

Raytracing with Maya Software

By default, the Maya Software renderer operates in a scanline mode. To activate raytracing, select the Raytracing attribute in the Raytracing Quality section of the Maya Software tab in the Render Settings window (see Figure 11.1).

Figure 11.1 The Raytracing Quality section of the Maya Software tab in the Render Settings window

Comparing the Scanline and Raytracing Processes

In general, the scanline process is as follows:

1. The renderer examines the objects in the scene. The objects within the camera frustum are added to a list and their bounding boxes are calculated.

2. The image to be rendered is divided into tiles to optimize memory usage. The complexity of the objects within a tile determines the tile's size.

3. Polygon triangles associated with visible objects are processed in scanline order. Each triangle is projected into screen space and is clipped to the boundaries of each pixel it covers. That is, the portions of the triangle outside the pixel boundaries are temporarily discarded. Each pixel is thus given a list of clipped triangle fragments. The fragments are stored in the lists as bit masks, which are binary representations of fragment visibility within a pixel. The algorithm responsible for this process is known as A-buffer.

4. The colors of each fragment are derived from the material qualities of the original polygons and the influence of lights in the scene. The final color of the pixel is determined by averaging the fragment colors, with emphasis given to those fragments that are the most visible. As part of this process, fragments are depth-sorted and additional clipping is applied to those fragments that are occluded.

In contrast to scanline rendering, the raytracing process fires off a virtual ray from the camera eye through each pixel of a view plane (see top of Figure 11.2). The number of pixels in the view plane corresponds to the number of pixels required for a particular render resolution. The first surface the ray intersects determines the pixel's color. That is, the material qualities of the surface are used in the shading calculation of the pixel.

If raytrace shadows are turned on, secondary *shadow rays* are fired from the point of intersection to each shadow-producing light (see bottom of Figure 11.2). If a shadow ray intersects another object before reaching a particular light, then the original intersection point is shadowed by that object. If the first surface is reflective and/or refractive, additional rays are created at the original intersection point. (A material such as glass can be both reflective and refractive.) One ray represents the reflection, and the other represents the refraction. If either ray intersects a secondary reflective and/or refractive surface, the ray-splitting process is repeated. This continues until the rays reach a predefined, maximum number of reflection and refraction intersections. When a reflection ray reaches a secondary surface, the shading model of the secondary surface is calculated and contributed to the original intersection point. Hence, the color of the secondary surface appears on the original surface as a reflection. A similar process occurs with a refraction ray, whereby the secondary surface shading model is contributed to the original intersection point. However, the direction that the refraction ray travels in is influenced by the refractive index. (Several Maya and mental ray material attributes set the refractive index value; these are discussed in this chapter and Chapter 12.)

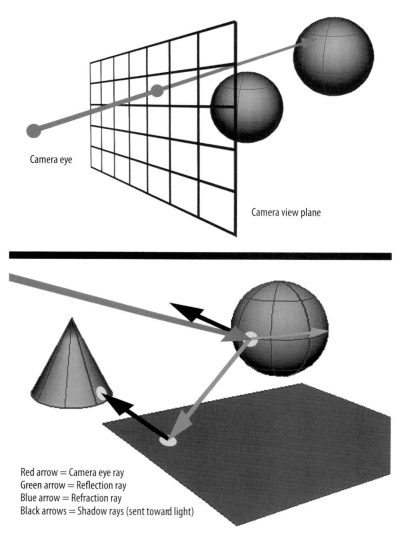

Red arrow = Camera eye ray
Green arrow = Reflection ray
Blue arrow = Refraction ray
Black arrows = Shadow rays (sent toward light)

Figure 11.2 Simplified representations of the raytrace render method

Maya Software Raytracing Optimization

Because a single camera eye ray can easily produce numerous shadow, reflection, and refraction rays, raytrace rendering is significantly more complex than the equivalent render with the scanline process. Consequently, the Maya Software renderer combines the scanline and raytrace techniques. If Raytracing is selected but a surface possesses no reflective or refractive qualities, Maya applies the scanline process and avoids tracing rays.

Another method by which Maya reduces raytrace calculations is through the creation of voxels. *Voxels* are virtual cubes created from the subdivision of a scene's bounding box (which includes all objects within the scene). Maya tests for ray intersections with voxels before calculating more exact surface intersections. This effectively reduces the number of surfaces that are involved with the intersection calculations. Without voxels, Maya would have to test every surface in a scene.

The Ray Tracing subsection of the Memory And Performance Options section in the Maya Software tab controls voxel creation through Recursion Depth, Leaf Primitives, and Subdivision Power attributes, which are described here:

Recursion Depth   Sets the number of available recursive levels of voxel subdivision. Values of 1.0 to 3 work for most scenes, with complex setups requiring higher numbers.

Leaf Primitives   Defines the maximum number of polygon triangles permitted to exist in a voxel before it is recursively subdivided.

Subdivision Power   The power by which the number of polygon triangles in a voxel is raised to determine how many times the voxel should be recursively subdivided (if recursion is deemed necessary by the Leaf Primitives attribute). For example, if there are 1,000 triangles in a voxel and the Subdivision Power value is changed from 0.25 to 0.5, the following math occurs:

```
1000 ^ 0.25 = 5.62
1000 ^ 0.5 = 31.62
```

Large Subdivision Power values lead to large results, which in turn create a greater number of recursive subdivisions and a greater number of subdivided voxels. Small subvoxels are inefficient if the majority of their brethren are wasted on empty space. On the other hand, a limited number of large subvoxels are also inefficient if they contain a high number of triangles.

Because Subdivision Power is not intuitive, it's best to change the attribute value by small increments. Maya documentation recommends a setting of 0.25 for most scenes.

> **Note:** A voxel is a form of octree, a data structure in which a node has up to eight children. An octree child is called an *octant*.

Setting Up a Raytrace

The Raytracing Quality section of the Maya Software tab provides Reflections, Refractions, Shadows, and Bias attributes. The Reflections attribute sets the maximum number of times a camera eye ray will generate reflection rays before it is killed off. The Refractions attribute sets the maximum number of times a camera eye ray will generate refraction rays before it is killed off (see Figure 11.3). The limit for both attributes is 10, which is generally satisfactory for a water glass, bottle, or vase.

The Shadows attribute, on the other hand, sets the maximum number of times a camera eye ray can reflect and/or refract and continue to generate shadow rays. The higher the value, the more recursive the shadows—that is, shadows will appear within reflections of reflections and refractions of refractions. This attribute has an effect only if raytraced shadows are used. Depth map shadows, whether they are generated by Maya

Software or mental ray, automatically show up in all recursive reflections. If Shadows is set to 0, all raytrace shadows are turned off. A value of 10 renders shadows within nine recursive levels of reflection or refraction (see Figure 11.4). If Shadows is set to 10 and no raytrace shadows appear in reflections or refractions, increase the Ray Depth Limit attribute in the Raytrace Shadow Attributes subsection of the light's Attribute Editor tab. (See Chapter 3, "Creating High-Quality Shadows," for more detailed information.)

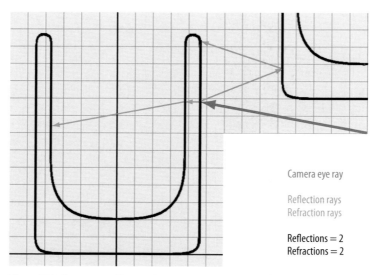

Camera eye ray

Reflection rays
Refraction rays

Reflections = 2
Refractions = 2

Figure 11.3 Rays generated by a single camera eye ray while the Reflections and Refractions attributes are set to 2

The Bias attribute serves as an adjustment for 3D motion blur in scenes with raytrace shadows. Often, raytrace shadows create dark bands around the center of rapidly moving objects. You can increase the Bias value to remove this artifact (see Figure 11.5).

Controlling Reflections

As soon as the Raytracing attribute is selected, the Maya Software renderer creates reflections for all objects. The amount of reflectivity is controlled on a per-material basis by the the Reflectivity attribute of Maya materials. (mental ray shaders are discussed in Chapter 12, "Working with mental ray Shaders, Global Illumination, and Final Gathering.") This attribute works in conjunction with the Specular Roll Off and Specular Color attributes. If Specular Roll Off and Specular Color are set to 0, there is no reflection. A material's Eccentricity attribute has no effect on the strength of a reflection and can be set to 0.

Note: Anisotropic materials offer an Anisotropic Reflectivity attribute, which overrides the standard Reflectivity attribute when selected. With Anisotropic Reflectivity, the strength of the reflection is determined by the Roughness attribute. The higher the Roughness value, the more quickly the reflection fades off (distant objects no longer appear as part of the reflection).

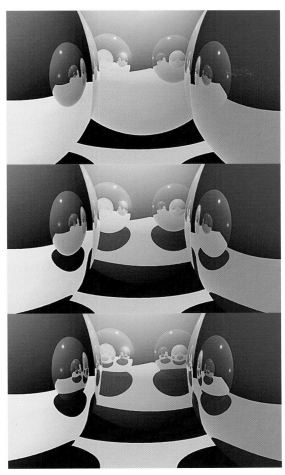

Figure 11.4 Top to Bottom: Spheres rendered with the Shadows attribute set to 1, 2, and 5, respectively. This scene is included with the Chapter 11 tutorial files as shadows.ma.

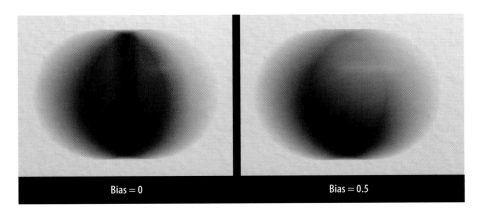

Bias = 0   Bias = 0.5

Figure 11.5 Left: Sphere rendered with raytrace shadows and 3D motion blur; Right: The same render with the Bias attribute set to 0.5. This scene is included with the Chapter 11 tutorial files as bias.ma.

In contrast, the Reflected Color attribute found on Blinn, Phong, Phong E, and Anisotropic materials does not require raytracing. If the Reflected Color value is set to a color other than black or is mapped, a simulated reflection is applied directly to the assigned surface. If the mapped texture is an environment texture, the results are quite convincing (see Chapter 5, "Applying 3D Textures and Projections," for a demonstration). Although a raytraced reflection is more accurate than a texture mapped to the Reflected Color attribute, raytracing is considerably less efficient. In any case, you can map the Reflected Color attribute *and* raytrace at the same time (see Figure 11.6). The color of light reflected in the raytrace process is multiplied by the Reflected Color attribute.

MODEL CREATED BY TORB, AVAILABLE VIA TURBOSQUID

Figure 11.6 Left: Raytraced chrome rim with the camera's Background Color set to blue; Middle: Same rim with an environment texture mapped to the Reflected Color attribute, but without raytracing; Right: Same rim with an environment texture and raytracing.

The Reflection Limit attribute (found in a material's Raytrace Options section; see Figure 11.8 in the next section) is a per-material attribute that sets the number of times a camera eye ray is allowed to reflect off the assigned surface before it is killed. Maya compares the Reflection Limit to the Reflections attribute in the Raytracing Quality section of the Maya Software tab and uses the lower value of the two.

The Reflection Specularity attribute (also found in a material's Raytrace Options section) controls the contribution of specular highlights to reflections. For example, in Figure 11.7 a car rim is assigned to two materials. In both cases the outer rim is assigned to a gray Blinn with its Reflection Specularity set to the default 1.0. On the left the spokes are assigned to a red Blinn with its Reflection Specularity set to 0. Thus, the reflection of the spokes in the rim does not include the specular component. However, if the spokes' Reflection Specularity is returned to 1.0, as on the right, the specular highlights of the spokes become visible in the rim reflection. When set to a value below 1.0, the Reflection Specularity attribute can help reduce anti-aliasing artifacts resulting from recursive reflections that contain a high degree of detail.

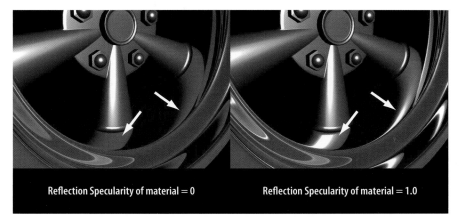

| Reflection Specularity of material = 0 | Reflection Specularity of material = 1.0 |

Figure 11.7 The Reflection Specularity attribute of a Blinn material determines whether specular highlights appear in reflections.

Managing Refractions and Aberrations

Refraction is the change in direction of a light wave due to a change of speed. When a light wave crosses the boundary between two materials with different refractive indices, its speed and direction are shifted. The human brain, unaware of this shift, assumes that all perceived light travels in a straight line. Hence, refracted light is perceived to originate from an incorrect location and objects appear bent or distorted.

A *refractive index* (also known as *index of refraction*) is a constant that relates the speed of light through a vacuum to the speed of light though a material (such as water or glass). The constant follows:

```
speed of light through a vacuum ÷ speed of light through a material
```

Water has a refractive index of 1.33, which equates to 1/0.75. The speed of light through water is only 0.75 times as fast as the speed of light through a vacuum. The refractive index of air is extremely close to 1.0 and is considered 1.0 when working in 3D. In contrast, glass has a refractive index of approximately 1.4 to 1.8 (depending on the manufacture of the glass). (You can find refractive index tables listing values for various materials by searching for "index of refraction table" online.)

In Maya, refractions are defined on a per-material basis in the Raytrace Options section of the material's Attribute Editor tab. Refraction attributes include Refractive Index, Refraction Limit, Light Absorbance, Surface Thickness, Shadow Attenuation, and Chromatic Aberration (see Figure 11.8):

Refractive Index   Sets the refractive index of the assigned surface. The default value of 1.0 creates no refraction and is the same as nondistorting air.

Refraction Limit   Sets the per-material maximum number of times a camera eye ray is refracted through the assigned surface before it is killed off. Maya compares this attribute to the Refractions attribute in the Raytracing Quality section of the Maya Software tab and uses the lower of the two.

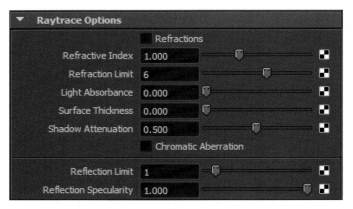

Figure 11.8 The Raytrace Options section of a material's Attribute Editor tab

Light Absorbance   Describes the amount of light that is absorbed by transparent or semitransparent objects. All real-world materials absorb light at different wavelengths (in which case the light energy is converted to heat). When set to 0, the Light Absorbance attribute allows 100 percent of the light to pass through the object. The higher the value, the more light is absorbed by the object's surface and the darker the surface appears (see Figure 11.9).

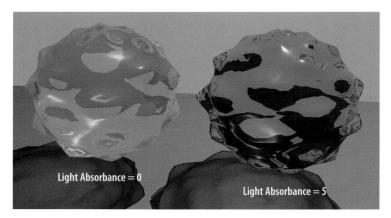

Figure 11.9   Left: A glass material with its Light Absorbance attribute set to 0; Right: The same material with its Light Absorbance attribute set to 5. This scene is included with the Chapter 11 tutorial files as `absorbance.ma`.

Surface Thickness   Determines the simulated thickness of a surface that possesses no model thickness. For example, in Figure 11.10 two primitive NURBS planes are given different Surface Thickness values. Because the left NURBS plane has a Surface Thickness value of 100, the sky color is not visible in its refraction; in addition, the high value creates a magnifying glass effect, which enlarges the table's checker pattern.

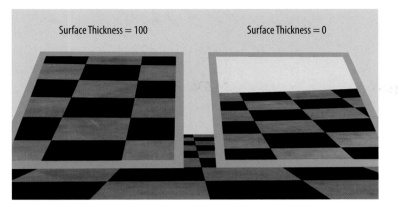

Figure 11.10 The refraction of a NURBS plane is adjusted with the Surface Thickness attribute. This scene is included with the Chapter 11 tutorial files as `thickness.ma`.

Shadow Attenuation Replicates the brightening of a shadow's core and the darkening of the shadow's edge when the shadow is cast by a semitranspar-ent object. A high Shadow Attenuation value creates a high-contrast transi-tion within the shadow (see Figure 11.11). A value of 0 turns the Shadow Attenuation off. The Refractions attribute does not have to be selected for Shadow Attenuation to work.

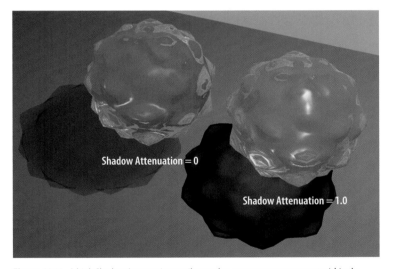

Figure 11.11 A high Shadow Attenuation attribute value creates greater contrast within the shadow. This scene is included with the Chapter 11 tutorial files as `attenuation.ma`.

You can also use the Shadow Attenuation attribute to adjust raytraced shadows that involve materials with Transparency maps. If Shadow Attenuation is left at the default value of 0.5, the part of the Transparency map that is 100 percent white will sometimes cast a soft shadow. At other times, a high Attenuation value may cause the shadow artifact to appear. For example, in Figure 11.12 a directional light casts the shadow of a plane that has a bitmap of a star symbol mapped to its material's Transparency attribute. The black lines in the figure represent the position of the shadowed plane. The red lines represent the edges of the plane as they appear as part of the shadow. The area within the red lines is darkened slightly, even though the Transparency map should provide nothing to shadow around the edges of the star. Attenuation is set to 1.0. When Attenuation is reduced to 0, however, the darkened area disappears appropriately.

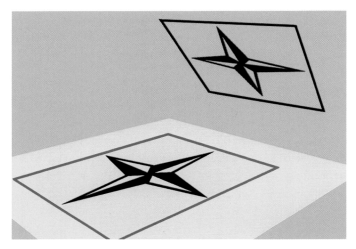

Figure 11.12 A Transparency map applied to the material of a plane casts a raytraced shadow. The red lines represent the edges of the plane as they appear as part of the shadow. An adjustment of the Attenuation attribute prevents this area from rendering inappropriately dark. This scene is included with the Chapter 11 tutorial files as `attenuation_trans.ma`.

Chromatic Aberration Refers to the inability of a lens to focus different color wavelengths equally. This is an artifact of dispersion, in which different wavelengths of light travel through a medium, such as glass, at different speeds. In effect, this causes a lens to have a different refractive index for each wavelength. The Chromatic Aberration attribute distorts refraction rays, causing colors to shift as shading models are invoked. Points closer to the light source shift toward cyan, while points farther from the light shift toward red and yellow (see Figure 11.13). The aberration is visible only if the Chromatic Aberration and Refractions attributes are selected.

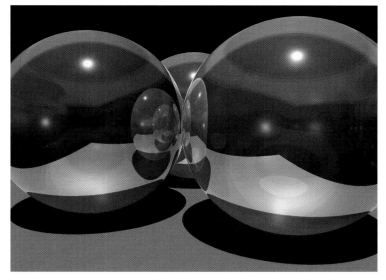

Figure 11.13 The Chromatic Aberration attribute introduces color shifts in raytraced geometry.

Raytracing with mental ray

With the Maya 2015 mental ray renderer, raytracing is activated by default. The only way to deactivate raytracing is to switch to the legacy rasterizer. Although there is a Raytracing attribute located within the Raytracing section of the mental ray Quality tab, you cannot change its state unless you switch to the rasterizer.

To switch to the legacy rasterizer, change the Sampling Mode menu, in the Sampling section of the Quality tab, to Legacy Rasterizer Mode. At that point, you are free to deselect the Raytracing attribute in the Raytracing section of the same tab. The legacy rasterizer uses scanline techniques to render and is specifically optimized to render motion blur. With older versions of Maya, you are free to deactivate the Raytracing attribute without switching to the legacy rasterizer.

Because many mental ray attributes are unique—or at least different in name— it is worth examining additional common settings in the Render Settings window. As part of this review, unified sampling, motion blur, and shadows are detailed.

> **Note:** The legacy rasterizer offered by mental ray treats motion blur in an efficient manner. Instead of sampling and shading each visible point of a moving object multiple times along its motion path for a single frame, the rasterizer samples all objects at a fixed position. The shading information is cached, and then is allowed to "travel" with the object when it is placed at the end of its motion path for a particular frame. Because each visible point has only one shading sample taken per frame, the calculation time is sped up significantly.

Understanding mental ray Unified Sampling

You can find the quality settings for mental ray in the Sampling section of the Quality tab of the Render Settings window (see Figure 11.14). (The mental ray tabs are visible only if mental ray is selected as the renderer.) Through the Sampling Mode menu, you can choose three main modes of operation: Unified Sampling, Legacy Rasterizer Mode, and Legacy Sampling Mode. Legacy Rasterizer Mode uses scanline techniques and is briefly discussed in the prior section. Legacy Sampling Mode offers anti-aliasing attributes used with earlier versions of Maya—these may be useful if you are working with an old Maya file. Unified Sampling Mode is designed to work with the majority of mental ray renders.

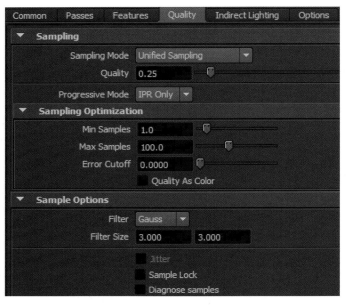

Figure 11.14 The Sampling and Sample Options sections of the mental ray Quality tab, as seen in Maya 2015

Unified Sampling Mode combines spatial and temporal sampling to increase the efficiency of anti-aliasing. As such, the mode offers an easy way to fine-tune scenes that include motion blur without having to resort to the legacy rasterizer. In addition, Unified Sampling works efficiently with mental ray shaders, lights, and shadows by reducing the need to adjust individual material, light, and shadow shading samples. On a technical level, Unified Sampling uses QMC (Quasi-Monte Carlo) sampling. QMC creates a semi-random sample distribution that optimizes the distance between subpixels, thus preventing uneven subpixel clustering that may degrade the resulting render by missing some aliasing artifacts.

Note: *Anti-aliasing*, as it's used in 3D programs, is any technique that attempts to minimize image distortions due to resolution mismatches. The distortions, referred to as *aliasing*, often occur when texture maps are represented by lower resolution renders. That is, the pixels present in the rendered area may be far fewer than the number of pixels in the corresponding texture map. This problem is exacerbated when the textured surface is not oblique to the camera or when the surface and/or camera are in motion. Aliasing artifacts include buzzing (flickering pixel color when the camera moves) and stairstepping (where diagonal edges appear blocky or jaggy). In general, anti-aliasing techniques employ *subpixels*, which are additional scene samples that fall within the domain of a single rendered pixel (subpixels are also referred to as *supersamples*). The additional samples are used to create a more accurate color for the associated pixel and thus minimize the appearance of aliasing.

Unified Sampling Mode includes a Quality slider. The higher the Quality value, the more accurate the anti-aliasing. The higher the Quality value, the greater the number of subpixel samples are taken in areas of the render that are flagged by an aliasing "error" detection algorithm. Error-prone areas include those that contain changes in contrast (due to texture color, lighting, and/or shadowing), points where surfaces meet in screen (raster) space, or points where surface edges meet the empty background in screen space.

In general, a Quality value of 1.0 is equivalent to "production quality." Values higher than 1.0 will slow the render exponentially. A value of 0.01 essentially turns the anti-aliasing off. The default value of 0.25 is sufficient for initial testing and fine-tuning of a scene.

> **Note:** If you use the IPR mode of the Render View window, you can increase the speed of the render by setting the Progressive Mode menu, in the Sampling section of the mental ray Quality tab, to IPR Only. This forces the renderer to use fewer subpixel samples during its initial calculations. This is dependent on the selection of the IPR > IPR Quality > IPR Progressive Mode option through the Render View menu.

You can further optimize Unified Sampling by adjusting Min Samples, Max Samples, Error Cutoff, and Quality As Color found within the Sampling Optimization subsection of Maya 2015. (Maya 2014 includes these attributes within the Samples section.) If an increased Quality setting fails to improve the render quality, you can increase Max Samples above the default 100. (*Samples* refers to subpixel samples.) Conversely, you can lower Max Samples to decrease the render quality for previews. Note that Unified Sampling is adaptive in that it varies the samples taken based on aliasing error values. Hence, the Min Samples and Max Samples values set the permitted sample range. The Error Cutoff attribute determines the sensitivity to errors. Error Cutoff values above 0 reduce the overall render quality but may improve render times. For many renders, the default settings with the Sampling Optimization section are suitable. However, to help determine appropriate values, you can use the mental ray diagnostic work flow, which is described in the next section. You have the option of setting Quality, Min Samples, and Max Samples per color channel if you select Quality As Color (Maya 2015) or Contrast As Color (Maya 2014).

If you use the Unified Sampling or Legacy Sampling Mode, a convolution filter is also activated. The filter further averages pixels in the resulting render as a post-process step. This helps reduce any aliasing artifacts (essentially, the render becomes slightly softer). You can control the aggressiveness of the filter and the resulting softness by adjusting the Filter Size X and Y in the Samples Options section. Lower values reduce the averaging. The style of convolution filter is controlled by the Filter menu. The Gauss (Gaussian) option offers a good combination of sharp edges and interior softness. Box and Triangle are crude but mathematically efficient filters. Mitchell and Lanczos apply minor variations to the Gauss model.

The Sample Options section also includes the Jitter, Sample Lock, and Diagnose Samples attributes. Jitter, available to the Legacy Sampling Mode, introduces systematic variations in subpixel sampling locations within pixels. (This feature is supplanted by the superior QMC sampling method of the Unified Sampling system.) Sample Lock ensures that the sampling pattern is consistent across multiple frames of an animation. Sample Lock overrides Jitter. If neither Jitter nor Sample Lock is selected, samples are taken at pixel corners when using the Legacy Sampling Mode. Diagnose Samples is described in the following section.

Diagnosing Samples

You can visualize the Unified Sampling mode by selecting the Diagnose Samples attribute, found in the Sample Options section of the Quality tab in the Render Settings window. When the attribute is selected, a multichannel OpenEXR file is rendered with RGB representations of aliasing errors, sampling rates, and render buffer times. To examine and interpret the OpenEXR file, follow these steps:

1. Leave the Sampling Mode set to Unified Sampling. Select the Diagnose Samples attribute. Create a render through the Render View window.

2. Through the Render View menu, choose File > Load Render Pass > Diagnose Samples. The Imf_disp window opens.

3. Initially, Imf_disp shows a beauty pass. However, several additional render passes are available. Choose Layer > mr_diagnostic_buffer _error. This displays the render with special color coding (see Figure 11.15). Where values are the highest, aliasing errors are the most intense. Such areas may have highly detailed textures; a high degree of surface variation dues to bump maps, lighting, or shadows; or surface edges that cross over empty space or other surfaces from the view of the camera.

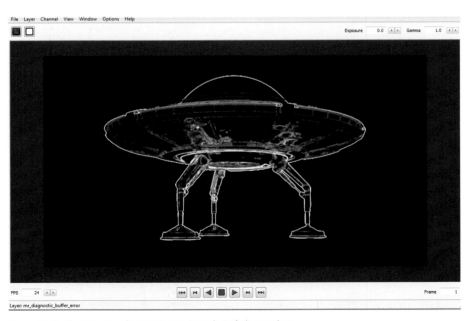

Figure 11.15 The error view of a spaceship render in the Imf_disp window

4. Close the Imf_disp window. Alter the sampling values in the Render Settings window (for example, raise the Quality value). Re-render in the Render View. In the new Imf_disp window, choose Layer > mr_diagnostic_buffer _error. The view updates with the current OpenEXR render. The color values change based on the sampling settings. For example, when the Quality value is raised, the pixels in the error view lose intensity. This is due to increased subpixel sampling reducing the amount of residual aliasing.

5. Specific error values are assigned to the pixels in the mr_diagnostic_buffer error view. You can view these by running your mouse over the view. The values are read out at the bottom-right of the window. Each color channel has its own set of values. If the error values are close to 0, the subpixel sampling is sufficient to suppress aliasing. If the error values are close to 1.0, the subpixel sampling is insufficient to suppress aliasing.

6. You can examine the density of subpixeling sampling by choosing Layer > mr_diagnostic_buffer_samples. Initially, the layer appears pure white because of the values stored as superwhite. Nevertheless, you can display the values by lowering the Exposure cell, found at the top-right of the window. For example, set the Exposure to −6. With this view, subpixel samples are indicated by bright pixels (see Figure 11.16). You can see the sample value assigned to a particular pixel by dragging your mouse over the view. The values are read out at the bottom right of the window. If a value is 1.0, no subpixel samples are taken. The higher the values, the more subpixel samples are taken.

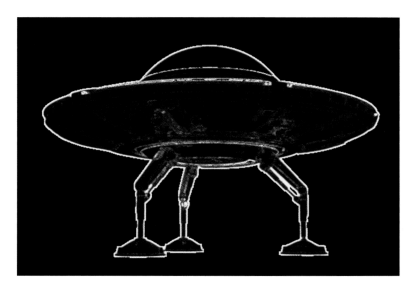

Figure 11.16 The samples view of the spaceship render

Using the samples view of the diagnostic render as a reference, you can follow these basic guidelines for adjusting the Quality tab settings:

- If the sample values are consistently low across the entire scene, the render may suffer from unnecessary aliasing artifacts. Try incrementally raising the Quality value and determine if the resulting render improves. If there is little or no perceptible change, return the Quality to its previous value.

- If the samples values are consistently high across the entire scene, there may be redundant subpixel sampling. Try incrementally lowering the Quality value and determine if the resulting render is acceptable. If the quality degrades, return the Quality to its previous value.

- If the sample values consistently plateau at the Max Samples limit (100 by default), consider raising the Max Samples value. The highest values usually occur where surface edges meet empty space.

Note that the OpenEXR file is stored as `diagnostic.exr` within the project's `\renderData\mentalray\` directory.

Using mental ray Motion Blur

Two forms of motion blur are employed by the mental ray renderer: No Deformation and Full. No Deformation motion blur is equivalent to the 2D motion blur provided by Maya Software in that it ignores surface deformation. Full motion blur, on the other hand, plots the motion vectors of each surface vertex and is thus sensitive to deformation. Attributes for mental ray motion blur are located in the Motion Blur section of the mental ray Quality tab and include Motion Steps, Motion Blur By, Displace Motion Factor, and Keyframe Location (see Figure 11.17). Note that neither No Deformation nor Full motion blur can incorporate rapid changes in object motion. That is, the motion blur streak is always drawn in a straight line. In this situation, Maya Software 3D motion blur is more accurate.

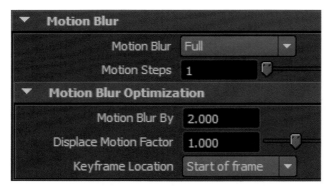

Figure 11.17 The Motion Blur section of the mental ray tab in the Render Settings window

The Motion Steps attribute determines the number of incremental time steps used to plot the motion blur streak for a frame. The higher the value, the more accurate the result. Higher values are particularly important for Full motion blur with a surface that deforms as it moves. Higher values may have little or no impact on the motion blur streak with No Deformation motion blur.

The Motion Blur By attribute serves as a multiplier for the current time interval. Higher values exaggerate the motion blur streak. Ultimately, the length of the streak is dependent on the Shutter Angle attribute, which is located in the Special Effects section of the camera's Attribute Editor tab. For more information on the Shutter Angle attribute and how it relates to exposure, see Chapter 10, "Prepping for Successful Renders."

By default, the blur streak is centered at the current frame. However, you can start the blur streak at the previous frame position by changing the Keyframe Location to End Of Frame (see Figure 11.18). You can start the blur streak at the next frame position by changing Keyframe Location to Start Of Frame. The ability to offset the blur streak is useful for matching animation to live-action video, which may include a different variation of motion blur based on the camera mechanism. You can further adjust the blur streak start and stop by adjusting the Shutter Open and Shutter Close attributes, located in the Legacy Options section of the Quality tab. For example, you can move the blur streak forward in time by one-quarter frame by changing Shutter Open to 0.25 and Shutter Close to 1.25.

With default render settings, mental ray motion blur streaks tend to appear grainy. However, you can adjust the Unified Sampling settings to create a smooth blur. For example, a Quality setting of 1.0 and a Min Samples setting of 50 generally make the grain disappear.

The Displace Motion Factor setting manages geometry reduction so as to speed up the render process. High values temporarily simplify the geometry during the blur calculation, with the most aggressive simplification occurring for areas with the greatest amount of motion (creating the longest blur streak). A value of 0 turns this feature off.

Controlling mental ray Depth Map Shadows

A light's Use Ray Trace Shadows attribute functions in the same manner for the mental ray renderer as it does for the Maya Software renderer. (Maya Software shadows are discussed in Chapter 3.) However, mental ray supplies separate attributes that control depth maps. These are found in the Shadows section of the mental ray tab in the Render Settings window (see Figure 11.19). Additional controls are located in shadow-specific sections of each light's Attribute Editor tab.

The Shadow Method attribute controls the method of depth shadow calculation and has four options: Disabled, Simple, Sorted, and Segments. The Simple method creates fast, efficient shadows and is appropriate for most animation. The Sorted method determines shadow order if multiple objects obscure the rendered point from the point-of-view of the shadowing light. With the Simple and Sorted methods, shadow rays are generated by the light from the light's origin. Unless a custom mental ray shader is used, Sorted offers no advantage over Simple.

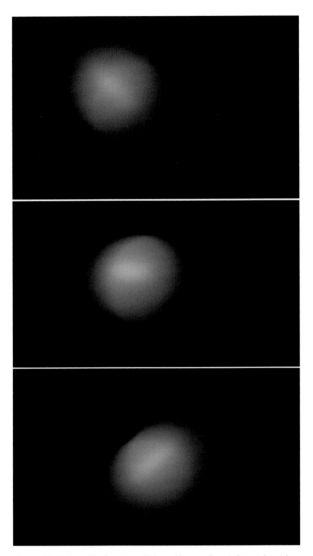

Figure 11.18 Top: A ball makes a V-shaped bounce from left to right with Keyframe Location is set to End Of Frame; Middle: Keyframe Location is set to Middle of Frame; Bottom: keyframe Location is set to Start Of Frame. Note the linear nature of the Full motion blur streak.

Figure 11.19 The Shadows section of the mental ray tab in the Render Settings window

With the Simple and Sorted methods, each shadow ray is terminated when it intersects a surface. With the Segments method, a new shadow ray (a *segment*) is born at each intersection. The rays also travel in the opposite direction, from the camera eye to the light. This approach makes the method suitable for depth map shadowing volume effects, such as Fluid Effects, nParticles that use volume shaders, and fur (if fur is simplified by treating it as a volume). Simple and Sorted methods are not able to cast shadows within volume materials.

Raytrace shadows, by their very nature, understand object transparency. However, if depth map shadows are used with the mental ray renderer, object transparency information is ignored. This holds true for standard Maya depth maps, controlled by the Depth Map Shadow Attributes section of a light's Attribute Editor tab, as well as mental ray depth maps (also known as *shadow maps*), controlled by the mental ray > Shadows subsection of a light's Attribute Editor tab. (For more information on depth map shadows, see Chapter 3.) Nevertheless, you can impart transparency to the depth map shadows by adjusting the Format attribute in the Shadow Maps subsection of the Render settings Quality tab (see Figure 11.19 earlier).

If the Format attribute is set to Detail, mental ray takes into account surface properties, such as transparency, when building the depth map shadows (see Figure 11.20). In addition, the Detail option provides superior depth map shadows for motion-blurred objects. Much like the Segments style of standard shadow map, detail shadow maps call a mental ray shadow shader when shadow rays intersect a surface. If Use Ray Trace Shadows is selected in a light's Attribute Editor tab, the Format option is ignored for that light (again, raytrace shadows automatically understand object transparency).

Shadow Method = Simple
Shadow Maps = On

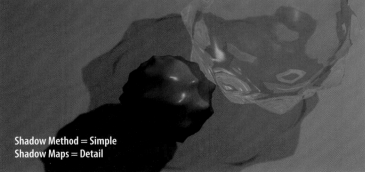

Shadow Method = Simple
Shadow Maps = Detail

Figure 11.20 A mental ray depth map with and without the Detail option. This scene is included with the Chapter 11 tutorial files as `mental_detail.ma`.

You can also access the Detail option through the mental ray > Shadows subsection of a spot, point, or directional light's Attribute Editor tab. If you switch the Shadow Map Format attribute from Regular Shadow Map to Detail Shadow Map, the light overrides the Format attribute in the Shadows section of the Render Settings Quality tab. When selected, the Detail Shadow Map option opens three additional attributes in the Detail Shadow Maps Attributes subsection (directly below the mental ray > Shadows > Shadow Map Overrides subsection). The Samples attribute controls the number of pixel samples taken at the intersection points of shadow-casting objects. The Accuracy attribute controls the quality of the shadow. Low Accuracy values increase quality but slow the render. An Accuracy value of 0 allows Maya to choose the best solution for the scene. The Alpha attribute, when selected, forces a scalar (grayscale) shadow.

Returning to the Shadows section of the mental ray tab, the Shadow Maps Disabled option of the Format attribute overrides light shadow settings and turns off every depth map in the scene. The Regular option turns on standard depth maps (unless overridden by the Detail Shadow Map option of the light). The Regular (OpenGL Accelerated) option attempts to use OpenGL acceleration to speed up shadow calculations (if available through the system graphics card).

When the Format attribute is switched to Regular, Regular (OpenGL Accelerated), or Detail, the Rebuild Mode attribute becomes available in the same section. The Reuse Existing Maps option retrieves previously rendered depth maps where feasible. The Rebuild All And Overwrite option creates shadow maps from scratch with each render. The Rebuild All And Merge option retrieves previously rendered shadow maps and updates the maps wherever any visible points have shifted toward the shadowing light.

All mental ray depth map shadow types create motion-blurred shadows when Motion Blur is set to No Deformation or Full and Motion Blur Shadow Maps, in the Shadow Maps subsection of the Render Settings Quality tab, is selected. Reflected and refracted shadows are also subject to mental ray motion blur.

Creating Reflections and Refractions with mental ray

As discussed earlier in this chapter, mental ray automatically raytraces. You can control the global raytracing quality through the Raytracing section of the Quality tab in the Render Settings window (see Figure 11.21).

Figure 11.21 The Raytracing section of the mental ray Quality tab in the Render Settings window

The following attributes control the rays used for the render:

Reflections   Sets the maximum number of times a camera eye ray can be reflected off reflective surfaces. This attribute is overridden on a per-material basis by the Reflection Limit attribute of Maya materials. (Reflectivity and refractivity settings for mental ray shaders are discussed in Chapter 12.)

Refractions   Sets the maximum number of times a camera eye ray can be refracted through refractive surfaces. This attribute is overridden on a per-material basis by the Refraction Limit attribute of Maya materials. (Refractions are not created by mental ray unless the Refractions attribute is selected for a Maya material.)

Max Trace Depth   Controls the maximum number of times a camera eye ray can reflect off *or* refract through surfaces. This attribute trumps both the Reflections and Refractions attributes. For example, if Max Trace Depth is set to 5, a ray can reflect twice and refract three times before it is killed off.

If a scene is fairly simple and there aren't multiple semitransparent or transparent surfaces, you can lower Reflections and Refractions to optimize the render. For example, if you're rendering a plate glass window in an otherwise nonreflective room, you can set Reflections to 2 and Refractions to 0 (which disables unneeded refractivity). However, if the scene involves something more complex, like a glass vase with an inner and an outer surface, Reflections and Refractions should be left at 10 so that the reflective and refractive rays pass through the surfaces and reach any objects behind the vase and then return to the camera. Errors created by incorrect raytracing settings are discussed in the next section.

Additional mental ray raytracing attributes control recursive shadows and blurs:

Shadows   Sets the maximum number of times a camera eye ray can reflect and/or refract and continue to generate shadow rays. The higher the value, the more recursive the shadows—that is, shadows will appear within reflections of reflections and refractions of refractions. The default value of 2 allows shadows to appear in a reflection or refraction, but not in a reflection of a reflection or a refraction of a refraction.

Reflection Blur Limit and Refraction Blur Limit   Represents the maximum number of times a camera eye ray can reflect or refract and still be considered for a blur. Unlike Maya Software, mental ray can blur reflections and refractions. With the default value of 1.0, mental ray blurs only the first reflection or refraction but does not progress recursively (see Figure 11.22). The degree of blurriness for Maya materials is controlled on a per-material basis by the Mi Reflection Blur and Mi Refraction Blur attributes, found in the mental ray section of the material's Attribute Editor tab. Reflection Rays and Refraction Rays, in the same section, control the quality of the blur by providing additional shading samples when their values are raised. Because a blurred reflection within a blurred reflection is difficult to distinguish from a reflection with a blurred reflection, a Reflection Blur Limit of 1.0 works in many situations. Additionally, per-material Reflection Blur Limit and Refraction Blur Limit attributes are provided in the mental ray section of the material's Attribute Editor tab.

Figure 11.22 A mental ray–blurred reflection and refraction

For additional information on per-material raytracing settings, see the "Controlling Reflections" section earlier in this chapter. See Chapter 12 for information on mental ray shaders and their ability to render glossy reflections.

Solving Raytrace Errors

Complex raytrace scenes may produce errors when reflectivity and/or refractivity is present. The errors often appear as black voids or blackish reflections along the surface. There are two common causes:

- Reflections of Maya empty space
- Refraction rays dying before they reach background surfaces.

Empty space within Maya is rendered as black in RGB. (In the alpha channel, the empty space is assigned 100 percent transparency.) Hence, blackish reflections may show in the raytraced render. For example, in Figure 11.23, reflective white tubes display dark gray areas despite the addition of a plane in the background that is assigned to a red material (the black of empty space reflects off the white surfaces to become gray). You can alter the empty space color by changing the Background Color of the rendering camera. (Choose View > Camera Attribute Editor from the viewport menu and go to the Environment section of the camera's Attribute Editor tab.) One option is to choose a Background Color that more closely matches the materials assigned to other geometry in the scene. With the Figure 11.23 scene, red is suitable. In this example, the mental ray Reflections attribute is set to 1.0. Alternatively, you can change Background Color to match a desired location (for example, blue for an exterior sky).

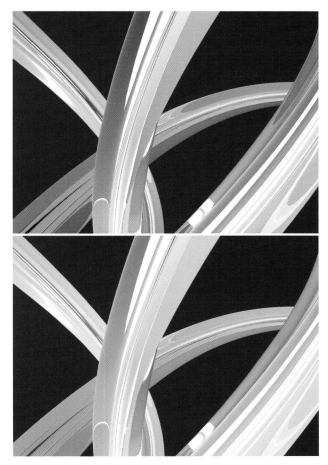

Figure 11.23 Top: White tubes reflect back empty space, creating gray reflective areas; Bottom: Same setup with Background Color set to red.

To avoid the empty space, you can surround the reflective surfaces with additional geometry. For example, you can add four walls, a floor, and a ceiling to emulate an interior space. If a surrounding the objects is not feasible, you can also map an environmental projection to the assigned material's Reflected Color attribute. In this way, the colors of a bitmap texture help to disguise the lack of surrounding geometry. For additional information on the Reflected Color attribute, see the "Controlling Reflections" section earlier in this chapter.

Aside from the reflection of empty space, errors occur when refractive rays fail to find background surfaces. This causes Maya to substitute the Background Color where no refractive information is available. For example, as seen in Figure 11.24, a convoluted polygon tube is assigned a Blinn material with 100% transparency but 0% reflectivity. Although the Maya Software Refractions attribute is set to 4 and the material's Reflection Limit is set to 4, black areas remain. For the refraction rays to successfully penetrate the tube surface, reach the background (a large cube surrounding the tube and camera), and return to the camera (sometimes passing back through the tube), a higher Refractions value is necessary. With this example, a value of 24 removes the majority of the black areas. If you cannot raise the Refractions value to a sufficiently high number due to long render times, you can lessen the impact of the black areas by changing the camera's Background Color.

Figure 11.24 Top: Black areas show up on a transparent tube when the Refractions value is not high enough; Bottom: Same setup with Refractions set to 24.

When you're rendering with mental ray and using Maya materials, a higher Refractions value may not remove all of the black areas. In this situation, it's necessary to switch to a mental ray shader. For example, you can assign the surface to a mia_material_x shader. Chapter 12 discusses mental ray shaders in detail.

Note that the mental ray Refractions attribute is clamped by Max Trace Depth. Max Trace Depth limits the total reflection and refraction rays. If you set Reflections to 5 and Refractions to 15, set Max Trace Depth to 20 to avoid stopping refraction rays before they reach their limit of 15.

Rendering with Dynamic Effects Systems

Several effects systems within Maya require special techniques for texturing, lighting, and rendering. These include the Bifröst simulation system, Fluid Effects, and nParticle meshes.

An Introduction to Bifröst Liquids

Bifröst is a new procedural platform included with Maya 2015 that is designed to create liquid simulations. You can preview Bifröst with the Viewport 2.0 renderer. You can render Bifröst simulations with mental ray.

To set up a simple Bifröst simulation, follow these steps:

1. Create a new scene and create a polygon cube. Scale the cube in the X and Z directions so that it has relatively little height. Create a primitive plane. Scale it so that it's wider and longer than the cube. Move the plane down in Y so it sits below the cube without touching it. Use Figure 11.25 as a reference.

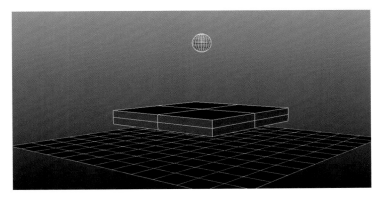

Figure 11.25 A primitive cube is used to generate Bifröst particles. A primitive sphere and plane are used as collision objects.

2. Create a primitive polygon sphere. Move it up in Y so that it sits above the cube without touching it. Keyframe animate the sphere dropping downward so that it touches the lower plane over 10 frames. Set the timeline duration to 30 frames. To play back the simulation accurately, set the Playback Speed to Play Every Frame (Window > Settings/Preferences > Preferences > Time Slider section).

3. With the cube selected, choose nDynamics main menu > Bifrost > Create Liquid. Bifröst particles appear in the volume of the cube. (If they fail to appear, make sure the viewport is set to Renderer > Viewport 2.0.) Additional Bifröst nodes are added to the scene. The BifrostLiquidContainer shape node serves as the liquid simulation solver. This node includes a long list of attributes that control internal gravity, simulation resolution (via voxels), and subparticle generation (in the form of droplets).

4. Select the original cube and go to its shape node tab in the Attribute Editor. Scroll down to the Bifrost section, which was added with the Create Liquid tool. Expand the Liquid Emission subsection and deselect Continuous Emission. This prevents additional particles from being born as the timeline moves forward. In the Conversion subsection, change the Mode menu to Solid. This causes the volume of the cube to be filled with particles; if Shell is selected, particles are born solely along the surface of the cube.

5. Shift-click the sphere and the Bifröst container in a viewport. (The container appears as a larger, unshaded cube surrounding the polygon cube; the container is generated by the bifrostShape node.) Choose Bifrost > Add Collider. Shift-click the plane and the Bifröst container and choose Bifrost > Add Collider again. The sphere and plane are tagged as a Bifröst collision object. Select the polygon cube and hide it.

6. Select the Bifröst container and play back the timeline. The timeline goes into a color mode, showing yellow or green frames. Maya information is sent to Bifröst, which is actually an external program. The Bifröst simulation is then reimported. When the timeline becomes fully green, the simulation is complete and you can play it back normally. With these steps, the sphere pushes a hole into the particle mass as the entire mass falls to the plane and spreads outward (see Figure 11.26).

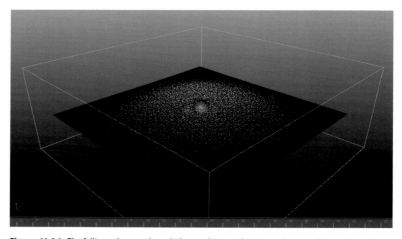

Figure 11.26 The falling sphere pushes a hole into the particle mass as the mass falls and spreads out on the plane. The Bifröst container is selected.

After you've created a Bifröst simulation, you can render it with the mental ray renderer. There are three main ways to interpret the simulated liquid surface:

Voxel Isomesh   You can render a virtual surface using the simulation's voxel information. For this to work, you must place the camera within the Bifröst container. In addition, the Auto Volume attribute must be selected (Render settings window > Features tab > Extra Features section).

Bifröst Mesh and Liquid Material   You have the option to convert the Bifröst particles into a triangulated, polygonal mesh. To do so, select the Enable attribute within the Bifrost Meshing section of the bifrostShape node tab. In this section, you can control the mesh detail. For example, you can raise the Resolution Factor value to make the mesh denser and more prone to reveal tiny undulations in the simulation. You can also reinterpret the cohesiveness of the surface. If you lower the Surface Radius value, the solid mass of water breaks into myriad drops (this is demonstrated in Figure 11.26). The mesh is assigned automatically to a Bifrost Liquid Material. Although the material includes common attributes to control diffuse color, reflectivity, and refractivity, it's designed to develop color and strength variation based on the particle simulation. The Diffuse Remap, Foam Remap, Reflection Remap, and Refraction Remap sections include ramp graphs that alter values based on particle velocity and vorticity (churning motion). Like other uses of ramp graphs in Maya 2015, the left of each graph equates to the low end of the input scale and the right side equates to the high end of the input scale. For example, you can use this feature to lighten the liquid color when the particles move quickly. Alternatively, you can make the water more transparent as it becomes idle.

Bifröst Mesh and Maya Material or mental ray Shaders   If a Bifröst mesh exists, you are free to assign the surface to other materials or shaders, as illustrated in Figure 11.27. Although these lack the ability to alter shading qualities based on velocity and vorticity, they offer reliability and familiar shading workflows. Regardless of the shader or material assigned, Bifröst meshes support reflections, refractions, shadowing, and motion blur.

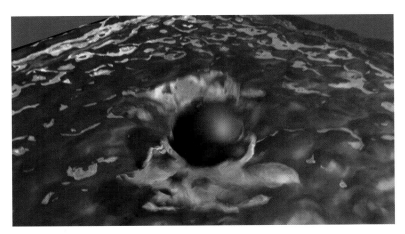

Figure 11.27 A Bifröst simulation is converted to a mesh and assigned to a Blinn material with reflectivity and refractivity. The shot is rendered with mental ray and motion blur. An example scene is included as bifrost.ma with the Chapter 11 tutorial files.

Note: As of this writing, the Bifröst system required the latest Maya service pack to function properly. For service pack information and documentation, visit the Autodesk Knowledge Network at knowledge.autodesk.com.

Shading and Lighting Fluid Effects

The Dynamics Fluid Effects system reproduces a wide range of fluid systems, including those that replicate atmospheric and viscous liquids. You can render Fluid Effects with either the Maya Software or the mental ray renderer. The Fluid Effects system relies on the Fluid Shape material, which provides shading controls that establish common shading qualities such as color, incandescence, and opacity of the fluid. The material is unique, however, in that you can pin the shading qualities on the simulation itself. Fluid Effects simulations incorporate fluid temperature, density, velocity, pressure, and fuel (combustive potential).

To create a simple Fluid Effects system and set its basic shading qualities, follow these steps:

1. Switch to the Dynamics main menu set and choose Fluid Effects > Create 3D Container. The fluid container is placed in the scene. At this point the container is empty.

2. Select the container and choose Fluid Effects > Add/Edit Contents > Add Emitter. A fluid emitter is added. Interactively move the emitter downward so that it sits near the bottom of the container (the fluidEmitter node is parented to a fluid transform node). Increase the timeline duration to 300. Play back the timeline. Blue–green dots, which represent the fluid, are drawn in the unshaded viewport. With shading activated, the fluid mass is roughly drawn. With default settings, the fluid mass slowing floats upward and gathers at the top of the container (see Figure 11.28). The container confines the simulation.

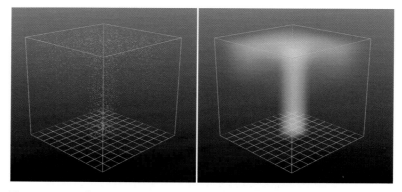

Figure 11.28 Wireframe and shaded views of the initial fluid simulation

3. Test-render a late frame with the Render View. The fluid renders as a flat-shaded smoke. Select the container and go to the fluidShape tab in the Attribute Editor. In the Contents Method section, note that the Density and Velocity menus are set to Dynamic Grid. This means that the fluid contents of each voxel in the container are calculated using dynamic simulation calculations. Other menu options include Static Grid and Gradient, in which case the fluid content does not shift or flow through dynamic simulation. The number of voxels in the container is determined by the Base Resolution attribute in the Container Properties section. The higher the Base Resolution value, the more intricate and detailed the simulation becomes. Although the unshaded viewport displays small, particle-like dots, the fluid mass is divided into cube-like voxels for dynamic calculations and rendering.

4. Expand the fluidShape tab's Shading section. In the Color subsection, note that the color ramp graph is pure white and the Color Input menu is Constant. Change Color Input to Density. Insert an additional handle into the ramp at Selected Point 0.2. Change the left handle to black and the new right handle to white (see Figure 11.29). By default, the fluid takes on additional orange and yellow colors through the Incandescence ramp graph. To remove this, delete the orange and yellow handles. Color changes to the fluid are visible in shaded viewport view. Play back from frame 1. Stop at a late frame. Render a test frame. The fluid now takes on more varied shades of gray, where denser areas are brighter and less dense areas are darker.

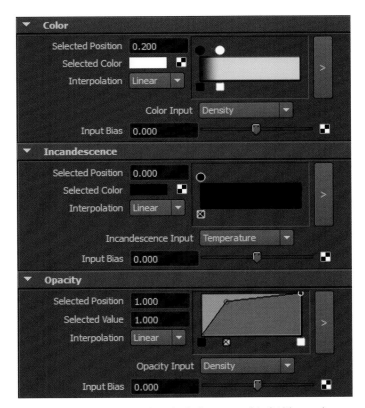

Figure 11.29 Adjusted ramp graphs in the Shading section of the fluidShape node

5. To make the fluid more intricate, raise Base Resolution to a higher value, such as 32. To make the fluid shape more convoluted, you can adjust various built-in dynamics properties in the Turbulence subsection. For example, expand the Contents Details section and Turbulence subsection of the fluidShape tab and raise the Strength value above 0. Play back from frame 1. Increased turbulence causes the fluid mass to become more erratic and form "arms."

6. By default, the fluid is trapped by the container and the fluid tends to collect along its walls and ceiling. You can automatically expand the container by selecting the Auto Resize attribute in the fluidShape node's Auto Resize section. To reduce the transparency of the fluid and make it appear denser, adjust the Opacity ramp graph in the Shading section. For example, insert an additional handle into the center of the ramp and give it a high value such as 0.8. You can also darken the color assigned to the Transparency attribute (at the top of the Shading section). To improve the overall render quality of the fluid, slowly raise the value of the Quality attribute, found in the Shading Quality section (see Figure 11.30). Note that the mental ray renderer generally creates a smoother fluid mass when rendering.

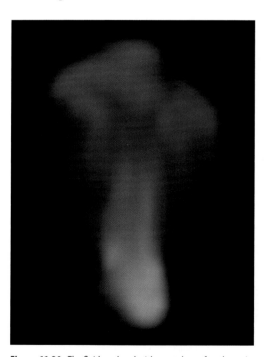

Figure 11.30 The fluid rendered with mental ray after the various shading and quality adjustments discussed in this section. A Maya scene is included as `fluid_effects.ma` with the Chapter 11 tutorial files. After opening the file, play back the timeline from frame 1 to see the fluid.

When you create a Fluid Effects system, the fluid interacts with lights any lights present in the scene. The more intense the lights, the brighter the fluid. However, the light's interaction with the fluid is diffuse so that the exact light direction is difficult to perceive. The fluid also reacts to depth map shadows—the shadows are also diffuse and darken areas of the fluid without creating distinct shadow shapes. Raytrace shadows, on the other hand, create more distinct shadow patterns and shadow streaking through the fluid mass. The fluid also casts diffuse shadows over other surfaces (see Figure 11.31).

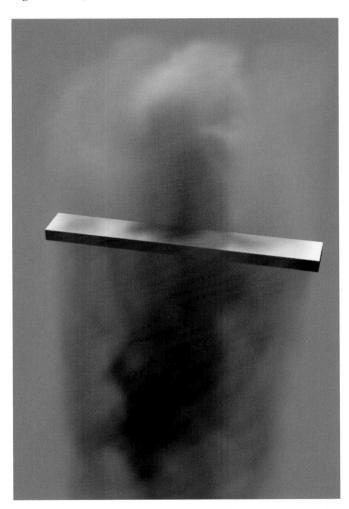

Figure 11.31 A cube is placed at the top of the fluid. The fluid is lit by a down-pointing directional light with raytrace shadows. The cube darkens the fluid directly below it. A Maya scene is included as `fluid_effects_lit.ma` with the Chapter 11 tutorial files. After opening the file, play back the timeline from frame 1 to see the fluid.

The fluidShape node also offers self-generated lighting and shadowing. This allows you to light the fluid independently of the scene lighting, which is sometimes desirable to achieve an aesthetic result. To activate this, deselect the Real Lights attribute in the Lighting section (see Figure 11.32). The fluid's internal light direction is controlled by the Directional Light XYZ vector. You can activate self-shadowing by selecting the Self Shadow attribute. Self-shadow softness and darkness are set by Shadow Diffusion and Shadow Opacity, respectively. For additional information on Fluid Effects simulation setup, see the "Modifying Fluids" page in the Maya Help files or at the Autodesk Knowledge Network (knowledge.autodesk.com).

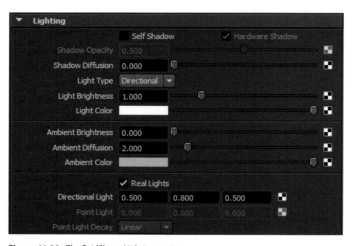

Figure 11.32 The fluidShape Lighting section

Rendering nParticle Meshes

You can convert a Blobby Surface nParticle simulation into a polygon mesh. The mesh follows the outer contours of the particle mass. This technique provides a way to create cohesive bodies of water with distinct, continuous surfaces and helps disguise the individual particles within the simulation. To create the surface, select the nParticle node and choose Modify > Convert > nParticle To Polygons. The nParticles are hidden and a triangulated mesh appears. As shown in Figure 11.33, the mesh updates as the nParticle simulation progresses. The mesh actively incorporates any changes you make to the simulation. (To see any updates, always play back from frame 1.)

You can assign the polygon mesh to any Maya Software or mental ray shader. The quality of the mesh is controlled by the output Mesh section of the nParticleShape node. Max Triangle Mesh sets the mesh resolution. Higher values follow the particle placement more carefully and thus show smaller undulations as individual "drops." The relative size of the resulting faces is set by Mesh Triangle Size, with smaller values creating a more intricate surface. For additional information on nParticles, see Chapter 7, "Automating a Scene with Sampler Nodes."

Figure 11.33 A nParticle simulation is converted to a polygon mesh with the nParticle To Polygons tool. The mesh is assigned to a reflective and refractive Blinn material and rendered with mental ray. This Maya scene is included as `nparticles_mesh.ma` with the Chapter 11 tutorial files. After opening the file, play back the timeline from frame 1 to see the simulation.

Chapter Tutorial: Texturing and Rendering an Ice Cube

In this tutorial, you will texture and render an ice cube with the mental ray renderer. You will employ reflections, refractions, and custom shading networks to help make the render more realistic (see Figure 11.34).

1. Open `icecube.ma` from the Chapter 11 tutorial directory.

2. Create two new Blinn materials in the Node Editor window. Name the first Blinn material **Inner** and the second Blinn material **Outer**. Assign Outer to the OuterIce polygon surface. Assign Inner to the InnerIce polygon surface.

3. Open the Outer material in the Attribute Editor. Set Transparency to 100% white, Eccentricity to 0.1, and Specular Color to 100% white. The material Color values do not matter because the materials are completely transparent. In the Raytrace Options section, select the Refractions attribute. Set Refractive Index to 1.3, Refraction Limit to 2, and Reflection Limit to 1.0. Note that real-world ice has a refractive index of 1.31, whereas water has a refractive index of 1.33.

4. Click the Bump Mapping attribute Map button. Choose a Noise texture from the Create Render Node window. Open the Attribute Editor tab for the new bump2d node. Set the Bump Depth attribute to 0.1.

Figure 11.34 An ice cube rendered with mental ray

5. Add a new Ramp texture and a Sampler Info utility to the Node Editor. Connect the Facing Ratio of the samplerInfo node to the V Coord of the ramp node. Note that connection to the V Coord attribute does not affect the appearance of the ramp in the Attribute Editor or in the Hypershade and Node Editor texture swatches. Nevertheless, different Facing Ratio values are fed to V Coord during the render, causing different color samples to be taken from different V-positions along the ramp (with Maya 2014 this is down to up and with Maya 2015 this is left to right). Connect the Out Color of the ramp node to Incandescence of Outer. Use Figure 11.35 as a reference.

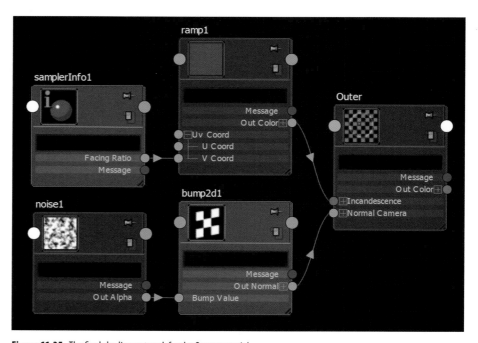

Figure 11.35 The final shading network for the Outer material

6. Open the ramp node's Attribute Editor tab. Change the Interpolation attribute to Smooth. Delete the middle color handle (if it is present). Change the top handle (Maya 2014) or right handle (Maya 2015) to dark gray. Change the bottom handle (Maya 2014) or left handle (Maya 2015) to medium gray. Position the top/right handle two-thirds of the way to the top/right of the ramp. The ramp controls the bright edge of the ice cube. Where the surface points away from the camera, low Facing Ratio values are returned, which causes the ramp to provide a medium gray color to the Incandescence. Where the surface points toward the camera, high Facing Ratio values are returned, which causes the ramp to provide a dark gray color to the Incandescence. If the cube edges render too brightly, darken the colors of the ramp. The Outer material is now complete.

7. Open the Inner material in the Attribute Editor. Set Reflection Limit to 2. Leave Refractions off. Leave the Specular Shading attributes at their default settings. Click the Bump Mapping attribute Map button. Choose a Fractal texture from the Create Render Node window. Open the Attribute Editor tab for the new bump2d node. Set the Bump Depth attribute to 0.2. The bump maps make the inner cube bumpy and convoluted and thus create the illusion of cloudy inner ice.

8. Create new Sampler Info, Reverse, and two Multiply Divide nodes in the Node Editor. Connect the Facing Ratio of the samplerInfo node to the Input X of the reverse node (use Figure 11.36 as reference). Connect the Facing Ratio of the samplerInfo node to the Specular Roll Off of the Inner material. Connect the Facing Ratio of the samplerInfo node to the Input1 X of the multiplyDivide1 node. Connect the Output X of the multiplyDivide1 to the Incandescence R, Incandescence G, and Incandescence B of Inner. Connect the Output X of the reverse node to the Input1 X of the multiplyDivide2 node. Connect the Output X of the multiplyDivide2 node to the Transparency R, Transparency G, and Transparency B of Inner.

9. Open the Attribute Editor tab for multiplyDivide1. Set the Input 2X attribute to 0.3. Increasing this value will create a stronger incandescence around the inner cube's edge (that is, the part that points away from the camera).

10. Open the Attribute Editor tab for multiplyDivide2. Set the Input 2X attribute to 2.75. Decreasing this value will make the inner cube edges cloudier and less transparent. The custom shading networks are now complete!

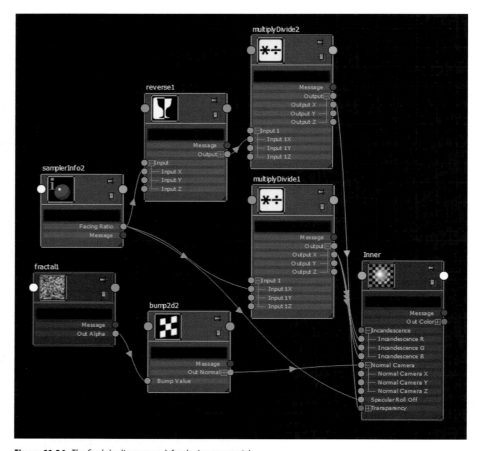

Figure 11.36 The final shading network for the Inner material

11. The scene file contains a single directional light named Key. Open the Attribute Editor tab for Key and select Use Ray Trace Shadows. Set Light Angle to 5. Set Shadow Rays to 32. This creates a soft-edged shadow. Set Ray Depth Limit to 3. This limits shadows to two recursive reflections or refractions.

12. Open the Render Settings window. Switch the Render Using attribute to mental ray. In the Quality tab > Raytracing section, set Reflections to 1.0, Refractions to 2, and Max Trace Depth to 2. This limits the raytracing to a maximum of 2 reflections and/or refractions per camera eye ray. Set Quality to 0.1. In the Common tab, choose a small resolution, such as 640×480, and render a test frame. If the render is acceptable, slowly raise the Quality, Refractions, material Refraction Limit, and light Shadow Rays and re-render and compare the results. Your result should look similar to Figure 11.33 at the start of this section.

The tutorial is complete! If you get stuck, a finished version is included as `icecube_complete.ma` with the Chapter 11 tutorial files. Keep in mind that this is not the only means with which you can create an ice-like look. For example, you can employ more advanced mental ray shaders, such as mia_material_x. The mia_material_x shader includes additional attributes to control reflectivity based on angle-of-view. Nevertheless, you can combine such a shader with your own custom network, as was described in this tutorial. For more information on mental ray shaders, see Chapter 12.

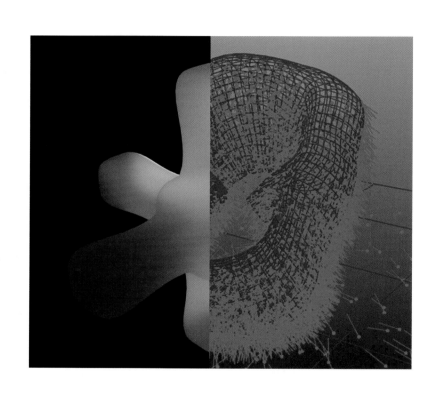

Working with mental ray Shaders, Global Illumination, and Final Gathering

Global Illumination and Final Gathering are powerful rendering algorithms that duplicate many real-world physical and optical events. For example, the Caustics attribute re-creates reflected specularity. Irradiance attributes, found on standard Autodesk® Maya® materials, illuminate a scene in which no lights are present. Global Illumination and Final Gathering are available through the mental ray® renderer. In addition to a long list of specialized attributes, mental ray provides custom mental ray shaders.

12

Chapter Contents

A review of mental ray shaders, including the mia_material_x shader
Introduction to subsurface scattering and contour rendering
Rendering with Global Illumination, Caustics, and Final Gathering
Activation of importons and irradiance particles
Application of lens, volumetric, and photonic shaders
Overview of mental ray light shaders

Applying mental ray Shaders

By default, mental ray works with all standard Maya materials. However, the best results are usually achieved by using shaders optimized for mental ray, and so a large number of mental ray shaders are included with the program. (You can use the term *material* and *shader* interchangeably.) You can find the shaders in the Create > mental ray section of the Hypershade, Create Render Node, and Create Node windows. You can assign a mental ray shader to a surface as you would a Maya material. However, you must use the mental ray renderer for the shader to be used. If mental ray is not activated, the mental ray shader thumbnail receives a red bar, indicating that it will be ignored. Many of the attributes of the mental ray shaders are not intuitive and don't correspond to their Maya counterparts. Therefore, I'll describe the most useful shaders and their attributes.

Using the mia_material_x Shader

The mia_material_x shader is a flexible shader designed for architectural and product design rendering. The *mia* prefix stands for the Mental Images Architectural shader library. It replaces the older dgs_material and dielectric_material shaders by incorporating advanced reflective and refractive qualities. The mia_material_x shader is referred to as *monolithic* in that it is able to reproduce a wide variety of dissimilar real-world substances and surfaces. The shader maintains physical accuracy and is therefore *energy conserving*, meaning that the incoming light intensity is equal to the light intensity the assigned surface reflects, refracts, and transmits.

Keep in mind that there are several shader variants that use the *mia_material* prefix. Descriptions of these are included here:

mia_material_x (2014 and 2015)   These versions carry all the attributes at their creation and are found in the Create > mental ray > Materials section of the Hypershade, Create Render Node, and Create Node windows. The *x* suffix denotes expanded bump map and ambient occlusion settings.

mia_material (2015)   Found in the Materials section of Maya 2015, this shader builds on the prior versions by including additional reflective and transmissive qualities. However, with this version, you must select the attributes you wish to work with so they can be added to the shader. Note that Maya 2015 moves the 2014 version of the mia_material into the Create > mental ray > Legacy section. The 2014 version of mia_material is similar to mia_material_x.

mia_material_x_passes (2014 and 2015)   This shader includes upgrades and improvements to the mia_material_x shader, including expanded framebuffer support. In addition, the shader can produce render passes (called *outputs*). The ability to create render passes is explored in Chapter 13, "Color Management, HDR Workflow, and Render Passes."

Diffuse and Specular mia_material_x Attributes

The Diffuse section of mia_material_x's Attribute Editor tab determines basic surface properties (see Figure 12.1). Surface color is set by the Color attribute. The Weight attribute is equivalent to the Diffuse attribute of a Maya material and sets the degree of diffuse reflectivity. Weight values below 1.0 darken the surface.

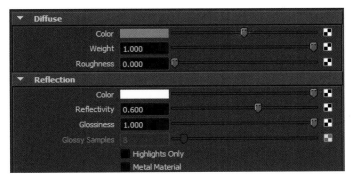

Figure 12.1 The Diffuse and Reflection sections of a mia_material_x shader

The Roughness attribute, on the other hand, determines the randomness of the diffuse reflection. If Roughness is left at 0, the shader is similar to the Maya Lambert material. The diffuse reflection of a Lambert material is relatively random, creating a matte-like surface with no specular highlights (that is, cohesive reflections forming hot spots). Raising the mia_material_x Roughness value above 0 exaggerates the randomness of the diffuse reflections, thus making the surface appear more powder-like. This may be appropriate when you're re-creating clay, flour, and similar substances. The higher the Roughness value, the flatter and less volumetric the surface appears; in other words, the surface appears evenly lit, with less variation in shading (see Figure 12.2).

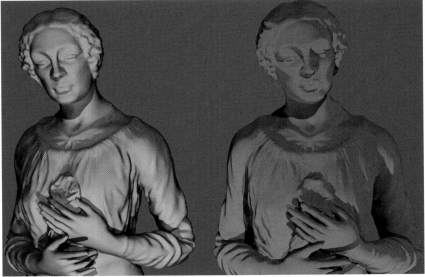

Figure 12.2 Left: Model assigned to mia_material_x with Roughness set to 0; Right: Same model assigned to mia_material_x with Roughness set to 1.0. In both examples, the Reflection section Color is set to black.

The mia_material_x controls specular reflections through the Reflection section. Specular reflections take the form of specular highlights as well as mirror-like reflections of neighboring surfaces and the surrounding environment. The Color attribute in this section sets the reflection intensity. You can tint the reflection by choosing a nonwhite or nongray Color value. The size and edge quality of the specular highlight is set by Glossiness. This attribute is equivalent to the Eccentricity attribute of a Blinn material. A high Glossiness value creates a hard-edged highlight; a low Glossiness value creates a soft-edged highlight. At the same time, Glossiness sets sharpness of reflections. When Glossiness is set to 1.0, the reflections are mirror-like with little or no degradation. If Glossiness is set to a value below 1.0, you have the option to adjust Glossy Samples to improve the quality of the blurred reflections. The lower the Glossy value, the higher you may need to go with Glossy Samples to produce a satisfactory result. For example, in Figure 12.3 the left model is given a Glossy value of 1.0. The right model is given a Glossy value of 0.5, with Glossy Samples set to 64. The lower Glossy value blurs the reflections while softening and enlarging the highlights. A single directional light illuminates the scene.

Figure 12.3 Left: Model assigned to mia_material_x with Glossy set to 1.0; Right: Same model assigned to mia_material_x with Glossy set to 0.5. A simplified version of this scene is included with the Chapter 12 tutorial files as `glossy.ma`.

Note: To reduce the intensity of the mia_material_x specular reflection, lower the Specular Balance value. Specular Balance is located in the Advanced section and serves as a multiplier for specular reflection intensity. You can also turn off reflections, in the form of specular highlights and mirror-like reflections, by setting the Color attribute, in the Reflection section, to 0-black.

The intensity of reflections is set by the Reflectivity attribute. You have the option to select the Metal Material check box, which blends the base surface color with the hot spot color; this is often useful for simulating colorful metallic surfaces such as copper.

> **Note:** The mia_material_x shader does not include an Ambient Color attribute. However, the Additional Color attribute, found in the Advanced section, provides the same functionality. The ambient light component represents the net reflected light in the scene beyond direct light provided by existing lights.

Refracting with mia_material_x

You can find attributes that control transparency and refractivity in the Refraction section of the mia_material_x Attribute Editor tab (see Figure 12.4). By default, refractivity is activated for the mia_material_x shader, even when the surface is opaque. However, the Index Of Refraction attribute has no visible effect on the surface unless the Transparency value is set above 0 or you choose to use anisotropic reflectivity (discussed later in this chapter).

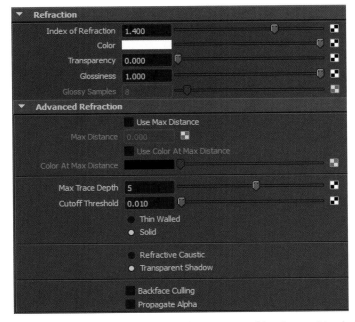

Figure 12.4 The Refraction and Advanced Refraction sections of the mia_material_x shader

The Refraction section also carries a Glossiness attribute, which determines the sharpness or blurriness of the refracted area. A Glossiness value of 1.0 creates an undistorted refraction; values below 1.0 blur the refraction. You can improve the quality of the blur by raising the Refraction section's Glossy Samples value. When recreating water, you can set Index Of Refraction to 1.33 (see the left of Figure 12.5). To reproduce glass, set the value between 1.4 and 1.8 (see the center of Figure 12.5.)

To disable refractivity when the surface is transparent, set Index Of Refraction to 1.0. You can create stylistic refractions by setting the Index Of Refraction value below 1.0 (see the right of Figure 12.5). In this case, the surface appears to take on a secondary, inner surface. You can tint the refracted area by setting the Refraction section Color attribute to a nonwhite color. This creates the illusion of colored glass.

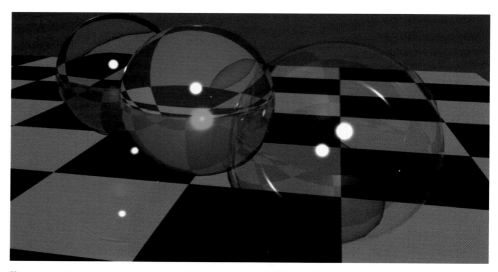

Figure 12.5 The left sphere is given an Index Of Refraction value of 1.33. The middle sphere receives an Index Of Refraction value of 1.6 and a green color. The right sphere is given an Index Of Refraction value of 0.6 and has the Thin Walled attribute activated. This scene is included with the Chapter 12 tutorial files as `mia_refract.ma`.

Note: You can selectively "remove" a portion of a surface during a mental ray render by mapping the Cutout Opacity attribute in the Advanced section of a mia_material_x shader. Where the map is white, the surface and shader are treated normally. Where the map is black, the surface is ignored and rendered as if it does not exist.

Using Advanced Reflectivity and Refractivity

By default, all surfaces are reflected and refracted by a mia_material_x shader. However, you can filter these surfaces by activating the Use Max Distance attributes in the Advanced Reflection and Advanced Refraction sections (see Figure 12.6). At that point, reflected/refracted objects must be a distance less than the Max Distance attribute values to appear as a reflection/refraction. You can choose to fade a surface that crosses the Max Distance value into a solid color by selecting the Fade To End Color attribute (Reflection section) or Use Color At Max Distance attribute (Refraction section) and choosing the color through the End Color or Color At Max Distance field. If you choose Use Max Distance, switch to Segment shadows so that the shadows are properly calculated (see Chapter 11, "Raytracing, mental ray, and Effects Rendering," for information about mental ray shadows). You can use the End

Color attribute to map a mental ray environment shader; this is demonstrated in the "Using mental ray Environment Shaders" section later in this chapter.

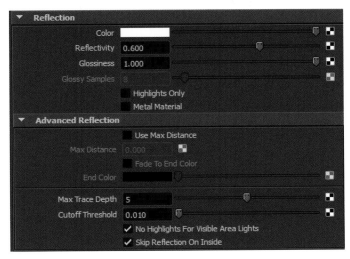

Figure 12.6 The Reflection and Advanced Reflection sections of the mia_material_x shader

The mia_material_x shader also supports per-material raytracing limits. In the Advanced Reflection subsection, the Max Trace Depth sets the maximum number of reflection rays and overrides the Max Trace Depth attribute found in the Raytracing section of the Render Settings window Quality tab. (If you set the mia_material_x Max Trace Depth to 0, it defers to the Render Settings window.) The Advanced Refractions subsection carries its own Max Trace Depth. In addition, you can select the Thin Walled attribute to render the surface as if it has significant thickness (see Figure 12.5 in the previous section). This option is suitable for creating a soap bubble or piece of thin plastic. You can also activate refractive caustics via the Refractive Caustic attribute. *Caustics* are specular highlights created when light refractively passes through a transparent surface and strikes a different surface. (You can also create caustics with the Global Illumination system, discussed later in this chapter.)

Using mia_material_x Anisotropy and BRDF

As discussed in earlier chapters, an anisotropic substance creates specular reflections that are not cohesive. This is commonly seen on real-world surfaces as streaked or elongated specular highlights. When you lower the Glossiness attribute, in the mia_material_x Reflection section, reflections take on an anisotropic look with streaking and blurring. For example, on the left side of Figure 12.7, a ground plane is assigned to a mia_material_x shader with a Glossiness value set to 0.5. The reflection of the sphere's specular highlight is streaked as well as the brighter specular highlight of the plane itself. This emulates a surface that is rough with myriad small imperfections. A simplified version of this scene is saved as glossy_streaked.ma with the Chapter 12 tutorial files.

Figure 12.7 Left: A Glossiness value of 0.5 streaks and softens specular highlights on the ground plane; Right: A Anisotropy value of 1000 elongates the specular highlights on the blue objects. The anisotropic Direction is mapped with a Noise texture, creating squiggly lines.

In addition, you can create anisotropic specular highlights by raising the Anisotropy attribute, in the Anisotropy section, above 1.0. You can adjust the resulting orientation of the elongation by altering the Rotation value. You can map the Rotation attribute and thus vary the direction of the specular elongation across the surface. (Note that Anisotropy does not affect reflections.) Nevertheless, you can use a lower Glossiness value and a higher Anisotropy value in conjunction. For example, on the right side of Figure 12.7, a mia_material_x assigned to the sphere and statue is given an Anisotropy value of 5. A Noise texture is mapped to the Rotation, producing squiggly specular highlights that emulate surface imperfections or surface features. With this example, Glossiness is set to 0.4, which increases the size of the highlights. A simplified version of this scene is saved as `anisotropic_streaked.ma` with the Chapter 12 tutorial files. Note that cylindrical surfaces naturally create elongated specular highlights, even when Anisotropy is set to 1.0 (this can be seen at the left of Figure 12.7 along the statue legs).

On the other hand, the mia_material_x shader integrates bidirectional reflectance distribution function (BRDF). BRDF alters the strength of reflectivity based on the angle of incidence (the angle of view). There are two BRDF modes: Fresnel mode and manual mode. The Fresnel mode, activated by the Use Fresnel Reflection check box in the BRDF section, bases reflectivity strength on the angle of incidence and the Index Of Refraction value (see Figure 12.8). The Fresnel mode is suitable for real-world transparent, refractive materials such as water or glass.

The manual BRDF mode is activated when Use Fresnel Reflection, in the BRDF section, is deselected. With this mode, reflections are stronger at glancing angles (where the surface does not point toward the camera but is perpendicular to it). (See the middle of Figure 12.8 for an example.) However, you can manually set the reflectivity for the glancing angle by changing the 90 Degree Reflection value. Values below 1.0 reduce the reflectivity in that region. Conversely, you can adjust the reflectivity of the surface facing the camera by altering the 0 Degree Reflection value. The reflective transition from glancing to nonglancing is set by the Brdf Curve value. Higher Brdf Curve values cause the reflectivity to taper off more rapidly (see the right side of Figure 12.8). Low Brdf Curve values cause the reflectivity strength to stay higher even as the viewing angle approaches 0 degrees. Using a low Brdf Curve value causes reflections within reflections to be more visible. The manual BRDF mode is suitable for a wide range of real-world materials, including metals and layered surfaces, such as lacquered wood. Note that the Figure 12.8 scene file uses a mental ray environment shader, which is described in the section "Using mental ray Environment Shaders" later in this chapter.

Figure 12.8 Left: A rotated, red cylinder rendered with Fresnel reflections; Middle: Cylinder rendered with Brdf Curve set to 1.0; Right: Cylinder rendered with Brdf Curve set to 6. This scene, with settings that match the middle cylinder, is included as `brdf.ma` with the Chapter 12 tutorial files.

Activating Translucency with mia_material_x

As discussed in earlier chapters, translucency allows light to penetrate a surface diffusely. You can activate this feature with the mia_material_x shader by selecting the Use Translucency attribute in the Translucency section.

The shader considers translucency as special subset of transparency, so the Transparency attribute, in the Refraction section, must be set above 0 for translucency to function. The color of the translucent light is set by the Color attribute in the Translucency section. (If the light is colored, Color serves as a multiplier.) The Weight attribute, in the same section, sets the mixture of transparency and translucency. If Weight is set to 1.0, the surface is translucent with no transparency. For example, in Figure 12.9, a sphere and statue are assigned to a mia_material_x shader with Weight set to 1.0. A directional light arrives from the back and is tinted red. Part of the sphere fails to gain translucency because the shadow of the statue falls over that region, thus blocking the translucent light. Lower Weight values reduce the translucency and increase the transparency.

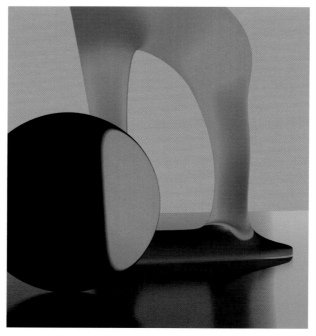

Figure 12.9 A sphere and statue are given translucency with a Weight value of 1.0. A simplified version of this scene is included as `mia_translucency.ma` with the Chapter 12 tutorial files.

Bump and Normal Mapping with mia_material_x

The mia_material series of shaders supports bump mapping. However, mia_material_x simplifies the process. To add a bump map, click the checkered Map button beside the Standard Bump attribute, found in the Bump section. A Bump 2d node is automatically connected. In the Bump 2d node's Attribute Editor tab, click the checkered Map button beside Bump Value and select a texture node from the Create Render Node window. You can control the intensity of the resulting bump by altering the Bump 2d node's Bump Depth attribute. For example, in Figure 12.10 a brick wall texture is mapped to the Standard Bump and Diffuse attributes of a mia_material_x shader.

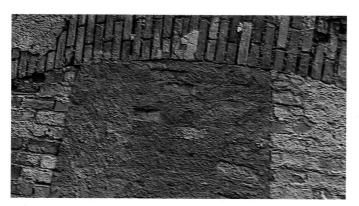

Figure 12.10 A flat wall is given bumpiness with a mia_material_x bump map. This scene is included as `mia_bump.ma` with the Chapter 12 tutorial files.

You can use the same process to apply a normal map. To activate the normal map, switch the Use As menu of the Bump 2d node to the correct space—either tangent space or object space—to match the style of normal map.

By default, the mia_material_x shader affects all the shading components with the bump or normal map—that is, the diffuse, specular, translucent, reflective, and refractive aspects of the assigned surface take on the bumpiness. However, if you select the No Diffuse Bump attribute, found in the mia_material_x's Bump section, the bump is withheld from the diffuse component. If the surface is opaque, this creates the illusion that the surface has a bumpy clear coating, such as shellac.

Note: The mia_material_x shader also provides an Overall Bump attribute in the Bump section. This attribute is designed to work with the mia_roundcorners shader, which bevels geometry during the render.

Note: The Bump Depth attribute of a Bump 2d or Bump 3d node does not affect the intensity of a normal map. To alter the rendered height of a normal map, adjust the Color Gain and Color Offset values of the normal map's File node.

Some mental ray shaders include a list of presets. In particular, the mia_material_x shader includes a long list that re-creates various real-world substances. Because of the complexity of the shader, the presets offer a valuable means to save time. To apply a preset, click the Presets button and choose *Preset* > Replace. You can also average the preset attribute values with the current shader values by choosing *Preset* > Blend *Percentage*. Blending allows you to create unique results; for example, you can blend a transparent shader with an opaque preset to emulate a semitransparent substance.

Note: The Attribute Editor includes a Presets button at the upper right of its frame. You can create your own preset by clicking the Presets button and choosing Save *Material* Presets from the menu. The current attribute settings of the material or shader are saved under the Preset Name that you choose.

Introduction to the Maya 2015 mia_material Shader

The mia_material found in the Materials section of Maya 2015 offers a different workflow from the mia_material_x shader. The main shading components are divided into different virtual layers. By default, only the diffuse component exists when you create the shader. Thus, the shader is similar to a Maya Lambert material. However, you can either switch to a different base shading component or add additional component layers. For example, you can change the Base Component menu, in the Base section, from Diffuse to Reflective. When you change the base component, the attributes in the Base section update to control that component. Hence, when Base Component is set to Reflective, Glossy Blend (specular intensity) and Glossy Roughness (specular spread) attributes are added.

You are not limited to a single shading component. To add an additional component as a new layer, click the +Layer button at the top of the Attribute Editor tab. A Choose Layer Type window opens, where you can choose between Weighted Layer, Fresnel Layer, or Custom Layer. Fresnel layers increase the component strength at glancing angles and reduce the strength in areas that face the camera. Custom layers employ the same Fresnel technique, but let you choose the strength values. After you choose the layer type, a Choose Elemental Component window opens and allows you to choose the shading component. When you make a choice, a new layer section is added to the Attribute Editor with a new set of component attributes (see Figure 12.11). The degree to which the component is mixed with other layers and/ or the base layer is controlled by the Weight slider (higher values increase the layer's strength). You also have the option to add multiple components to a single layer by clicking the +Mix button (to the left of the +Layer button).

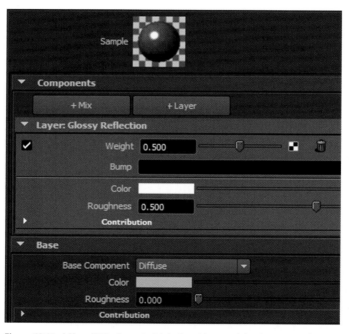

Figure 12.11 A Maya 2015 mia_material shader with one weighted component layer, Glossy Reflection

This unusual approach to shader adjustment allows you to mix a wide variety of shading components and shading techniques while using a single mia_material shader. For example, you can combine dissimilar styles of specular reflections.

Applying *mi* Series Shaders

The *mi* series of mental ray shaders are designed to re-create layered paint surfaces that combine clear, opaque, flaked, and dirt-like substances. There are two main shaders: mi_car_paint_phen_x and mi_metallic_paint_x. These are found in the Create >

mental ray > Materials section of the Hypershade, Create Render Node, and Create Node windows. This section will serve as a brief introduction to these shaders.

The mi_metallic_paint_x shader is a stripped-down shader designed to create paint with embedded metallic flakes. However, in its default state it lacks the ability to produce reflections. Therefore, it must be connected to additional shaders to become fully functional. As an alternative, you can use mi_car_paint_phen_x, which includes built-in reflection, flake, and dirt parameters. Here are brief descriptions of each of the mi_car_paint_phen_x attribute sections:

Diffuse Parameters   This section includes Base Color, which is equivalent to the Color of a standard Maya material. However, it also includes Edge Color, which defines the color of the assigned surface at a glancing angle (part of the surface that is perpendicular to the camera). With the clear coatings of modern automotive paints, the perceived color of the paint often shifts with a change of the viewing, or incident, angle. (This is handled by the BRDF section of a mia_material_x shader, discussed earlier in this chapter.) This section also includes the Lit Color attribute, which defines the color of the surface facing the camera. The Edge Color Bias and Lit Color Bias attributes control the transitions between the Edge Color and Lit Color values, with higher values narrowing the range in which the colors are visible. In contrast, Diffuse Bias defines the shader's diffuse specularity.

Specular Parameters   This section defines the primary specular highlight quality through Spec (specular color), Spec Weight (specular intensity), and Spec Exp (Phong-like specular size) settings. Additionally, the section supports a second specular highlight through Spec Sec, Spec Sec Weight, and Spec Sec Exp. Multiple specular reflections create the illusion that a base color coat and a secondary clear coat are each creating a unique reflection. You can take this further by selecting the Spec Glazing attribute, which creates an additional specular layer that re-creates polished glaze or wax.

Flake Parameters   This section establishes the color, size, and reflective intensity of metallic flakes suspended within the paint. Metallic flakes break the specular highlights into numerous, smaller specular hot spots (see Figure 12.12). To disable the flakes, set Flake Reflect to 0.

Reflection Parameters   This section sets the reflectivity at glancing angles through the Reflection Edge Weight attribute and the reflectivity of the surface facing the camera through the Reflection Base Weight value. The cohesiveness of the reflection is controlled by Glossy Spread; lower values create a more mirror-like refection. The quality of the reflection is set by Samples. Edge Factor defines the area of high reflectivity at glancing angles, with higher values making this region larger.

Dirt Parameters   Optionally, you can add noisy, nonreflective "dirt" to the underlying base paint and top clear coat layer by raising Dirt Weight above 0. The dirt color is set by the same-named attribute, which you can map with a texture.

Figure 12.12 The mi_car_paint_phen_x shader creates the appearance of metallic flakes within the specular highlights.

Note: A number of mental ray shaders carry the *phen* suffix. This stands for *phenomenon*, which is a mental ray group of shaders represented by a single node. For information on constructing your own phenomenon, see the "Build Phenomena" page of the Maya Help files. or at the Autodesk Knowledge Network (`knowledge.autodesk.com`)

Using mental ray Environment Shaders

The mental ray renderer provides a set of environment shaders, located in the Create > mental ray > Environments section of the Hypershade, Create Render Node, and Create Node windows. Much like their Maya material counterparts, the shaders offer a means to project a texture.

There are different methods you can use to employ mental ray environment shaders in a scene. For example, you can map a shader to the Environment Shader attribute of the rendering camera. This attribute is located in the mental ray section. With this technique, all reflective surfaces reflect the projected image. In addition, the image appears in the background in place of empty space.

Alternatively, if you are working with a mia_material_x shader, you can map the End Color. Follow these steps:

1. In the Advanced Reflection section of the mia_material_x's Attribute Editor tab, select Use Max Distance. Set Max Distance to 0. Select the Fade To End Color check box.

2. Click the checkered Map button beside End Color. Select one of the environment shaders, such as mib_lookup_spherical. (Maya 2015 moves the *mib_ lookup* environment shaders into the Create > mental ray > Legacy section). In the Attribute Editor tab for the shader, click the checkered Map button beside Texture. Choose a File texture (Create > Maya > 2D Textures) or the

mentalrayTexture (Create > mental ray > Textures) in the Create Render Node window. Load a bitmap texture into the new file node. Render a test frame.

With this type of network, the projection does not show up in the background of the render (see Figure 12.13). To increase the strength of the reflection, raise the Reflectivity value in the mia_material_x shader's Reflection section. You can also increase the reflection strength by using superwhite values for the Color attribute in the Reflection section. To do this, click the color swatch, switch the Color Chooser window's lower-right menu to HSV, and enter a value above 1.0 into the V (Value) cell.

Figure 12.13 The mib_lookup_spherical shader is mapped to the End Color of a mia_material_x shader to create a fake reflection of a desert landscape. A simplified version of this scene is included as `lookup_spherical.ma` with the Chapter 12 tutorial files.

A third method of adding an environmental projection is to create an image-based lighting setup. This is described in Chapter 13.

The mib_lookup_cylindrical, mib_lookup_cube1, and mib_lookup_cube6 shaders are similar to mib_lookup_spherical in that they are infinite projections. The mib_lookup_cube6 shader requires six different maps, whereas the other shaders require only one. The shaders do not use interactive placement nodes, as do Maya projections. Therefore, the shaders include built-in transform attributes to rotate or otherwise orient the projections. The mia_envblur shader works like mib_lookup_spherical. However, mia_envblur includes a Blur attribute that you can alter to blur the projected image.

Using mental ray Lens Shaders

Maya cameras include a Lens Shader attribute, found in the mental ray section of the camera's Attribute Editor tab. The attribute is designed for shaders that simulate various artifacts produced by real-world cameras, including depth-of-field and exposure adjustment. These shaders are described briefly here:

mib_lookup_background and mib_lens_stencil   If mapped to the Lens Shader attribute, mib_lookup_background renders a mapped texture to the foreground of the render, occluding geometry in the scene. This shader may be useful for adding motion graphics elements, such as text, to a render. The mib_lens_stencil shaders cut out a portion of the render based on a texture mapped to its Stencil attribute. This offers one means of creating a matte effect otherwise created through the render pass process (discussed in Chapter 13). These shaders are located in the Create > mental ray > Legacy section of Maya 2015 and the Create > mental ray > Lenses section of Maya 2014.

mia_exposure_simple, mia_exposure_photographic, and mib_lens_clamp   These shaders provide color grading tools that let you adjust the brightness, contrast, and saturation of the resulting render. These shaders are useful for color management and the adjustment of renders that contain superwhite values. These shaders and color management are discussed further in Chapter 13. The mib_lens_clamp shader was moved from the Lenses section to the Legacy section in Maya 2015.

mia_lens_bokeh and physical_lens_dof   These shaders create a depth-of-field, where the range within the render that is sharply in focus is narrowed. The physical_lens_dof shader has two attributes: Plane (the distance from the camera that represents the focal plane) and Radius (the degree of "out-of-focusness"). (The physical_lens_dof shader was moved from the Lenses section to the Legacy section in Maya 2015.) In contrast, mia_lens_bokeh adds more advanced controls that determine the shape of resulting *bokehs* (the shapes of out-of-focus points of lights). For example, in Figure 12.14 a narrow depth-of-field is added to a cylinder that recedes from the camera. In addition, three spheres are in the distant background. The out-of-focus spheres take on polygonal bokehs. In this case, Plane is set to 5 (at the front of the cylinder), Radius is set to 0.4, Samples (blur quality) is set to 128 (which is relatively high quality), Bias (bokeh sharpness) is set to 0.9, and Blade Count (the number of polygonal bokeh sides, emulating the shape of camera iris) is set to 5. Optionally, you can map a grayscale texture to the Bokeh attribute of the shader to define the bokeh shape. Although depth-of-field created by a mental ray lens shader is fairly accurate, it is significantly slower than the approximated Maya Software postprocess controlled by the Depth Of Field section of the camera's Attribute Editor (see Chapter 10, "Prepping for Successful Renders"). You can also create depth-of-field with a Z-depth render pass (see Chapter 13).

Applying Subsurface Scattering

The mental ray renderer provides a series of shaders with the *misss* prefix, where the *sss* stands for Sub-Surface Scattering. Subsurface scattering creates translucency. With translucency, light is permitted to scatter through a solid object. Although you can create translucency with standard Maya materials or a mia_material_x shader, the misss series shaders can create a more accurate and realistic result. Subsurface scattering is often employed when creating photorealistic skin or other translucent materials such as wax, soap, and plant material. For example, in Figure 12.15 a candle is lit by two lights: a directional key from screen-left and a point light placed above the wick. The top of the candle glows from scattered light traveling from the point light through the lip and body of the candle. The candle is assigned to a misss_fast_simple_maya shader with Diffuse Color set to tan. The point light color is orange.

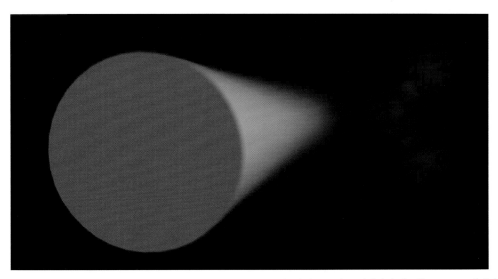

Figure 12.14 A receding cylinder and three distant spheres are rendered with the mia_lens_bokeh shader. This scene is included as dof_shader.ma with the Chapter 12 tutorial files.

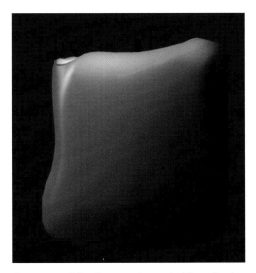

Figure 12.15 Subsurface scattering on a backlit candle using the misss_fast_simple_maya shader. This scene is included as sss.ma with the Chapter 12 tutorial files.

The misss series shaders are located in the Create > mental ray > Materials section. Of these, misss_fast_simple_maya is designed for easy setup. When you assign the shader to a surface, it automatically connects a mentalrayTexture node to the shader's Light Map input. The mentalrayTexture node is also connected to a misss_fast_lmap_maya node (see Figure 12.16). The misss_fast_lmap_maya node determines the amount of light bounce at the front and back surfaces of assigned geometry and writes the information to a temporary file using the mentalrayTexture node. mentalrayTexture varies from the Maya File texture in that it includes a Writable attribute, which allows a connected node to write out a file. The File Size Width and File Size Height attributes of mentalrayTexture are automatically connected to the project render resolution Width and Height via an expression. File Size Width is kept twice the width of the render because a front-surface and back-surface view of the scene is generated and placed side by side.

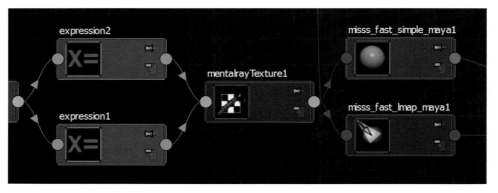

Figure 12.16 The subsurface scattering shading network created when misss_simple_fast_maya is assigned to a surface.

misss Shader Review

Additional misss shaders possess unique qualities. Here are brief descriptions:

misss_fast_skin_maya This shader builds on misss_fast_simple_maya by adding a large set of attributes that controls specular highlights. The attributes support a secondary highlight, which emulates the specular reflectivity of multiple, translucent layers, such as those present in dermal and subdermal skin layers. This shader makes use of the misss_fast_lmap_maya node when added to the scene (see the previous section).

misss_fast_shader_x Series The misss_fast_shader_x series shaders share many attributes with misss_fast_simple_maya. However, the shaders' specular quality is dependent on the mapping of separate shaders. For example, you can map a Blinn material to the Specular Shader attribute of the misss_fast_shader_x shader and thereby transfer the specular shading component.

misss_fast_shader2 Series The misss_fast_shader2 shader series offers a slight improvement over the misss_fast_shader_x series by adding greater physical accuracy. In particular, the misss_fast_shader2 series creates wavelength-sensitive color "bleed," in which scattered light shifts in color as each wavelength refracts differently. However, you must manually make all the necessary connections to make the shader function. The critical connections include the following:

mentalrayTexture.message > misss_fast_shader2.lightmap

mentalrayTexture.message > *lightmap_shader*.lightmap

material.message > misss_fast_shader2.diffuse_illum

With these connections, the diffuse shading component is defined by a Maya material or mental ray surface shader such as mia_material_x. Light map shaders are located in the Create > mental ray > Light Maps section. You can use misss_fast_lmap_maya for any misss shading network.

> **N o t e :** If you manually connect a mentalrayTexture node to an misss shader Lightmap attribute, select the texture's Writable check box. Failing to do so will cause the render to abort. Set File Size Width to twice that of the render resolution. Set File Size Height to match the render resolution. Set the File Size Depth menu to 32 Bits to ensure accuracy.

Adjusting misss Attributes to Improve Quality

Each misss shader includes a long list of attributes (see Figure 12.17). Many of these are shared across misss shaders.

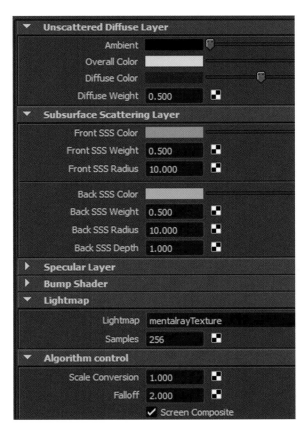

Figure 12.17 A portion of the attributes carried by the misss_fast_simple_maya shader

Here are brief guidelines for adjusting the attribute values:

- In the Lightmap section, Samples defines the quality of the light scatter. Higher values, such as 256, smooth out any graininess caused by the scattering process.

- Subsurface scattering shaders are sensitive to scene scale. Therefore, you can alter the intensity of the scattered light by adjusting the Scale Conversion attribute, which is in the Algorithm Control section. For example, reducing the value raises the intensity of the scattered light.

- Front SSS Color defines the color of scattered light at the front side of the object. Back SSS Color defines the color of scattered light at the back side of the object. Light often shifts in color as it is scattered through a surface. For example, white light becomes red as it's scattered through human flesh. The front side is the side that the light first strikes. The back side is the side the light reaches after scattering through the object.

- The front and back colors each carry their own SSS Weight attribute, which controls the intensity of the scattered light, as well as the SSS Radius attribute, which sets the distance scattered light travels (in scene world units).

Contour Rendering

Several Create > mental ray sections contain contour shaders. These shaders are designed to render stylized wireframes or toon-like outlines of geometry. This feature may be useful for creating modeling demo reels or futuristic displays. To contour render, follow these basic steps:

1. Select the Enable Contour Rendering attribute in the Contours section of the Features tab in the Render Settings window.

2. Select the Enable Contour Rendering attribute in the mental ray > Contours subsection of the shading group node belonging to surfaces you wish to contour render.

3. Set the Sampling Mode menu, in the Quality tab of the Render Settings window, to Legacy Sampling Mode.

4. To fine-tune the resulting contours, adjust the attributes in the Draw By Property Difference and Draw By Sample Contrast subsections of the Features tab in the Render Settings window. These attributes control where the contour lines appear on the geometry. You must select at least one option in the Draw By Property Difference section for the contours to appear in the render. In addition, you can adjust the attributes in the mental ray > Contours section of the shading group node. These attributes set the contour line color and line width (see Figure 12.18).

Shading group nodes also include a Contour Shader attribute in the mental ray > Custom Shaders subsection. Although you can manually map a contour shader to this attribute, this is generally unnecessary as the steps outlined here produce high-quality results.

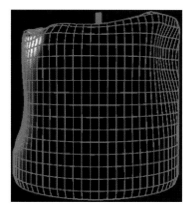

Figure 12.18 A candle is rendered with mental ray contours. The Around All Poly Faces option is selected in the Draw By Property Difference section. This scene is included as `contours.ma` with the Chapter 12 tutorial files.

Understanding Indirect Illumination

In the real world, light mixes and "bleeds." For example, a brightly lit red object "bleeds" red onto the white of a tabletop (see Figure 12.19).

Figure 12.19 Indirect illumination causes the red of an object to "bleed" onto the white of a tabletop.

Scanline rendering and raytracing are unable to replicate color bleeding. Nevertheless, several mental ray rendering systems, including Global Illumination and Final Gathering, possess this capability. Before I discuss these systems, however, a closer look at the mechanics of light is warranted.

Light is a form of electromagnetic radiation that exists as a continuous range of wavelengths. Specific wavelengths are visible to the human eye and are perceived by the human brain as specific colors. At the same time, light is quantified as photons. A *photon* is an elementary particle that represents a quantum of light or other form of electromagnetic radiation. When a light wave with a particular wavelength strikes an object, it is absorbed, reflected, or transmitted. Absorption occurs when the energy of a photon is captured by an atom. The capture causes an orbiting electron to temporarily jump to a higher energy level. As the electron returns to a lower energy level, it releases the excess energy as a new photon, which equates to a longer wavelength of radiation. The longer wavelength is felt as radiant heat.

Transmission, on the other hand, occurs when the photon is absorbed by an atom at a material boundary. The energy is not released by the material immediately, however. Instead, the energy is transferred from one atom to a neighboring atom. This continues until the energy is passed through the bulk of the material to an opposite material boundary. At the opposite boundary, the energy is released as a photon with energy similar to the original photon. Since the energy, and the wavelength, is inherently the same, the light remains visible. Thus, transmission makes glass and similar materials transparent.

Note: All transparent materials incur some degree of refractivity. Refraction occurs when a light wave crosses the boundary between two materials with different refractive indices. As the wave enters the second material, its wavelength, speed, and direction are altered. Therefore, refracted objects appear bent or broken. For more information on refraction and refractive indices, see Chapter 11.

Ultimately, color is not contained within the materials of objects. Instead, color is the result of particular wavelengths of light reaching the viewer through reflection or transmission. Different materials (wood, stone, metal, and so on) have different atomic compositions and thereby absorb, reflect, and transmit light differently. Hence, the red of a red object represents a particular wavelength that the object reflects. In the scenario illustrated in Figure 12.19 earlier in this section, the white light of a light source is reflected off the object as a red wavelength. (White light contains the full spectrum of color wavelengths; therefore, the non-red wavelengths are absorbed and converted to radiation interpreted as heat.) The reflected red wavelength strikes the white table, which is made of a different material and has a different atomic structure. Nevertheless, the table reflects pink wavelengths that are closely related to the original red of the object.

Global Illumination can replicate the absorption, reflection, and transmission of light and the resulting mingling of colors. Therefore, the system can produce extremely realistic renders.

Note: *Wavelength* is the distance between repeating features of a waveform cycle. *Frequency* is the number of cycles that occur during a particular period of time. When discussing light, frequency is explicitly dependent on the wavelength and speed of the light wave (roughly 300,000 kilometers per second). Hence, the formula is frequency = speed of light / wavelength. Light is considered to have dual properties, simultaneously existing as a wave and as photons.

Tracing Photons with Global Illumination

Global Illumination is provided by the mental ray renderer. You can activate the system via the Global Illumination attribute in the Indirect Lighting tab of the Render Settings window. To successfully use the system, you must employ virtual photons. In Maya, spot, point, area, and directional lights generate photons when the light's Emit Photons attribute is selected (see Figure 12.20). You can find Emit Photons in the mental ray > Caustic And Global Illumination subsection in the light's Attribute Editor tab.

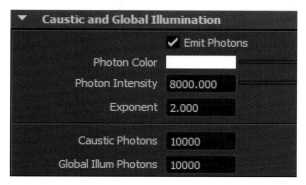

Figure 12.20 The Caustic And Global Illumination subsection of a spot light's Attribute Editor tab. The Caustics Photons and Global Illum Photons attributes are accessible only if those systems are activated in the Render Settings window.

When a scene is rendered, photons are traced from each photon-emitting light to objects in the scene. If a photon "hits" a surface, it is absorbed, reflected, or transmitted (refracted) based on the qualities of the material assigned to the surface. If a photon is reflected or transmitted, it survives with only a portion of its original energy. The amount of energy is determined by the reflection coefficient, which is established by the Reflectivity attribute of a Maya material or mental ray shader. The photons that are absorbed by the surface have their position, incident direction, and energy stored in a special photon map written to disc.

Note: To simplify the photon-tracing process, many Global Illumination systems, including the one employed by mental ray, randomly cull photons in a process known as *Russian roulette*. Photons that survive a surface hit through reflection or refraction are given an increased energy that is proportional to the potential energy of all the photons generated by the light source.

Note: When you render with Global Illumination, the render happens in two phases. During the initial phase, photons are traced and stored in the photon map. Depending on the number of photons generated and the Max Photon Depth value, this phase may take a significant amount of time. The status of the render is printed on the MEL command line at the bottom-left of the program window. During the second phase, the render appears in the Render View.

The absorption, reflection, or transmission of a photon is affected by the shading components of the assigned material. Changes to the Diffuse and Reflectivity attributes affect photon scattering; in addition, Color, Eccentricity, and similar specular attributes have an equal impact. If a photon survives a hit and is reflected or transmitted, it continues through the scene until it hits another surface. Once again, the photon is absorbed, reflected, or transmitted. This process continues until the surviving photons are stopped by the Max Photon Depth attribute, which defines the number of hits permitted per photon. (Max Photon Depth is discussed in the section "Adjusting Global Illumination Attributes" later in this chapter.) Ultimately, the information stored in the photon map is combined with the direct illumination model, which in turn determines the color and intensity of each rendered pixel.

Note: Although directional lights can generate photons, they are not recommended. Directional lights possess direction, but no true position. Therefore, when tracing photons, a potentially large number of photons may never reach the geometry of the scene and the render is thereby made inefficient.

Adjusting Photons

The number of photons generated by a light is set by the light's Global Illum Photons attribute. You can lower or raise the default value of 10,000 to decrease or increase quality. In addition, you can change the qualities of photons generated by a light with the following attributes, which are located in the light's mental ray > Caustic And Global Illumination subsection:

Photon Color Represents the red, green, and blue components of a photon's energy. Photon Color is a "dummy" attribute. The RGB values of its color swatch are multiplied by the Photon Intensity attribute to produce Energy R, Energy G, and Energy B attributes. You can access these attributes in the Script Editor (for example, `getAttr spotLightShape1.energyR;`).

Photon Intensity A scaling factor used to determine the intensity of photons produced by a light. The default value of 8000 tends to be too high and will often wash out a render. A value of 0 will turn off photon tracing for the light. Photon Intensity should be changed through the Attribute Editor and not through the Script Editor or with a MEL script.

Exponent Simulates light falloff over distance. The default value of 2 replicates natural, quadratic decay. A value of 1.0 effectively prevents falloff from occurring. Values higher than 2 create a more rapid falloff by artificially decreasing photon energy with distance.

Adjusting Global Illumination Attributes

You can create a Global Illumination render with mental ray as long as the Global Illumination attribute is selected and at least one light is generating photons. In general, initial Global Illumination renders appear rough and unrefined. You can fine-tune the result by altering the attributes within the Global Illumination section of the

Render Settings window (see Figure 12.21). Of all the attributes, Radius and Accuracy are perhaps the most critical for creating a refined render.

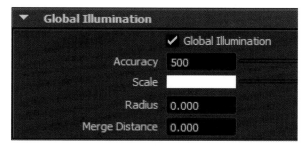

Figure 12.21 The Global Illumination section of the Indirect Lighting tab in the Render Settings window

The Radius attribute controls the maximum distance from a photon hit that the renderer will seek out neighboring photon hits to determine the color of the hit in question. The default value of 0 allows Maya to automatically pick a radius based on the scene size. Although the default value produces a satisfactory render in many cases, it will often create spottiness (see Figure 12.22). The spottiness is exaggerated in scenes containing complex reflective or refractive surfaces, as the photons are scattered to an even greater degree. The spottiness is also more apparent when few photons are produced by the lights in the scene.

Figure 12.22 Photon hits appear as colored circles. For the left render, each of the two lights generates 10,000 photons. For the right render, each of the two lights generates 200 photons.

In this situation, each circle corresponds to the location of one photon hit. The color of a given circle, however, is derived from the average energies of all the photon hits discovered within the circle. The areas between the circles receive no indirect illumination and are thus darker. The circles vary in color because the photon energy levels, stored as RGB, are influenced by the Color/Diffuse value of the materials they encounter while reflecting off and transmitting through surfaces. For example, if a material is green, the energy of the reflected or transmitted photon is biased toward green. Hence, the mingling of colors and color bleeding is possible.

Ideally, the individual photon hits should not be visible in the render but should blend seamlessly with each other and the direct illumination. If the default Radius value is producing spottiness, follow these steps:

1. Gradually increase the Global Illum Photons value for each photon-producing light. If higher Global Illum Photons values are unable to improve the quality without drastically affecting the render time, manually set the Radius attribute. Gradually increase the Radius value until the photon hits begin to disappear. Gradually increase the Accuracy value to further blend overlapping photon hits. If Accuracy has no significant impact on the render, continue to raise the Global Illum Photons and Radius values.

2. If a few photon hits remain visible despite high Global Illum Photons, Radius, and Accuracy values, consider using Final Gathering, described later in this chapter, which does an excellent job of smoothing out Global Illumination renders.

Balancing the number of photons in a scene with the Radius value is an important aspect of the Global Illumination process. An excess of photons will cause a redundant overlapping of photon hits and an unnecessarily slow render. On the other hand, a limited number of photons with a large Radius will lead to inaccurate indirect lighting calculations.

The Accuracy attribute sets the maximum number of neighboring photon hits included in the color estimate of a single photon hit. The search for neighboring photon hits is limited to the region established by the Radius attribute. In general, the higher the Accuracy value, the smoother the result (see Figure 12.23). However, Accuracy only affects overlapping photon hits—that is, if the photon count is low or the Radius value is set small so that the photon hits do not significantly overlap, the Accuracy attribute will have no effect on the render.

The Scale attribute serves as a multiplier for the Photon Intensity attribute of all lights in the scene. If the slider is set to 50 percent gray, all the photons in the scene will be at half intensity.

The Merge Distance attribute sets the world distance within which multiple photon hits are merged into a single photon hit. Adjusting this value can significantly reduce the complexity of the photon map. If left at 0, no merging occurs.

The Photon Map section in the Indirect Lighting tab in the Render Settings window determines how the maps are employed. By default, the Rebuild Photon Map attribute is selected, which forces the map to be rebuilt each time a frame is rendered. If the attribute is deselected, the program looks for the map listed in the Photon Map File field. By default, the maps are written to the `\renderData\mentalray\photonMap\` project directory.

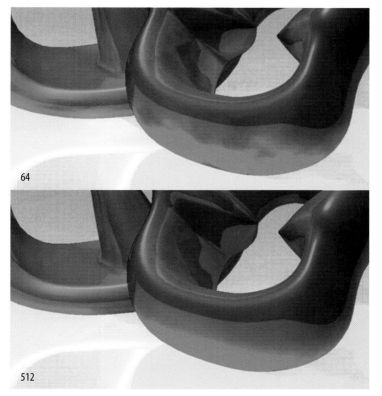

64

512

Figure 12.23 Top to Bottom: Accuracy set to 64 and 512. This scene is included with the Chapter 12 tutorial files as `simple_global.ma`. You can further improve the quality by raising the Accuracy or activating Final Gathering.

The Photon Tracing section of the Indirect Lighting tab sets the number of permitted photon surface hits due to reflections and refractions. Photon Reflections and Photon Reflections limit the number of hits that occur due to reflectivity and refractivity, whereas Max Photon Depth sets the maximum number of reflective and/or refractive hits. The higher the value in this section, the greater the degree of color bleeding and the more time-intensive the render.

> **Note:** The first surface that a photon hits is ignored in the creation of a photon map. Nevertheless, the first hit is considered part of the direct illumination calculation.

> **Note:** The Direct Illumination Shadow Effects attribute, in the Photon Map section, combines direct illumination shadows and photon shadowing via a shadow shader. The use of this feature leads to more subtle variation in shadowed areas.

Reviewing Photon Hits

Unfortunately, photon maps cannot be viewed with FCheck. Photon maps are not image files but data files that contain a 3D spatial search structure called a *kd-tree*.

The kd-tree stores the location, incident direction, and energy of each absorbed photon. (The *kd* in kd-tree stands for k-directional, where *k* is an axis within the data structure.) Nevertheless, mental ray provides a special window to examine data with the maps. Follow these steps:

1. Select the Enable Map Visualizer attribute in the Photon Map section. Optionally, enter a new map name in the Photon Map File attribute field.

2. Render a test frame using Global Illumination.

3. Choose Window > Rendering Editors > mental ray > Map Visualizer. The mental ray Map Visualizer window opens. Generally, the new photon map is preloaded into the Map File Name attribute field. If not, click the browse button and retrieve the photon map from the following directory:

   `project_directory\renderData\mentalray\photonMap\`

4. Select the Globillum Photons check box (if unselected). The photon hits are rendered as colored points in the viewport. Each point includes a direction line to indicate the direction of photon travel (see Figure 12.24).

Figure 12.24 Map Visualizer points and direction lines representing photon hits, as seen in a viewport

You can control how photon hits are displayed in the viewports by changing various settings within the mental ray Map Visualizer window (see Figure 12.25).

You can change the point and direction line scale with the Point Size and Direction Scale sliders. If you wish to compare the direction lines with the surface normals, raise the Normal Scale value above 0. The Search Radius Scale attribute is designed for Final Gathering renders using irradiance and is discussed in the section "Using Irradiance Particles" later in this chapter. You can also view caustic photon hits and volume photon hits by activating the same-named attributes in the Photon Visibility section. Caustics are discussed in the next section. Volume photon tracing is discussed in "A Note on Photonic Shaders" later in this chapter.

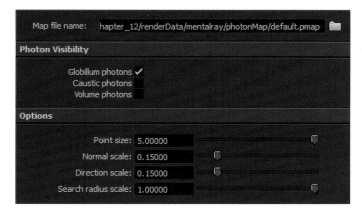

| Map file name: | hapter_12/renderData/mentalray/photonMap/default.pmap | |

Photon Visibility

Globillum photons	✔
Caustic photons	
Volume photons	

Options

Point size:	5.00000	
Normal scale:	0.15000	
Direction scale:	0.15000	
Search radius scale:	1.00000	

Figure 12.25 The mental ray Map Visualizer window

Applying Photon-Traced Caustics

A major advantage of the mental ray renderer is its ability to provide caustics. Caustics are focused specular reflections that form highlights on other surfaces. For example, caustics are commonly produced by shiny metal, water, diamonds, and glass (see Figure 12.26). If a 3D material or shader does not possess specular properties, no caustics will be generated by that material.

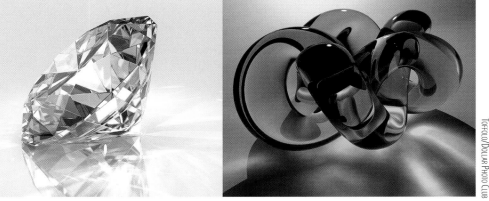

Figure 12.26 Real-world caustics created by a cut diamond and a glass sculpture

A special set of caustic photons is used to create caustics in Maya. A caustic photon is emitted by a light during the initial rendering phase and is traced through the scene until it is reflected or refracted a maximum number of times set by the Max Photon Depth attribute. If a caustic photon encounters a diffuse, nonreflective, nonrefractive surface, it is absorbed and its energy contribution is stored in a photon map.

Global Illumination photon maps do not store specular reflection and specular refraction information. Nevertheless, if the Caustics and Global Illumination attributes are selected for a render, the caustic photon and Global Illumination photon information is stored side by side in the same file. You can view the caustic photon hits with the mental ray Map Visualizer window (see the previous section). You can render caustics without Global Illumination if need be. You can activate caustics by selecting the Caustics attribute in the Caustics section of the Indirect Lighting tab in the Render Settings window (see Figure 12.27).

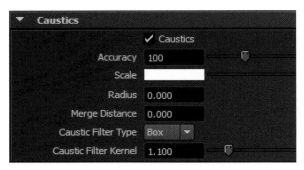

Figure 12.27 The Caustics section of the Indirect Lighting tab of the Render Settings window

The number of caustic photons generated by a given light is set by the Caustic Photons attribute in the mental ray > Caustics And Global Illumination subsection of the light's Attribute Editor tab. The Caustics tab in the Render Settings window also includes the additional caustic attributes. These include Accuracy, Scale, Radius, and Merge Distance, all of which function in a manner identical to their counterparts within the Global Illumination section. (See the "Adjusting Global Illumination Attributes" section earlier in this chapter.)

Note that it's not necessary to match the Radius attributes in the Caustics and Global Illumination sections. In general, caustic photon hits occur in small pockets and are not as spread out as their Global Illumination brethren. Nevertheless, stray caustic hits will occasionally pepper a render. So, take great care when balancing the Caustic Photons and Radius attributes (see Figure 12.28).

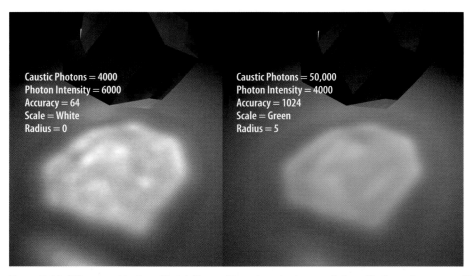

Figure 12.28 Different combinations of Caustic Photons, Photon Intensity, Accuracy, Scale, and Radius attributes create different degrees of caustic detail. This scene is included with the Chapter 12 tutorial files as `caustics.ma`.

To improve the caustic quality, you can follow these two basic steps:

1. Incrementally increase Radius until there is little change in the render.

2. Incrementally increase Accuracy until the caustic is suitably smooth.

The Caustics section also includes several unique attributes. Caustic Filter Kernel affects the sharpness of the caustic with the application of a filter. The attribute sets the strength of the filtering. Caustic Filter Type determines the style of filter. The Box and Gaussian options produce sharper caustic edges, whereas the Cone option produces softer results. The effect is subtle unless the total number of photons used in the scene is fairly low.

Keep in mind that the reflective, refractive, and specular qualities of assigned materials and shaders affect the look of the caustics. Thus, the caustics produced by a Blinn material vary from those produced by a mia_material shader. In addition, changes in the attribute values may alter the caustic shape (this is particularly true for less sophisticated Maya materials).

Activating Importons

Importons are similar to photons in that they "bounce" off surfaces in a scene. However, importons are emitted from the rendering camera toward the scene lights. Importons do not have a virtual energy; instead, they have a color value that represents the lighting contribution of the surface point they interact with. Ultimately, importons determine what indirect illumination contributions are "important" in a scene. In Maya, you can use importons in conjunction with photons to reduce the size and complexity of photon maps.

To use importons, follow these steps:

1. Set up a scene to use either Global Illumination or Caustics (or both systems). In Maya, importons require the existence of traced photons.

2. In the Indirect Illumination tab of the Render Settings window, expand the Importons section and select the Importons check box (see Figure 12.29).

Figure 12.29 The Importons section of the Indirect Lighting tab

3. Set the Global Illumination and/or Caustics Merge Distance attribute to 0. Set the Merge Distance attribute, in the Importons section, to a non-0 value, such as 0.1. This allows the importon data to eventually determine which photons are merged within the photon map.

4. Render a test frame. Importons are traced in a pre-rendering stage before the photon-tracing. The importon information is discarded during the creation of the photon map.

To fine-tune the result, you can alter the attribute values in the Importons section. The Density attribute determines the number of importons created per pixel of the render resolution. If it is set to 1.0, one importon per pixel is created. Higher values create a more accurate indirect illumination result but slow the render.

You can raise the Merge Distance value to simplify the photon map or lower the value to raise the photon map accuracy. If Merge Distance is set too high, the indirect illumination component may become visibly inaccurate. If Merge Distance is set to low, the render may become unacceptably time-intensive. Thus, it's important to test different values to determine what creates an acceptable result.

The Traverse attribute, which is selected by default, allows importons to "bounce" between multiple surfaces. For each surface intersection, importon color information is noted. If Traverse is deselected, only the first surface intersection is stored for an importon. However, if Traverse is deselected, you can choose the number of permitted bounces by setting the Max Depth attribute to a non-0 value.

To compare the impact of importons, you can use the mental ray Map Visualizer. Although the visualizer does not display importon hits, it does display photon hits, which vary in density and distribution based on the disuse or use of importons. For more information on the map visualizer, see the "Reviewing Photon Hits" section earlier in this chapter.

Final Gathering

Although Final Gathering is often used in conjunction with Global Illumination, it is not the same system. Final Gathering employs a specialized variation of raytracing in which each camera eye ray intersection creates sets of Final Gather rays. The Final Gather rays are sent out in a random direction within a hemisphere (see Figure 12.30). When a Final Gather ray intersects a new surface, the light energy of the newly intersected point and its potential contribution to the surface intersected by the camera eye ray are noted. The net sum of Final Gather ray intersections stemming from a single camera eye ray intersection is referred to as a Final Gather point. The Final Gather points are stored in a Final Gather map and are eventually added to the direct illumination color calculations. The end result is a render that is able to include bounced light and color bleed.

During a render, the creation of Final Gather points occurs in two stages. During the first stage, prior to computation, camera eye rays are projected in a hexagonal pattern from the camera view. Wherever a camera eye ray intersects a surface, a Final Gather point is created. In the second stage, which occurs during the visible render, additional Final Gather points are generated whenever the point density is discovered to be insufficient to calculate a particular pixel.

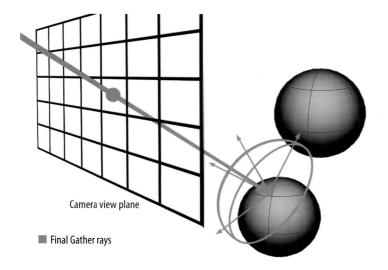

Camera view plane

■ Final Gather rays

Figure 12.30 A simplified representation of the Final Gathering process

Ultimately, Final Gathering is an efficient alternative to Global Illumination. Final Gathering is particularly well suited for scenes in which diffuse lighting is desirable. For example, in Figure 12.31 a character is lit with a single spot light from frame right. The Maya Software render of the scene (left) produces dark shadows. The Final Gathering mental ray render (right), however, brightens the dark areas with bounced light. In addition, the yellow of the wall and the red of the stage spotlight bleed onto the character's hair, cheek, and torso.

Figure 12.31 Left: Scene rendered with the Maya Software renderer; Right: Same scene rendered with mental ray Final Gathering.

Adjusting Final Gathering Attributes

To use Final Gathering, select the Final Gathering attribute in the Final Gathering section of the Indirect Illumination tab of the Render Settings window (see Figure 12.32). You must use the mental ray renderer.

Final Gathering

✔ Final Gathering

Accuracy	100
Point Density	1.000
Point Interpolation	10
Primary Diffuse Scale	
Secondary Diffuse Scale	
Secondary Diffuse Bounces	0

Final Gathering Map

Rebuild	On
Primary Final Gather File	
Secondary Final Gather File	Add New Item

☐ Enable Map Visualizer
✔ Preview Final Gather Tiles
☐ Precompute Photon Lookup
☐ Diagnose finalgather

Figure 12.32 The Final Gathering and Final Gathering Map sections of the Indirect Illumination tab

The Final Gathering section includes the following attributes:

Accuracy Sets the number of Final Gather rays fired off at each camera eye ray intersection. Decreasing this value will reduce the render time but introduces noise and other artifacts. Values less than 200 work for most test renders, whereas the maximum of 1024 is designed for renders that require maximum quality. For example, in Figure 12.33 lowering the Accuracy and Point Density values creates a rougher render with the indirect illumination contribution appearing blotchy. In this example, the Primary Diffuse Scale value is set to 2, 2, 2 in RGB to exaggerate the color bleed intensity. The floor, back wall, and ceiling are assigned to a gray material.

Figure 12.33 Left: Final Gathering render with default Accuracy and Point Density attribute values; Right: Same scene with Accuracy set to 16 and Point Density set to 0.25. This scene is included as final_gathering.ma with the Chapter 12 tutorial files.

Point Density   Serves as a multiplier for the density of the projected hexagonal grid created during the pre-render stage. Values between 1 and 2 generally suffice. Higher values increase the amount of detail.

Point Interpolation   Sets the number of Final Gather points that are required to shade any given pixel. Higher values produce smoother results.

Primary Diffuse Scale   Serves as a multiplier for the Final Gathering contribution to the render. You can tint the contribution by choosing a nonwhite color.

Secondary Diffuse Bounces   Allows additional bounces for each Final Gathering ray. Raising this value increases the amount of light bounce and color bleed but significantly slows the render.

Secondary Diffuse Scale   Serves as a multiplier for the secondary Final Gather contribution, as determined by the Secondary Diffuse Bounces attribute.

Working with Final Gathering Maps

The Final Gathering Map subsection (see Figure 12.32 in the previous section) has additional attributes that affect the Final Gathering map:

Rebuild and Primary Final Gather File   If Rebuild is set to On, a new Final Gathering map is computed for each rendered frame. If Rebuild is set to Off, the renderer will use the preexisting Final Gathering map listed in the Primary Final Gather File attribute field. The map file is stored in the *Project_Directory*\renderData\ mentalray\finalgMap\ directory. If Rebuild is set to Freeze, the renderer will rely on the Final Gathering map calculated for the first frame of an animation and will not update the map as the animation progresses. The Freeze option is suitable if there are no animated cameras, lights, or objects.

Secondary Final Gather File   You can combine multiple Final Gathering maps, either from different cameras or different frames, by clicking the Secondary Final Gather File Add New Item button and browsing for the additional Final Gathering map. This option may be useful for smoothing out the Final Gathering result by averaging multiple maps.

Enable Map Visualizer   Creates temporary Final Gathering maps that may be used with the mental ray Map Visualizer (see "Reviewing Photon Hits" earlier in this chapter). Final Gathering points are displayed as dots in the viewports. Point Size and Normal Scale attributes in the Map Visualizer window control the size of the dots and their corresponding surface normals.

Diagnose Finalgather   Renders Final Gathering points as green dots through the Render View. Useful for visualizing Final Gathering point density.

Precompute Photon Lookup   If Global Illumination is activated, you can select this attribute to optimize the Final Gathering process. In this case, the photon map irradiance information is used to reduce the number of required Final Gathering rays and points.

Controlling Final Gathering Quality

The Final Gathering Quality subsection, in the Indirect Illumination tab, has additional attributes that affect the resulting render quality:

Filter Controls a special filter that eliminates or reduces speckles created by skewed Final Gathering samples. If a surface in a scene is brightly lit, it can unduly influence energy calculations when intersected by Final Gather rays. A value of 0 turns the filter off. Values between 1 and 4 soften the render but reduce artifacts.

Falloff Start and Falloff Stop Define the world distance from a camera eye ray intersection that Final Gather rays are allowed to travel. Thus, these attributes determine the size of the hemispherical region associated with a Final Gather point. If a Final Gather ray reaches the Falloff Stop distance before intersecting a new surface, the contribution of the ray is derived from the camera's Background Color attribute.

Normal Tolerance Sets the maximum angle, in degrees, that a Final Gather point may deviate from the associated surface normal and still be considered as part of the indirect illumination calculation. Lowering this value reduces the number of considered Final Gather points.

In addition, the Final Gathering Tracing subsection controls its namesake (see Figure 12.34).

Figure 12.34 The Final Gathering Quality and Final Gathering Tracing subsections of the Indirect Illumination tab

This subsection includes these attributes:

Max Trace Depth Sets the number of subrays created when a Final Gather ray intersects a reflective or refractive surface. A default value of 0 kills the Final Gather ray as soon as it intersects a surface (although the energy contribution from that intersection is noted). A value of 1.0 allows a Final Gather ray to generate one additional reflection or refraction subray. Since Final Gather rays are searching for surfaces that might contribute light energy, the Max Trace Depth attribute can be left at 1.0 or 0 with satisfactory results for many renders.

Reflections and Refractions   Respectively set the number of reflection and refraction subrays created when a Final Gather ray intersects a reflective or refractive surface. These attributes are overridden by the Max Trace Depth attribute, which controls the total number of subrays permitted per ray intersection.

Final Gather Mode   This menu includes several options that control the Final Gathering functionality. The Automatic method relies on the Accuracy and Point Density attributes, in the Final Gathering section, to control the Final Gathering render quality. The Optimize For Animations option averages Final Gather points across multiple frames. This option reduces the flickering sometimes present with Final Gathering renders. Such flickering may be present if an animated camera is used or objects are in motion. The No FG Caching option prevents disc caching and forces Final Gathering to make a brand-new Final Gathering calculation for the current frame. This option may speed up simple Final Gathering scenes. The Use Radius Quality Control option uses Min Radius and Max Radius attributes instead of Accuracy and Point Density to control quality.

Min Radius and Max Radius   These attributes are available if Final Gather Mode is set to Use Radius Quality Control. Min Radius and Max Radius define the region in which Final Gather points are averaged to determine the color of a pixel. If an insufficient number of points are discovered within a region, additional points are created during the render for that region. Maya documentation suggests that the Max Radius should be no larger than 10 percent of the scene's bounding box. Along those lines, the Min Radius should be no more than 10 percent of the Max Radius. If a scene involves intricate or convoluted geometry, however, you can decrease the Min Radius and Max Radius to improve quality. The default value of 0 for both attributes allows Maya to select a Min Radius and Max Radius based on the scene bounding box.

View (Radii In Pixel Size)   This attribute is available if Final Gather Mode is set to Use Radius Quality Control. View forces the Min Radius and Max Radius attributes to operate in screen space and not world space.

Final Gathering with Irradiance

Final Gathering does not require lights to render a scene. The system can use irradiance alone. Technically speaking, *irradiance* is a measure of the rate of flow of electromagnetic energy, such as light, from a per-unit area of a surface. The ambient and incandescent attributes of Maya materials and mental ray shaders represent irradiance. Irradiance differs from glow in that irradiance employs bounced light. Glows, such as those created by the Glow Intensity attribute of standard Maya materials or by Optical FX nodes, are added as a postprocess blur and are placed on top of the render.

For example, in Figure 12.35 a scene is rendered with Final Gathering. The Enable Default Light attribute is deselected in the Render Options section of the

Common tab of the Render Settings window. A Fractal texture with an orange Color Gain attribute is mapped to a Blinn material's Incandescence attribute, which provides the only light for the scene. Although the ground plane is assigned to a second Blinn material with Ambient Color and Incandescence values set to 0, it reflects the orange energy.

Figure 12.35 A primitive object lights a scene with orange irradiance. This scene is included with the Chapter 12 tutorial files as `irradiance.ma`.

In addition, standard Maya materials include Irradiance and Irradiance Color attributes in the mental ray section of their Attribute Editor tab. If the Irradiance attribute is mapped, the map becomes an irradiant light source. Irradiance Color serves as a multiplier for the resulting irradiant light.

You can view irradiant Final Gather points, as well as Final Gather points in general, through the mental ray Map Visualizer window. If a valid Final Gather map is listed in the Map File Name field, the points are automatically displayed in the viewports as colored dots. The Point Size attribute controls the size. Search Radius Scale controls the density of displayed points; in most cases, it is not necessary to adjust this attribute.

Using Irradiance Particles

Irradiance particles employ importons and virtual particle tracing to calculate indirect illumination. However, irradiance particles are not compatible with Global Illumination or Final Gathering systems in Maya (although they do work with the Caustics system).

The irradiance particle system follows these basic steps when rendering:

- Importons are traced. At intersection points, direct and indirect illumination contributions are noted. (See the "Activating Importons" section earlier in this chapter.)

- Based on the importon information, irradiance particles are traced as rays. Each ray determines the amount of irradiance (emission of visible light) created by each shaded point in the scene from the view of the camera. A special irradiance particles map is written to disc.

Irradiance particles offer a system that is potentially more accurate than the Final Gathering system. This is particularly evident when low-quality settings are used. For example, on the left side of Figure 12.36 Final Gathering is used with Accuracy and Point Interpretation set to 32. On the right side of Figure 12.36, irradiance particles are used with Rays and Interpoints set to 32. The irradiance particles produce color bleed directly below the red and green shapes, whereas the Final Gathering render fails to add color to those areas. Even if Final Gathering and irradiance particles produce a similar render, irradiance particles offer unique attributes with which to adjust the indirect illumination.

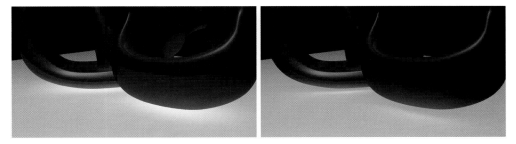

Figure 12.36 Left: Final Gathering render with low-quality settings misses the color bleed below the red and green objects; Right: Irradiance particle render with similar low-quality settings includes the color bleed. This scene is included with the Chapter 12 tutorial files as `irradiance_particles.ma`.

To use irradiance particles, select the Irradiance Particles check box in the Irradiance Particles section of the Indirect Lighting tab of the Render Settings window (see Figure 12.37).

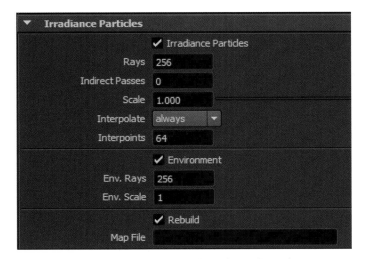

Figure 12.37 The Irradiance Particles section of the Indirect Lighting tab

The following attributes influence the resulting quality:

Rays   Specifies the total number of irradiance particle rays shot from the camera view. In contrast, the Final Gathering Accuracy attribute sets the number of rays per Final Gather point, making the Final Gathering process significantly more complex.

Indirect Passes   Sets the number of indirect illumination passes that occur through ray bounces. If this attribute is set to 0, the irradiance particles system determines the direct lighting contribution and skips indirect lighting.

Scale   Serves as a multiplier for the irradiance particle light contribution to the scene.

Interpolate   Controls the contribution of the irradiance particles to the render. The Secondary option removes the initial surface intersections from the contribution, and the Always option includes all intersections.

Interpoints   Sets the numbers of irradiance particle ray intersections used to calculate a shading point.

Environment, Env. Rays, and Env. Scale   If the Environment attribute is selected, the renderer incorporates any environment shaders or Image-Based Lighting (IBL) setups that may be present in the scene to influence the irradiance particles. A separate irradiance map is created for the environment. Env. Rays sets the numbers of irradiance particle rays used for the environment. Env. Scale is a multiplier for the environment contribution. For more information on environment shaders, see the "Using mental ray Environment Shaders" section earlier in this chapter. For more information on IBL workflow, see Chapter 13.

Rebuild and Map File   By default, a new irradiance particles map is created with each render. However, if you deselect Rebuild, you can force the render to reuse a map defined by the Map File field.

Working with Volumetric Shaders

The mental ray renderer includes several volumetric shaders, which are designed to place a virtual atmosphere within a volume area. The atmosphere emulates participating media such as water vapor, fog, smoke, and so on. Participating media occludes objects that are far from the viewer; objects that are closer to the viewer are occluded to a lesser degree. You can find volumetric shaders in the mental ray > Volumetric Materials and mental ray > Photon Volumetric Materials sections of Maya 2015 (photonic shaders are described in the next section).

The most direct way to apply a volumetric shader is to map it to the Volume Shader attribute, found in the mental ray section of the rendering camera. For example, in Figure 12.38 a mib_volume shader is mapped to Volume Shader, producing a purple fog that partially occludes objects that are further from the camera.

The mib_volume shader has three attributes. The Color attribute sets the color of the fog. The Max attribute determines the world distance from the camera where the fog is at 100 percent opaqueness. The Light Rays attribute, if selected, uses a more accurate but more expensive rendering technique.

Figure 12.38 A purple fog is created with the mib_volume shader. This scene is included as `volume_fog.ma` with the Chapter 12 tutorial files.

You can also map a volumetric shader to a shading group node via the Volume Shader attribute (see Figure 12.40 in the next section). This attribute is located within the Custom Shaders section of the shading group node's Attribute Editor tab. This places the volumetric effect *within* the volume of the assigned surface (this assumes that the geometry is closed, as is the case with a sphere or torus). For example, in Figure 12.39 a parti_volume shader is mapped to the Volume Shader attribute of the shading group associated with the giraffe sculpture geometry. The sculpture is assigned to a mia_material_x shader. The mia_material_x shader is given 100 percent transparency and no reflectivity so that the volumetric effect shows through the surface. Note that it's necessary to add at least one light to the scene for the volumetric effect to be visible in the render.

Figure 12.39 Fog-like participating media is placed within a surface with the parti_volume shader. A simplified version of this scene is included as `parti_volume.ma` with the Chapter 12 tutorial files.

Whereas the mib_volume shader renders the participating media with even illumination, parti_volume reacts to lighting. The part of the media closest to light is illuminated, and the neck and head are not. In this scene, the sole light—a point light—has its light decay set to Linear. The part_volume shader emulates light scatter through the participating media. The color of the scattered light is set by the Scatter attribute (which you can map with a texture). The degree of scattering is controlled by the Extinction attribute, with higher values emulating a denser medium and thus creating a darker result.

Note that you can map volumetric materials designed for the Maya Software renderer to the Volume Material attribute of the shading group node (this is located in the Shading Group Attributes section, as illustrated by Figure 12.40 in the next section).

A Note on Photonic Shaders

The mental ray renderer includes several shaders with the _photon suffix. These shaders are designed to work with Global Illumination and/or Caustics renders and react correctly to photon-tracing. For example, parti_volume_photon works in the same way as parti_volume but supports photon-tracing so that photonic rendering systems work correctly with participating media. In Maya 2015, parti_volume_photon is located in the Create > mental ray > Photon Volumetric Material section (the section was previously named Photonic Materials).

The Custom Shaders section of shading group nodes (Figure 12.40) has a Photon Shader attribute. You can use this attribute to map a photonic shader. For example, you can map parti_volume to Volume Shader and parti_volume_photon to Photon Shader. Some advanced shaders, such as mia_material_x, automatically map themselves to the Material Shader, Shadow Shader, and Photon Shader attributes. Thus, such materials react correctly to Global Illumination and Caustics in their default state. (Whereas Maya materials are mapped to the Surface Material attribute, similar mental ray shaders are mapped to the Material Shader attribute.)

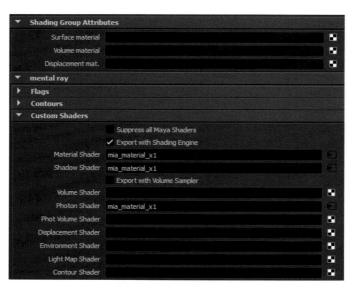

Figure 12.40 The Shading Group Attributes and Custom Shaders sections of a shading group node. A mia_material_x shader is assigned to a surface.

Using mental Ray Light Shaders

The mental ray renderer includes a set of physically accurate lights. Although the use of these lights may not be necessary for Maya scenes that contain imaginary or otherwise fantastic locations, they are often employed for architectural visualizations and other situations where a high degree of accuracy is mandatory. These are located in the Create > mentalray > MentalRay Lights section of the Hypershade, Create Render Node, and Create Node windows.

Although some mental ray lights mimic Maya standard lights, such as mib_light_infinite (directional), mib_light_point, and mib_light_spot, others are designed for specific advanced lighting and rendering situations, such as rendering photo-real locations or working with fur. The light shaders do not create light icons and cannot be manipulated directly with the viewports. Instead, you must map the shader to the Light Shader attribute of a standard Maya light. The Light Shader attribute is located in the mental ray > Custom Shaders subsection of the light's Attribute Editor tab. Brief descriptions of the most useful lights follow:

mib_light_infinite, mib_light_point, and mib_light_spot   Although it may seem redundant to map one of these shaders to the Light Shader attribute of a Maya light, the shaders offer additional controls for light decay. With these shaders, the Factor attribute tapers shadows by letting light penetrate occluding surfaces when Factor is set above 0. The Attenuation attribute, when selected, creates light falloff within the light distance set by the Start and Stop values. By default, these shaders create their own shadows (as set by the Shadow attribute). These shaders are located in the Legacy section in Maya 2015.

mib_light_photometric and mia_photometric_light   The mib_light_photometric shader is similar to mib_light_point but includes a Profile attribute that accepts an IES (Illuminating Engineering Society) light profile. You can generate a mental ray Light Profile node by clicking the checkered Map button beside Profile. The resulting mentalrayLightProfile node accepts an IES text file through the File Name attribute. IES files define light intensity distribution (that is, light falloff patterns) and are designed to replicate specific light fixtures. Because of the high degree of falloff accuracy, these shaders are well suited for architectural visualization. The mia_photometric_light shader expands on mib_light_photometric by adding intensity and light distribution controls. The mib_light_photometric shader is located in the Legacy section in Maya 2015. IES profile files are often available for download from the websites of light fixture manufactures.

physical_light   This light shader replicates the light intensity falloff present in the Earth's atmosphere, where the light intensity is the inverse square of the distance. Although you can create a similar falloff with a standard by setting Decay Rate to Quadratic, this shader offers additional fine-tuning with its Cone (cone falloff with spot lights), Cosine Exponent (width falloff for area lights), and Threshold (removal of light intensities below Threshold value) attributes.

mib_cie_d The mib_cie_d shader produces a color tied to a chosen kelvin temperature on the CIE D illuminant scale. CIE stands for Commission on Illumination and is an international standard for color management. (For more information on color temperature, see Chapter 1.) For example, you can use the shader to produce a color temperature that matches a certain time of day or specific light source, such as a particular manufacturer and model light-bulb. The shader includes two attributes: Temperature (degrees in Kelvin) and Intensity (color multiplier). Note that you can combine multiple light shaders. For example, you can map mib_light_photometric to the Light Shader attribute of a spot light and map the mib_cie_d shader to the Color attribute of the same spot light. See Figure 1.25 in Chapter 1 for a simplified kelvin color chart.

mia_portal_light This shader is designed specifically for Global Illumination simulations where a door or window is allowing light to penetrate an interior space. This light is commonly used to create photo-real interior spaces.

Chapter Tutorial: Using Global Illumination and Final Gathering with the Cornell Box

A *Cornell box* is an enclosed 3D set used to create Global Illumination tests. Some objects within the set are colored whereas others are gray or white, allowing you to test color bleeding. In this tutorial, you'll apply Global Illumination, Caustics, and Final Gathering with the mental ray renderer. Follow these steps:

1. Open the box_start.ma file included with the Chapter 12 tutorial files. The scene includes a set with walls, floor, and ceiling, two abstract sculptures, and two point lights.

2. Open the Render Settings window and change the Render Using menu to mental ray. Switch to the Indirect Illumination tab. Select the Global Illumination attribute in the Global Illumination section. Leave the other Global Illumination attributes at their default settings.

3. Select the BulbLeft point light. In the mental ray > Caustics And Global Illumination section of its Attribute Editor tab, select Emit Photons. Do the same with the BulbRight light.

4. Render a test frame. The scene appears overexposed. To reduce the influence of the indirect illumination, set the Exponent attribute of each light to 2. This causes the photon energy to decay more rapidly. Render a test frame. The exposure is better, but (as shown in Figure 12.41) the photon hits are visible as large colored dots.

5. Increase the Global Illum Photons value of each light to 25,000. Render a test frame. The quality improves but the walls, floor, and ceiling do not appear smooth. Increase the Global Illum Photons value of each light to 50,000. Return to the Indirect Lighting tab of the Render Settings window and set the Global Illumination Radius to 0.5. Render a test frame. This time, many small photon hits appear. Radius sets the world size of each photon "dot" within

which multiple photons hits are blended into a single color. Increase the Radius to 2. Render a test frame. The quality improves but the pools of color bleed are still fairly rough (see Figure 12.42).

Figure 12.41 A low number of photons creates visible colored dots.

Figure 12.42 Settings of 50,000 photons per light and a Radius value of 2 improve the render quality.

6. You can use Final Gathering in conjunction with Global Illumination to create a more refined render. Final Gathering will further average the indirection illumination component, blending the photon hits together. In the Render Settings window, go to the Final Gathering section and select the Final Gathering

attribute. Render a test frame. The render becomes smoother, even with default Final Gathering settings. The color bleed becomes more subtle thanks to the Final Gathering algorithm.

7. In the Final Gathering section, change the Primary Diffuse Scale value to 1.5. You can enter a higher value through the Color Chooser window color fields. You can enter **1.5, 1.5, 1.5** in RGB or **0, 0, 1.5** in HSV. This exaggerates the contribution of the indirect illumination component and thus increases the strength of the color bleed. For each light, reduce the Intensity value to 0.75 so that the scene does not become overexposed. Render a test frame. As shown in Figure 12.43, the scene becomes smoother with a greater degree of red and green spill from the side walls.

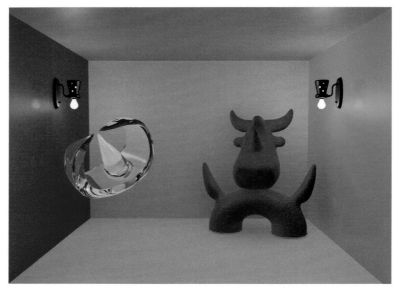

Figure 12.43 Final Gathering improves the render quality. An increased Primary Diffuse Scale value increases the intensity of color bleed.

8. At this point, there are no cast shadows. Go to each light and select the Use Ray Trace Shadows attribute (in the Shadows > Raytrace Shadow Attributes section). Set each light's Light Radius to 2 and Shadow rays to 40. This creates soft shadows. Render a test frame.

9. Although the abstract C-shape object is transparent, it fails to produce a caustic. In the Render Settings window, go to the Caustics section and select the Caustics attribute. Leave the other Caustics attributes at their default values. Go the Caustics And Global Illumination section of each light and change Caustic Photons to 50,000. Render a test frame. A caustic highlight appears on the floor beneath the C-shape. Due to the high Caustic Photons value for each light and the presence of Final Gathering, the caustic is relatively smooth.

The tutorial is complete! Your render should look similar to Figure 12.44. Feel free to experiment with the Global Illumination, Caustics, and Final Gathering attributes. Recommendations for adjusting these attributes to increase render quality are discussed earlier in this chapter. Keep in mind that you can use Global Illumination, Caustics, or Final Gathering systems by themselves to add indirect lighting to a scene. Each system has its own sets of advantages and disadvantages. A finished version of this scene is included as box_final.ma with the Chapter 12 tutorial files.

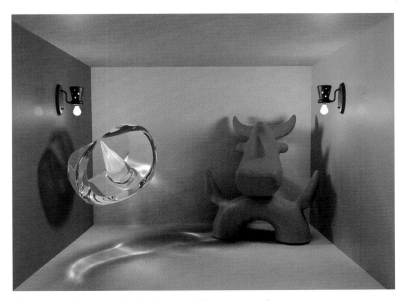

Figure 12.44 The final render with shadows and Caustics activated

Color Management, HDR Workflow, and Render Passes

Color management is an important part of 3D rendering, and the Autodesk® Maya® program provides built-in tools for color space selection and conversion. You can also work with 16- and 32-bit floating-point textures, renders, and lighting systems to increase the accuracy of your project. In addition, setting up render passes gives you even greater control when fine-tuning your renders in postproduction.

13

Chapter Contents
Working with color space conversions
Employing Maya color management
Rendering 16- and 32-bit images
Using HDR textures
Understanding image-based lighting
Setting up render passes

Managing Color Spaces

As discussed in Chapter 1, "Understanding Lighting and Color," color management is an important part of digital image creation. In addition to the color calibration techniques discussed in that chapter, you can activate the color management system built into Maya. Through this system and the color management attributes of individual shading nodes, you can choose among various color profiles. Color profiles interpret and convert color spaces. Maya allows you to work with multiple color spaces with gamma correction or within a linear space that lacks gamma correction. Maya also supports multiple bit depths by reading 8-, 16-, and 32-bit image formats. You can render 16- and 32-bit formats through the mental ray® frame buffer.

Color Space Overview

In Chapter 1 you saw that Maya uses the RGB color model to make its calculations. More specifically, Maya operates in sRGB color space by default. A *color space* is a set of colors that a system or device can display. sRGB is a widely used color space standard developed by Microsoft and Hewlett-Packard in the 1990s. The default sRGB color space used by Maya is gamma-corrected—that is, a gamma power function is applied to make the images more suitable for human vision (which is more sensitive to darker value ranges). (See Chapter 6, "Creating Custom Connections and Applying Color Utilities," for additional information on gamma correction.)

Maya supports other color spaces through various functions discussed in this chapter. Brief descriptions of these color spaces follow. Later in the chapter, we'll look at selecting a color space.

Linear sRGB   This color space is the same as sRGB but does not apply gamma correction. Note that color models use primaries to describe the primary colors. *Primaries* are coordinates within the color space. Hence, sRGB and Linear sRGB use the same RGB color model and same red, green, and blue primaries.

HDTV (Rec. 709)   Defines the color space commonly used for HDTV broadcast and recording. *Rec. 709* refers to an international standard.

Linear Rec.709   This color space is the same as HTDV (Rec. 709) but does not apply gamma correction.

CIE XYZ   With this color space the Y component is luminance (brightness), whereas X and Z are chromatic (color) components. The space is supported by Maya for node outputs through a Color Profile node (see the next section). CIE stands for the International Commission on Illumination. (See Chapter 12, "Working with mental ray Shaders, Global Illumination, and Final Gathering," for information on the mental ray mib_cie_d light shader.)

Cineon Log   This format is logarithmic and is designed to match motion picture film. Using this format makes the image appear low contrast. A rendered image of this format generally requires additional color manipulation in postproduction.

Choosing Color Profiles for Textures

Maya File and Movie textures, as well as the mentalrayTexture shader, include a Color Profile menu (see Figure 13.1). You can set this menu to a color profile and thus convert the loaded file's color space to that of the chosen profile. (This ability depends on the mental ray renderer and is not supported by the Maya Software renderer.) This option is useful for converting dissimilar files into the same color space. For example, set the Color Profile menu to HDTV (Rec. 709) to convert the file to HDTV color space. By default, the menu is set to Use Default Input Profile, which prevents a conversion and reads the file RGB values without alteration.

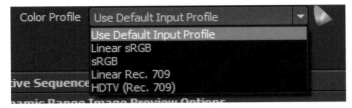

Figure 13.1 The Color Profile menu, as carried by a File texture, and the list of available color spaces

A Create A New Color Profile button is located at the right side of the Color Profile menu. When you click this button, a new Color Profile utility node is connected to the File, Movie, or mentalrayTexture node. This places the definition of the preferred color space outside the original node. By separating the definition, you can use the Color Profile node in a more complex shading network. For example, you can connect the output of the Color Profile node to multiple File, Movie, or mentalrayTexture nodes. As such, you can connect the Color Profile Type output channel of the Color Profile node to the Color Profile input channel of the File, Movie, or mentalrayTexture node. When a Color Profile node is connected, you can set the Color Profile menu to the name of the Color Profile node, such as *colorProfile1*. The Color Profile node carries a Color Profile Type menu, which lists all the color spaces discussed in the previous section.

> **Note:** You can manually add a Color Profile utility to your scene at any time. The utility is located in the Create > Maya > Utilities section of the Hypershade, Create Node, and Create Render Node windows.

Using the Color Management System

As we discussed earlier, Maya operates in sRGB color space by default. However, you can activate the Color Management attribute through the Common tab of the Render Settings window to alter the color space workflow (see Figure 13.2). (This ability depends on the mental ray renderer and is not supported by the Maya Software renderer.) When Color Management is selected, the Default Input Profile and Default Output Format attributes become accessible. Default Input Profile defines the default color space interpretation applied to all incoming texture files. Default Output Profile defines the color space interpretation applied to all outgoing renders. If these two attributes are the same, no color space conversion is applied during the rendering process. If these two attributes are different, a color space conversion is applied during the render. You can use Color Profile nodes in conjunction with the Color Management system.

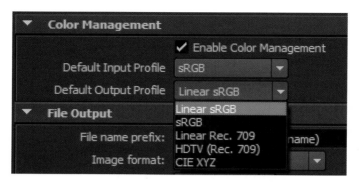

Figure 13.2 The Color Management section of the Render Settings window and the list of available color spaces for the Default Output Profile attribute

Note: Node swatches (thumbnail images) in the Hypershade and Node Editor are not affected by color management within Maya. Hence, the swatch colors may not be accurate.

Working with HDR

High-dynamic range (HDR) commonly refers to 16- and 32-bit floating-point color spaces and digital images that use those color spaces. *Floating-point* describes the image format architecture that defines a value with a fixed number (a *significand*) and a scaling exponent. For example, a floating-point definition might be 1.234×10^6, which is equal to 1,234,000. Thanks to their unique architecture, HDR images can store potentially large dynamic ranges (ranges of color values). In other words, an HDR image can have extremely high values, such a 2.3×10^{32}, and extremely low values, such as 2.3×10^{-6}, or 0.0000023. By default, Maya operates in 8-bit color space. The 8-bit color space does not use floating-point architecture and thus only stores integer (whole number) values. The highest value an 8-bit image can store is 255.

You can switch from 8-bit color space to a 32-bit floating-point color space in Maya 2014 by following these steps:

1. Choose Window > Settings/Preferences > Preferences. Go to the Settings > Rendering section of the Preferences window and select mental ray from the Preferred Renderer menu.

2. Select the 32-bit Floating Point (HDR) radio button beside Render View Image Format. A warning dialog box opens, explaining that the change will take effect the next time Maya is started.

3. Click the Preferences window's Save button. Restart Maya. The Render View window now operates in 32-bit floating-point color space.

If you are using Maya 2015, switch to the mental ray renderer. No additional steps are necessary to switch to 32-bit color space.

To batch-render an image sequence in 16- or 32-bit color space, you must use the mental ray frame buffer, which is described in the next section. Renders created in the Render View do employ the full 32-bit dynamic range; however, a color space conversion is necessary to display the image on a standard monitor. This is explored in the "Creating a Linear Workflow" section later in this chapter. The way in which 32-bit textures are interpreted is controlled by additional attributes; this is discussed in the "Using HDR Textures" section later in this chapter.

Rendering 16- and 32-Bit Image Sequences

By default, the Maya Software and mental ray renderers render 8-bit image sequences. Although this is suitable in many situations, some professional projects require the render of 16- or 32-bit images. You can use the mental ray renderer to achieve this with the following steps:

1. In the Render Settings window, switch the renderer to mental ray. In the Common tab, change the Image Format to OpenEXR, HDR, or TIFF. These formats support 16-bit and 32-bit renders. (The 16-bit floating-point format is often referred to as *half float*.) (If one of these formats is missing from the list, make sure its associated plug-in is activated in the Plug-In Manager window.)

2. Switch to the Quality tab and expand the Framebuffer section (see Figure 13.3). Change the Data Type menu to either RGBA (Half) 4x16 Bit for a 16-bit render or RGBA (Float) 4x32 Bit for a 32-bit render.

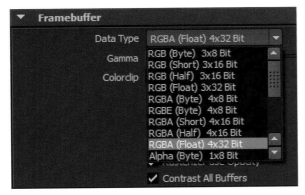

Figure 13.3 The Framebuffer section of the Quality tab with the list of available bit depths

3. Launch a batch render. The resulting image sequence renders as 16- or 32-bit.

To take full advantage of a floating-point workflow in Maya 2014 before you batch render, follow the steps listed in the previous section to change the Maya working color space to 32-bit. Note that the Default Output Profile setting, in the Render Settings window, does add a final color space conversion to batch-rendered files if the Enable Color Management attribute is selected. See the "Using the Color Management System" section earlier in this chapter.

Note: It's not necessary to use HDR images to create superwhite values in Maya. You can adjust lights, materials, and shaders to create such values. For example, raising the intensity of a light to an excessively high value, such as 10, may produce superwhite specular highlights on a surface assigned to a material with an excessively high specular color value such as 5.

Note: You can adjust the superwhite values produced by batch render by adding a lens shader to the rendering camera's Lens Shader attribute. For example, you can map the mia_exposure_photographic shader and use the shader to lower the values within the rendered image. In this way, the mia_exposure_photographic and mia_exposure_simple shaders serve as color grading tools that you can apply as the final step of a render. For more information on lens shaders, see Chapter 12.

Creating a Linear Workflow

A *linear* color space is one that is not gamma-corrected. Working within a linear color space may be necessary when re-creating a photorealistic render or with other projects that demand a high degree of color accuracy. Gamma-corrected images may suffer from overexposed highlights and improper light decay. This may be particularly problematic when working in the default 8-bit Maya sRGB color space, which has a value range of 0–255 (often expressed as 0-to-1.0). With 8-bit space, the highlights may be clipped, where values over 255 are thrown away.

To create a linear workflow in Maya, you can follow these steps:

1. Change the renderer to mental ray. If you are using Maya 2014, select the 32 Bit Floating-Point (HDR) option in the Rendering section of the Preferences window. The necessary steps are described in the "Working with HDR" section earlier in this chapter.

2. In the Render settings window, change the Image Format menu to a format that supports 32-bit renders, such as OpenEXR or TIFF. Change the Data Type menu to RGBA (Float) 4x32 Bit. The necessary steps are described in the previous section.

3. In the Common tab of the Render Settings window, select the Enable Color Management attribute. Set the Default Input Profile menu to sRGB. This reads texture bitmaps in the sRGB color space, which is the most common color space used by texture bitmaps. Optionally, you can interpret textures individually by using the File, Movie, or mentalrayTexture node's Color Profile menu (see the section "Choosing Color Profiles for Textures" earlier in this chapter). Set the Default Output Profile menu to Linear sRGB. This prevents the application of gamma correction during the renders or batch renders.

4. In the Render View window, select Display > Color Management. In the Attribute Editor tab for the defaultViewColorManager node, change the Image Color Profile node to Linear sRGB (see Figure 13.4). This ensures that the

Render View window interprets incoming linear color space color values correctly. Leave Display Color Profile set to sRGB to match the standard color space used by most computer monitors.

Figure 13.4 The defaultViewColorManager node attributes in Maya 2015

This procedure places the entire Maya workflow, from the ingestion of textures to the export of images through rendering, in a linear color space. Note that renders created in linear space generally appear with reduced contrast. Also note that the full dynamic range available to 32-bit color space is not visible on a standard 8-bit or 10-bit monitor. Nevertheless, the color values stored in rendered 32-bit files may be superwhite (values over 1.0 in 0-to-1.0 space).

> **Note:** The defaultViewColorManager node supplies a LUT File attribute. You can load a LUT (look-up table) file to make a color space conversion. The attribute accepts LUT files created by commonly used color grading software packages, such as Discreet Lustre and Avid Media Composer.

Even if you choose not to work in linear color space, you can continue to use the defaultViewColorManager node to control the Render View display. For example, you can set Display Color Profile to HDTV (Rec. 709) to preview the render in HDTV color space.

> **Note:** If you are working in a gamma-corrected, nonlinear color space, you can remove the gamma correction from a specific node by connecting a Gamma Correct utility to its Out Value output channel. If you set the utility's Gamma RGB attribute values to 0.455, the gamma correction is roughly neutralized. You can then connect the utility's Out Value output channel to a useful input channel of another node, such as a material's Color.

Using HDR Textures

You can use 16- and 32-bit OpenEXR and TIFF bitmaps in Maya as textures. You can load them into a File or Movie node as you would an 8-bit texture. However, because of the wide dynamic range available to a floating-point image, the full range of color values is not visible through the Hypershade and Node Editor swatches.

Maya provides the Float To Fixed Point attribute to convert the HDR values into a range usable by the swatches. It is located in the High Dynamic Range Image Preview Options section of a File or Movie texture's Attribute Editor tab. The Float To Fixed Point attribute has three options. The Clamped option clamps the HDR values to the standard 0-to-1.0 range, thus throwing away superwhite values. The Linear option normalizes (remaps) all the values within the HDR image so they fit within the 0-to-1.0 range. This may cause the texture to take on a high degree of contrast. The Exponential option retains the lowest and highest values, while providing an Exposure slider that you adjust to select different exposure (brightness) levels within the HDR file. Any changes to the Float To Fixed Point and Exposure attributes cause the texture swatch to update in the Hypershade and Node Editor windows.

The Float To Fixed Point attribute settings do not affect batch renders. If you batch-render with an image format that supports floating-point values, the render uses the full range of values within the original HDR texture. Hence, the resulting batch-rendered images may contain superwhite values. That said, the Default Output Profile setting, in the Render Settings window, does add a final color space conversion to batch-rendered files if the Enable Color Management attribute is selected. See the "Using the Color Management System" section earlier in this chapter.

The Float To Fixed Point attribute settings do not affect renders created with the Render View window. The full range of values in the HDR texture is used automatically in Maya 2015. (If you are using Maya 2014, you must switch to 32-bit render mode as described in the "Working with HDR" section earlier in this chapter.) However, the defaultViewColorManager node settings affect the look of the Render View render because the node applies a color space conversion before displaying the rendered image. This means that the Render View render may appear different from a batch-rendered image. Ultimately, you should refer to the batch-rendered image to properly judge the result of the HDR workflow.

Applying Image-Based Lighting

The mental ray renderer provides a means to light a scene with image-based lighting (IBL). An IBL system emulates the ambient light arriving from a sky, an interior space, or similar surrounding environment. The light generated by an IBL system is dependent on a mapped texture file, where bright parts of the texture produce areas of bright light. IBL systems are generally used with photographs of real-world locations. Although you can use 8-bit textures with an IBL system, it's more common to use 32-bit HDR photo bitmaps.

To create an IBL system with mental ray, follow these steps:

1. In the Render Settings window, go to the Indirect Lighting tab. In the Environment section, click the Image Based Lighting button.

2. A mentalrayIblShape node is added to the scene. This creates a yellow environment sphere at 0, 0, 0 (see Figure 13.5). You can find the node listed in the Lights tab of the Hypershade window.

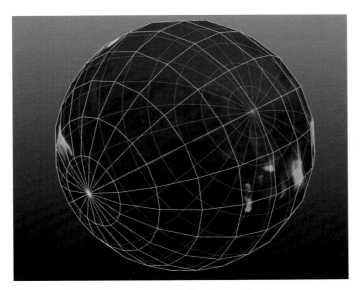

Figure 13.5 An IBL environment sphere with Mapping set to Angular

3. In the Attribute Editor tab for the new mentalrayIblShape node, click the file browse button beside Image Name (see Figure 13.9 in the "Adjusting the IBL System" section later in this chapter). The node is able to read any standard image format supported by mental ray. It can use an 8-, 16-, or 32-bit image. However, to map the image onto the environment sphere correctly, you must use a spherical or angular HDR projection mapping. HDR images that are intended for 3D lighting generally possess one of several standardized mappings. Specialized HDR programs, including HDR Shop and HDRsoft Photomatix, are able to create the mappings. You can identify spherical and angular projection mappings by the following criteria:

   - Spherical mappings appear rectangular, with the horizon line laid horizontally (these are also known as equirectangular, latitude/longitude, or lat/long mappings).

   - Angular mappings look like flattened spheres (these are also known as light probes). An example angular HDR file (see Figure 13.6) is included as room.hdr with the Chapter 13 tutorial files.

4. Change the Mapping menu to Spherical or Angular to match the mapping style of the loaded HDR file. You can use a non-HDR image with the IBL system; however, the image may appear stretched due to improper mapping. In addition, a non-HDR image will provide a limited value range with no superwhite values.

Figure 13.6 An angular HDR bitmap

Note: In general, HDR images designed for 3D lighting use spherical, angular, or cubic cross projection mappings. (Cubic cross projections look like unfolded cubes.) That said, it's possible to create an HDR image that has no special mapping. Such an image may be useful when applying an HDR texture to the color of a 3D light (see Chapter 2, "Applying the Correct Maya Light Type," for more information on light attributes).

In contrast, photographers often use HDR as a means to combine multiple exposures into a single photograph. The combination and adjustment of HDR exposures is known as *tone mapping*. Tone-mapped photographs are given a lower bit depth, such as 8-bit.

5. The IBL system does not affect the lighting in the scene unless an additional indirect lighting system is used. Return to the Indirect Lighting tab of the Render Settings window. In the Final Gathering section, select the Final Gathering attribute.

6. To prevent the default light from interfering with the render, go to the Common tab, expand the Render Options section, and deselect the Enable Default Light attribute. Render a test frame. Final Gathering uses the IBL HDR file as a light source by tracing rays from the IBL sphere to the objects within the scene. In addition, the HDR image appears by default in material and shader reflections (see Figure 13.7). (For information on Final Gathering quality settings, see Chapter 12.)

Figure 13.7 Default render with Final Gathering using the `room.hdr` bitmap. This scene is included as `default_ibl.ma` with the Chapter 13 tutorial files.

Indirect Lighting Options with IBL

It's not mandatory that you use Final Gathering with the IBL system. Instead, you can use IBL with Global Illumination and/or Caustics. In this situation, you must emit photons from the IBL projection. To do so, expand the Photon Emission section of the mentalrayIblShape node and select Emit Photons. In this section you can set the number of Global Illumination and caustic photons generated.

The mentalrayIblShape node also includes its own indirect lighting system, known as light emission. To activate this system, go to the Light Emission section and select Emit Light. In this case, the IBL projection acts like an array of directional lights that point toward 0, 0, 0. The quality of the light emission is set by the Quality attribute in this section. Note that the light intensity created by light emission may be less than the default IBL settings.

The mental ray IBL system works in conjunction with standard Maya lights. IBL naturally produces soft shadows. However, you can activate Maya and mental ray depth map or raytraced shadows if you need shadows with more distinct edges.

Adjusting the IBL System

By default, the IBL environment sphere is considered to be infinitely far from 0, 0, 0. Hence, all scene objects are affected. Nevertheless, you are free to rotate the environment sphere by selecting the sphere in a viewport or by selecting the mentalrayIbl transform node in the Hypergraph or Outliner window. The image mapped to the IBL node rotates with the sphere; thus changes to rotation alter the scene lighting.

You also have the option of deselecting the Infinite attribute in the mentalrayIblShape Attribute Editor tab and then adjusting the scale of the sphere to alter the lighting.

When you render a scene with the IBL system, you may find that the indirect lighting contribution is too dark or too bright. You can alter the intensity of the contribution by going to the Render Stats section of the mentalrayIblShape node, selecting the Adjust Environment Color Effects attribute, and changing the Color Gain and/or Color Offset values. For example, you can set the Color Gain to 0, 0, 2.0 in HSV to double the IBL lighting contribution. If you are using Final Gathering, you have the additional option of selecting the Adjust Final Gather Color Effects attribute and changing a secondary set of Color Gain and Color Offset sliders (see Figure 13.8).

Figure 13.8 Updated IBL render with increased Final Gather Color Gain value and deselected Primary Visibility. This scene is included as updated_ibl.ma with the Chapter 13 tutorial files.

By default, the HDR image appears in the background and in reflections. (However, the HDR image is rendered as transparent in the alpha channel.) You can hide the image by deselecting Primary Visibility in the Render Stats section of the mentalrayIblShape node (see Figure 13.9).

Although the IBL system is generally used with photo bitmaps, you can use it with texture nodes instead. To do this, change the Type menu, in the Image Based Lighting Attributes section of the mentalrayIblShape node, to Texture. You can then choose a texture by clicking the checkered Map button beside the Texture attribute.

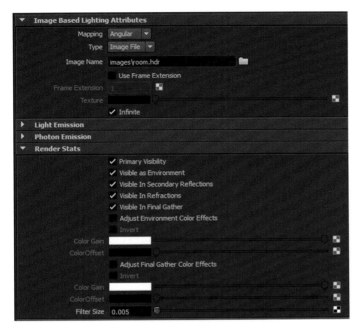

Figure 13.9 The Image Based Lighting Attributes and Render Stats sections of the mentalraylblShape node

Using Physical Sun & Sky

The Physical Sun & Sky system is unique in that it creates a complete light system that emulates an outdoor sky. The system relies on the mental ray renderer and Final Gathering. With a limited number of steps, you can use the system to create a realistic lighting scenario that matches an outdoor location.

To set up Physical Sky & Sun, follow these steps:

1. In the Render Settings window, go to the Indirect Lighting tab. In the Environment section, click the Physical Sky & Sun Create button.

2. The system adds a new shading network to the scene (see Figure 13.10). The network includes a mia_exposure_simple lens shader, mia_physicalsun, and mia_physicalsky nodes. You can use the mia_exposure_simple node to make final color grading adjustments to the render. The mia_physicalsun node determines the color and intensity of the virtual sun light. This node is linked automatically to the mia_physicalsky node via expressions. The mia_physicalsky node generates an atmospheric sky dome. You can adjust the atmospheric quality and remotely alter the sun light through this node. You can find the mia_exposure_simple, mia_physicalsun, and mia_physicalsky shaders in the Utilities tab of the Hypershade window.

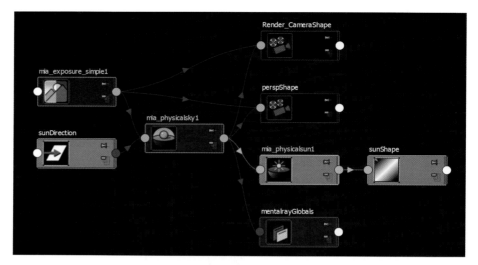

Figure 13.10 The shading network created for the Physical Sun & Sky system

3. The system also adds a directional light, named *sun*, to the scene. You can rotate this light to set the direction of the system's virtual sun (see Figure 13.11).

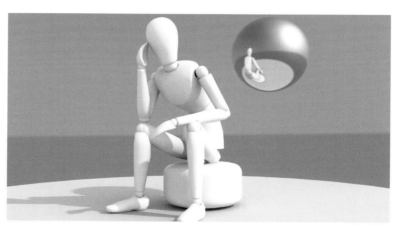

Figure 13.11 A render using Physical Sun & Sky with the sun directional light pointing down and toward the mannequin's screen-right side. This scene is included as sun_and_sky.ma with the Chapter 13 tutorial files.

4. When you create a Physical Sun & Sky system, Final Gathering is automatically activated. You can adjust the Final Gathering attributes to improve the resulting render quality. Essentially, the entire Physical Sun & Sky system is an indirect lighting tool.

The mia_physicalsky node produces a long list of attributes you can adjust (see Figure 13.12).

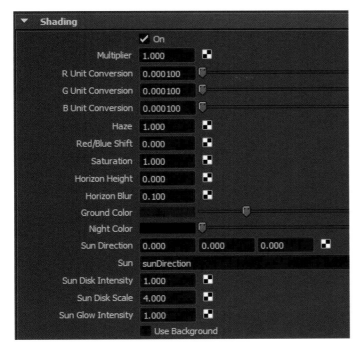

Figure 13.12 The mia_physicalsky attributes

Here's a brief review:

Multiplier and Red/Blue Shift   Multiplier controls the intensity of the virtual sun. Red/Blue Shift sets the sun light color; a value of 1.0 creates red light and a value of –1.0 creates blue light.

Haze   Creates an environmental, fog-like haze. The higher the value, the thicker the haze.

Horizon Height, Horizon Blur, and Ground Color   These attributes control the height, blurriness, and color of a virtual ground plane that extends to a distant horizon line, as seen through the camera.

Sun Disk Intensity, Sun Disc Scale, and Sun Glow Intensity   These attributes alter the look of the virtual "sun" created in the sky when the sun direction light is pointed toward the camera.

You can use the Physical Sun & Sky system in conjunction with Global Illumination. To do so, select the Emit Photons attribute of the *sun* directional light. The system also works in conjunction with Maya lights and depth map and raytraced shadows.

Rendering Passes

The Render Layer Editor, as discussed in Chapter 10, "Prepping for Successful Renders," allows you to split up a scene so that objects are rendered separately. You can take this one step further by rendering separate shading components for each object in a series of *render passes*. A *shading component* is a particular surface quality created by a material or shader. For example, you can create render passes that seprarate the diffuse, specular, ambient, and shadow shading components. Render passes give you even greater flexibility in compositing. For example, you can brighten a specular highlight without affecting other surface qualities of an object if you create a specular render pass.

You can create render passes in Maya by using the mental ray renderer and the Render Layer Editor. Before detailing this process, I'll review some of the render passes that are used commonly in the animation and visual effects industries.

Note: An additional render pass variation is a lighting pass. A lighting pass renders objects with a subset of all the available lights. Splitting a scene into multiple lighting passes allows you to adjust light intensities in the composite. To create lighting passes with the Render Layer Editor, selectively assign lights to different layers. See Chapter 10 for more information about the Render Layer Editor.

Overview of Common Render Passes

Here are brief descriptions of commonly used render passes:

Beauty This pass creates a render you normally see in the Render View with all the shading components present (see the left of Figure 13.13). The mental ray renderer creates a beauty pass automatically when you activate render passes and batch render.

MODEL BY BRIAN BUTLER, AVAILABLE VIA TURBOSQUID.COM

Figure 13.13 Left to right: Beauty pass, diffuse pass, and specular pass

Diffuse This pass includes the surface color without specularity or reflectivity (see the center of Figure 13.13). A variation of this pass omits basic shading (light and dark areas), making the result appear flat-shaded.

Specular This pass renders specularity by itself (see the right of Figure 13.13). The specular highlights appear by themselves over black.

Reflection This pass renders reflections by themselves (see the left of Figure 13.14).

Figure 13.14 Left to right: Reflection pass, matte pass, and shadow pass

Matte   This pass renders the alpha information in RGB, where opaque objects are white and empty areas are black (see the center of Figure 13.14). You can use a matte pass in a compositing program to cut out a layer or an input. This pass may be referred to as a *holdout*.

Shadow   This pass renders cast shadows by themselves. There are several variations of this pass. One variation places the shadow in the alpha channel with black RGB. Another variation captures the shadow in RGB, where the shadow colors are taken from the surface, and non-shadow areas are rendered black (see the right of Figure 13.14). Depending on the type of shadow pass, additional adjustments may be required in a compositing program to make the pass useful.

Ambient Occlusion   This pass captures subtle, soft shadows that form within cracks, crevices, and locations where surfaces are close together. The pass is similar to a shadow pass in that you can use it to darken parts of other renders. See the "Rendering Ambient Occlusion Passes" section later in this chapter for an example.

Motion Vector   This pass encodes object motion as values in RGB. In general, X motion is encoded to the red channel and Y motion to the green channel. The motion is captured in screen space. A special plug-in or node is needed in the compositing program to convert the motion vector pass into 2D motion blur. Creating motion blur as a motion vector and not an actual blur in Maya can speed up the render time. In addition, using a motion vector pass in a compositing program allows you to fine-tune the resulting blur in an efficient manner.

Depth   This pass encodes Z-buffer depth information in RGB. Using this pass is an alternative to rendering the depth information to a Z channel. For more information on Z-buffers, see Chapter 10.

This list of render passes is by no means complete. However, these passes are used consistently on professional projects.

Creating Pass Contribution Maps and Render Passes

To create render passes with mental ray, you must create at least one pass contribution map. A pass contribution map associates render passes with specific render layers. You can follow these steps to create a pass contribution map and a series of render passes, and to batch-render the result:

1. Switch to the mental ray renderer. Go to the Render Layer Editor. RMB-click over layer a name and choose Pass Contribution Map > Create Empty Pass Contribution Map. A pass contribution map is added to the layer (see Figure 13.15). You can access this map by clicking the small arrow that appears to the left of the layer name. You can add a pass contribution map to the masterLayer and/or any additional custom layer.

Figure 13.15 A pass contribution map is added to the masterLayer, as seen in the Render Layer Editor.

2. Open the Render Settings window and switch to the Passes tab. Click the Create New Render Pass button. (This is the button highlighted with a red square in Figure 3.17.) The Create Render Passes window opens and lists all the available render passes (see Figure 13.16). Ctrl/Cmd+click one or more render pass names and click the Create And Close button.

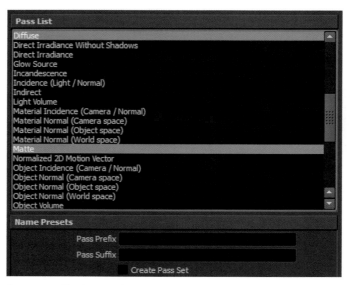

Figure 13.16 The Create Render Pass window with two passes selected

3. The render passes are listed in the Scene Passes section at the top of the Passes tab (see the top of Figure 13.17). While the passes are selected and appear with blue bars, click the Associate Selected Passes With Current Render Layer button. (This is the button highlighted with a green square in Figure 3.17.) The render passes are moved down to the Associated Passes section (see center of Figure 13.17).

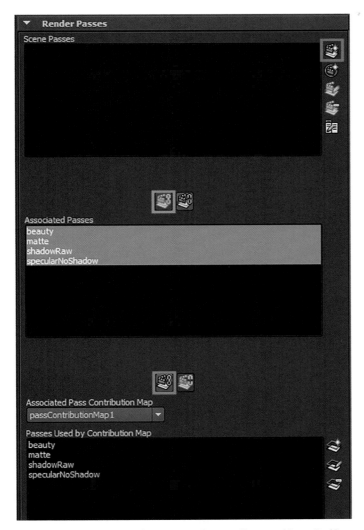

Figure 13.17 The Passes tab with Scene Passes, Associated Passes, and Passes Used By Contribution Map sections

4. Ctrl/Cmd+click the render pass names in the Associated Passes section. Change the Associated Pass Contribution Map menu to the pass contribution map you wish to attach to the render passes. Click the Associate Selected Passes With Current Pass Contribution Map button. (This is the button highlighted with a blue square in Figure 3.17.) The render passes appear in the Passes Used By Contribution Map section. Passes listed in this section render when a batch

render is launched. You can remove a pass from any section in the Passes tab by selecting the pass name and pressing the Delete key.

5. Batch-render the scene as an image sequence. By default, each render pass is placed in its own directory. For example, a matte render pass is rendered to the `project\images\matte\` directory. Each render pass image sequence takes its name from the File Name Prefix set by the Render Settings window. In addition, mental ray renders a beauty pass, which is placed in a `project\images\MasterBeauty\` directory. Keep in mind that every render layer that is marked as renderable in the Render Layer Editor, along with each renderable layer's render passes, is rendered. (For more information on the Render Layer Editor, see Chapter 10.)

You can add new render passes at any time by clicking the Create New Render Pass button in the Passes tab. You can also RMB-click a layer name in the Render Layer Editor and choose Add New Render Pass > *render pass*; this places the new render pass directly into the Associated Passes section of the Passes tab. You can remove a pass contribution map from a layer by RMB-clicking the pass contribution map name in the Render Layer Editor and choosing Remove Pass Contribution Map From Layer.

Note: To avoid creating multiple render passes with the identical file names, add name tokens to the File Name Prefix field of the Render Settings window. For example, if you add **<RenderPass>** to the field, each resulting rendered image will incorporate the render pass type into the file name. For a complete list of available tokens, see the "Subfolders and Names of Rendered Images" page of the Maya Help files or at the Autodesk Knowledge Network (`knowledge.autodesk.com`).

Rendering Passes to Multichannel Formats

The OpenEXR image format supports the ability to render multiple passes to a single file, where each pass becomes a special channel within the file. You can access, copy, and rearrange the channels in a compositing program such as Adobe After Effects or The Foundry's Nuke. When you batch-render an OpenEXR sequence with render passes, each frame is rendered as single EXR file that uses the File Name Prefix set by the Render Settings window.

In a similar fashion, the PSD Layered image format renders passes to a single file. However, each pass is placed on a Photoshop layer. When you batch-render a PSD Layered image sequence with render passes, the passes are temporarily placed in individual folders as Maya IFF files. As a final step as each frame is rendered, the Maya IFF renders are combined into a single PSD file. The PSD file is placed in the `project\images\` directory. Many compositing programs are able to access individual PSD layers or offer the option to merge the layers together. For more information on image formats and batch-rendering image sequences, see Chapter 10.

Creating Material Overrides

Although the list of render passes provided by mental ray is quite long, it sometimes pays to create your own custom render pass. One method of creating a custom pass is to assign a particular material or shader to all the objects belonging to a render layer. For example, you can assign a Use Background shader to a layer and thus trap shadows in the alpha channel. Alternatively, you might assign a mia_car_paint_phen_x shader to a layer and adjust the shader so that physically correct reflections appear on the surfaces. You can then combine the custom render passes with standard passes, such as diffuse or specular, to create a more complex result in the compositing phase.

Using the Render Layer Editor, you can create a material override that assigns a material or shader to all the objects on a layer. This assignment does not affect other layers, including the masterLayer. To create an override, RMB-click over a layer name and choose Overrides > Create New Material Override > *material/shader name*. A new copy of the material or shader is added to the Hypershade and Node Editor. You are free to alter the attributes of the new material or shader. A layer that's using a material override does not require the addition of a pass contribution map or a render pass. You can see the result of the material override when rendering through the Render View window. With batch rendering, the layer is treated as a standard render layer. (See Chapter 10 for more information on batch rendering with the Render Layer Editor.)

You can remove a material override at any time by RMB-clicking over the layer name and choosing Overrides > Remove Material Override.

Rendering Ambient Occlusion Passes

There are several methods of rendering ambient occlusion passes with the mental ray renderer. An ambient occlusion pass is included with the pass list in the Create Render Pass window. An Ambient Occlusion section is also included in the Indirect Lighting tab of the Render Settings window. In addition, the mia_material_x shader includes an ambient occlusion functionality. Because of its ease of use and reliability, I recommend using the shader to create such a pass. You can follow these steps:

1. RMB-click over a layer in the Render Layer Editor and choose Overrides > Create New Material Override > mia_material_x. The override is created and the new shader is assigned to all surfaces on the layer.

2. Through the Hypershade or Node Editor, open the new mia_material_x shader in the Attribute Editor. In the Reflection section, reduce the Reflectivity value to 0. Reflections are not desirable when creating an ambient occlusion render pass.

3. Expand the Ambient Occlusion section and select the Use Ambient Occlusion attribute (see Figure 13.18). Change the Ambient Light Color to white. Render a test frame with mental ray.

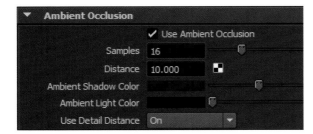

Figure 13.18 The Ambient Occlusion section of a Maya 2015 mia_material_x shader

4. In general, a useful ambient occlusion render is one where the non-shadow areas are bright gray or white (see Figure 13.19). If the render appears too dark, raise the Ambient Light Color. You can set the color to superwhite values by entering values into the numeric fields in the Color Chooser window (for example, set the values to 0, 0, 2 in HSV). You can also adjust the shadow darkness by altering the Ambient Shadow Color attribute. You want to maintain high contrast between the shadows and the non-shadow areas while keeping soft edges on the shadows.

Figure 13.19 An ambient occlusion render. This scene is included as `mia_material_ao.ma` with the Chapter 13 tutorial files.

5. If the render appears grainy, raise the Sample attribute. With the ambient occlusion algorithm, soft shadows are created wherever two surfaces or multiple features of a convoluted surface are within a particular distance. This distance is set by the Distance attribute. If you wish to have fewer surfaces or surface convolutions considered for shadowing, lower the Distance value. With a lower value, the soft shadows shrink.

 Note: To avoid seeing the empty space rendered as black with an ambient occlusion render, set the rendering camera's Background Color to white.

Rendering Passes with a _passes Shader

Maya materials support the majority of render passes listed in the Create Render Pass window (see the "Creating Pass Contribution Maps and Render Passes" section earlier in this chapter). However, mental ray shaders support a smaller subset of these. In fact, mental ray supplies shaders with a *passes* suffix specifically to work with the render pass system. Those that do not have the _passes suffix will not produce passes.

When mental ray renders a frame, it discretely renders various shading components as separate threads (ordered sequences of instructions sent to a computer's CPU). The renderer then combines the threads into a final composited frame, which is displayed in the Render View or is written to disc through a batch render. You can convert the individual shading component threads to render passes by using a shader with a *passes* suffix (for example, mia_material_x_passes). The shading component threads are often referred to as *outputs*.

To create passes with a _passes shader, follow the steps outlined in the "Creating Pass Contribution Maps and Render Passes" earlier in this chapter. However, to successfully create the passes, you must limit yourself to supported passes. For example, mia_material_x_passes supports the following passes: beauty, diffuse, direct irradiance, indirect, reflection, refraction, specular, and translucence. The mia_metallic_paint_x_passes shader supports ambient color, beauty, diffuse, direct irradiance, indirect, reflection, refraction, and specular passes. For more information on _passes shader outputs, see the mia_material_x page (titled "Architectural Material") in the Maya Help files or at the Autodesk Knowledge Network (`knowledge.autodesk.com`).

Overview of Third-Party Renderers

Maya supports additional renderers, which are available via plug-ins. Although coverage of these renderers is far beyond the scope of this book, it pays to be familiar with tools that are commonly used in the animation and visual effects industries.

Here is a brief review of several of these:

V-Ray for Maya   V-Ray is a physically based lighting, shading, and rendering tool. V-Ray optimizes difficult rendering tasks, such as raytracing, subsurface scattering, and fur and hair. V-Ray supports advanced systems such as Ptex layouts, render masks (to render specific portions of frames), and built-in in color management and color grading. V-Ray is used on a wide array of projects, ranging from architectural visualization to commercial production to visual effects work. For more information, visit `www.chaosgroup.com`.

RenderMan for Maya   RenderMan is a shading and lighting system developed by Pixar. RenderMan boasts a long history and is optimized to handle physically based lighting effects, such as global illumination. It also supports newer developments such as deep textures, whereby every pixel carries Z-depth samples, allowing more flexibility in the compositing phase. RenderMan for Maya includes RenderMan Slim, which allows you to create and edit RenderMan shaders. For more information, visit `renderman.pixar.com`.

messiahStudio The messiahStudio package provides a wide array of tools, ranging from character rigging to particle simulation to shading and rendering. The shading ad rendering components support advanced raytracing (for photoelectric glass), volumetric effects (such as clouds), and optimized global illumination. For more information, visit `www.projectmessiah.com`.

Book Wrap-Up

Maya is a complex program with a seemingly endless list of tools, nodes, functions, and attributes. While it's almost impossible to cover every aspect of Maya in a single book, I've attempted to touch on the most critical aspects of texturing, lighting, and rendering. Hopefully, this has given you enough information to come up with your own interesting solutions. Always remember that there are probably a dozen ways to tackle any given problem in the program. Although I may approach a task in one particular way, you may find a different but equally useful method. This is not necessarily a bad thing—I consider it the most rewarding part of 3D animation. Creativity and hard work always pay off in this realm.

Thank you for reading this book.

Index

Note to the reader: Throughout this index **boldfaced** page numbers indicate primary discussions of a topic. *Italicized* page numbers indicate illustrations.

H

I

M